DATE DUE

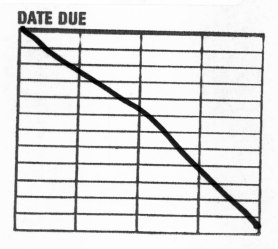

DEMCO

The Democratic Wish

THE
DEMOCRATIC
WISH

*Popular Participation and
the Limits of
American Government*

James A. Morone

BasicBooks
A Division of HarperCollinsPublishers

Morone, James A., 1951—
  The democratic wish : popular participation and the limits of
American government / James A. Morone.
    p. cm.
  Includes bibliographical references and index.
  ISBN 0-465-01603-0 : $22.95
  1. Political participation—United States—History.
2. Bureaucracy—United States—History. I. Title.
JK1764.M67   1990
323'.042'0973—dc20

90-80250
CIP

For Deborah

Five years have passed; five summers with the length
    Of five long winters. And . . .
    Oft in lonely rooms, and 'mid the din
    Of towns and cities, I have owed to them, . . .
    Sensations sweet,
    Felt in the blood, and felt along the heart
                    Wordsworth, *Tintern Abbey*

Contents

Contents

II. THE PEOPLE AND REFORM: THE POLITICAL RECONSTRUCTION OF CLASS, RACE, AND PROFESSION

Contents

Preface

By the time I finished it, this book was late. And, needless to say, there was trouble as I raced to the Goshen (New Hampshire) post office. A large maple tree was down, blocking the road. A logging truck was already sitting there—the driver and I gave the tree a try, but it barely budged. A minute later my neighbor, Dave Brenner, came along followed by a car packed with boys from the Goshen-Lempster school. Together (the kids whooping, the rest of us groaning) we wrestled the tree aside, gave ourselves a hearty cheer, and went back to the cars. My first thought went straight to Tocqueville (yes, I know it's an obsession) on the spirit of New England townships: "If some obstacle blocks the public road halting the circulation of traffic, [an] improvised assembly . . . of neighbors . . . remedies the trouble." Some things don't change. On the other hand, in Tocqueville's day, the Goshen post office was a plum—a reward for service to the winning political party. Now the postmaster is a civil servant; and he is a she. All of which is *The Democratic Wish* in a nutshell: How citizens "in the street," participating directly in public life, created and reformed the American state (which, for a long time, was mainly the post office).

As long as I'm on the subject of trees, a brief note about methodology. Sawing a tree down by hand is an old metaphor for writing history—

cutting across years chronicled by the lines that remain on the stump. In reality, historians do the fine work—probing carefully at a few years, a decade, an era—rather than whacking across great swaths of time as I do here. This book is a study in politics rather than history. I have paid more attention to historiographic issues and controversies than political scientists generally do (I believe that the great debates between historians mark the fault lines of American political development). But my purpose is to make sense of a political dynamic that evolves through American history rather than to contribute to the historical literature on specific periods. (Naturally, I hope the results are provocative all around.)

If I have a methodological ax to grind it is that politics cannot be understood outside their historical context—past patterns illuminate present policies; and not just as "background" but as explanations for why things happen. In my view students of public affairs should spend more time looking back. My book is organized to demonstrate this principle. Part I traces a political theme through the episodes that built up the American state; part II puts that pattern to work, reinterpreting twentieth-century political events. I suspect that variations of the pattern I describe—the democratic wish—could also illuminate political issues which I did not pursue here.

Along the way I got a great deal of help. The following people all read the manuscript. They made the book sharper, clearer, more accurate, more interesting, and more fun to write. I wish I had a more effusive way to communicate my gratitude to them: Thomas Anton, Lawrence Brown, Roger Cobb, Andrew Dunham, Peter Eisinger, Robert Evans, Daniel Fox, Ira Katznelson, Bryan Jones, William Macallister, Sidney Milkis, Eric Nordlinger, Kenneth Prewitt, Harvey Sapolsky, Robert Shapiro, Deborah Stone, Steve Stone, Frank Thompson, Nancy Rosenblum, Aaron Wildavsky, Alan Zuckerman. Thomas James read it twice—with great care and wonderful comments.

And two special intellectual debts: Ted Marmor—mentor, colleague, friend—really got me going on all this when we did some work on citizen representation more than a decade ago. "Why were they so nutty when they designed this program, Jim?" he kept asking me. It drove me crazy that I couldn't say. It never occurred to me that his question would send me back to colonial America. Anyway, Ted, here, finally, is my answer.

More than 15 years ago, in one of those graduate seminars that meet long into the night, David Greenstone burst out, "I'm just trying to work out Louis Hartz." Walking out, I told Andy Dunham, "Such a big deal about Hartz—I don't get it. I can't imagine being so stuck on him." (Well, I was wrong, but that's a different story.) "You missed the point," said Andy; "You and I are going to be working out Greenstone." Andy was right, of course. *The Democratic Wish* is an effort to work out ideas David threw at us years ago. David died just as I was finishing. His many students, colleagues, and friends all miss him terribly.

Special thanks to student researchers who helped with chapter seven (which balances the rest of the book with some concrete cases): Stephen Ornstein, Steven Sidel, and Chris Swistro. I am grateful to my students at Brown and Yale for sampling this material as I was developing it. The Hastings Center offered a wonderful intellectual home for the first stirrings of my idea. Brown University helped it along with a sabbatical. Eileen Evans heroically kept the rest of my obligations afloat while the last revisions stretched on. Bob Hackey negotiated computer connections between Brown and Yale.

I am convinced that Martin Kessler, president of Basic Books, runs a successful publishing house because it gives him an excuse to play with ideas all day. It was a genuine pleasure playing along—this book is far better for his gentle, penetrating suggestions. And Phoebe Hoss is—as other authors have already testified—the world's best editor. Heartfelt thanks to Phoebe for flushing me out from dull academic equivocation in the final chapter. And anyone who spends any time foraging in my endnotes ought to be thanking her too.

Finally, some personal connections: As soon as Sally and Steven Brenner could walk down the road, Judy had taught them: If the curtains are closed, Jim was up till dawn and nobody should be knocking on the door. Thanks to Andy Dunham for years of talk (not to mention miles jogged and bottles of wine emptied). And to Jo Hart and Linda Cook for working the night shift back at the office with me. Jim and Stasia Morone taught me to love politics, to tell stories, and to see things from more than one angle. Deborah Stone prefers private ceremonies to public ones; so here I'll just say thanks and offer her the small bouquet from Wordsworth on the dedication page.

Introduction

The Democratic Wish

At the heart of American politics lies a dread and a yearning. The dread is notorious. Americans fear public power as a threat to liberty. Their government is weak and fragmented, designed to prevent action more easily than to produce it. The yearning is an alternative faith in direct, communal democracy. Even after the loose collection of agrarian colonies had evolved into a dense industrial society, the urge remained: the people would, somehow, put aside their government and rule themselves directly.

The story I tell is how Americans master their antistatist trepidations by pursuing their democratic wish. In the recurring quest for the people, Americans redesign political institutions and rewrite political rules. The direct results have been uneven; some efforts enhance popular control, some attenuate it, some seem to manage both. Paradoxically, the unanticipated consequences are more constant. The institutions designed to enhance democracy expand the scope and authority of the state, especially its administrative capacity. A great irony propels American political development: the search for more direct democracy builds up the bureaucracy.[1]

1

INTRODUCTION

DREAD AND YEARNING

The Dread of Government

The American suspicion of government—rooted partially in ideology, partially in institutional design—forms the background for the democratic impulse. Here is a state that occupies an unusually ambiguous place in its society. The grudging stance toward government comes from the perception that public power threatens civic liberty; the tension is especially sharp in administrative agencies, for they wield power unlegitimated by formal mechanisms of representation. In the traditional view, now familiar after two centuries of repetition, the American difference comes from the way citizenship rights developed in the first place.

In Europe, citizenship rights were dispensed in the struggles that defined nations. As kings centralized authority, they stripped control over suffrage or jury trials from aristocrats, clerics, and estates. Of course, it was a complex process. Kings gave commoners a share in the government in order to "humble aristocrats"; nobles sometimes fought back by granting the common people "political weight"; peasants and workers often sped the process (and sometimes retarded it) by rebelling. Nevertheless, successful state building meant subordinating the political intermediaries that stood between citizen and state. The act of creating nations was tied up with winning the power to define and defend civic privileges from the political center.[2]

While Europeans sometimes mobilized to win rights from the state, Americans revolted to block the crown from meddling with rights they were already exercising. Alexis de Tocqueville articulated what would become the analytic standard when he observed "Americans were born equal without having to become so." They did not need to overcome feudal and clerical oppressions, to displace an entrenched aristocracy, to negotiate citizenship rights with the crown, or to mobilize collective power to clear paths of social and economic mobility. The political center was more a menace to rights than their source. Madison contrasted the American Constitution with the European experience as "a charter of power granted by liberty rather than a charter of liberty granted by power."[3]

Recent scholarship significantly qualifies Tocqueville's egalitarian picture of early America. In many ways, Puritan and planter élites carried old world hierarchy across the Atlantic. But though there is dispute about its origins, the preoccupation with limiting government remains a vivid feature of American political life. "The long train of abuses and usurpations" allegedly perpetrated by George III's "multitude of offices" and "swarms of officers" would prove an enduring image of tyranny, a kind of national birthing trauma.[4]

The fear of public power has been a fixture on the American political scene ever since. The first American constitutions avoided ministerial power altogether. A half-century later, Tocqueville reported, "The society acts by and for itself . . . so feeble and restricted is the part left to administration, so vividly is the administration aware of its popular origins." No European, he concluded tartly, would find the consequences tolerable. Hegel thought the United States no state at all, absent a bureaucratic class, a national culture, or a monarch to stand for the permanent interests of the national community. Decades later, Henry James was still ticking off the inventory of American statelessness: "No sovereign, no court, no aristocracy, no church, no army, no diplomatic service . . . no state . . . indeed, barely a specific national name."[5]

Even as American public administration began to take its contemporary form (most scholars detect a modern administrative state somewhere between the two Roosevelt administrations), the antigovernmental contrast to other nations lingered on. Take, for example, the development of social insurance. In Europe, programs were generally proffered from the political center by statesmen bidding for the allegiance of workers. Bismarck designed his welfare monarchy (in the same spirit with which he suppressed the Social Democrats) in order to pacify German labor. Napoleon III, along with some of the factions in the Second Republic, anticipated Bismarck's approach, though they were less successful in securing the programs. Lloyd George was explicit about maintaining working-class support for the Liberals when he promoted similar reforms in the early 1900s.[6]

In the United States, the political payoff is not often noted, and new social welfare programs not often proposed. They are likely to provoke the same ideological reflex that shackled the government's early development—now replete with great outcries about looming socialism. Granting old-age benefits, publicly financing health care, legitimating labor unions, legislating civil rights, fluoridating the water, regulating industry, and a multitude of other policies have all elicited the response. New forms of state authority—even, at times, for the extension of narrow benefits to broad constituencies—are likely to evoke the battle cry of the American founding: a tyrannous state threatens the rights of free people.*

And yet, dread or no, the American government grew and changed. The regime that disdained all ministers (and tried to govern through state legislatures) in its first decade had 200 gentlemen administrators by 1800 and 2.8 million civil servants by its bicentennial. In fact, the antistatist rhetoric failed to bury any of the examples in the preceding paragraph. Reformers won Medicare (though not national health insurance, and it took them three decades); black citizens won voting rights (though as a group, their economic status has improved only marginally). The dread of government matters, but it is only half the story.

The question I address is how the Americans negotiated their dread of public power as they constructed their administrative institutions. The answer lies in the myth of communal democracy. Reformers— oppressed groups, public officials, policy entrepreneurs—have repeatedly overcome the checks and balances of a polity biased against the expansion of government by promising to restore power to the people. The mass movements that develop around the democratic idea yield mixed results. One that has often escaped notice is the introduction and development of institutions originally designed to the specification

*Examples are easy to collect. These are among my favorites: The National Association of Manufacturers said about big government in 1953: Americans "face the prospect of complete . . . domination by the federal government. And complete federal domination IS totalitarianism." School desegregation left southern newspapers speculating "How the communist masses in Russia and China must have howled with glee." The Kennedy administration's scaled-back Medicare proposal would lead us to "wake up . . . one day . . . and find that we have socialism. . . . We will spend our sunset years telling our children and our children's children what it was like in America when men were free."[7]

of populist yearning. First, consider the nature of the ideology itself, then how it operates to remake American politics.

The Democratic Wish

As the American Revolution broke out, hastily organized committees grabbed political power away from startled British governors. Groups like the Sons of Liberty and the Committees of Public Safety, backed by mass meetings and mobs, bypassed formal political authorities and conducted public business themselves. They enforced boycotts, levied fines, issued licenses, and held open-air courts. They left American reformers an enduring ideal—the people taking charge of their own communities in the face of a distant and usurpative state. Here is the central image of the democratic wish: the direct participation of a united people pursuing a shared communal interest.

The key to the ideology is an image of the people—a single, united, political entity with the capacity, as John Adams put it, to "think, feel, reason and act."[8] The people are wiser than their governors; they will solve the troubles that plague the nation. This populist ideal is not simply the rhetorical flourish that strikes the modern ear. Nor is it merely a call for more responsive government. The people would be governors as well as constituents, political agents as well as principals. They will act by and for themselves. Here is nothing less than an alternative locus of political authority. Somehow, power will be seized from the government and vested in the people themselves.

The democratic wish involves three additional features; what might be called the method, the assumption, and the setting. First, the celebrated method is direct citizen participation in politics. Direct democracy will foster better citizens and frame better policies. The process of participation itself transforms "private into public," "conflict into cooperation," "bondage into citizenship." Government for the people must be government by them.[9]

Thomas Jefferson made perhaps the best remembered (or, at least, the most often quoted) American argument for direct democracy: "I [conclude] every opinion with the injunction, 'divide the country into wards.'" In these small, autonomous, constituencies—little republics,

Jefferson called them—free men could control their own political destinies. Citizens would meet, deliberate, decide, and implement.[10] In time, a romantic, yeomen democracy was imputed to New England towns, and these "peaceable kingdoms" became the reflexive illustration of Jeffersonian principle. Tocqueville found in them a communal spirit that seemed to "spring directly from the hand of God." In his portrayal, citizen action obviated the need for public hierarchy. An "improvised assembly of neighbors" remedied troubles "long before anyone thought of the possibility" of appealing to formally constituted authority. Years later, the Progressive reformers were still sighing for this "ideal of a civilization" where citizens enjoyed "fresh, primary thoughts, feelings, beliefs, [and the] life of simple, homely, genuine men."[11]

Americans would return to citizen participation in a wide variety of ways. The Left pursues it in, perhaps, its purest form, through neighborhood democracy, worker participation, and community organizing.[12] More often, reformers have promoted political changes that might at least approximate the ideal within government institutions. Antifederalists resisting the Constitution, Jacksonians remaking the federal bureaucracy, Progressives attacking corruption, New Left students seeking a democratic society, segregationists resisting one, officials in regulatory agencies searching for legitimacy, and many others, each in their own fashion, pursued the democratic aspiration of stretching beyond representation to direct citizen participation.

Second, the usually implicit assumption is that the people agree with one another. The democratic ideal is founded on consensus. The people form a homogeneous body with a shared, discernible, public interest that transcends narrow individual concerns. Only malefactors ("idiots" and "self-murderers" as observers at the Founding put it)[13] would spurn the common good for private gain. Reforms introduced amid celebrations of the people are rarely designed to accommodate conflict among them.

Precisely when American politics grows most contentious, Americans look beyond adversary democracy and expect to find a consensus about shared interests residing in the people. A Rousseauian common good seems to beckon from beyond the Lockean status quo—from the grass roots and the moral economy of the mob. For example, when the racial crisis of the 1960s swept northward, driving the difficult issues of the Southern movement into the northern ghettos, the Johnson administration launched a war on poverty that assumed local consensus about community needs. The program's designers were soon wondering why nobody in Washington had anticipated the conflict that followed. As we shall see, they stood in a long line of reformers pondering the same question.[14]

Third, the people dwell in communities. In its original formulation, these were small, homogeneous, rural communities—Jefferson's wards, for example. However, with time, the notion of community grew beyond these boundaries and began to encompass a great variety of political settings: artisan communities in the Jacksonian city, professional communities of "affinity" in the Progressive imagination, neocorporatist national community in Bull Moose and Blue Eagle rhetoric. Such communities pushed beyond geographical place altogether. The idea of community itself took on a powerful metaphorical meaning, vaguely recalling Jefferson and serving as a kind of democratic Genesis myth—a shared memory of a purer collectivity that, somehow, holds the key to contemporary troubles.

"The old principle of local community," as Franklin Roosevelt put it, offers Americans a potent political symbol. Leaders repeat the word in a kind of litany that seems widely understood without being defined. In fact, the power of community lies in an intimation of shared values and societal solidarity. Calling for community is the acceptable form in which to cast collectivist sentiment in a society of state bashers.[15]

Taken together, the democratic wish imagines a single, united people, bound together by a consensus over the public good which is discerned through direct citizen participation in community settings. It is a utopian image. To be sure, many features of the ideology might be practicable. Lively cases have been made for citizen participation. And the notion of common good, of getting beyond adversary self-interest, holds important lessons for contemporary American public policy. However, this particular manifestation of the democratic idea— the persistent democratic wish—cannot be achieved. Ultimately, "the people" is a reification, a powerful political fiction. In the end, I will argue, a less grandiose democratic conception might offer more real power to real people.

INTRODUCTION

The recurring democratic myth is easy to overlook. The romance of the people deteriorates swiftly into the clash of stubbornly narrow political interests. So improbable an idea is often ascribed to the naïveté (in the 1960s, for example) or the guile (the 1900s, the 1830s) of political reformers. However, we shall see how this image of a collective, participatory people has formed a most useful myth in the most liberal of nations.

After all, here is a direct counter to every aspect of liberalism. The authors of *The Federalist*, for example, debunk it throughout. To the hope of a united people, Madison responds that "the latent causes of faction are sown into the nature of man." Direct participation makes it easy to mobilize power "adverse to the rights of other citizens" or the "aggregate good of the community," for "there is nothing to check the inducements to sacrifice the weaker party." And consensus about (or "unperplexed pursuit" of) the public good is "more ardently to be wished for then seriously to be expected"; even if "the people commonly intend it," they often fail "to reason right about the means of promoting it." To the people, participation, common good, and community, American liberalism (there are other kinds) responds with individuals, representation (in a limited government full of checks and balances), private interest, and individualism.[16]

Still, there is a crucial feature the democratic ideology shares with its liberal antithesis. As they have evolved in political practice, each rests on a suspicion of government. Each promises an alternative to centralized political authority. The democratic wish offers a communitarian counter to individualism without triggering the fear of governmental power.

When reformers frame their proposals as efforts to restore power to the people, they sidestep the American suspicion of collective action with an alternative, symbolically potent ideology. Movements that focus more bluntly on a raw redistribution of power—Loco Focos, the Industrial Workers of the World, the Socialist party, the Student Non-Violent Coordinating Committee, Franklin Roosevelt's Supreme Court packing—are more likely to provoke hostility and charges of illegitimacy. Redefining the issue of the moment into a question of enhancing democracy facilitates—indeed, it permits—the deployment of new kinds of public power in a polity biased against government action. In short, the democratic wish is the ideology of reform and change, a legitimate, populist counter to the liberal status quo.

The democratic ideal, then, is well constituted as a mechanism of change. It poses a legitimacy test that the existing regime inevitably fails. It offers a standard for political mobilization, complete with powerful symbols (like frontiersmen or town meetings), revered forefathers (Thomas Jefferson, Andrew Jackson), and great expectations (the restoration of the people). It carries a blueprint for political reform: more "actual" government, more direct participation, a restoration of community. And it is profoundly ambiguous, facilitating broad (even bizarre) political coalitions.

Through the reforming generations, the hunt for the people yields large changes but small victories. The major legacies are unanticipated—the development of an administrative apparatus and the legitimation of new groups. In the end, Jeffersonian aspirations yield Madisonian, even Hamiltonian ends. A closer look at the political mechanics of the democratic wish explains why.

DYNAMICS OF THE DEMOCRATIC WISH

The American democratic ideology sets a recurring pattern into motion. Each successful call to the people progresses, roughly speaking, through four stages.

First, the process begins (as it ends) in the political stalemate of American liberalism. Ideology, institutions, and interests all block change. The antistatist ideology, noted earlier, is reflected in chaotic institutional fragmentation (celebrated as checks and balances). No other nation, report Peter Marris and Martin Rein, "organizes its government as incoherently as the United States." The political chaos "leaves most reforms sprawling helplessly in a scrum of competing interests."[17] The executive and the two chambers of Congress each pursue its own agenda; in the past century and a half, the three institutions have been split by party 40 percent of the time, by sectional rivalry almost constantly.[18]* Together, they operate in a tenuous equilibrium with courts, state governments, and the bureaucracy.

Privileged political interests can usually find protection from change somewhere in the fragmented political apparatus. For example, when Congress moved to legitimate labor (1933), it had to tread gingerly around a skeptical Supreme Court; when the Court took a leftward turn and championed civil rights (1954), it was frustrated for more than a decade by Congress, state governments, and local officials. In addition, groups resisting change summon up the antistatist ideology to rouse conservative allies. Both capital in the 1930s and white supremacists in the 1950s and 1960s did so by proclaiming their indignant opposition to "federal totalitarianism," "communism," "Hitler," and "Stalin." The conclusion is not that the state does nothing but that what it is doing is difficult to change.

With time, pressures for political reform mount. The economy develops; both the organization of labor and the nature of capital formation evolve; the population shifts westward; social élites rise (and fall); the underprivileged articulate grievances. The imperatives for change—for new forms of government action, new regulations, new fights, the legitimation of new groups—are blunted by the bias toward the status quo. The stalemate is broken when proponents of change transform the debate by invoking the democratic wish.

We reach the second stage when the call for the people provokes a popular response. If there is no reaction, the democratic imagery can be dismissed as inflated rhetoric. At critical moments throughout American history, on the other hand, broad political movements take up the populist call; Americans attack the status quo and demand changes that will empower the people.

The story I tell does not impute independent power to the democratic idea. As we shall see in the chapters that follow, underlying social and economic conditions help propel the people "out of doors" or "into the streets" (as the reformers of the 1760s and 1960s would, respectively, describe their mobilizations). Rather, the democratic wish offers

---

*Of the seventy-four Congresses since 1840, thirty have seen a party division in control of the Presidency and the two houses of Congress. Remove the administrations of Franklin Roosevelt and those of Lincoln through Grant—the two greatest periods of crisis—and the figure is precisely 50 percent, or thirty of sixty.[19]

a rhetorical and ideological pattern through which Americans have converted vague social tensions into concrete political change.

Scholars perpetually debate the matter of who, precisely, issues the call for reform. Oppressed classes? Public-sector officials aiming to expand their authority? Private élites searching for social control?

I argue all three can be true. The democratic ideology enables many interests to push reform simultaneously. Different, even contending classes can find their own aspirations within the ambiguous promise of the people. The democratic vision mobilizes powerful symbols in a vague way. The ambiguity itself invests the wish with political force; it facilitates broad (if brief) coalition and grants a fleeting verisimilitude to the hope of communitarian consensus. "The people" covers a multitude of factions. This helps explain why the democratic wish introduces change more easily than do movements based explicitly on the redistribution of wealth or power. Even when social tensions are sharp, contending factions can converge on a set of symbols that appear to promote the interests of each.

For example, Jackson's rhetorical celebration of the common man (and his roasting of the moneyed interest) appealed to republican artisans fearful of threats to their way of life. At the same time, it reassured entrepreneurs making their way up. And party leaders resorted to both democratic rhetoric and rule changes as they jockeyed for power. Thus, the same events have been interpreted as the struggle of a gathering working class, the stirring of incipient capitalists, and the search for hegemony by political élites—what social scientists would designate class, consensus, and state-centered explanations.

The democratic ideals run through the reforming generations. Naturally, each era articulates its own variations—new rhetorical turns, new grievances, new images of the people. And, crucially, each generation introduces new democratic rules and administrative institutions in pursuit of its vision. Those institutional changes hold the key to the political results; they are the mechanism through which Americans form and reform their administrative state. The innovations may be inspired—indeed, politically enabled—by democratic myth. However, even political organizations designed with chimerical aspirations carry real political consequences.

The third stage begins with the implementation of new political institutions. Once the reforms are in place, the image of a united republican *volk* evaporates into the reality of classes and interests scrapping for partisan advantage. The revolutionaries' "unity," the antebellum "common man," and the War on Poverty's "community" all swiftly proved to be cumulations of clashing interests. When the people and their consensus fail to materialize, the aspirations of the democratic wish are done in. However, the institutions designed (and won) in the name of the people remain. Like all political organizations they have biases; they alter the old political alignments and break the stalemate imposed by the dread of government. Across the reforming generations, we shall see these institutions both legitimate and limit previously suppressed political constituencies; at the same time, they permit the state to claim new powers and take on new tasks.

Since populist ideals and rhetoric shape the new institutions, their organizational biases tend to differ from those of existing agencies. Precisely because they were designed to empower the people, the new organizations facilitate the participation of new groups and permit the articulation of previously ignored or suppressed conflicts. Moreover, new institutions are less likely to have entrenched constituents resisting change (and more likely to attract the attention of reformers lobbying for it). "New men" entered American politics through the assemblies of the 1770s and the people's bureaucracy of the Jacksonian era. Organized labor rushed in through the organizations forged under the enigmatic aegis of the National Industrial Recovery Act (1933); black Americans, through the Community Action Agencies (1964). One result is a more open political system, marked by newly legitimated groups and new kinds of conflicts.

At the same time, the democratic institutions restrain the reforms they introduce. Assuming democratic consensus, they often fail to define constituencies and offer them formal mechanisms of political accountability. Instead, the new organizations extend participation largely to groups that seize the opportunity to mobilize. Moveover, the reforms focus great protest movements on organizational matters within the American state. Reformist energy that might have been mobilized on more radical purposes are spent on (newly legitimated) conflicts within a narrow institutional context. Jacksonian-era workers (and immigrants) won suffrage and were swept up in the elections and spoils scrambles of the party state; when organized labor finally won recognition during the New Deal, it fought for "fair representation" rather than a restructured political economy. Potentially radical forces gain participation and focus on the limited (and limiting) conflicts of organizational life. If the institutions introduced by the democratic wish often enhance liberal democracy (a heartily debated point, as we shall see), they also co-opt more fundamental challengers to the status quo.

Finally, the organizational innovations expand the boundary of government power. The limits imposed by the American suspicion of government are lifted in the rush of democratic sentiment. The institutions introduced in those moments offer the state its opportunities to expand and change. The Jacksonians constructed a party state and a rudimentary national bureaucracy; the Progressives transformed that apparatus into a roughly modern administrative state; the Community Action Agencies propelled federal authority into urban racial politics.

There is no single analytic key to the winners and losers in these conflicts for democracy. Images of popular consensus ease the way for political reform, then evaporate before the conflicts the new organizations themselves introduce. They leave behind new institutions with new political rules which, to varying degrees, restructure the conflicts of the era.

The fourth step is a return to the first—the reassertion of a liberal political equilibrium (around a new political status quo). In order to empower the people, reformers design new political rules and institutions. Once the political smoke has cleared, those are what remain. The American democratic moments introduce new bureaucracies, new public powers, new political privileges, and newly legitimated groups. The institutional forms that were intended to mobilize a communitarian people ultimately remake the liberal state.

Put the other way round, American public institutions were shaped through the political dynamics of American populist myth. The irony of the process is that democratic aspirations have been crucial for the development of public administration. The often-noted antinomy between the two is more a creative dialectic than a static tension.

It is always tempting to impute intention to the interests that ultimately benefit, and conclude that they masterminded the reforms. In *The Democratic Wish*, I tell a different story. Reforms are introduced in a groping, trial-and-error process. Some of those cast in democratic form gather more support (or encounter less resistance) and, often impelled by underlying pressures for change, progress through the stages described here, one trial-and-error step at a time. The outcomes—winners and losers, suppressed classes and rising groups, burgeoning state powers and bungled opportunities—vary with the political maneuvers of the era. Every organization has biases; however, they are not often self-consciously computed in advance. The ruling class is rarely so prescient.[20]

Different aspects of the process generally trouble observers on the Left and the Right. Conservatives are critical of the democratic tumult that accompanies the introduction of new interests (and their previously ignored conflicts). The Right does not hear the republican echoes: Revolutionary assemblies were "chaotic," even "despotic." "Hot and heady" Jacksonians populated public office with "wild Irishmen and French refugees."[21]* Poverty Warriors in the 1960s were "inarticulate," "irresponsible," "unsuccessful."[22] On the other side, the Left is likely to cheer the process and lament the outcome. The politics of democratic participation contrast wanly with the promises of the democratic vision. Leftists often criticize the failure to empower the people, to reorient American institutions, or to usher in a more egalitarian political culture.

The democratic wish is not a complete explanation of American institution building. It works, in effect, to overcome the political bounds imposed by the suspicion of the state; when those limits are relaxed, the democratic ideology is not relevant—without a thesis, there is no antithesis. For example, that universal state builder, war, promotes the expansion of government authority unaccompanied by democratic wishes. A comprehensive history of American institutional development would dwell on wars and their aftermath. The ideological tension, however, which is my central focus is generally eclipsed by the imperatives of wartime mobilization. (Perhaps that is why when American public officials wish to signal particular emphasis on a problem—

---

*"Wild Irishmen and French refugees" was actually the description of the partisan changes Jefferson put through after the American presidency changed party hands for the first time; it aptly characterizes the reformers' view of the Jacksonians.

14

poverty, illegal drugs, even inflation—they declare the "moral equivalent of war"; it is as if they would suspend the limits of the American state for just one policy task.)

RIVAL VIEWS OF AMERICAN
POLITICAL DEVELOPMENT

Social scientists tell the story of American political development in different ways, engaging in spirited controversies about the underlying dynamics. Were early Americans liberal individualists or republican communitarians? Is the nation's progress marked more fundamentally by shared values or by economic fights? How, more generally, should we characterize growth and change in American public administration? The pattern of dread and yearning offers a perspective on each of these familiar debates.

The Soul of American Politics: Liberal or Republican?

The dread of government, described earlier, rests on a reading of America as a liberal polity. In this view, Americans designed their regime to protect private rights from public meddling. Rejecting classical notions of public good, the Founders left individuals to define and pursue their own self-interest.

Accordingly, government is carefully limited; it is organized to protect private rights and promote fair interplay among self-interested individuals. The liberal vision seems a distinctly modern one, calculated to work harmoniously, even among citizens who are less than virtuous (or men who are not angels, as Madison had it).[23] Indirect elections are designed to set the people at a distance from their limited state which is, itself, constituted with checks and balances so that ambitions for power offset one another.

There are multiple variations of the liberal paradigm. Some emphasize idealistic social obligations; all give primacy to liberty. However, the dominant interpretation of liberal America focuses on the pursuit of self-interest. From this perspective, it is easy to see why Americans took readily to commerce and capitalism. Indeed, scholars in this tradition often lament the depth and power of the liberal ideology in American culture. Liberalism is not, in their view, merely a set of institutional arrangements. It is a mind-set so pervasive as to eclipse every alternative; it impoverishes American politics by truncating the range of possibilities Americans find in their social world.[24]

The liberal orthodoxy has recently been challenged by an interpretation known as classical republicanism. Rather than a polity founded on modern liberalism, these revisionists see a backward-looking ideal drawn from classical antiquity. To them, the spirit of Machiavelli runs as deep in Americans as that of John Locke.

In the republican view, the colonial and Revolutionary ideal lay, not in the pursuit of private matters, but in the shared public life of civic duty, in the subordination of individual interests to the *res publica*. Citizens were defined and fulfilled by participation in political community. To the first American generation, the political community was a single organic whole, binding each of its members into a civic body of shared interests that transcended individual concerns. Natural leaders were expected to rise up among the people; others would acknowledge their place within the natural order and contribute their own talents to the common good.

Rather than institutions framed to harness self-interest, the revisionists see a social vision that demanded (and fostered) virtue in its citizens. Rather than holding people at a distance from their government, republican American expected them to participate directly. Instead of a nation primed for commerce, the new view finds one clinging to small homogeneous communities and the yeoman self-reliance of agriculture. Here, then, is an image of a virtuous, united people, bound together by a shared public good, active in civic affairs, and populating rural communities outside historical time. Americans, conclude the proponents of this analytic perspective, were not liberals but republicans, not individualists but communitarians, no longer celebrants of self but participants in a shared public life.[25]

Though the debate is lively, the issue at stake has grown murky.

Proponents of the republican interpretation began with an important but limited claim. This world view, argued Bernard Bailyn, informed the colonists as the English began to meddle in New World politics; the imperial menace to republican ideals helps explain why the settlers moved so swiftly to revolution. The next step was Gordon Wood's powerful exposition of how the classical images of communal republic shaped the first American decade until they were swamped by factional conflicts and displaced by the Constitution. Most political scientists emphatically concur, at least regarding the factionalism of the 1780s. It is difficult to find aspirations of community or public-interested consensus on either side of the ratification debate. Citing the *Federalist* papers, the Antifederalists, the Constitution itself, many political scientists conclude that, whatever the colonial experience, the new order introduced a profoundly liberal set of rules.[26]

And yet, by the early nineteenth century, other scholars find a vibrant republicanism. The paradigm has proved a powerful heuristic, organizing new interpretations of working-class formation, the role of women in the cities, models of public school education, debates over the national bank, the organization of political parties, and a host of other topics.[27]*

In its most sweeping form, articulated by J. G. A. Pocock, the republican view would displace the liberal interpretation of America. For Pocock and the scholars who follow him, the republican paradigm is an analytic key to American history and culture. From the other side, social scientists who see a liberal nation have been long and loud in their critique.

What are we to make of this passionate intellectual debate? The democratic wish suggests one way the two paradigms might fit into a single conceptual story. The civic republicanism of the 1770s is, I argue, the first manifestation of the recurring American ideology of revolution and reform.

The Revolution was mobilized by the republican image of the people. The revolutionaries tried to institutionalize the ideal, pushing for participatory (or "actual") governments and reducing their ministers to ciphers; the governments would "think, feel, reason and act" like the

---

*On the eclipse of republican community, see pages 62–65.

people. Once the institutions were in place, the people proved contentious and factious (though whether this was maladroit institutional design or the rush of new participants is in dispute). In 1789, the utopic republican assumptions of a united people were swept aside by a more "realistic" new order—not liberalism exactly, but an early relative. I argue that this was the first iteration of the political cycle described earlier.

Much, though not all, of the republican world view discovered in the 1770s can be rediscovered in the 1830s or the 1900s; I will suggest that it has resurfaced (in a narrower form) throughout American history. What we have, then, is two political paradigms that are almost mirror opposites of one another. Liberalism is dominant. The story I tell is how it is repeatedly challenged by a recurring, subordinate ideology. As I suggested in the preceding section, the shared consensus of a united people does not survive the attempt to achieve it. Each effort collapses into the liberal clash of interests organized around a new institutional status quo which is, itself, eventually challenged in the name of the people.

This explains how the republican spirit can be vivid in 1776, eclipsed by 1789, and stirring once again in the early nineteenth century. Recent scholarship reflects the persistent tension between liberalism and republicanism, between private pursuits and civic good, between narrow individualism and broad communitarianism. The debate about the "soul of American politics," as John Diggins characterizes it, obscures the polarity that lies there.

Of course, the democratic impulse has evolved from its early republican form. Natural hierarchy faded with the decline of the old gentry; by the 1830s, the common man knew best—those who sought to subordinate him would have to become more artful. And although elaborate images of good and evil would shape public policies from abolition to abortion and prohibition to poverty, these have often involved far broader notions of virtue than the republican meaning of deference to natural order. Moreover, the American vision of community would evolve from yeomen working their own land. We still speak of "grass roots"; however, even by the Revolution, Jefferson's "chosen people of God" were mingling as a patriotic ideal with the crowds mobbing customs officials in the cities. Although the democratic aspirations of participation, community, and the people recur through American history, we shall see each generation articulate them in its own way. Classical republicanism offers an early instance, not an unchanging pattern.

The March of Democracy: Consensus or Conflict?

The periodicity of American democratic reform is hard to miss. But where do the great outbursts come from? What are they really about? What do they accomplish? The answers divide theories of American democracy—crudely speaking—into two schools: class conflict and ideological consensus. The debate has been long and lively, for the two schools see the same phenomena in almost precisely opposite ways. In one view, a profound agreement about democratic principles has led to the steady expansion of citizen rights; in the other, powerful economic conflicts often (but not always) preserved the status quo. Americans either concur about democracy or clash over class. Consider each in turn.

The consensus argument rests, of course, on the liberal tradition. Samuel Huntington has articulated the most forceful recent version. Ideas matter, argued Huntington. Ideas like equality, freedom (Americans, uniquely, believe in both simultaneously), inalienable rights, and the consent of the governed form a powerful "American Creed." When political reality diverges too widely from these ideals, Americans rebel. (They have done so four times.) The reformers win, more or less, because the reforms they seek accord with what Americans believe. However, democratic triumphs never fully achieve democratic ambitions; when they fall short, they establish the conditions of the next outburst.[28]

Before Huntington's contribution, political scientists who saw an American consensus appeared to have written their theory into a historical dead end, with no places for large-scale change. Americans, they said, agreed on the big matters; American politics were the petty adjustments of incremental pluralism. While Huntington gave pluralists a consensus theory with historical dimensions, historians had long been employing the consensus approach. Consider, for example, what they made of two great American reformations undertaken two centuries apart.[29]

While political science was rediscovering consensus in the American present, scholars like Edmund and Helen Morgan were finding it in the past. Never mind class conflict, wrote the Morgans. When Americans demanded rights and representation from George III, that is precisely what they wanted. Americans united in a "glorious cause" dominated by such bold new ideas as popular sovereignty. Though their first efforts at self-government may have been excessive in populism (and deficient in administrative "energy"), the new nation checked its "drift toward anarchy" with the Constitution of 1789. (This story may sound like the one normally put out for popular consumption, but it was distinctly out of favor with historians till the consensualists restored it in the 1950s.)[30]

Or take the civil rights movement in the 1960s. The condition of American black people violated the American creed. Despite agonizingly slow progress against an implacable white minority, civil rights protesters eventually won both legislation and voting rights because they articulated ideas that Americans believe in and, generally, agree on.

The consensus approach finds similar cases throughout American history. Universal male suffrage (in the Jacksonian era), Emancipation, the Fourteenth and Fifteenth Amendments (after the Civil War), the extension of the franchise to women (the Progressive era), or the legitimation of labor (1930s) all illustrate the steady progress of citizenship rights.[31]

The alternative tradition was originally formulated by the Progressive historians and is now carried on by social scientists loosely identified as New Left. In their view, class conflict has propelled social and democratic progress in America. The Progressives put it starkly. The movements celebrated by the liberals as a kind of unfolding of the American idea were, in reality, fights about economic interest. Ideas counted for little, they were obfuscations or propaganda. Consensus, where it appeared at all, was illusory.[32]

The perspective has grown increasingly sophisticated in the hands of such diverse authors as Lawrence Goodwin, Gary Nash, Edward Pessen, Eric Foner, Sean Wilentz, and Gordon Wood. They have updated the Progressive interpretation. They replace the brute class categories with a more dynamic view. Class continues to matter, but it is embedded in social and political relationships that go far beyond simple economic categories. Still, the American political development remains a series of struggles between haves and have-nots. In this view, clashes prompted by democratic reform movements reflect the working out of socio-economic tensions in the structure of society. As the nation evolved, these underlying tensions repeatedly drove reform to the surface of American political life. There, ideas may have played a role; but each case was profoundly shaped by underlying social and economic imperatives.

For example, the Progressive revision of the American Revolution pictured a colonial society racked by tensions as settled regions began to mimic European social patterns. Amid a development crisis marked by growing disparities of wealth and status, the colonial gentry managed to deflect the people's ire toward the British. After independence, they snatched political control away from the rising plebes by replacing the republican state governments (under the Articles of Confederation) with a counterrevolutionary Constitution.[33]

New Left scholars tell a similar story about the civil rights movement. A rising, oppressed class was partially bought off (with welfare benefits) and partially manipulated into the bureaucratic backwaters of the administrative state (like the War on Poverty agencies). For all the agony of that reform campaign, the economic status of black Americans relative to whites has shown only marginal improvement.[34]

The same pattern, say the New Left scholars, was repeated in each step of the "march of democracy." The celebrated rise of the common man during the age of Jackson meant subordination to party hierarchy, to new forms of labor organization, and to new accumulations of capital (with little of the economic mobility long celebrated in American myth). Reconstruction ended cruelly when the American majority tossed aside their "creed" and permitted the reassertion of white supremacy. Progressive reforms enfeebled political parties and urban immigrants while empowering economically based interest groups. Though judgments about winners and losers vary among proponents of the conflict tradition, the process invariably involves entrenched élites struggling to maintain (or extend) their privileges from the challenge of the have-nots.[35]

The two traditions are almost exact opposites. They examine the

21

same political episodes and see different causes (democratic ideas or economic differences) and different political processes (consensus or conflict). Recent work also differs about the outcomes. Consensualists look at the progress of formerly suppressed interests and celebrate the American promise; the New Left weighs the same promise by the economic progress of the have-nots and declares it a fraud (or, in more moderate hands, an exaggeration).

Once again, an argument debated as long as this one is likely to have insight on each side. In this case, each view concedes merit to the other.[36] There is evidence of both conflict and consensus, of both material forces and ideas that matter. The question (besides which matters more fundamentally) is, once again, how the evidence on each side can be pieced together. The politics of the democratic wish offers the following perspective.

The American democratic ideology fosters a consensus that permits new conflicts. The ideology is not propaganda (as the Progressives had it); nor is it an idea with the reforming power that consensualists ascribe to democracy. Rather, it is myth. The people that American reformers pursue is a chimera. However, it is a most significant illusion precisely because it conjures up the consensus that liberals ascribe to the "American creed."

The consensus introduced by the democratic hope is real. Here, after all, is an image that repeatedly proves acceptable to American élites without appearing trivial to their challengers. This, again, is why the democratic ideology wins acceptance while more explicit assaults on privilege and power do not. Still, the consensus introduces conflict. It facilitates the introduction of new rules and new institutions which, in turn, offer a locus for the underlying conflicts the Progressive school has focused on.

In this way, a political system biased toward the status quo has negotiated extraordinary change. Consider the evolution: frontier society, a mercantile political economy, bourgeois capitalism, corporate capitalism, welfare state capitalism, and a post- (alternately, "late" or "new") industrial system. Each of these transformations (and many others) created wholesale social and economic tensions, propelled new interests up, and threatened established classes with decline. From legislative government in the 1770s to regulatory agencies two hundred years later, a consensus over the mirage of the people cut through the political factions and enabled the creation of new political institutions which, in turn, provided a locus for the political fights that come with change.

But who wins? Different social scientists investigate the same democratic movements and draw entirely different conclusions: the Founding, the Jacksonian reforms, and the civil rights movement are alternatively pictured as triumphs of democracy or élite manipulation of the people. How can these conclusions be reconciled? The answer is simple: they cannot be. The outcomes are fundamentally ambiguous.

The democratic ideals that inspire reformers are, like any myth, unattainable. Judged by the hope of restoring the people, the movements—from the Founding to the civil rights crusade—all failed. Moreover, as I suggested in the preceding section, the reforms simultaneously introduce and limit political change. The former enable optimistic conclusions; consensus theorists can measure the political progress of previously shunned groups and celebrate the American process. On the other hand, the limits generate conclusions of co-optation and defeat. Neo-Progressives can measure the same events by social and economic indicators and judge them failures.

Of course, there is an entirely different criterion of success. The democratic revolts built up the capacity of the American state. Did they do so in an effective way? The question moves us to a final set of analytic traditions and an overview of the cases discussed in the chapters that follow.

Roundabout State Building

In contrast to the vast literature on democracy, the development of an administrative state has drawn sparse attention till recently. The work that has been done falls roughly into two types.

First, traditional histories of public administration offered broad and detailed studies of the agencies themselves. Leonard White's magisterial four-volume history still dominates the field (after four decades, here is a prime topic for a revisionist look). While the traditional works often demonstrate impressive historical sweep, they do not go far in explaining why things happened as they did. Administrative changes, though minutely detailed, emerge out of the events of the moment: Hamilton pressed his plans in the Washington administration; Garfield's assassination increased the cries for civil service reform.[37]

Second, recent work penetrates deeply into single moments in the development of administrative state building, illuminating the structural conditions and political imperatives. The focus shifts to such matters as the changing patterns of political recruitment (Matthew Crenson on the Jacksonians); the intricate play of party, politics, and power (Stephen Skowronek on the Progressives); the capacity and experience of the state itself (Theda Skocpol and her co-authors on the New Deal); and—more generally—the pressures of class, status, and new modes of organization.[38] Of course, rich detail in the study of a single era comes at the cost of pursuing the common links between the periods.

The traditional scholars focus narrowly on their dependent variable, public administration. The state-building approach turns the emphasis onto the independent variables, the underlying causes of change in each period. This book might be said to address a recurring intervening variable which links the two. The democratic ideology permits Americans to convert social pressures into policy-making institutions. If administrative state making is ultimately impelled by the imperatives of an evolving political economy, it has been negotiated by variations in the hunt for the people. In a sense, the chapters that follow each reinterpret a state-building moment through the analytic prism of the democratic wish.

OVERVIEW

The logic of my arguments differs slightly in the two parts of the book. In part I, I demonstrate how the democratic impulse negotiated the American dread of government and built up the administrative state; and, in part II, how the populist dynamic persists through the twentieth century, securing reforms when the government does not have the legitimacy (or the capacity) to act directly. In each case—across two hundred years—new state powers are secured and new groups legitimated through the mobilization of the people.

Each era described in part I saw the character of American public administration change in some fundamental way. The changes go beyond a mere jump in the number of officials (though their ranks grow in each case) and include reforms in the logic and rules governing public service. The choice of cases is a traditional one; these have generally been regarded as the state-building moments. (Wars are ignored for the reason noted earlier—though this omission, too, echoes the traditional histories of public administration.)

The Founding (chapter 1) set the political legacy and the constitutional rules. Here was the first effort to square public administration with democracy. The New World republicans rebelled against administrative usurpations, dispensed with ministers, and tried governing through popular assemblies. I argue that the delegates in Philadelphia reacted directly against this democratic wish. Eventually the Federalists split the difference between crown tyranny and legislative tumult (as they saw it) and designed an administrative apparatus populated by gentlemen trustees.

The gentlemen remained in place (despite adjustments during "Jefferson's revolution of 1800") till the Jacksonian period. Then, as I discuss in chapter 2, they were overthrown for a "people's bureaucracy," which formed the cornerstone for the nineteenth-century party state. Public administration plums (or jobs) lent coherence to both the parties and the polity in the tumult of mid-nineteenth-century America. The ambiguous pursuit of the people remade American institutions. The Jacksonians introduced a rudimentary bureaucracy to accommodate the rotation of "common men" into and out of office; the early try at centrally controlled administration was placed at the disposal of political parties. The United States has, quite distinctly, denied its public officials independence or stature. As we shall see, it was the people's bureaucracy that first negotiated their subordination.

The Progressive movement, described in chapter 3, eventually destroyed the party state and replaced it with a rough framework of contemporary administration. The Progressives linked efforts to restore power to the people (initiative, recall, referenda, extensions of suffrage, attacks on judicial review) to distinctly undemocratic administrative reforms (scientific management, civil service). Recent interpretations stress the latter and dismiss the democratic impulse that seemed to contradict it. I argue that the Progressives cannot be understood—indeed, their reformist oxymorons do not make sense—outside the context of the democratic wish. Reinterpreting the movement as an effort to reconstruct the direct participation of a consensual people demonstrates coherence (though not realism) in Progressive aspirations.

Precisely because they organized their reforms around a myth, the Progressives repeated the American reforming cycle: they mobilized a broad revolt against the "new aristocrats of plunder and patronage";[39] introduced their reforms as a way to restore government to the people; fought narrow political fights couched in the grandiloquent terms of democracy; and succeeded in creating the institutions of a new administrative state while new forms of private power subverted their populist innovations. The Progressives left behind a large but weak institutional apparatus which extended the constitutional checks and balances throughout the administrative system. Americans continue to struggle with this political legacy.

The New Deal is, as we shall see in chapter 4, a partial exception that illuminates both the argument and its limit. The Roosevelt administration extended the Progressive state without calling on the people. Roosevelt did not need them. The liberal fear of government had collapsed along with the economy. Without the dread, there was no call for the yearning. However, when the Democrats meddled in labor relations and industrial policy, they ran into the limits of their legitimate authority and a political stalemate, as I show in chapter 5. Roosevelt and his advisers negotiated the limits by calling on the people. I locate FDR's democratic wish in part II because it reformed one policy sector—labor politics—rather than reconstructing the administrative state.

In part II, I argue that the populist dynamics that built up the administrative state are now used to secure reforms within it. The legitimation of organized labor (chapter 5), the political empowerment of black Americans (chapter 6), and the end of professional domination of American medical politics (chapter 7) were all negotiated through the democratic wish.

These cases are narrower in scope than those of part I. They focus on movements that remake policy areas rather than on those that reconstruct American administration. Each chapter uses the democratic wish to reinterpret a political event; taken together, the cases are meant to demonstrate the broad applicability of the democratic process to contemporary America. There is no established analytic tradition drawing the three cases together. Still, they represent some of the central social cleavages in the United States—class, race, and professional status. The pattern (shaped in the eighteenth and nineteenth centuries) that I trace across class, race, and medical politics might help illuminate a variety of other topics. For example, environmental politics, the women's movement, disability rights, industrial policy, and the gay mobilization prompted by AIDS might all, in different ways, be explicated in terms of the democratic wish.

The questions of labor and race are roughly similar. Both involve the violent "redistributive" politics that surround the struggle of oppressed groups. Each presents clear parallels to the issues at stake in past democratic rebellions (say, conflicts over suffrage). Health care offers a contrast and a "least likely case." It shifts from the pyrotechnic politics of class and race to the cool complexities of medical policy. Rather than the legitimation of the most oppressed Americans, health care in the 1970s involved the subordination of the most privileged. This last case shows the democratic wish operating far from the ideological context normally associated with calls for popular participation.

If the political settings differ, however, the political processes are all variations on the same democratic themes. In each case, pressures for government action (which range from medical inflation to race riots) are blocked by the checks of a liberal state. Entrenched interests shout "socialism" to mobilize conservative allies. Multiple layers of federalism, overlapping bureaucratic jurisdictions, oversight by competing authorities (furiously balancing one another), and a multitude of other institutions all reinforce the limits to government action. Reformers—in these cases, usually within government—overcome the stalemate between imperatives for action and the limits on government by

27

re-creating the conditions of American state building. They call on the people.

The political process is distinctly recognizable. Public officials return hot issues to the "communities" (anything from neighborhoods to industrial sectors). There, the people will make choices. The democratic imagery creates a broad consensus; the program seems more or less acceptable on all political sides. (The War on Poverty, for example, may have been the only program of the civil rights era which was credible to black activists and yet did not provoke a Southern filibuster.)

The new programs create new agencies that muster up and modernize old town-meeting ideals. They offer an exuberant mix of democratic images and contemporary organizational methods: open meetings, civic education, broad opportunities to participate, professional staff support. The one thing they lack is political authority (after all, if the state could have mandated the authority, the exercise in democracy would have not been necessary).

Once the programs are implemented, the imagined consensus of the people deteriorates into the clash of groups and interests. Previously suppressed or inchoate groups mobilize to win a place in the program, their entrée into the political system. The new participants challenge established élites. The new institutions enable them to fight previously suppressed fights (ranging, in these chapters, from conducting labor union elections to controlling hospital construction).

The definition of the issue and the bias of the institutions not only legitimate the conflict, they limit its scope. The battles that were introduced by images of democracy are fought over the terms of representation in a program on the political periphery. Underlying the questions of representation lie the more vexing issues of power and such indivisible benefits as the bias of the state. However, battles of representation do not easily grow into conflicts over economic status. As we shall see, the politics of democratic yearning promote political change while deflecting fights about economic relations.

As new groups contend for political legitimacy, the imperatives of organizational maintenance begin to displace the fervor of mobilization. The moment of democratic possibility is followed by retrenchment, even within apparently radical groups. Political élites learn, in weak participatory agencies on the periphery of the state, that the incorporation of new groups promotes stability. White urban officials learned to negotiate with black leaders in the Community Action Agencies, capitalists first negotiated with labor leaders in the relative safety of NRA code negotiations that nobody but "the people" (or alternatively, the "American housewife") would enforce. Even authority over health politics was reconstructed in such a setting.

In the process, new forms of government power are legitimated. The tasks allowed the people (without sanctions) are, in each of these cases, incorporated into the workings of the administrative state. Political rules are recast, government powers extended. The search for the people continues to yield its ironic result: new administrative powers.

The search for the people enabled Americans to negotiate their liberalism and build up a public sphere. The process is full of ironies: democratic wishes produced bureaucracy; communal hopes reinforced liberal institutions. One question that runs through the following chapters is about the consequences. What kind of government did this roundabout state-building style leave the United States?

I argue that, in the end, the government lacks precisely the communitarian sentiment that reformers repeatedly championed. The democratic ideology is legitimate and consequential partially because it offers an alternative to government. However, this means that in America both liberal and communitarian traditions eschew state action—one in favor of private choices, the other for an imaginary people.

The result is that Americans have failed to institutionalize a communal spirit—an active notion of the people—within their government. We shall see that as American institutions were built up, the dilemma grew sharper. Communal sentiment remained a recurring challenge to the state rather than one of the features it was designed to represent. The lingering tension between democracy and public administration reflects the final irony of the American state-building process: democratic aspirations built a bureaucracy largely beyond popular control

This is not a failure of ideas. It is a dilemma of political practice and institutional design. Both classical liberalism and some communitarian thought offer alternative notions of shared common good. Americans may need to draw on them. Contemporary problems may require Americans to mobilize national energy, to centralize the discourse about ends and means, values and mechanisms. However, neither liberal nor democratic traditions, as they have been practiced, offer a guide for pursuing the public interest within the state itself. The task for the future is to replace the longing for imaginary community with a communal imagination that is part of the government.

Still, these are speculations of future politics. The story that follows is about past ideology and the evolution of the American administrative state. Whether or not the democratic wish is sufficient for contemporary problems, it has exerted a powerful influence throughout the American past. In a polity that never lost its Whiggish suspicion of government and governors, here is an alternative ideal offering its elusive chimerical promise: somehow, power can be taken away from the state and restored directly to the people. That ideal, rooted in the crucial instant of the Revolutionary conflict, may be the most important false hope in American history.

I

STATE BUILDING AND THE PEOPLE

1

Representation, Revolution, and Republic

The representative assembly . . . should be in miniature an exact portrait of the people at large. It should think, feel, reason and act like them.

—John Adams, 1776

The proposition that {the people} are the best keeper of their liberties is not true. They are the worst conceivable, they are no keepers at all. They can neither act, judge, think, or will.

—John Adams, 1787

Americans broke from England expressing a democratic wish. It interpreted confusing social changes, shaped colonial grievances, mobilized the population, inspired their politics, and defined their institutions. It was what the state constitutions of the 1770s aimed for and what the one of 1789 was aimed against.

My central theme is the communal vision of the people (or, for this period, classical republicanism) and its relationship to administrative power. This may seem an odd juxtaposition, for at the core of republicanism lay a dread of ministers. However, the tension was a dynamic one: it drove the American state builders. When imperial ministers seemed to violate colonial rights, Americans countered with revolutionary governments that abjured administrative authority altogether. Instead, they called on the people to rule directly (first mobbing in the streets, then mirrored in the assemblies). Although the Federalists eventually found a synthesis, reconstructing the people (in a more liberal fashion) and designing a more energetic administrative apparatus to govern them, they never resolved the tension between the people and their administrators. It would erupt again in the 1820s, sparking the next state-building moment.

The definition of "the people" is at the center of the two major analytic disputes about the Revolutionary era. First, the rediscovery of classical republicanism has prompted the debate described in the preceding chapter: Were the revolutionaries looking backward to ancient notions of civic participation in the common good? Or did they point forward to a modern liberalism founded on individual self-interest? A second, older, intellectual cleavage turns on whether the American Revolution was marked by a consensus that united colonial classes and factions against England (proponents of this view are, willy-nilly, tagged conservative). Or was it, at bottom, an internal conflict which colonial élites managed to redirect against the English?[1]

The overlapping debates ultimately raise the matter of American self-identity, both at the Founding and beyond. The same question—the colonists' political self-image, their definition of the people—is central to the three sections of this chapter: the clashing meanings of representation, the logic of revolution, and the definitions of the new republic. Each, I argue, began with a quest for a utopian community; in the end, the process left Americans an ambiguous definition of liberty and an unresolved anxiety about how to make it fit with their state's administrative institutions.

REPRESENTATION

The Political Setting at Midcentury

When England defeated France in 1763, colonists celebrated both the military triumph and "the glorious fabric of Britain's liberty," "the most perfect form of government . . . that ever existed."[2] The cheers echoed for their own institutions since the colonists believed that their governments replicated the English Constitution. Governors, upper chambers, and assemblies reflected the Crown, Lords, and Commons. In each case, the branches of government represented and balanced the orders of society—the monarchial (embodying order and energy), the aristocratic (wisdom), and the democratic (honesty and goodness). The trouble with the analogy was that it was not doubted on one side of the Atlantic and not taken seriously on the other. In fact, the English got it right; the similarities were superficial, the contrasts profound.[3]

Eighteenth-century English politics were stable, hierarchical, and ultimately harmonious. If there were elaborate court intrigues and at times a dizzy procession of ministers, the underlying political principles were settled. Members of Parliament were elected from fixed districts with restricted franchises. Ridings (or electoral districts) had not been added or withdrawn in almost a century. Thirty voters in Lewes sent two members; growing commercial centers such as Birmingham and Manchester, none. Members often answered to private patrons (who controlled "pocket boroughs"). Though the Glorious Revolution had circumscribed Crown authority over Parliament, the King owned some boroughs outright (electors held Crown posts and could be dismissed) and dispensed patronage to control others (a third of the members held Crown posts). Parliament did not permit lobbying in the modern sense; it could be petitioned only through formally prescribed, traditional outlets such as magistrates or universities.*

These representational mechanisms rested on a conception of fixed, corporate political interests. Members stood for local communities

---

*Samuel Beer calls the pattern "Old Whig Politics" and illustrates the mores of private patronage with a line from the younger Pitt about his patron: "if ever our lines of conduct should be opposite, I should give him the opportunity of choosing another member."[4]

bound together by "ancient ties of interest" and for broad functional orders such as "the landed classes," "commercial centers," or social "ranks." The patterns of representation reflected the essentially aristocratic politics of the English Augustan age. The state played a limited role in domestic matters; most issues turned on the perquisites of court or the affairs of empire.[5]

Colonial politics offered a vivid contrast. They were unsteady, fractious, and open. William Penn crystallized the political ethos in his well-known plea: "For the love of God, me and the poor country, be not so governmentish." The settlers ignored him and remained "open and noisy in dissatisfactions."[6]

Colonial representation contrasted with English practice at almost every point. Assembly seats generally reflected the flux in the populace. The Massachusetts constitution of 1691 required each town of forty voters to send a representative—resulting in an average of one addition every fifteen months for the next half-century. The Privy Council finally (in 1767) sought the stability of English politics by forbidding new constituencies; but this only provoked the colonists, who would declare their mode of representation "a right inestimable [to the people] and formidable to tyrants only."[7]

Moreover, recent analysis supports Thomas Hutchinson's piquant exaggeration about the breadth of the franchise: "anything with the appearance of a man" was entitled to vote. Across the colonies, between 50 percent and 70 percent of the white, adult males qualified. The consequences were generally obscured by widespread political deference to "big men"; however, the broad suffrage facilitated the spread of political contagion. Voters, as William Shirley prophetically observed, "have it in their power upon an extraordinary emergency to double and triple their numbers which they would not fail to do if . . . they suspect their ordinary members."[8]*

---

*Compare Shirley's observation with E. E. Schattschneider's classic epigram: "The central political fact in a free society is the tremendous contagiousness of conflict. . . . The outcome of all conflict is determined by the scope of its contagion."[9] Shirley was the royal governor of Massachusetts from 1741 to 1749 and from 1753 to 1756; Hutchinson was lieutenant governor of Massachusetts (appointed in 1758), chief justice (appointed 1760), and governor (from 1771 to 1774).

The political rules led legislators to take a distinctly local view of their role. Constituencies were small, many colonies (New York, Maryland, and all New England) imposed residency requirements, elecions were held annually, instructions on specific matters were common. William Smith, an eighteenth-century historian, judged the assemblymen themselves: "Plain, illiterate husbandmen whose views seldom extend further than to the regulation of highways, the destruction of wolves, wild cats and foxes and the advancement of other little interests of the particular counties which they . . . represent."[10]

The patterns of colonial representation reflected the nature of the society and the tasks before its governments. An unsettled nation with an undeveloped economy required active politics. Public choices had to be made about the distribution of land, the development of an economic infrastructure (wharfs, roads, ferries, civic buildings), and the design of social institutions (towns, schools, colleges, public libraries). William Smith was exactly right: colonial politics was about highways and wild cats.

In short, the colonists' metaphor about "balanced constitutions" obscured powerful differences between England and its colonies. On the one hand, a stable social order represented ancient interests in highly formalized ways; on the other, a new society wrangled over the shape of its social order and the nature of its political economy. Where the colonists saw a mirror of the English Constitution, English officials saw "oversees ordinance-making municipal corporations."[11] Each prospered from their relationship as long as neither looked closely at the others' assumptions about it.

Colonial affairs lay, loosely, in the hands of the ministry. Edmund Morgan charts the bureaucratic intricacies of the neglect that generally characterized English administration:

[The King left administration of the colonies] to his Secretary of State for the Southern Department. . . . The Secretary left it pretty much to the Board of Trade and Plantations. . . . The Board of Trade told the Secretary what to do; he told the royal governors;

the governors told the colonists; and the colonists did what they pleased.[12]

The royal governors were not in a position to do anything about it. Three thousand miles eviscerated most of their power. The chronic disarray of colonial charters was emblematic of the thin lines of authority that stretched back to London.[13] Instructions concocted at court were often irrelevant to New World conditions. Patronage posts were limited (and the assemblies often seized control over those that existed). There were few ways in which to establish local loyalty without investing personal fortunes (which the governors came to the colonies to seek, not spend). Their weak political hand was further undercut by frequent challenges from the assemblies which, like Parliament, had won control over public finances.

In 1763, the loose policy of indifference came to sudden end. The Crown decided to maintain a standing army in the colonies. With an inexperienced king, a sharply divided Parliament, and no majority coalition (four ministers stepped up to form governments between 1763 and 1770), power devolved onto the administrators at the subministerial level. They moved to rationalize colonial administration in earnest. They wrote new regulations, tried to enforce old ones, acquired new taxes, and moved to rein in the assemblies. When England introduced its more vigorous colonial policy, the clashing political visions rose swiftly to the surface. The colonists responded to each administrative innovation from London—and, as James Q. Wilson points out, most of George III's "abuses and usurpations" were administrative policies—with outcries about representation.[14]

Two Concepts of Representation

England and her colonies moved toward their break articulating sharply different theories of political representation, each embedded in the style and mores of their respective social orders. The debate mixed traditional ideas, rationalizations of contemporary practice, and wishful thinking. The English theory never fully addressed colonial objections and lasted, as J. R. Pole put it, "only so long as it escaped detection and definition."[15] On the other side, the colonists went to war loudly pronouncing a different representational ideal, though the peace treaty was signed long before they had a workable theory.

When Parliament imposed taxes on the colonies (and what was worse, tried to collect them), the Americans charged that their own assemblies had not approved the levies—taxation without representation. Thomas Whateley (the secretary to George Grenville who had drafted the stamp tax) responded with the doctrine of virtual representation: "None are actually, all are virtually represented; for every member of Parliament sits in the House, not as a Representative of his own Constituents, but as one of the August Assembly by which all the Commons of Great Britain are represented."[16] The members from Bristol spoke for Birmingham sixty-five miles distant and Boston across the sea as well. A decade later, Burke made the best-remembered statement of the theory:

> Parliament is not a congress of ambassadors from different and hostile interests which interests each must maintain, as an agent and advocate, against other agents and advocates; but Parliament is a deliberative assembly of one nation, with one interest, that of the whole—where not local . . . prejudices ought to guide, but the general good. . . . You choose a member, indeed; but when you have chosen him he is not a member of Bristol, but he is a member of Parliament.[17]

Today Burke is usually cited for his dictum on how representatives ought to behave: they should be trustees, pursuing the best interests of others; they owe constituents their good judgment, never their votes. However, the argument speaks with equal force to the other side of the representational relationship, to the definition of constituency. Burke insisted that the constituency was a single entity bound together by a single interest—the general good. Representatives stood not for individual citizens or cities or causes, but for the country. Once representation is construed in this way, direct electoral accountability to individual citizens—which is what the colonists had been clamoring for—can be talked down. Burke would loosen the linkages between citizenry and state. He would limit voting to the natural leaders, who could thoughtfully judge the representatives' conduct. The implicit vision of society is one of stability, aristocracy, deference, and only a small number of political interests (the last assumption protects the nonvoters—and the representational scheme—if self-interested factions creep in).

The colonists' response to virtual representation evolved over three decades as they thought, fought, and reconstructed their governments. They began with what is sometimes called the microcosm view of representation. As John Adams put it, the legislature "should be an exact portrait, in miniature, of the people at large, . . . it should think, feel, reason and act like them." And later, "the perfection of the portrait, consists in its likeness."[18] The colonists constantly repeated the metaphor and added others: the assembly as portrait, as mirror, as microcosm. Here was the reverse of the Burkean view: not the wisest doing what is best for the people, but the typical doing what the people themselves would have done.

Contemporary theorists criticize the microcosm view for offering no guide to representative action. Burke's theory instructs representatives how to behave; the colonists' only tells them whom to be like. The lack of specificity illuminates a critical point. The colonists were sceptical of representation altogether. Assemblies were a necessary inconvenience, tolerated only because it was not (always) practical for the people to act "directly and personally," as Jefferson put it. Their theory pushed up against the boundary of what counts as representation, shading into a metaphorical form of direct citizen participation in government.[19]

Within this quasi-participatory rubric, the colonists linked constituents as closely to their representatives as they could. The revolutionaries broadened their franchises, multiplied constituencies (on average, the assemblies doubled in size), mandated periodic reapportionment of seats (in five states), guaranteed the right to instruct representatives (in four states), erected visitors' galleries in the assemblies. One proposal, in Pennsylvania, would have all laws posted for a year in the public houses before the legislature acted on them (critics jibed that the taverns had become the second House of the Commonwealth).[20]

The real trouble with the colonial counter to virtual representation lay neither in the ambiguous mandate to the representatives nor in the sometimes impractical mechanisms linking representatives to their constituencies. Rather, the problem was its murky delineation of the constituency itself. What (or whom) should the assemblies mirror? Individual citizens? Property holders? Towns? Counties? The populace of an entire state, taken together? The answer, of course, would instruct the behavior of the representatives in the most fundamental ways.

Clearly, some sort of natural social hierarchy was implied. Women, black people, native Americans, and men without property did not generally vote (although there were exceptions in all four cases). Most colonists still expected commoners to defer to their natural leaders—but such distinctions only complicated the "portraiture" of the people. The issue was exposed when Massachusetts apportioned an assembly delegate for every hundred voters. Small towns, especially those in the Connecticut River Valley, protested: many would have to share delegates with other towns (might as well share a soul with other individuals, they said). The citizens of western Massachusetts turned the colonial critique of virtual representation on the people of Boston, with whom they claimed to have no more in common than they had with the citizens of London.[21] The problem, of course, is that "the people" is not a concrete entity. The colonists were seeking an assembly that would "think, feel, and reason" like a fiction, a reification.

It took decades to fully work out the problem. Americans had, however, an implicit (if ultimately unworkable) answer to questions of constituency and representative behavior: it lay in the larger world view of classical republicanism. This political paradigm makes sense out of the colonial view of representation by filling in the assumptions and expectations that framed the theory. Taken as a whole, republicanism can be read as an idyllic rationalization of colonial politics; but alter just a few elements of the paradigm, and it turns into a revolutionary ideology.

At the heart of republican politics lay the subordination of individual interests to the common good, the *res publica*. The ideal was not simply the sum of individual private interests, but a distinct public interest with an objective existence of its own. Like Rousseau's general will, the common good would harmoniously integrate the entire community. The community was a single organic body which united all its members in "common feeling, founded on a common consent." The communal bond rendered the good of the whole in the interest of each individual. "That the great body of the people can have any interest separate from their country . . . is not to be imagined," commented William Smith; unless, added John Sullivan, "we suppose them idiots or self-murderers."[22]

Republics operated through direct citizen participation in civic affairs. Liberty was public; sharing in communal decisions, both a right and an obligation. "One or few could never be better judges [of the common good] than was the multitude." Once the people participated directly in politics, all could contribute their own virtues (wisdom, for example, or courage) to the common good; the natural rulers would "emerge from the midst of them."[23]

Classical republicanism was by no means egalitarian. Members of the community were expected to acknowledge their place in the natural order; common people would defer to the "natural aristocracy." The expectation reflected the colonial experience, marked by paternalistic hierarchy and deference to "big men." But there was a hidden catch. The existence of natural leaders implied an objective standard by which existing leaders (and their ascent) might be weighed; natural hierarchy implied the reverse—an artificial one.

Republics demanded virtue. Monarchies could rely on coercion and "dazzling splendor" to suppress self-interest or factions; republics relied on the goodness of the people to put aside private interest for public good. The imperatives of virtue attached all sorts of desiderata to the republican citizen: simplicity, frugality, sobriety, simple manners, Christian benevolence, duty to the polity. Republics called on other virtues—spiritedness, courage—to protect the polity from external threats. Tyrants kept standing armies; republics relied on free yeomen, defending their own land. (It was thought that republican citizens made the fiercest armies, though General Washington would soon testify to the contrary.)[24]

Citizens were, by definition, independent and self-reliant. They were yeomen farmers who owned their own land (and, as a result, were not dependent on anyone else). When Jefferson suggested that every Virginian be given fifty acres, he was articulating the republican ideal of independent yeomen as the bulwark of liberty. When he repeated "after every speech" that the nation be divided into wards of fifty citizens, he was affirming the usual wisdom that republics had to be small and homogeneous in order to permit men to govern themselves.[25]

Republics had proven the most fragile form of government, always declining from virtue to corruption and self-interest (proving "spectacles of turbulence and democracy," wrote Madison, "as short in their lives as they have been violent in their deaths"). They existed outside historical time; development, cities, manufacturing, capitalism— modernity—would rip the fabric of the small self-reliant communities. However, optimists followed the French philosophes and articulated a kind of frontier myth to suggest why the new world was different: here was a special people inhabiting a vast continent with an apparently inexhaustible stock of land.[26]

In short, the republican idyll involved consensus about the common good, direct citizen participation in civic affairs, rural independence, small homogeneous communities, natural hierarchy, and popular virtue. The ideology offers a largely implicit framework which helps to clarify the colonial analysis of representation. Consider how it illuminates the definition of constituencies, the role of the representative, and the link between them.

The colonists had something definite in mind when they claimed "the people" as their political constituencies. This was not the rhetorical fillip that strikes the modern ear; nor was it only the undifferentiated "democratical" element of traditional mixed constitutions. To the colonists, "the people" also evoked the republican expectation of a powerful, shared common interest that the representative would articulate and pursue. The ubiquitous appeals to "the people" during the Revolutionary crisis reflect an effort to anchor representation in the elusive world of classical republicanism.

However, the underlying dilemma remained. The members of a community might share a single interest; but, in order to secure it, the community would have to be small, homogeneous, and rural. How were the people of, say, Massachusetts to square the interests of the many communities across their state? And what to do about a metropolis like Boston? How about relationships to the communities of the other states? These dilemmas of constituency were inherent in the application of classical republicanism to the New World.

Republicanism also illuminates the representative's role. Calling for a "portrait" of the people was an effort to reproduce the communal political process that was capable of ascertaining the public good. The republican image fills in an implicit step in the representational syllogism: if the representatives "think, feel, reason" like the people, they will act like the people; and—furthermore—the people participating in civic affairs is how the public good is discerned. Adams was not only telling representatives what they should *be* (as contemporary theorists of representation assume); he was also suggesting that if they could be like the people—if communal republicanism could somehow be reproduced in the assembly chamber—they were more likely to think, feel, and reason their way to the common good.

Finally, the many participatory devices with which representatives were linked to the people reflected the republican emphasis on civic participation. At the same time, they also reflected the decidedly noncommunal legacy of colonial politics with its emphasis on particularistic, self-interested political agendas. The gap between theoretic promises and traditional politics was wide.

At first glance, what is most striking about the republican idea is its wholesale denial of the entire colonial experience. Republicanism imagined a selfless, united people; colonial politics was racked, as Wood puts it, by a "bitter and kaleidoscopic factionalism." Republicanism posited an underlying, organic public interest as the object of politics; colonial politics was marked by the narrow pursuit of petty interests. Republicanism imagined homogeneous rural communities; the New World was, as we shall shortly see, rapidly developing social classes and commercial centers. One conclusion is that the "revolution was one of the great utopian movements in American history."[27] The same would be said of every political movement described in this book. It is precisely during the periods of political turmoil that the republican promise of unity and common interest seems most alluring.

At the same time, the tenets of classical republicanism also formed a powerful ideology by which to mobilize revolutionary sentiment. Here is an idea that the people share a true common interest which can be discerned only when they participate directly in politics, when their "rulers . . . proceed from the midst of them." What if the rulers were, somehow, artificially imposed on the people? Once the logic (and habit) of deference evaporated, the bias of the ideology would shift radically. Torn from its agricultural context and set in the cities, the republican idea offered a justification for direct action, for revolution. If, as John Adams announced, "democratical despotism is a contradiction in terms,"[28] then Tory sympathizers deserved whatever justice the mobs of Boston meted out. The republican image would prove an implausible ideal by which to shape a regime; mixed with disorienting social conditions and a tradition of mobbing, it proved a most effective one by which to spark a revolution.

Finally, the nature of early American republicanism has excited considerable intellectual ferment. After powerfully reshaping our understanding of the American Revolution, it is now challenged by a new wave of scholarship.[29] The claim made here is that the republican paradigm clarifies colonial arguments about representation; I will argue that it illuminates their revolutionary impulse, the success and failures of the first American governments (under the Articles of Confederation), and the arguments that the framers of the Constitution were arguing against.

REVOLUTION

A Changing People: Demography and Democracy

Beneath the theories of representation lurked a bundle of social tensions. The colonies were changing as they matured. Their economy was growing more complex and differentiated; so was the society, as new forms of wealth and hierarchy emerged. Both trends quickened during the French and Indian War; by the time it ended in 1763, the colonies were experiencing a crisis of development.

The republican myth offered both a paradigm through which to interpret the new developments, and a set of strategies with which to escape from them. At the same time, however, social and economic dislocations inverted the political bias of republicanism: they turned it into a challenge to the status quo.

Consider three types of tension confronting the Americans: regional, rural, and urban. First, regional conflicts developed as the colonies grew. The population doubled every twenty-five years in the northern colonies, every fifteen years on the frontier. T. R. Malthus judged this "a rapidity of increase probably without parallel in history." Growth was complicated by mobility. Migrants from Massachusettes established ninety-four towns in Maine in the fifteen years prior to the Revolution; twenty thousand settlers moved into Vermont in a decade; farmers created a Connecticut colony in central Pennsylvania. The flux played havoc with political boundary lines and constituencies. Governors resisted new representatives in order to stabilize their provinces while the settlers clamored for a local voice.[30]*

More serious political consequences emerged as the seaboard differentiated itself from the frontier, a distinction that became clear about 1725. Tensions developed as their interests diverged. By the 1760s, sectional violence was flaring across the colonies. For example, the Paxton Boys mobilized to fight native Americans in frontier Pennsylvania, then turned their guns on the eastern establishment which, they insisted, had grown hostile to their interests. The Regulators (in South Carolina), the Vigilantes (North Carolina), the Green Mountain Boys (Vermont), and other frontier groups challenged the colonial leaders with similar patterns of violence.[32]

Second, large landowners were reconstructing rural society. While the conditions of social mobility were being renewed on the frontier, they were receding in the settled areas. New England, argues Kenneth Lockridge, was "rapidly becoming more and more an old world society." Tenant farming, landlessness, poverty, and social hierarchy were all increasing. Outside New England, old colonial proprietors revived long-dormant land claims (and the quitrents, or payments, attached to them), sparking a "feudal revival." In the simpler colonial society of

---

*Overall, the colonial population grew 22 percent in the 1740s (reaching 1,170,760 by 1750), 26 percent (1750s), 25 percent (1760s), and 22 percent (1770s).[31]

the past, absentee landlords could not make their titles pay; now the London landholders collected rents comparable to those of the great English estates. The long-settled districts throughout the colonies, conclude Rowland Berthoff and John Murrin, "were approaching the demographic pattern of Western Europe": population density, economic stratification, labor specialization, and declining social mobility.[33]

Third, these changes were particularly vivid in the cities. There, the top 10 percent of the wealth holders controlled 70 percent of wealth (compared with just 40 percent in the northern farming communities). An identifiable poverty class (numbering between 10 and 20 percent of the population) developed in Boston by 1740, in New York and Philadelphia by 1760. Gary B. Nash illustrates its rise by charting the taxpayers dropped from the revenue rolls because of poverty: in Philadelphia they grew from 3 percent in 1740 to between 6 and 7 percent in 1750 and 10 percent by the 1760s. Boston was worse. Colonial wars exacerbated the disparities by creating both profits and victims (such as disabled veterans and widows). The cities, concludes Nash, "were becoming centers of frustrated ambition, propertylessness, and genuine distress."[34]

Urban tensions regularly erupted into violence. Richard Brown counts twenty-eight riots in the eight largest cities between 1760 and 1775. What is striking about the outbursts is their political ambiguity: they challenged both English policy and colonial élites. The best-known instance followed the stamp tax (in 1765). The people were mobilized by patriot leaders but ran out of their control and sacked the mansions of the city tax collector (Andrew Oliver), the lieutenant governor and chief justice (Thomas Hutchinson), a clerk of the admiralty court, and two customs officials. Governor Francis Bernard reported "a war of plunder, of general levelling and taking the Distinction of rich and poor." He warned about the "insurrection of the poor against the rich, those that want the necessity of life against those that have them." Wealthy patriots brought out their own arms, leading General Thomas Gage to comment on the swift change in their outlook: "Each fears he might be the next victim of the rapacity . . . and there has been as much pains taken since to prevent insurrections of the people as before to excite them."[35]

What to make of the turmoil? The republican framework offered the colonists two overlapping explanations. It fixed the blame on both the colonists and the Crown, on both internal malaise and imperial malice.

One trouble was colonial corruption. After the French war, as social hierarchies grew more vivid and rigid, an old American jeremiad against wealth and luxury became especially urgent. Americans were being "carried away by the stream of prosperity," by wealth, ostentation, pride, "fêtes champêtres," and "Asiatic Amusements." Northern sermons, newspapers, and pamphlets resentfully protested the emerging—distinctly unrepublican—social order; in the South, they articulated a social disorientation within the ruling élite. Throughout the colonies, socio-economic development was interpreted as the loss of republican virtue.[36]

Second, the colonists blamed England as it began to meddle in the New World. The imperial influence—court, courtiers, and bureaucrats—was overturning the natural order. Corrosive Old World vices were corrupting the New World republicans. Men rose, not by their natural endowments, but by currying favor with royal authorities. English officials exacerbated colonial fears by suggesting than an indigenous American nobility might impart social stability and political balance on the rambunctious settlers: "How eagerly they wish to form distinctions among us, that they may create a few more tools of oppression. They wish to see us aspire to nobility and are ready to gratify us whenever we do."[37] Here was a simple, conspiratorial explanation for the changes that seemed to be transforming seaboard society into a rude mirror of the Old World.

These colonial diagnoses are well known; what is not often recognized is how they anticipate contemporary explanations for the Revolution. Today there are two major lines of analysis. Either the colonists fought to defend their potent ideas from British interference; or the "little" men, driven by (equally potent) socio-economic developments, rose up and challenged colonial élites. The Revolution was marked either by a consensus over the democracy or by a conflict rooted in demography.

There are traces of both in the colonial explanations. The cry against corruption is a challenge to the legitimacy of the new social hierarchies; the critique of imperial meddling sticks the frightening social changes on English "innovations," as John Dickinson referred to them.[38] The republican paradigm linked the two and shaped a response to each.

On its face, the dream of rural virtue and natural order seems a romantic escape beyond historical time which appealed to the colonists' imagination precisely as modernity was crashing in on their society. However by the 1770s, the paradigm that once rationalized traditional politics was evolving into an ideology of political mobilization. Republicanism instructed common men to defer to natural leaders; what was now thrown into doubt was just who was which. New social and economic hierarchies were unsupported by "ancient ties" or "the growth of ages," as Dickinson would put it. "The most opulent families have risen from the lowest rank in our memory," reported a New Yorker.[39] The emphasis on corruption and declension from virtue challenged the political status quo; leaders could be weighed by the unlikely republican criterion: had they emerged from "the midst of the people" on the strength of their natural endowments and fitness to rule? The franchise had always been generous in the colonies; commoners had been bound more by social checks than by political rules. Now, both the logic and the habits of deference were eroding. As they did so, the logic of republicanism changed: now such republican injunctions as civic participation in search of the communal good were precisely what the Boston mobs or the Green Mountain Boys could profess to be doing.

Of course, growing economic stratification or declining social mobility are amorphous secular trends. They may have stirred up the underlying political tensions, but the colonists had a far more concrete source on which to pin the disorienting changes. English efforts to impose a new administrative regime provided a political focus and brought the issues to a crisis. And the republican paradigm offered ostensibly lost ideals to regain—a government that would "think, feel, reason, and act" like "the people."

The Long Train of Abuses

When the English reorganized colonial administration, their view of the American governments (which was, at bottom, bureaucratic) collided with the colonists' own interpretation (thirteen balanced constitutions). England pursued its rationalizing contrivances; the colonists resisted with their republican contentions. That tension—administration against representation—would repeatedly prove to be the thesis and antithesis of the American state-building dialectic.

The ministers tried to impose efficiency on the patchwork of departments, boards, and agencies which concocted colonial policy. A new office, secretary of state for the North American colonies, now oversaw imperial administration and offered the royal officials in America a direct avenue for complaints. Administrators drafted revenue bills. They overhauled the notorious American customs (which had systematically winked at the trade and tariff violations that marked the bulk of colonial trading). New tax agents arrived in the colonies waving bureaucratic forms at the colonial merchants; they implemented increasingly stiff restrictions, wielded growing powers (to inspect ships, seize cargo), and met mounting hostility. Edmund Morgan articulates a popular colonial perspective when he pictures the new officials as "a rapacious band of bureaucrats who brought to their task an irrepressible greed and vindictive malice."[40]

What made this a "despotic administration of government," however, was the effort to run it independently of the uncooperative colonial institutions. The Privy Council began to oversee (and overrule) colonial legislation in earnest. It instructed the governors to prorogue defiant assemblies. The ministers struck at the core of colonial representation when they forbade the seating of new constituencies. They stripped the legislatures of their trustiest weapon—the power of the purse—when the Townshend tariffs* were earmarked as salaries for royal officials (from tax collectors to governors). Moreover, London further liberated its officials from the litigious colonists (who seemed to sue, says Morgan, as often as they ate and slept) by replacing jury trials with administrative (or admiralty) courts.[41]

Bernard Bailyn has demonstrated how colonial suspicions were already aroused by the strident warnings of the radical Whigs: Crown

---

*The Townshend Acts, sponsored by chancellor of the exchequer, Charles Townshend, imposed duties on paper, glass, lead, and tea; strengthened the hand of imperial officials; and asserted the right of Parliament to tax the colonies.

ministers craved power; they would corrupt assemblies, create standing armies, run up debts, heap taxes on the people, and wreck republican manners.[42] Consider how the tension between imperial reforms and republican ideals framed three early "abuses" in the progress toward war.

In 1763, the Crown closed the frontier, drawing a crude western boundary to the American colonies. The effort to secure the territories newly won from France restricted American migrants seeking land. On a practical level, it threatened to exacerbate the growing regional tensions in the colonies. As a symbolic matter, it threatened the New World expanses which, in the colonial imagination, promised to regenerate republican societies of independent yeomen farmers. Even worse than the prohibition on settlers was the prospect for speculators. The English repeatedly allowed exceptions to their boundaries. Each time they redrew the lines, London speculators with political pull (and their colonial agents) made a fortune. The apparently straightforward matter of a colonial boundary raised all the complications of corruption and virtue: here were court politicians creating new forms of wealth (gained through political machination) while they threatened the mainspring of republican renewal.

The Quartering Act (April 1765) required the colonial assemblies to billet British troops in empty barns and warehouses. This mandate, too, raised the echo of Whig alarms. Standing armies typified ministerial oppression; true republics relied instead on militias of armed yeomen, defending their land with their own muskets. Worse, Parliament was ordering a tax; in a free nation, taxes were offered by the people, sitting in assembly. The levy raised the most contentious issue: Who represented the colonists, local assemblies or Parliament? London tried to finesse the matter by ordering the colonial assemblies to order the tax. However, Charles Townshend exposed this fig leaf by introducing a measure to suspend the New York Assembly when it balked. The issues of standing armies, taxes, political authority, and precisely who represented whom were all crammed into the quarrel over where the soldiers were going to sleep.

The stamp tax (March 1765) ignited the first really national outcry over precisely the same issues. On the most superficial level, it was an economic clash. Prime Minister Grenville and the parliamentary majority set out to defray "the expenses of defending . . . the British colonies." Colonial leaders reasoned that taxes levied in America were taxes avoided in England (where politicians might hear more directly from electors and mobs). Of course, it was not the money. Colonial assemblies had long struggled with governors over control of public finance; in colonial eyes, the battle mirrored Parliament's own conflict with the Crown over the same matter (finally settled by the Glorious Revolution in 1688). However, the English leaders missed the parallel and saw, instead, just another challenge to their authority. They refused to hear colonial petitions before the vote. They insisted on the right to tax, even as they finally repealed the levy. The clash between institutions was elevated into the celebrated debate over representation when Whateley conjured up the notion of virtual representation as a theoretic legitimater.[43]

The response among the colonists went beyond discussions of revenue, republicanism, or representation. Boston leaders mobilized artisans and mechanics to protest the act. As we saw, the mob ran out of control. Mobs were also active in Newport, New York, Philadelphia, Charleston, and elsewhere. We do not need to convert the Stamp Act into a nineteenth-century class rebellion to acknowledge the "ill defined feelings of class and defiance of authority" that were touched off by the English tax.[44]

The Stamp Act brought the colonists "out of doors." Local committees, national congresses, mass meetings, and mobs began to act in the name of the people. They bypassed formally constituted institutions, seized political authority and vested it in ad-hoc, extragovernmental, political organisms such as the Sons of Liberty. The search for extralegal mechanisms to empower the people directly would animate the revolutionary struggle and become one of its major political legacies.

The Revolution introduced a pattern that would be repeated, in all kinds of variations, throughout American history. Underlying tensions create dissatisfaction and unease. The myth of a lost era in which political and social mobility rested on virtue gains popular currency. The tensions are converted into political action after a villain is charged with violating the (always evolving) norms of popular rule. Often, as in the Revolutionary era, the perceived usurpations come from administrators reaching beyond the legitimate boundaries of their power. The indictment against them is cast in the name of "the people" who are repeatedly, almost ritualistically, called on to reassert their rightful place. The people—that united, consensual collectivity of classical republicanism—forms the linchpin of this democratic wish and the American pattern of political revolt.

The People Out of Doors (1774–76)

For a stunning moment, a republican vision of the people seemed to materialize among the colonists. The people appeared to wrest political authority from the Crown officials; they bypassed formally constituted institutions, threw up ad-hoc, extralegal political bodies, and began to govern themselves directly. The row with England seemed to promote "a remarkable and unexpected union . . . throughout all the colonies," "a degree of public spirit among all ranks of men."[45]* The image of a unity lasted only while the imperial challenge eclipsed internal conflicts. Nevertheless, the colonists went to war touting the image of a united people rising up to challenge a tyrannous encroachment on their rights.

The people of the 1770s acted through a variety of mechanisms: provincial assemblies, conventions, mass meetings, mobs, and—perhaps most important—citizen committees. Consider each in turn.

By 1773, nearly every colony had devised bodies to stand for prorogued assemblies. "If the governor will not convene the Assembly," explained a member from North Carolina, "then the people will call themselves." Free from the Privy Council's restrictions, the new bodies tended toward broader suffrage, the incorporation of new (usually western) constituencies, and substantially larger memberships (South Carolina jumped from 42 delegates to 104; Massachusetts, from 105 to 293).[47]

Along with their ad-hoc assemblies, the people called a multitude of

---

*"Those few years, before the actual conflict," comments Gordon Wood, "marked the time and spirit which best defined the Americans' Revolutionary objectives and to which they clung throughout the war with increasing nostalgia."[46] It is my point that the same urge, so distant by 1780, would repeatedly return to tantalize American democrats.

conventions. Some drew deputies from across the colonies—the Stamp Act and the Continental Congresses are the best remembered. These bodies claimed no formal political authority beyond the "name of the people"; yet both patriots and Crown officials testified that they appeared to have the "same regard paid to them as used to be paid to laws enacted in form."[48]

The people also met and mobbed. Public meetings were called on every kind of matter—quieting the Boston crowds after the stamp tax riot, rousing them before the Tea Party, electing delegates to assemblies or conventions, forming new committees, or roasting Crown officials. The mob, shuddered Gouverneur Morris after a New York gathering, "began to think for itself." ("Poor reptiles," he added, "ere noon they will bite.")[49]

Mobbing was a fixture of eighteenth-century communal life, both in the New World and the Old. Crowds extinguished fires, acted as police, enforced quarantines, and imposed morality on the wayward; when times were hard, the crowd set "just prices," punished price gougers and hoarders, and drove off outsiders who threatened to compete for jobs. This was the social and political weapon of the ordinary people, grounded in the republican logic of corporatism—the notion that the community was a single body with a common interest. The concept was set in a larger moral framework (or "moral economy") of mutual obligation.[50]

Crowds are evanescent. In the Revolutionary crisis, citizen committees formed a kind of political vanguard which mobilized and led them. The Sons of Liberty organized in response to the stamp tax. As the crisis spread, the network of committees grew: the Committee of 28, of 60, of 43, of Inspection, of Observation, of Safety, of Merchants, of Privates; the Loyal Nine; the South End Caucus Club. Most were organized by community leaders, though with time they began to call on associations of the "damn, dirty, mutinous . . . riff-raff."[51]

At the start, the committees mobilized the mobs to traditional corporatist ends. They fanned defiance of British policy, organized boycotts of English goods, harassed customs agents, and punished anybody with a mind to observe instructions from London. These semi-organized citizen bands managed to frustrate English colonial policy (gutting the stamp tax by managing broad noncompliance, for example). As war approached, the committees—in concert with both the Continental Congress and the crowd—began to exercise a broad array of state powers. They set the price of necessaries, boycotted colonial courts, formed alternative tribunals, examined the merchants' books, punished public offenders (for profiteering, petty crime, or cooperating with the British), regulated trade, intervened between debtors and creditors, issued licenses, and—as critics had it—directed "what we shall eat, drink, wear, speak and think."[52]

For a brief time, two separate sets of institutions operated in the colonies—one disintegrating, one barely organized. On the one hand were the English ministers, royal governors, military authorities, and customs officials; on the other, the Continental Association, provincial congresses, local committees, and mobs. By 1775, royal governors were reporting that "orderly government was no longer possible." In fact, the governing order had been wrenched out of their hands by the committees who managed to (more or less) run things despite "lacking the force of law."[53]

That brief revolutionary moment when the people seemed to govern without governments, without "the force of law," crystallizes the central image of the democratic wish. This is not simply an effort to topple a tyrannous government in order to establish a better, more popular one (in the traditional revolutionary manner). Rather, power would be seized from the government and vested in the people themselves. They would govern directly, outside the formal mechanisms of the state. The people comprise a concrete, independent political entity, capable of ruling by and for itself, even in opposition to the government.

When the colonists set out to establish formal political institutions, they continued to pursue the popular wish embedded in the people out of doors. Their first effort was not merely organized around a set of institutions that might deliver the public good; rather, they tried to organize governments that would reflect the public, that would reconstitute it within the organs of the state. Of course, the image of the people ruling themselves directly is a populist myth—one that the framers of the Constitution would rebel against. Nevertheless, this notion of the people would survive the Federalist effort to bury it.

The Revolutionary crowd was elevated into a mythic people. No comparable idealization would rub off on the Revolutionary parties that mobilized them. (The contrasting American myth, grounded in one variant of liberalism, would celebrate individuals acting in the marketplace.) The Sons of Liberty might receive their filiopietistic due. As a political form, however, organizational vanguards and committees would pass through American political iconology as a peril to populism.*

Even the scholarship on the Revolutionary committees is submerged within the larger analytic questions about the people: Did the committeemen élite mobilize the populace only to lose control of them (the conflict school)? Or did they attack the British in solidarity with people of all social classes (the consensus school)? Each tradition, in its own way, organizes itself around the American myth; each line of analysis turns on a judgment about the Revolutionary people as an independent force.

The politics of committees, crowds, and congresses lasted only a brief revolutionary moment. However, the image of collective, participatory politics would remain, an ironic (and, as we shall see, useful) myth for the most liberal of nations. Somehow the authority of the state would be seized from corrupt ministers and exercised directly by the people themselves.

CONSTITUTIONAL CONTENTIONS: RECONSTRUCTING THE REPUBLIC

The People Indoors

After declaring independence, Americans framed governments that reflected both the aspirations and the optimism of the early Revolution. They sought to institutionalize the principles that seemed so powerful

---

*Frances Fox Piven and Richard Cloward, arguably the most widely read American leftists, energetically propound this perspective: mass, grass-roots, popular protests win change; organizations stifle it. In their *Poor People's Movements: Why They Succeed, How They Fail*, they trace repeated cycles of populist victory undone by organizations.[54]

in the revolutionary moment—popular consensus, actual representation, protection from magistrates.

Operating under state constitutions and the Articles of Confederation, Americans won the war, negotiated a favorable peace, muddled through a depression, sorted out the tangled land claims on the frontier, and secured—as Patrick Henry put it—"a territory greater than any European monarch possessed." Gordon Wood judges the new assemblies "as equal and fairly representative of the people as any legislature in history." And yet, by the mid-1780s, America reverberated with talk of crisis. The delegates to the Annapolis Convention reported that "the situation of the United States [is] delicate and critical." This, wrote Jefferson about Virginia, "is not the government we fought a revolution for." Added Washington, "we have probably had too good an opinion of human nature in the formation of our confederation." And more melodramatically, "to be fallen! So lost! It is mortifying."[55] Less than five years after their victory at Yorktown, Americans were debating an entirely new kind of government. What went wrong with the first ones?

The answers fall into two analytic categories: shoddy constitutional design and class conflict. Though the interpretations draw radically different conclusions, recent analysis demonstrates that both capture important features of the "critical period." What has received less notice is how both chaos and social conflict flowed directly from the same source—the revolutionaries' idea about what it meant to represent the people. Before we see how this is so, consider the partial truths in the traditional interpretations.

The view generally put out for popular consumption pictures awkwardly designed political institutions which blundered from chaos to legislative tyranny. The revolutionaries framed their governments to mirror the people. They vested almost all public power in the assemblies and shaped them with the mechanisms of actual representation I have described. Whig theorists had warned the colonists about the ministerial lust for power; sure enough, trouble had come from the Crown ministers. Now, the Americans carefully subordinated executive officers to the legislatures. The new constitutions, reported Jefferson, "absolutely divested . . . the kingly office . . . of all its rights, powers, and prerogatives." The enfeebled magistrate became a mere "administrator." Pennsylvania dropped the office altogether: "having no rank above that of freeman, she has but one interest to consult." If the governments were less efficient, this would be a small price. "Energy in government," John Page of Virginia would later argue in Congress, "is the doctrine of tyrants"; in comparison, "indecision, delay, blunders, nay villainous actions in the administration of government are trifles." The states were left with only a vestigial administrative apparatus, the national government with almost none. "It would seem to be a maxim of democracy to starve the public servants,"[56] Elbridge Gerry would tell the Constitutional Convention. In the decade following 1776, Americans sank public administration in their conception of the people.

Legislative government soon proved tumultuous and chaotic. The assemblies passed and repealed laws, sometimes to accommodate single individuals. Madison charged that the first decade of independence witnessed as much legislation as the preceding century. Laws did not last long enough for "trial to have been made of their merits" or even for "knowledge of them to have reached the remoter districts."[57] The critical litany is well known: states violated the treaty with Britain, delayed payment of public debt, issued cheap paper money (creditors hid to avoid being paid off in worthless specie), refused to pay their share of national expenses, raised their own salaries, cut those of other officials, and so on. Of course, many of the lapses have a distinctly contemporary flavor: "salary grabs," inflation financing, public debts, and government deficits remain trusty political outrages.

The national level offered no stability or check to the turmoil in the states. The Articles of Confederation were not so much a central authority as a "firm league of friendship" among the sovereign states— the amateurish minute man of government, as Norman Jacobson put it. Important action required approval of nine states; constitutional changes, unanimity (ratification alone took five years). The national government operated almost without administrative capacity. All action fell on the Congress—even naval strategy was plotted by committee.[58]

Ultimately, concludes the traditional interpretation, flaws in constitutional design led from anarchy to tyranny. The legislative department, wrote Madison, is "everywhere . . . drawing all power into its impetuous vortex." Even Jefferson worried that "concentrating . . . all the power of government . . . in the legislative body . . . is precisely the definition of despotic government. . . . Seventy-three despots would surely be as oppressive as one." Critics charged that the assemblies reversed court judgments, stayed executions after judgments were rendered, legislated ex post facto, and ruled "under the bias of anger, malice, or thirst for revenge."[59]

The revolutionaries had confused the organs of rebellion with republican organization. Their governing theory was flawed. The American Revolution had to be redeemed by a new constitution grounded in a more workable vision of the people and their government.

The alternative interpretation was popularized by Charles Beard and the Progressive historians in the first decades of the twentieth century. They dismissed the charges of anarchy and, on the contrary, celebrated the first American governments. What really motivated the traditional critique was not poor constitutional engineering but constitutions that empowered the poor. The debate, according to the Progressives, turned on economic self-interest. Wealthy élites had lost control and feared the leveling power of a state in the hands of the people. The Constitution did not redeem the Revolution from chaos; it was a counterrevolution through which men of property seized the government back from the plebes.

There is substantial evidence for at least some portions of the Progressive revision. Traditional deference to societal leaders had been evaporating during the Revolutionary crisis; the new rules often seemed to accelerate the process. Jackson Turner Main's analysis takes one measure of the new regime: In New Hampshire, New York, and New Jersey, representatives who were "wealthy" or "well to do" comprised 83 percent of the assemblies before the revolution, 38 percent afterward. In Maryland, South Carolina, and Virginia, legislators characterized as wealthy tumbled from 52 percent to 28 percent. If the government did not exactly mirror the people, it bore a closer resemblance to them. The character of the delegates began to change ("not quite so well dressed or politely educated"), and they began to rotate more rapidly ("every new election in the States is found to change one half of the representatives" was Madison's observation).[60]

The most often repeated illustration of the class-conflict hypothesis is the uprising of indebted farmers led by Daniel Shays in western Massachusetts. The rebels followed all the traditions of the people out of doors; the state militia eventually suppressed the rebellion anyway. However, an enormous increase in turnout gave the Shayites control of the legislature in the next (annual) election (60 percent of the assemblymen were new). When they mandated debtors' relief, "big men" throughout the colonies were outraged: "sedition will sometimes make laws."[61] Here is a more ambiguous account of "legislative tyranny." If the political rules did not produce a mirror of the people, they at least facilitated popular penetration of state institutions.

Something was going on, but a bald class analysis oversimplifies what it was. The *New York Times* immediately hooted at Beard's rough treatment of the Founders; a generation later, social scientists were letting him have it for his treatment of the data. A closer look does not sustain the interpretation of simple class conflict. Both creditors and debtors tended to be wealthy speculators. Political disputes pitted not just rich against poor but every sort of faction against one another. New men entered politics, but property qualifications still marked most elections; almost everywhere, higher property qualifications became the test of wisdom (or aristocratic virtue) which the upper houses were supposed to embody. (The test generally failed: the upper houses proved as rowdy as the lower.) The new nation was torn by cross-cutting cleavages and factions; "the unequal distribution of property" may have been their "most durable source" (as Madison avers in *Federalist* 10), but few historians find evidence of sustained class struggle outside Massachusetts, North Carolina, and Pennsylvania.[62]

Still, Beard's simple political cleavage can be recast into a more subtle and persuasive form. As Gordon Wood put it (after the requisite caveats about cross-cutting tensions), the struggle was between traditional American élites and "socially insignificant men" of the "middling orders." Here were cosmopolites versus locals, aristocracy versus democracy, men of wealth and education against upstarts "without reading experience or principle." This was political and social upheaval as much as economic conflict.[63]

Revisionists charge proponents of the traditional interpretation with overstating the chaos. Some confusion was inevitable as Americans instituted a new political order with substantially more citizen participation. "Let us be patient," urged Benjamin Rush of Philadelphia; "our republican forms of government will in time beget republican opinions and manners. All will end well." Jefferson, writing from Paris, concurred. In fact, the same charges of tumult, unruliness, incompetence, and venality would greet new political participants throughout American history. We shall see establishment politicians repeating the lament when Jacksonian artisans mobbed political conventions or black Americans entered city politics.[64]

As with many long-standing analytic disputes, both conceptions capture part of the truth. Even the Antifederalists conceded that the political institutions of the 1780s were chaotic. Governments without administrators lacked energy and coordination. On the other side, the Federalists did not try to hide their contempt for the new men who had entered politics and provoked class and social tensions. The argument between interpretations—between the primacy of chaos and class—obscures their common source. Both followed from the false premises of the American idyll that guided the Framers of 1776.

The first American governments were designed to mirror a corporatist people. They were founded on manifestly false assumptions of unity, consensus, and virtue. However, even institutions founded on faulty premises have real consequences. Seeking the image of the people, the revolutionaries designed governments that fostered both the social mobility the Progressives celebrated and the institutional incapacity the Federalists deplored.

The conflicting interpretations each rest on a different unintended consequence of "actual" representation. On the one side, political institutions designed to operate within harmonious republican communities led by natural aristocrats faced instead the political faction and social upheaval of the Revolutionary period. In the unanticipated context, the new rules—a broader franchise, smaller constituencies, residency requirements, annual elections—facilitated the rise of new men. In effect, the rules of actual representation combined with a decline in traditional social checks to throw open the paths of political mobility.

However, the same assumptions of republican homogeneity resulted in maladroit institutions, ill equipped for the real political world of self-interested factions scrambling for advantage. The image of a corporatist people threatened by corrupted ministers led to simple

61

governments, without ministers, hierarchy, or—as it turned out—administrative competence. The practical result was "the lack of energy" which the Federalists tirelessly attacked.

In short, the republican myths embedded in the people out of doors were more effective for mobilizing the citizens than for governing them. The corporatist mob and the frontier yeomen were not metaphors that could plausibly organize an extended nation. Social historians who celebrate the political mobility of the first American governments sometimes echo the Antifederalists and argue that, given time, the Americans might have made their federation work. If so, they would have needed a more realistic political philosophy than the one that tried to mirror the people out of doors. Before any such conceptual revisions took place, supporters of the first governments were debating a new constitution rooted in a radically different vision of the people.

Reinterpreting the People

The first American generation traced a disjointed state-building pattern. Crown ministers had violated colonial conceptions of representation. When the Americans revolted, they went to the opposite extreme, establishing feeble magistrates who were subordinated to representations of the people; from administrative tyranny they lurched to administrative incapacity. In Philadelphia, the delegates to the Constitutional Convention propounded a synthesis to this dialectic. New modes of "energetic" administration were framed by a new view of the people.

George Mason kept the old concept of representation before the convention. The delegate from Virginia constantly reminded the others that governments should mirror the people, "think as they think, feel as they feel." But now Alexander Hamilton, representing New York, responded, this "will never happen. . . . The proposition has no meaning or an absurd one."[65] As soon as the convention got down to business, the delegates tore into the microcosm principle. "The people want information," are "constantly liable to be misled," are the "dupes of pretended patriots," and "should have as little to do [with governing] as may be." To the revolutionaries (and now the Antifederalists), usurpatious magistrates were the chief threat to liberty; to the men who framed the Constitution, a graver threat lay in the "turbulence," the "levelling spirit," and the "follies of democracy." The Constitution was constructed in opposition to the old conception of the people: the re-ification that had launched the Revolution now imperiled the regime.[66]

It is easy to find a conservative counterrevolution in the Philadelphia convention. For over a century, historians have pondered what the delegates most feared—rising classes or descent into chaos. (The fram-ers of the Constitution would have resisted such a distinction, but that resistance could be used to support either side.) This intellectual rubric obscures the debate over representation that was actually taking place. The Constitution challenged every dimension of the theory that had guided the Revolution. It offered a new conception of the people, their representatives, the link between them, and the role of administrators within a republican regime. The reconstruction triumphed, of course, and was organized into the American political system. However, the antinomy between administrative order and unruly democracy sur-vived to animate future political fights.

In the new view, representation offered a useful opportunity to im-prove on the people rather than an unfortunate necessity to improvise for them. As Madison told the delegates, "refining the popular appoint-ments by successive filtrations" would produce "the men who possess the most attractive merit," and pronounce the public good more clearly than "if pronounced by the people themselves."[67] Here was a sharp change from representatives acting as delegates to those who behaved as trustees. Classical republicanism sought a microcosm; the Constitu-tion, a filter.

The new sort of representation would be institutionalized by loos-ening the links to the constituents, by raising "the Federal pyramid to a considerable level," as James Wilson (of Pennsylvania) put it. Only one house of one branch would be elected directly. And the constitu-encies were huge—no more than one representative for every thirty thousand people. (It took Washington's last-minute suggestion to re-duce it from one in forty thousand.) The House would be smaller than the assembly of every state but two; it was just one eighth the size of Commons. The Senate was smaller yet ("Seventeen men are all that is necessary to pass a law," cried the Antifederalists); Senators were to be selected by the state legislatures rather than the people. There were no annual elections anywhere in the new federal establishment.[68]

The clashing visions of representation were clearly articulated in the ratification debates. Patrick Henry, still seeking a mirror, bitterly criticized the Constitution's bias toward men of "conspicuous military, popular, civil or legal talents." This, of course, was precisely the point of filtration: "nothing but real weight of character can give a man real influence over a large district" was the way James Wilson put it.[69] The Federalists restored an older—hierarchical, even aristocratic—conception of leadership. Their institutional mechanisms replaced the social checks that had evaporated in the revolutionary tumult.

Madison articulated the new theory most clearly. However, a close reading exposes his uneasiness about its implications; he repeatedly appended qualification to the filtration idea. When he introduced the argument in Philadelphia, he cautioned that "it might be pushed too far." The most celebrated exposition, in *Federalist* 10, is studded with the same caveat: "the effect may be inverted"; "inconveniences will be found on . . . both sides."[70] Madison's temporizing is a harbinger of the political split that would rend the Federalists almost as soon as the Constitution was ratified. Just how high should the federal pyramid be? How (and how much) should the people participate in their government?

Recent historical scholarship has been framed by the effort to tag the republican (and, alternately, liberal) label on one side or the other: each has been characterized both ways.[71] Madison's growing preoccupation with civic participation reflects one tenet of the old republicanism; Hamilton's insistence on hierarchy and the deference to natural leaders reflects another. The flaw in some of the contemporary debate is an overly narrow focus on the role of the representatives and the mechanisms that link them to their constituents; what is sometimes overlooked is the delineation of the constituency itself. In this, both sides ultimately agreed on a conception markedly different from the revolutionaries' notion of the people.

The matter of defining constituencies had always been problematic in the New World. (Recall how the townspeople of western Massachusetts thought they could no more share a delegate with a neighboring town than they could share their souls with neighboring townspeople.)

The revolutionaries sidestepped the complex realities when they seized on the republican notion of a single, consensual people and used it to anchor their conception of government. The image legitimated the committees, mass meetings, and mobs. It held out the illusive hope that power could be vested in the people, and the unlikely ideal that public institutions could be framed in a way that, somehow, transported the people into the state apparatus (such as it was).

It did not take the Americans long to learn that a corporatist people offered no realistic basis for political representation. By 1789, even the Antifederalists had abandoned the construct. When they attacked the Constitution for favoring the "conspicuous" over those in "middling" circumstances, they were denying the homogeneity of the people (and undercutting the premise of their own theory).* The Constitution abandoned the pursuit of a corporatist people altogether. The Framers rested sovereignty, not in towns (the colonial reality) nor in the people as a whole (the Revolutionary ideal), nor in the states (the bias of the Articles), but in individual citizens. In order to support its "considerable altitude," the federal pyramid rested on a broad base.[73]

Within the *Federalist* papers, Madison and Hamilton seem to portray political constituencies in significantly different ways: contrast the relatively fixed social orders in Hamilton's *Federalist* 35 with the apparent flux in Madison's 10 and 51. However, each analysis abandons the notion of a single people with a shared interest and turns instead on factions applying the calculus of economic self-interest. The ideal of an "assembly of representatives with a sole view to the good of the whole" would swiftly become, as J. R. Pole put it, "almost as archaic as the royal prerogative." It would be several political generations before the implications were fully understood, before commerce truly replaced citizenship, to use Diggins's phrase.[74] However, the Constitution laid out both the philosophical and the legal framework for the shift. The Framers reconstructed the collective people seeking a shared interest into a pluralistic population pursuing its multitude of private concerns. They remade "the people" into a plural noun.

---

*On this point, Gordon Wood and Herbert Storing are in implicit agreement: Wood argues that the belief in a homogenous people evaporated in the conflicts of the 1780s and had disappeared by the ratification debates; Storing, commenting directly on Wood, finds the notion of "some organic common good . . . strikingly absent from Anti-Federalist thought."[72]

A Hesitant Energy

The Constitution, like the Articles, subordinated administration to representation. However, the Federalists' idea of representation offered executives a far more prominent role. Here, once again, was a broad base and a considerable height. The Federalists broke with the old Whig notion that magistrates stood for a different societal order than assemblies. The executive now represented the people, and in much the same way as representatives throughout the Federalist establishment—trustee governance by prominent men. The chief executive would be "filtered" through electors who were themselves chosen directly by the public in just four states by 1800. John Adams fancied "your majesty" as the proper mode of address.[75]

Both at the convention and on the hustings, the Federalists repeated their administrative catechism: energy, vigor, firmness, decision, steadiness. As Hamilton summed up, "the true test of a good government is its ability to produce good administration."[76] Efficient administration would be the antidote to the "turbulence" of the Articles. Federalists pictured an executive that penetrated American society in a way that seems distinctly modern—"comprehensive in its agency," reaching "matters of internal concern," "circulat[ing] through those channels and currents in which the passions of mankind naturally flow."[77]

When Antifederalists heard "energy," they cried "tyranny." The Federalists responded that efficient governance would win the attachment of the people. Hamilton's often-noted rhetorical progress during the New York ratification debate demonstrates the Federalist logic: He began by suggesting that local governments, being closer, will enjoy more popular affection than the national—unless the national offers "a much better administration" (the Constitutional Convention and *Federalist* 17). Later he suggested "the probability that the general government will be better administered" (*Federalist* 27); and still later offered "manifest and irresistible proofs" of its superiority (*Federalist* 46). At the New York ratifying convention, Hamilton took the tension between popular representation and efficient administration head on: "It is not necessarily true that a numerous representation is necessary to obtain the confidence of the people. The confidence of the people will easily be gained by good administration. This is the touchstone."[78]

66

An energetic executive, doing good for the people, was the Federalist touchstone; but—even in their own enthusiastic hands—it lay in uneasy tension with the American version of a government by the people. The conflict between active administration and popular representation spilled out of the Constitutional Convention to the ratification debates and then into the policy conflicts of the first administration. It is a tension that neither the Founders nor the succeeding generations fully resolved.

Wariness of executive power provided a regular counterpoint to the incantations about energy. Article II—which frames the executive branch—is the most loosely drawn of the Constitution. The basic representational issue, how to choose the president, was debated throughout the summer. (Edward S. Corwin argues that it took "more time and effort" than any problem before the convention.)[79] The still more fundamental question of whether executive authority would rest in a single person or a committee took just as long to resolve. The proposal for an executive council was argued almost as hard (and resulted in the odd constitutional stipulation that the president may require in writing the opinions of his subordinate officers). The power to hire cabinet officers was compromised (given to the executive with senatorial advice and consent); the power to fire them was sidestepped and took two months for the First Congress to resolve. Hamilton assumed incorrectly that the same rules would apply and used it as evidence of stability promised by the new order. The First Congress would vest the power to fire in the president (the "decision of '89"); however, the issue would flare up throughout the nineteenth century, repeatedly resurrecting the analytic tension between representation and efficiency (as well as the more political conflict between the branches).

The Whiggish hesitancy that marked the framing of the executive is neatly illustrated by Hamilton's use of Alexander Pope in *Federalist* 68: "For forms of government let fools contest/ That which is best administered is best." Always eager to reiterate the point, Hamilton added that the "test of a good government" is its "tendency to produce good administration." However, mindful of a republican legacy (which the Antifederalists were busy invoking), Hamilton cloaked his approval by introducing the couplet as a "political heresy" in which "we cannot acquiesce."[80]

The American revolutionaries had framed institutions that were meant to empower a republican people. The result was an equal measure of "new men" and chaos. In response, Americans revised their notion of representation and sought a new set of institutions which promised stability and energy. The Constitution's framers would replace the uproar of the people with an effective government. When the Federalists took office, they completed the state-building task; the administrative structures they elaborated would not be successfully challenged till the 1820s, when the entire process would begin again.

The Golden Age of Public Administration

The Washington administration implemented an executive apparatus, fleshing out the Constitution as it filled posts and formulated procedures. Washington announced clear criteria for federal officeholders: competence, loyalty, and fitness of character. The standard was not as unexceptional as it now sounds. Loyalty meant Federalists; fitness was reckoned by class. Officers were men of "honor," "esteem," and "standing." Natural aristocracy and social hierarchy, which were not always produced by the legislative filter, were eagerly pursued in the executive branch.[81]

The rules governing federal administrators reflected their social standing. Officials were gentlemen trustees, left independent to do the correct thing. They held their posts as long as they followed the strictures of proper behavior. In eight years, Washington replaced just seventeen men, all for deficiencies in "character." Public officials conducted business with unrepublican formality, decorum, and secrecy. The Federalist conception of public administration, concluded Leonard White, "although antimonarchical, was not warmly democratic." The Federalist philosophy was "government for the people . . . not government by the people." (Precisely Hamilton's choice when he dismissed "numerous representation" in favor of "good administration.") Still, future reformers—lamenting corruption or laziness or jobbing—would look to the "extraordinarily high moral standards" of "this . . . literate tribe" and imagine a golden era of nonpartisan public administration.[82]

At the time, critics took a different view (belying the myth of non-partisan competence that would later be projected onto Washington). Opponents clung to republican standards, rejecting the élitism implicit in Federalist "energy." Officers should be "not only of ourselves but as much as possible as ourselves." When Senator James Monroe was dispatched as minister to France, critics called it "degrading to citizens that . . . no man can be capable of office, but one that is already thrown up and in some department." When Chief Justice John Jay was sent to England, the "departure from any principle of republican equality . . . insulted the majesty of the people."[83]

Public administration remained embedded in larger arguments about representation and even national identity. The search for gentlemen trustees in the executive branch was one aspect of the broad Federalist project to restore hierarchy to American politics. For example, the social pace at the new capital was a dizzy "annual fatigue" of presidential levees, balls, dinners, parties, coaches, fashion, and ostentation.[84] It was as if public officials and their entourages could willfully reassert the social checks that had been lost in the revolution.

Federalist hierarchy required a loose linkage to constituencies. Like the old republicans, they denounced faction and partisan conflict; however, they overturned the expectations of actual representation, condemning public efforts to exert "control and influence upon the measures of government." "The Public's right to associate, speak and publish sentiments" were no longer representational mechanisms but "revolutionary means," "excellent . . . only when a government is to be overturned."[85] Federalists denounced the faction (and opposition) introduced by democratic-republican societies in vivid terms: "phrenzy," a "hateful synagogue of anarchy," "the sport of firebrands," a "hellish school of rebellion and opposition to all regular and well-balanced authority."[86]

The ambitious Federalist economic program can be interpreted as part of the same political project. Hamilton would promote domestic manufacturing and stabilize credit. Rather than pay off the Revolutionary debt, he gathered it—state as well as continental—into a permanent national debt designed to offer speculators a stable source of investment. Each feature of Federalist economics challenged a republican shibboleth: manufacturing, debt, credit, and speculation countered the ideals of rural, virtuous, self-reliant yeomen. Here was an effort to promote behavior that was directly antithetical to the republican ideal.[87] Ultimately, the Federalists were out to reconstruct the people themselves.

The clashing notions of American political identity were distilled by the Whiskey Rebellion of 1794. Once again, a popular uprising asserted the shared interest of a corporate people. The protesters self-consciously invoked the memory of the stamp tax rebellion; they articulated similar grievances in a similar way. The contrasts among uprisings neatly measure the progress of the people out of doors through eighteenth-century American politics. The Stamp Act rebellion defined and mobilized a people, exposing the tenuous grip of British authority in the process. Shays's rebellion illustrated the bias of actual representation when the rebels swiftly recouped their military losses through legislative action. In contrast, the Whiskey Rebellion was suppressed so conclusively that opponents charged the Federalists with engineering the entire episode in order to demonstrate the authority of the new government. The new regime commanded the power to suppress the rebellion (in contrast to 1765) and a philosophy that unambiguously condemned it (a contrast to Shays's in 1786).

Federalist opposition to popular politics was codified in the Alien and Sedition Acts (1798). The statute would control foreign agents (specifically Jacobins, the Federalists' archfiends), monitor immigrants (aliens), and punish libels against federal officers (seditions). The effort misfired. In 1800, Jefferson and the Democratic Republicans unseated Adams and the Federalists. Jefferson introduced a very different vision of the people and their role in national politics. However, the Federalist administrative apparatus survived the transition.

In Jefferson's variant of American republicanism, participation, civic virtue, "free discussion," rural freemen, and "frugal" government on the Potomac would dislodge deference, institutional checks, trusteeship, manufacturing, and the "social fatigue" of New York and Philadelphia. Jefferson thought it as real "a revolution in the principles of our government as that of 1776 was in its form."[88] He deflected the Federalists from their energetic nationalist agenda as well as their assault on popular politics. To chart just one measure of the political transformation, Adams had almost doubled federal spending in four years; Jefferson reduced it by a quarter in three.* He abolished the excise tax, reduced the debt, shrank the army and navy, and legitimated party competition.

Public administration was a different matter. The new party made only modest changes in the Federalist apparatus. Jefferson did not alter Washington's criteria for public office, though loyalty was reckoned by the standards of the new party. He quietly replaced Federalist incumbents with his own men, till he achieved a rough political parity in the executive. The same reformers who imagined a Federalist golden age would tag Jefferson the father of the spoils system; they would charge him with appointing "wild Irishmen and French refugees" (precisely the groups at which the Federalists had aimed their Aliens act). However, what is most striking about Jefferson and the Democratic Republicans is how little they meddled with the administrative institutions they inherited.[90]

Jefferson continued to call on "fitness of character." "Not only competent talents . . . but respectability in public estimation are to be considered," he wrote after his election. Republican gentlemen from Virginia replaced Federalist gentlemen from New England; but the style, background, and expectations of federal administration remained the same. By one count, 92 percent of the men Adams recruited to the higher civil service came from "status occupations"; for Jefferson, the figure was 93 percent.[91]

The Federalists had embedded their administrative apparatus in a broad political agenda. Jefferson may have rejected their principles, but he did not alter their processes or structures. "It mortifies me," he wrote, "to be strengthening principles which I deem radically vicious, but . . . what is practicable must often control what is pure theory." As Leonard White put it, the Republicans "found a system in full working order"; they took it over and maintained it "with hardly a ripple for over a quarter century. . . . The same laws were on the books, the same motions occurred within the administrative system."[92] Public officeholders developed a lifetime tenure and came to look on their places as a kind of personal property. Gentlemen found places for their

---

*The actual expenditure figures for selected years were: 5,727,000 (1796), 10,786,000 (1800), 7,852,000 (1803), and 9,932,000 (1808).[89]

relatives and were succeeded by their sons. They built up a small, rudimentary, administrative bureaucracy along the principles laid out by Hamilton during the first administration.

CONCLUSION

By 1800, Americans had negotiated their first cycle of administrative state building. The process was driven by the tension between popular rule and political authority.

The cycle began when Crown ministers moved to rationalize colonial administration; a tangle of causes led to war, but the one the colonists "declared to the world" was the "abuse" and "usurpation" of their republican rights.[93] In response, the Americans resorted to the people. Committees and mobs ignited the rebellion, wresting public authority from royal officials. The image of the people acting directly (and in unison) offered the revolutionaries their unlikely governing ideal. They framed institutions that would mirror the sentiments of the men in the streets (and on the farms, of course), unencumbered by magisterial power or administrative hierarchy. The result accelerated and underscored the upheaval of the Revolutionary period. The Federalist reaction was cast explicitly against the republican idea of an organic, collective people. The Constitution redefined the American vision of political constituency and linked it loosely to an independent and energetic governing structure.

The republican image of a corporate people was central to each stage of the American founding. It might be called the great antithesis, mobilizing opposition to British rule and provoking, in turn, the opposition of the Constitution's authors. In the end, the Framers cast the people outside the administrative apparatus they erected. Perhaps this helps explain why the Americans never resolved their Whiggish tension between ministerial authority and the people. It is easy to overlook the issue, for the executive apparatus was small: in 1800, there were more elected representatives than executive officers in the national capital.

However, the matter would cast a long intellectual shadow. American public administration never fully acquired political legitimacy. As administrative institutions and functions grew, questions about their status in a democratic regime would recur with renewed urgency.

Analyses of the Revolutionary period pay only occasional notice to Federalist administration. On the other hand, classical republicanism is the focus of the dominant intellectual dispute (though the collective definition of the people generally receives a less central place than I have given it here). The contemporary question is not where civic republicanism came from or what it achieved, but when it went. Was it the final expression of an antique, now vanished world view? Or does it hold clues about the American national identity?

My argument is that one strain of classical republicanism persisted— and persists still. It turns on the collective people, sharing a single interest, celebrating civic community, skeptical of executive authority. The contemporary version is by no means the same as eighteenth-century republicanism: it operates independently of the republican struggle for virtue or the emphasis on rural freeholders (though Americans still refer to grass-roots democracy). This democratic wish would offer Americans a counter to both liberalism and the state. It would be crucial for redefining and reconstructing American administrative institutions. However, the communitarian spirit would never find a place at the institutional center of American politics. Instead, the call to community and collectivism remains a perpetual alternative, a reformist counterideology—always elusive, always beckoning.

2

The Resistible Rise
of the Common Man:
Jacksonian Democracy

You may say to all . . . Adamsites that the barnacles will be scraped clean off the ship of state. Most . . . stick so tight that the process will doubtless be fatal to them.
— A Jackson supporter, 1828

The Democratic panacea, after all, was a fraud like any other. The young Republic had rid itself of one gang of political streptococci only to take on another.
— H. L. Mencken

On the face of it, Americans have rarely pursued their democratic wishes with the fervor they showed in the second quarter of the nineteenth century. Here was the frontier, "universal" (meaning white, male) suffrage, booming political participation, and an era named after "the common man."

The Progressive historians found in this period another clash between "the house of Have and the House of Want." In their view, Andrew Jackson articulated the democratic aspirations of "the plain people" and led a charge "against the privileges and perquisites of broadcloth." Still, the conflict historians differed over who the common man was and whom, precisely, he was fighting: frontier democrat against Eastern conservative? proletariat against capitalist? artisan against entrepreneur?[1]

74

On the other side, consensus historians see barely a fight at all. There were, in this view, hardly any really rich or poor Americans, just a rising middle class, throwing itself into enterprise. "No admission here," Richard Hofstadter quotes an immigrant, "except on business." The democratic tumult came from the middle class, opening every possible pathway for the ambitious and the talented.[2]

In either analytic tradition, it was not a tidy political event. The Jacksonian Democrats, for example, willingly accepted slavery; their ostensibly conservative rivals demanded immediate abolition. The Jacksonians fought for less government; Whigs wanted more. Both Louis Hartz and Arthur Schlesinger, Jr. (a consensualist and a neo-Progressive) offer the same metaphor to connote the turmoil: two wild fighters who accidentally knock one another out (the Hartzian version), two drunken brawlers who inadvertently fight themselves into one another's overcoats (Schlesinger).[3] Most observers hear the political commotion of the common man—the question is what to make of it.

This chapter tells the following story. Nineteenth-century Americans faced a dizzying set of dislocations. An essentially mercantile economy hurtled toward bourgeois capitalism. Americans spread across the continent. Foreigners began to press into the eastern cities. Each of these changes—and many others—offered opportunity to some Americans and posed a threat to others.

In this setting, Jackson advanced explanations and solutions. Rather than systematic policies and programs, he offered Americans their democratic wish. Invoking the rhetoric so persuasively he was often said to embody it, Jackson updated the "the people" for a new era. The image, still recognizable a half-century after the Revolution, summoned a broad political constituency and shaped new political institutions—mass political parties, rotation in administrative office. The search for more actual representation and more direct participation ultimately transformed the administrative apparatus for a new era. In the end, the new institutions managed simultaneously to raise and restrict the voice of the common man in the affairs of the republic.[4]

In the first part of this chapter, I examine the political setting, focusing on social tensions and how they challenged Americans' notions of their republic. Next I turn to Jackson's democratic wish and, finally, explore the state-building consequences.

THE SETTING: SOCIAL AND ECONOMIC TENSIONS

At first glance, suggested Marvin Meyers, the Jacksonian inventory yields "a troubled mind groping to find names to fit its discontent." The Jacksonians, added J. R. Pole, "felt that their world was in danger. But that was almost exactly what their enemies felt."[5] In the antebellum republic, political tension was rising from at least three different sources—emerging capitalism, the evolving frontier, and the arrival of immigrants; each introduced challenges to the conceptions of American self.

In the first half of the century, a revolution in transportation, new modes of economic organization, and new forms of technology reshaped the nature of work. The changes posed a threat to skilled artisans, who viewed themselves as republican freemen, independent and self-reliant. Artisans had resisted such "Tory" innovations as dividing labor because "we want no one person over another." Within the workshop, master and journeymen were bound both by their craft and by the journeymen's anticipation of becoming masters themselves. Traditional work rhythms reflected artisan independence. The craftsmen set aside their tools to engage in other work or to fight fires or fish or take their late-morning toddy. The neoclassical vision of civic republic had, of course, evolved. Jefferson's independent yeomen were to have worked the land; and these urban dwellers had developed a more heightened sense of equality than strictly fit with classical conceptions of republican society. Nevertheless, the skilled artisans self-consciously invoked notions of self-reliance and republican community.[6]

The new mills operated on entirely different principles. Owners divided labor, set hours, empowered overseers, and forbade drinking (often espousing temperance off the job as well). There was no pretense of equality in this world, and little expectation that workers could ever own the means of production as the artisans had owned their tools. Moreover, wages made men dependent; workers lost their status as republican freemen and fell into the category where they had formerly relegated women, children, and slaves. Indeed artisans viewed wages in themselves as a form of slavery. The mills also violated republican conceptions of collectivity. The constraints of distant markets eclipsed the concerns for local community.

Republican conceptions gave many Americans the categories for interpreting these developments and the language with which to voice their discontent. The loss of equality and independence, the decline of community, and the assertion of individual economic interest over the commonweal were all taken as signs of corruption, of decline into "tyrannies" and "monarchs." The nature of the laments can be illustrated by the following snippet of Rhode Island doggerel:

> *For Liberty our fathers fought*
> *Which with their blood they dearly bought*
> *The factory system sets at nought . . .*
> *Great Britain's curse is now our own,*
> *Enough to damn a King and Throne.*[7]

On the other side, the new entrepreneurs used another variation of the same ideology both to justify and to complain. Mill owners (reconstructing dormant models of paternalistic authority) justified their modes of organization by suggesting that they inculcated "punctuality, temperance, industriousness, steadiness, and obedience to mill authorities."[8] Like the Hamiltonian Federalists, the capitalists stressed order, natural hierarchy, and virtue.

Celebrants of Jacksonian capitalism see the entrepreneurs as part of an "almost universal ambition to get forward" in the American society of the period. "Go ahead is the real order of the day . . . the real motto of the country."[9] The new self-interested creatures of the market might appear to challenge the old republican order in fundamental ways. And yet the drive to "go forward" taps another mainspring of Revolutionary era republicanism, one that Jackson would play on: the idea of true and false hierarchy, the notion that citizens acknowledged their place in the social order and acted accordingly. The successful entrepreneurs regulated the society within the mill; the factory hand deferred and was ostensibly elevated. The ideas that had mobilized a political revolution could be molded into the justification for an economic one.

The new entrepreneurs saw a different set of threats to republican order: the dispensation of privilege by the government in the form of monopolies. Here, once again, were false hierarchies won through corrupted political influence that kept natural leaders from their rightful places.

In short, artisans expressed their fears with variations of the same ideology entrepreneurs used to speak their aspirations and voice frustrations of their own. As we shall shortly see, Jackson's rhetoric reshaped the language of republicanism in a way that spoke to both groups. By roasting the moneyed interest, he could articulate artisan fears and pin them on apparently specific malefactors; by balancing his attack with a celebration of "farmers, mechanics, and laborers," Jackson appeared to offer the restoration of republican society. At the same time, the rhetoric echoed entrepreneural complaints about political favors; the repeated assertion that "rewards" should go to "superior industry, economy and virtue" seemed to promise a clear way for those with the capacity to "get ahead."[10]

The frontier might have offered the solution to these economic tensions. Classical republican theory had warned about the development (and consequent corruption) the mill towns and cities were now experiencing. True republics existed outside historical time. But Americans had a counter to the corruption in the East: the West. The frontier offered to renew the conditions of yeoman independence. It seemed to offer a spatial solution to the republican problem of historical time. In Jefferson's well-known oxymoron, here was an "empire for liberty."[11]

To take just one measure of the westward motion, the Old Northwest held less than 1 percent of the American population in 1800, 4 percent by 1810, and over 12 percent by 1830.[12] Jackson himself, as his followers endlessly repeated, "was the very personification" of the frontier, the "embodiment of the whole west."[13] His Democrats* embraced

---

*The Democratic Republicans who had held the executive since Jefferson now constituted themselves the Democrats. The old Federalists ran their last presidential candidate in 1816; after that a similar political sentiment first rallied around the John Quincy Adams wing of the Democratic Republicans, then reconstituted itself the Whig party.

the promise of manifest destiny: after Louisiana, Democrats wanted Oregon, half of Mexico, Cuba. Expansion, however, raised the matter of free men in a dangerous way. With each new territory came the question of whether slavery would be allowed.

Rather than offering a haven from historical time, westward motion repeatedly raised the angriest issue confronting the American regime. The issue fractured the American discourse of community and liberty. Conscience Whigs adopted the message of moral community the religious fundamentalists of the Second Great Awakening were spreading across New England. Suddenly a gradual end to the sin of slavery was not enough; in the 1830s, these Northerners threw themselves into the movement for immediate abolition. Southern planters responded, of course, that theirs were the classically ordered communities—and added that they did not turn their workers out during hard times. The "lord of the lash" and "the lords of the loom" clashed over community and tyranny in their respective labor hierarchies. The Jacksonian Democrats dropped the matter of virtue and argued that local communities ought to decide for themselves. Their position only focused the fight on the admission of new states. Territorial expansion raised the same kinds of question as the economic transformation (though with greater urgency): What did it mean to be a free person in America? What was the nature of the American community itself?

A third development would soon complicate still further the issue of American community—of Americanism. In 1824, less than 8,000 immigrants arrived in the United States, a figure that had been declining for five years. By 1828, their numbers had more than tripled to 27,000 a year; they topped 60,000 four years later and reached 104,000 by 1842.[14] The new arrivals crowded into cities, often without useful skills or even English. What would they do to the ideology of independence, self-reliance, virtue, and communal public interest?

American society faced a series of disorienting changes that challenged its political discourse and self-image. Rising capitalism, manifest destiny, slavery, foreigners—all injected tensions and contradictions into the republic. Religious fundamentalists expressed the strains as the corruption of the era. They were echoed, again and again, by Jacksonian orators and journalists condemning "the moral depravity" of the society.[15] The changes—along with the confusion, disquiet, optimism, aspirations, and greed that accompanied them—provided the setting for Jacksonian democracy.

THE PEOPLE

Jackson fashioned vivid imagery to fix blame and offer correctives. Using the language of the people to explain and justify, Jacksonian Democrats reconstructed political institutions for a new era. In the next sections, I examine first the Jacksonian interpretation of American troubles, then his variation of the democratic wish; finally, I turn to the political institutions which the rhetoric introduced.

Jackson's Aristocrats

The revolutionaries had the luxury of an external enemy. They could project the sources of their own social upheaval on a tyrant three thousand miles away. In a sense, Jackson rhetorically reconstructed the trusty old enemy of the people, then led the new revolt. Once again, the "false, rotten, insubstantial world" of aristocracy and privilege offered the threat to "plain republican order."[16]

American troubles came from speculators and unproductive moneyed interests. This was a class that inverted all the republican virtues. They got on, not by their own hands, but by the "labor and earnings of the great body of the people." Rather than rise through "superior industry, economy and virtue," they became "intriguers" and "politicians." They upset the natural order by creating "artificial distinctions, titles, gratuities and privilege."[17]

The "antirepublican" forces crept "silent and secret" toward "tyranny and despotism." They dominated and corrupted the government.[18] Jackson's attack is sometimes interpreted narrowly, as an assault on the special monopolies that individual corporations won from the government—the politically savvy winning privileges that stifled new entrepreneurs. (Perhaps the best-known illustration is the Charles River Bridge case, in which the bridge operators sued to stop construction of a competing bridge, claiming that their state charter implied a monopoly.)* However, Jackson's language was far broader and more diffuse. It appeared to address the concerns of a wide range of constituents. The indictment of speculators and aristocrats could explain the threats to artisans in the cities, workers in the mill towns, and farmers in the old agricultural districts. At the same time, it seemed to promise the entrepreneurs an opportunity to "get ahead" by sweeping away old government-sponsored monopolies.

Still, if the rhetoric was usefully ambiguous, the institutions that Jackson attacked (and the ones his administration eventually put in their place) were inevitably concrete: the national bank, public administration, the old electoral forms.

The most flamboyant rhetoric surrounded Jackson's assault on the national bank, the essential embodiment of the "false, insubstantial world." When Jackson vetoed the recharter of the bank, he claimed to be protecting the "purity of our elections." When he withdrew the public funds, he did so for the "morals of the people, the freedom of the press, the purity of the elective franchise." The motif would be embellished by anti-banking Democrats for the next two decades: "Banks have been the . . . enemies of republican government from the beginning," "a legacy [of] the aristocratic tendencies of a bygone age," the source of "artificial inequality of wealth, pauperism and crime, the low state of public morals."[20] All but obscured in the republican bombast were the distinctly non-egalitarian opportunities for speculators implicit in moving the funds to state banks.†

The same logic and rhetoric fixed the Democrats' hostility on the old neo-Federalist administrative apparatus, "the final bastion of the aristocracy." Jackson's inaugural set the tone: the President scored incum-

---

*Hofstadter makes a great deal of the Charles River Bridge case—decided in 1837 against the monopolists and (thus for free enterprise) in an opinion written by Roger Taney, a Jackson appointee to the Supreme Court.[19]
†Cartoonists of the era used the battle as an opportunity to hone their skills at drawing hydras.

bent officers as "unfaithful," "incompetent," and—inevitably—a threat to the "freedom of elections."[21] Officers had neglected the "service of the people" and turned public office into a "species of property." The address was cheered for making "half the office holders in the country quake in their slippers."[22]

The critique of administration was part of a challenge to overreaching government (an objection that echoed the revolutionaries). John Quincy Adams had futilely championed a wide variety of administrative improvements: canals, roads, a national university, an executive office for the sciences, national observatories. The innovations lay in a framework of Hamiltonian republic: hierarchical, ordered, deferential. This Whig view looked to internal improvements rather than to outward expansion. Adams articulated the trustee view of representation which was the corollary when he cautioned Congress not to "fold up our hands and proclaim to the world that we are palsied by the will of our constituents." However, the Jacksonian Democrats were sweeping the nation in the other direction (and would, before long, take the Whigs with them).[23]

Jackson's Common Men

But what were the Jacksonians for? Ultimately, Jackson offered another variation of the democratic wish. He embraced the people, pictured consensus among them, wrestled with the conundrums of community amid the centrifugal forces of the era, and organized far more popular participation and actual representation into the regime. Consider each feature of the impulse in turn.

Jackson broadened the conception of the people for the new era of bourgeois capital and burgeoning cities. The "stout, upright, moral, common men" still formed a "hardy race of free men." However, the "planters and farmers" were now joined to "mechanics and laborers." Together, these broad classes constituted the "bone and sinew of the country." Repeatedly, Jackson returned to his expanded republican image. The laboring people exhibited all the old republican virtues— "independent spirit," "love of liberty," "intelligence," "high tone of moral character."[24]

In Jacksonian rhetoric, the people anchored a shared, discernible public will: "Never for a moment believe that the great body of citizens can deliberately intend to do wrong." Just as their polity was being strained by powerful disruptive forces, Americans postulated a shared common good which only the iniquitous (or "idiots and self-murderers" as the first American generation had it) would violate. Jackson acknowledged the likelihood of temporary lapses, "but in a community so enlightened and patriotic as the people of the United States, argument will soon make them sensible of their errors."[25]

Once again, American institutions would be propelled forward by rhetoric and argument that looked wistfully back to a lost, virtuous, republican order. The actual content of Jackson's shared public interest was, in Marvin Meyer's terms, "an idealized ancestral way." However, the vague yearning of republican restoration served a powerful political purpose: it mobilized and consolidated the wide variety of interests Jacksonian Democrats were trying to balance. Slavery, the tariff, or the deflationary policies of hard money were all potent sectional issues. Jackson negotiated the coalition, as Russell Hanson puts it, with "the lowest common denominator," with the will of the people.[26]

Like so many other democratic movements, the Jacksonians created a rhetorical community. However, the nature of the American community was precisely what was in question in the turmoil of the period. Once passed the rhetoric of "bone and sinew," it was not obvious who belonged to the community of the people and who did not. Of course, native Americans did not qualify: Jackson pursued a savage policy of "Indian removal." Slaves did not fit either: the Jacksonian Democrats were brutal in their race policies, playing frankly to racist bigotry in general elections. The immigrants, when they began to arrive, proved a different matter: the Democrats embraced them.[27] On the other side, many Whigs offered exactly the reverse—opposition to the headlong westward expansion that underlay Indian wars, powerful abolitionist sentiment, and a strong nativist prejudice against the immigrants. With nullification in the South, expansion and slavery in the West, growing cities beginning to fill with foreigners in the East, the issue of constituency—of community—bristled with contradictions.

Who was at the center of the Jacksonian (and Whig) constituencies? Though the differences are complex and cross-cutting, recent scholarship tends to find that the Whigs drew on citizens at "the core" rather than "the periphery," Americans who welcomed the changes of the era. The group is roughly analogous to those who turned to the Federalists in the first generation. On the other side, Jacksonian Democrats seemed to be, very roughly, citizens who faced the socio-economic tumult of the period with trepidation. This revises an older view which suggested that Jackson's effort "to clear the way" spoke to the rising entrepreneurs.[28] It may be, however, that the ambiguous logic of the democratic rhetoric once again facilitated broad, even paradoxical, coalitions. Sean Wilentz's study of artisans in New York City vividly demonstrates how republican rhetoric appeared on all sides and in all kinds of variations. It appealed both to the entrepreneurs who thought to "get forward" (echoing their faith in self-improvement) and to the workers (who sought communitarian sentiment as a buffer to exploitation).[29]

Beyond the rhetoric of common man and virtuous community, the Jacksonians tried to weld their disparate coalition by limiting national government and leaving controversial matters to the people in local communities. Jackson pictured activist policies and institutions as structures of privilege. His attack on protective tariffs, corporate charters, internal improvements, or a national bank were all portrayed as efforts to eliminate government favors; let the people make their own way. The logic of limited government and deference to local community led the Democrats to reject legislation for temperance, for observation of the sabbath, or for limitations on slavery.

Finally, Jackson's democratic wish sought more active, participatory forms of political representation. In fact, participation was already rising. On the state level, voting turnout surged to between 68 percent and 98 percent in the first two decades of the century. Moreover the states were putting aside formal restrictions. For example, legislatures had chosen presidential electors in ten (of sixteen) states in 1800; the number fell to nine (of nineteen states) in 1816, six in 1824, and just two (of twenty-four) in 1828.[30] By then, only five states retained property qualifications. Jackson himself helped bury "King Caucus," which had nominated presidential candidates behind closed congressional doors; it was replaced by party conventions (crowded with delegates "fresh from the people") beginning with the Anti-Masons in 1831 and the major parties a year later.

Local party élites pushed along the extension of suffrage in efforts to outflank one another. Local conflicts led groups to take advantage of the new rules and mobilize, especially during the depression that followed 1819. Groups like the New York Working Men demanded egalitarian workshops; grass-roots movements around the country demanded debt relief. In the process, traditional deference to local political élites declined. Its final passing away, comments Ronald Formisano, has been discovered in every decade between the Revolution and the Civil War.[31] Still, its progress in the 1820s and 1830s is striking.

Jacksonian rhetoric endorsed and promoted the movement toward direct participation. More significantly, between 1828 and 1840, the Democrats (followed by the Whigs) channeled the institutionalized popular participation onto the national level. They took a profusion of local groups, grievances, and governors and harnessed their energies to national electoral politics.

However, the Jacksonian Democrats faced a problem. Their party constituency (indeed, the polity itself) was an unstable amalgam of contending regional factions. Their message about national government was essentially negative. What were they going to mobilize participation for? The answer was participation itself.

The Democrats celebrated the mechanisms of participation, the political party. "Keeping the organizational faith," as Douglas Jaenicke put it, "became the watchword of the Democrats."[32] Unity, discipline, and subordination to the organization became the test of political virtue. Procedural norms replaced substantive goals. The contending factions of a heterogeneous nation were united through their participation in the party processes.

With party victory came rewards—and an opportunity to participate on another level. Martin Van Buren of New York offered his supporters government positions, proving (as he said) "that fidelity to the cause shall not go without its reward." Senator William Marcy (also of New York) gave the rewards their popular designation: "Politicians . . . preach what they practice . . . They see nothing wrong in the rule that to the victor belong the spoils."[33] The spoils of office would grow steadily, forming the cornerstone of the party and the principle by which administration would be reconstructed.

The Whigs at first jeered the Democrats' celebration of participation and the common man ("a manifesto to anarchy," thought Nicholas Biddle, president of the Bank of the United States). The Whigs offered their more ambitious vision of positive government. Before long, however, they sent their own candidates scrambling to pledge allegiance to Jackson's idyll. By 1840, the Whigs were ardent champions of the common man. William Henry Harrison left his Ohio mansion to pour hard cider and proclaim his log cabin heritage. Daniel Webster announced that though he had missed "the good fortune to be born in a log cabin, my brothers and sisters were. . . . That cabin I annually visit." Anyone who called him an aristocrat was a "liar and a coward."[34]

The parties evolved into noisy, tumultuous, unstable, shifting coalitions that organized national political participation in earnest. Less than 27 percent of the electorate (350,000 voters) had turned out in 1824; the numbers rose to around 57 percent for the Jackson and Van Buren elections, then to over 80 percent in 1840. With competitive national parties, the turnout averaged over 75 percent for the next five elections.[35]

The political imagery of the era turns on the roaring participation of the common man. "It must be seen to be believed," reported Tocqueville. "No sooner do you set foot on American ground than you are stunned by a kind of tumult. . . . Almost the only pleasure an American knows is to take part in the government and discuss its measures." The celebrated story of Jackson's inaugural is perhaps the most enduring emblem of the era: the White House furniture was allegedly trampled by "a rabble a mob, of boys, negroes, women, children, scrambling, fighting, romping . . . ladies fainted, men were seen with bloody noses." And all to shake hands with Jackson. "It was a proud day for the people," said Amos Kendall, formulating the caption to the myth. George Caleb Bingham's often-reproduced paintings of raucous young democracy capture the same tone—a mix of burlesque, hucksterism, exuberance, and populism. On the other side, men like James Fenimore Cooper were complaining that universal suffrage left "the power to control their governments, in the hands of the worst part of the community."[36]

However, as Formisano puts it, "beneath the hoopala of 'the age of the common man' lurks the iron law of oligarchy." It is not only that the imperatives of victory shaped hierarchical organizations that consolidated power at the top. Rather, careful local studies repeatedly suggest that the political parties obscured controversial issues; they suppressed the fights about the political economy for the pageantry of the common man. Repeatedly, local groups—real farmers, mechanics, and laborers—articulated grievances that were defused by the political parties.[37] The great tumult that "stunned" Tocqueville was political bread and circus as much as egalitarian politics. Once again, the democratic wish simultaneously amplified and muffled the popular voice.

THE PEOPLE'S BUREAUCRACY

The logic of democracy (and the imperatives of party) transformed American public administration. Jackson had assailed incumbent officials—"Adamsites"—as an aristocratic feature of the old order. His administration turned the American administrative apparatus from "fit character" to popular choice. At the heart of the reconstruction lay a fundamentally democratic principle:

> The duties of all public officers are, or at least admit of being made so plain and simple that men of intelligence may readily qualify themselves for their performance; and I cannot but believe that more is lost by the continuance of men in office than is generally to be gained by their experience.[38]

Any man—every man—could do the job. The populist spirit of Jacksonian rhetoric would infuse the national administration. Rather than relying on gentlemen doing the right thing for a lifetime, the Jacksonians would rely on common men doing what the people wished until the next election. With each vote, a new set of individuals would rotate from private life to public office. Officeholders would better understand the public; the public would be better protected from the "overbearing insolence of office." It "recognizes the equality which is so dear to the American mind," Lord Bryce would later report, "bidding an official that he is a servant of the people—not their masters like the bureaucracies in Europe." (How clearly this English visitor echoed Tocqueville.)[39]

In the Old World, as Pocock notes, Karl von Clausewitz was formulating a theory of war as an instrument of the bureaucratic state. In the United States, the people were still celebrating General Jackson and his Kentucky riflemen—the American Cincinnatus and his yeomen troops—who had left their plows to rout the professional British soldiers in the battle of New Orleans. (Never mind that in reality most of the Kentucky force had no rifles, that it was too dark to see, or that it was American artillery and British blunders that won and lost the day.)[40] The same republican virtue would infuse American statecraft when the common man took administrative tasks into his own hands.

Jackson articulated the principle and set the precedents. However, he moved with caution toward the system that so mortified future reformers. He replaced less than a fifth of Adams's incumbents. ("The slaughter of innocents," commented Charles Beard, "was not as great as the opposition alleged.") And as Sidney Aronson has demonstrated, Jackson's appointees were no more plebian than Jefferson's.[41]*

The significance of Jackson's innovation—and the extent of the jobbing—grew with the hair's-breadth elections that began to characterize American politics after his administration. Following Jackson, neither party won successive victories for twenty years. Only one presidential candidate polled more than 51 percent in the next twenty-eight. Just three of the next seven presidents mustered popular majorities. Ad-

*Aronson comments, "Although he did not succeed in democratizing the elite, everyone thought he had. Furthermore, Americans generally felt that Jackson's successors should do as he had done"—a last-ditch effort to save a hypothesis, perhaps, but still a testament to the rhetorical power of Jackson's democracy. Crenson follows Aronson. Their argument is disputed by Lynn Marshall.[42]

ministrative offices were central to the contests. Both parties seized on jobs as a device to nourish their organization and gain electoral advantage. The prospect of tangible rewards helped stir enthusiasm for the party cause. By Lincoln's administration, roughly 90 percent of the public service would be turned over to the spoils.[43]

The new system broadly expanded the party cadres. Prior to the spoils, wage earners and artisans were excluded from politics by economic necessity as much as by legal restriction. Political activism required an independent income and leisure time. Throwing public offices—federal, state, and local—open to political appointment permitted the recruitment of new social classes for party service. Men could now make a living out of politics. Electioneering and political activism were transformed from élite avocations to popular professions. New rules and rhetoric may have sanctioned broad participation, but the spoils of victory are what infused midcentury American politics with their proletarian vigor.

The result was a sort of people's bureaucracy. Citizens rotated from private life to public office with each election. Once again, public administration was enmeshed in issues of representation. The Revolutionary generation had restricted administration in favor of political representatives who would mirror the people. Now Americans were turning their administration itself into a kind of civic mirror—and one that served representatives more directly by working to get them elected.

Like the earlier effort to mirror, this one was widely criticized for chaotic inefficiency. Turning out the vote became a more important recruitment criterion than administrative agility. Americans help themselves, reported Bryce, and they "do not care whether their functionaries are skillful or not." He was, once again, echoing Tocqueville who thought that no European would find the consequences tolerable.[44]*

Chronicles of the period are filled with the spread of the spoilsmen through the executive branch. When Harrison and the Whigs finally won in 1840, the White House was allegedly so crowded with job seekers that the President could not find a free room in which to meet the cabinet. "They refused to quit," as Leonard White reports the

---

*"Democracy," Tocqueville goes on to note, "pressed to its ultimate limits, harms the progress of the art of government."[45] The American dread, of course, reverses the proposition.

story, until the President "would receive their papers and pledge to attend to them. . . . First his pockets were filled with papers, then his hat, then his arms." When Harrison died, the crush of jobbers was conjectured to have killed him. When Polk restored the Democrats (1844), he warned his cabinet officers that "so many bitter Whigs were retained in office"; the party men wore him down till he began to ask, "Will the pressure for office never cease? I most sincerely wish that I had no offices to bestow." Zachary Taylor returned the Whigs (1848) and unwhiggishly declared "rotation in office . . . is sound republican doctrine"; though he later noted that if he did not kick a party man downstairs, the man left thinking he had been offered a post. When Democrats won two successive elections (1852, 1856), Buchanan paid no mind and made a clean sweep of Franklin Pierce's Democrats. Senator Marcy clarified his aphorism: "To the victors belong the spoils . . . but I certainly should never recommend the policy of pillaging my own camp."[46]

The spoils became an important mechanism of social and political control. Lincoln, in particular, demonstrated the political potential of the system. For example, he cultivated loyalty by permitting rural districts to vote on their postmasters. He repeatedly traded offices for congressional votes. Lincoln negotiated passage of the Emancipation Proclamation by jobbing a half-dozen congressmen in exchange for their votes on Nevada's statehood, which, in turn, gave him the margin he thought necessary to submit the measure. Likewise, Congress passed the Thirteenth Amendment in 1864 largely on the strength of lame Democratic ducks whom Lincoln had induced with plums.[47]

Ultimately, the party system and its spoils offered a counterbalance to the centrifugal strains on American society. Matthew Crenson argues that the system shored up "the popular support and authority of the federal establishment" precisely where it had most "become a scarce commodity."[48] Frontier squatters were indifferent to a distant government. Other western settlers held land grants from Spain or France, and their loyalty was equally questionable. The southern nullifiers were still more likely to offer defiance. All were likely to show more deference to a public administration staffed by men who could command their votes. The spoils offered political élites a mechanism through which to negotiate some loyalty from the fast-spreading, increasingly diverse nation they were trying to govern.[49]

The same centripetal dynamic operated in the East. The cities were crowded with foreign laborers; during the 1830s, the nativists began to riot against them. The mill hands and artisans had their own discontents, sometimes expressed in brief leveler movements. By treating votes like a "marketable commodity," the parties induced potential rebels into politics structured on an unabashed market model. Apparent routs of upward political mobility beckoned ambitious individuals, regardless of their class, their education, or their national origin. Party politics accommodated and co-opted a national network of public-sector Horatio Algers. Political leaders could do well for themselves without pursuing systematic economic reform or articulating class grievances. And even when they tried to organize class-based movements, the mechanics of party politics often diffused the effort. The party system and its spoils of office roughly integrated divergent cultures, regions, and ideologies and turned them to the limited common purpose of winning elections. It linked recent settlers with the older ones and tied both to the state.

The spoils may have rendered the state more democratic and the polity more coherent. However, they also posed a dilemma. How were public offices to be organized and run? As the gentlemen were turned out, their administrative methods went with them. They had been selected for their reputations and guided by gentlemen's mores; long tenure permitted them to develop experience in office. Administrative style was rooted in the individual. Subordinates were more like apprentices than rank-and-file public officials. (When Samuel Swartwout, the New York Customs collector, embezzled over a million dollars in 1838, his subordinates all told Congress the same story: "I was Mr. Swartwout's clerk and would not betray the secrets of my employer.")[50] The administration of "fit characters" was highly idiosyncratic, shaped by the proclivities, morals, and talents of individual incumbents.

When the Jacksonians flung open the federal establishment, the clear expectations and common experiences of a class-based system evaporated. Political élites could no longer assume education, competence, sobriety, or—as Swartwout demonstrated—honesty. Correct conduct needed to be defined; at least a rude efficiency imposed. Jacksonian administrators had to negotiate the tension between sustaining the party and delivering the mail.

The problem of control was made more acute by the growth of the civil service: it increased almost sixfold in the four decades preceding the Civil War. Throughout the period, most positions (85 percent) were in the Post Office, which became the largest organization in the nation. This, of course, exacerbated all the dilemmas of distance and control, for it meant that public servants would be in towns and cities far from Washington. (A little under 6 percent of them operated in Washington between 1821 and 1861.)[51]*

The solution was a rudimentary national bureaucracy. As Michael Nelson points out, Jackson had instituted rotation declaring not that all jobs were simple but that "they admit of being made so." Public tasks could be routinized, governed by preformulated rules and regulations. The Democrats introduced a new administrative creed: "I want no discretion. I wish to be able to turn to some law or lawful regulation for every allowance I am called on to make." An impersonal apparatus—a rudimentary national bureaucracy—began to direct administration and impose a "mechanical adherence" to old norms of behavior upon public officials.[53]

The rationalization of administrative office was led by Amos Kendall during the Jackson administration. Kendall supervised his far-flung postal administration with the watchwords "organize, organize." He routinized relationships between subordinates, created an elaborate system of accounts, introduced quarterly reports and intricate systems of cross-checking. Similar reforms spread to the other departments. The Jackson administration imposed a wide range of related innovations: functional specialization, executive staffs, a bureaucracy of linked offices within each agency (resisted by Congress for its costs), and efficiency records that marked officials on "competence, faithfulness and attention" (resisted by the administrators for its intrusion). Jackson's ally Orestes Brownson lamented, "We are making more rapid strides

---

*Between 87.3 percent (in 1831) and 85 percent (1861) worked in the Post Office. The percentage of officials actually in Washington was 5.7 percent in 1831, 5.9 percent in 1861. Neither figure fluctuated more than 1 percent in the intervening years. The total number of civilian employees in the federal government was 11,491 in 1831 and 50,020 in 1861.[52]

towards . . . centralization and the bureaucratic system than even the most sensitive nullifyer has yet suspected." It was precisely that incipient bureaucratic system which permitted spoilsmen to be "placed and replaced without upsetting the integrity of the whole."[54]

In short, the rule of gentlemen had counted on their personalities; administration by the people was designed to counter theirs. The egalitarian revolt produced a rudimentary bureaucracy, fashioned to organize the growing federal officers and keep the incumbents roughly honest. The democratic aspirations of the Jacksonian age yielded not merely corruption or inefficiency but the systematic centralization of authority. Ironically, federal offices were rationalized in order to permit popular participation within them.

The change in public office mirrors the transformation in the economy. Artisans were losing control over their work. They, too, faced routinization, a division of labor, and the same hierarchically imposed spurs to "competence, faithfulness, and attention." Moreover, both forms of rationalization were justified primarily in terms of inculcating morality—both private and public sector managers dramatized the need for workplace standards by pointing to the danger of drink. In both cases, the high road of morality was used to justify new modes of social control designed to meet new standards of efficiency. In the process, both private enterprise and public service were reconstructed to the imperatives of bourgeois capitalism, regional market economies, and a continental polity.

The American public service bureaucracy was first fashioned to shore up the nineteenth-century party scramble for spoils. It is interesting to speculate about the implications of this genealogy for subsequent bureaucratic development.

Note, first, that the new administrative system was introduced in a blistering attack on administrators. Not only were the Adamsite officials personally corrupted and unrepresentative. The Adams notion of positive government was, in itself, a form of usurpation, an extension of government beyond its legitimate sphere. The governing bureaucracy was introduced amid a broad regime change that promised limited, negative government. The Jacksonians introduced new state capacities while articulating an antistatist faith. The public service has never managed to free itself of the sentiment.

Both the continuities and the contrasts with the Revolutionary moment are striking: The colonists, too, attacked corrupted ministers who had overreached the bounds of legitimate authority. The revolutionaries' reaction had been to limit administrative authority in favor of representative assemblies; the Jacksonians also limited administrative scope, more directly subordinating it to representation (or, more precisely, elections). Both efforts resulted in the threat of administrative chaos. The first American generation turned to Federalist administrative energy, though doing so left the public service with a tenuous link to the people. The Jacksonian resolution, on the other hand, bolstered the administrative link to the people, relying on its rude bureaucratic apparatus to organize the rotation of party men in and out of office. In this way, the Jacksonians enabled their administration to modernize and grow—without permitting it to grow strong or independent. The United States has distinctly denied its bureaucracy independence or stature. Ironically, it was the people's bureaucracy that negotiated the subordination.

Finally, the introduction of a national bureaucracy may have rendered the regime more coherent, at least temporarily addressing some of the tensions that confronted the society. It certainly advanced the capacity of the American state. However, it made little progress against the American dread of ministers. On the contrary, Jacksonian-era bureaucracy was introduced amid an attack on positive government. It fed on political self-interest and seemed to flaunt the ministerial corruption that had so concerned Americans. With time, the spoils may have even added a measure of contempt to the American wariness of administrative office.

CONCLUSION

I have argued that the Jacksonian period was organized around a democratic wish. Perhaps more than any other president, Jackson used the White House to preach for the people, the public interest, and more direct participation. One question about the effort is, ironically enough, whether the common man "rose up" during the period. In this chapter, I offer a definite answer: yes and no.

On the one hand, popular parties and the people's bureaucracy operated as mechanisms of social control. They co-opted political activists into the party melees of the period. The idea that the entire nation was scrambling to get forward—one great rising middle class—is questioned by studies suggesting that only a small number of citizens got very far. To take just one measure, Edward Pessen's study of four cities shows that the wealthiest 1 percent of the population owned 25 percent of the wealth in 1825 and 50 percent by 1850.[55] Though the matter is far from settled, Pessen suggests that the élite was small and did not much change.

On the other hand, the democratic rhetoric mattered. The plebes entered politics, trooped to the polls in unprecedented (and, in the twentieth century, unmatched) numbers, rotated in and out of the civil service, and dismantled the old gentry structures of exclusion and privilege.

Moreover, I have argued that the implications of the democratic ideology reached far beyond the common man. The pursuit of the people led to the institutional innovations of the era—particularly national parties and administrative bureaucracy. Once again, the democratic wish negotiated the reconstruction of American politics.

Democratic rhetoric offered a framework for coping with the emerging bourgeois capitalism. Both artisans and entrepreneurs heard their own message in the attack on aristocrats, in the celebrations of bone and sinew, and in the promise that real Americans would be liberated to make their own way. The institutional reality was the withdrawal of government from many market activities (most obviously, capital formation and monopoly charters). At the same time, the remaining public functions were rationalized, orienting public services to a larger, more fluid society. The search for the people led directly to a state that was organized to accommodate bourgeois capital.

Democratic rhetoric, along with parties and the spoils, also offered the regime centripetal forces to cope with geographic expansion in the West and immigrants arriving in the East. They were not, of course, sufficient for the issue of slavery. That crisis destroyed the Whigs and drove the Democrats out of the White House for the longest stretch in the party's history.

Even so, the administrative mechanisms that were introduced in order to permit the rotation of the people through public office would survive into the last decade of the century. When the Jacksonian system was attacked and finally brought down, it was with the same promise that had originally put it in place—the restoration of the people.

3

Administrative Science and the People: The Progressive Movement

By training in science, law, politics, economics, and history, the universities may supply from the ranks of democratic administrators, legislators, judges, and experts for commissioners who shall disinterestedly and intelligently mediate between contending interests.
—Frederick Jackson Turner

A young man who has gone to college may succeed in politics, but the chances are 100 to 1 against him.
—George Washington Plunkett

When the Union army ran at Bull Run, one wag attributed the rout to a rumor of three vacancies in the New York Customs House.[1] By the end of the Civil War, inexpert citizens, rotating in and out of office had begun to turn from a symbol of popular government to a symptom of political corruption.

The following half-century was cluttered with causes and reformers—Populists, Prohibitionists, Suffragettes, the National Short Ballot Association, the Antimonopolists, the Knights of Labor. Amid the political tumult, two successive movements attacked the spoils and struggled to reconstruct American public administration. First, in the 1870s and 1880s, avowedly élitist Mugwumps championed merit examinations and a neutral civil service. The innovation was designed to dislodge the "noxious counterfeits of statesmen."[2] Astonishing claims were made about the degradation of the spoils: "Some young women in despair, losing hope at the loss of their jobs, went wrong on the town, for Washington like other cities big and little had its red light district . . . Oh! the Pity of it."[3] Civil service would be a political purification; it would restore a "pure," "frugal," "good," "efficient" government. Civil service advocates won their reform but none of its promises. By the Benjamin Harrison administration of the late 1880s, the movement had given way to the far broader reforming impulse of the Progressives.

Armed with an enormous array of proposals, the Progressives carried the fight for a renewed democracy to every level of government. The sprawling movement drew on the aspirations of all the groups noted in the preceding paragraph.[4] At bottom, however, Progressive reform turned on two apparently contradictory ideals: First, the reformers would strip public power from corrupted political officials and vest it directly in the people. The people themselves would hold referenda, overturn unpopular judicial decisions, and recall unsatisfactory officials; here, once again, was the urge to constitute a more "actual" government. At the same time, experts would be responsible for administration; they would shun politics for scientific facts. At the heart of the Progressive agenda lay a political paradox: government would be simultaneously returned to the people and placed beyond them, in the hands of the experts.

Scholars sometimes resolve the apparent contradiction by dismissing its democratic aspirations as a ruse by which the people could be induced to throw over the bosses for the reformers.[5] Brushing aside Progressive democracy, however, distorts the movement and disregards its continuities with the reformations that came before and after. Like the colonists and the Jacksonians, the Progressives rooted their political vision in a democratic wish. Both their administrative science and their direct democracy rested on the assumption of united, virtuous, communitarian people sharing an objective public interest. Once again, the ambiguous image of "the people" served to meld an uneven coalition of interests and philosophies. It provided an indictment of the party state, new political ideals to win (offered as old legacies to be regained), and a wide array of institutions that promised to do the trick. Even as the frontier (and its promise of republican yeomen) was receding into memory, the Progressives struggled to synthesize their neo-Hamiltonian notions of positive government with the neo-Jeffersonian democratic ideal.* The Progressives failed to secure their ends, more because of false (but politically potent) premises than because of false promises.

In this chapter, I begin with a look at the historical setting, briefly sketching the long contest between party leaders and reformers over control of American public administration. The struggle stretched, very roughly, from the Grant administration (1869–77) through Woodrow Wilson's first term (1913–17). That conflict—ultimately about the nature of the American state—set the political rules and helped define the coalitions of the Progressive era. In the next section, I turn to the Progressive agenda itself, unpack its odd mix of populism and science, and trace the communitarian yearning that lies under the welter of apparently self-contradictory reforms. Finally, I consider the consequences. The Progressives won many of the devices they championed and, in the process, founded a new order, the contemporary administrative state. However, neither their democratic nor their administrative innovations yielded the anticipated results. Instead, the Progressives left behind a fragmented, unresponsive public administration dominated by narrow, private groups and self-interested state officials. Two decades later, Franklin Roosevelt extended the Progressive institutions without resolving their structural flaws. Contemporary policy choices are still made within the chaotic political establishment the Progressives fashioned around their version of the fictitious people.

---

*In 1893, Frederick Jackson Turner began his celebrated essay by quoting the superintendent of the census: "At present . . . there can hardly be said to be a frontier line. . . . It cannot, therefore, any longer have a place in the census reports."[6]

THE POLITICAL SETTING

Corruption

The most often told story about the rise of reform features the pervasive corruption of party politics. During the Grant administration (1869–77), fraud engulfed the executive branch. The vice president; the secretaries of war, navy, treasury; the attorney general; the second assistant postmaster; Grant's private secretary; and the ministers to England and Brazil were all caught at financial chicanery. Congressmen freely participated, both individually and—in the retroactive 50-percent "salary grab" of 1873—as a group. One observer tabulated the political wreckage after a railroad scandal: "total loss, one Senator; badly damaged and not serviceable for future political use, two Vice Presidents and eight Congressmen."[7]

The traditional judgment is that public regard for government had never sunk so low.[8] However, the scandals were only the most theatrical lapses of the era. Ultimately, they reflected the spirit of party politics, organized by bosses and driven by the spoils. "What are we here for if not offices?" was the often-quoted question put to the Republican Convention in 1880. When necessary, electoral strategies were brazenly fraudulent. The Republican National Committee issued clear instructions to their men in Indiana: "Divide the floaters into blocks of five, put a trusted man with necessary funds in charge of these five and make him responsible that none get away." "Men of standing" priced their votes at fifteen to thirty dollars, the less reputable went for two.[9] In fact, buying votes in national elections was practical because, as Walter Dean Burnham notes, only a small number of areas (in roughly five states) were politically fluid. With electoral victory (occasionally a negotiable political commodity, too, as Rutherford Hayes demonstrated in 1876) came the "orgy of office seekers." President James Garfield complained, "The stream of callers became a torrent and swept away my day. I felt like crying out in the agony of my soul against the greed for office." His lament was repeated by each chief executive (though not, of course, with the same macabre portent, for Garfield would be shot by one of the job seekers). Those who secured posts paid their "assessments"—the cornerstone of party finance—and started working on the next election. The system effectively mobilized the party faithful. Election turnouts were huge (ranging from 72.8 percent to 87.3 percent between the Civil War and the turn of the century). Of course, the political advantage came at the cost of administrative competence.[10]

The first reformers on the national scene were the gentlemen Mugwumps. (With their lack of party loyalty, they sat on the political fence, their mugs facing one way, their wumps another.) These patricians were offended by the corruption of party politics—as well as by their exclusion from it. They repeatedly invoked "the civil service established by George Washington"—and its fit gentlemanly characters—as their uncorrupted ideal. They insisted that civil service reform would restore it. (Of course, it would also restore them.)[11]

Civil service advocates constantly invoked the rhetoric and imagery of American reform: Traditional democracy had been usurped by "a new aristocracy of plunder and patronage." These "few bad men" defied the will of the people. Reforming civil service was "the people's cause," "the people's reform." Many of the arguments that had cheered Jackson's system in were now used to run it down. Once again, a change in administrative design would free the government from the grasp of "the new aristocrats" and restore it to the people.[12] The Civil War injected a fresh motif into the reformist rhetoric. Some abolitionist groups turned to the new cause, comparing party bosses to slaveholders and dubbing civil service reform the "second emancipation."

The midcentury political establishment had a sturdier response than the Crown administrators or the Adamsites. In contrast to the neo-Federalists who first condemned the "reign of King Mob" before rushing to mimic Jackson's frontier iconology, the spoilsmen held their political ground, turning the arguments about the people back on the Mugwumps. Reformers were "namby-pamby goody-goody gentlemen who sip cold tea," or gentlemen "who forget that parties are not built by deportment or by ladies magazines or gush."[13]* They were prissy aristocrats, their reform (dubbed "snivel service") was something for-

---

*The most flamboyant denunciations came from Roscoe Conkling, senator and spoilsman from New York. The pejorative that stuck, of course, was *goo-goo*, a shortened form of *goody-goody*.

eign, even Prussian; it would create an educated aristocratic class. College boys were contrasted with maimed Civil War veterans and judged inferior, regardless of merit exams or civil service rules. In fact, for all the plundering and corruption, the parties remained a major force of social integration and cohesion, particularly among the immigrants in the cities.[14] The Mugwump call for the people did not provoke a popular response. The party oligarchs may have not shared much power with the rank and file, but this time both sides had some claim on the people.

The Politics of Administrative Reform (1865-96)

Because administrative jobs were the cornerstone of the party state, the fracas over offices occupied each president in the three decades following the Civil War. Andrew Johnson's administration illustrates the wide range of conflicts that could be fought out on administrative ground.

Johnson used patronage to shore up both his power and his reconstruction policy (which would reconstruct the white Southern élite). Congressional Republicans moved to block him and extend their own authority with the Tenure of Office Act, which required Senate approval before public officials could be dismissed. The administrative issue that had been deferred at the Constitutional Convention and disputed during both Washington and Jackson administrations now confronted Johnson. He defied Congress and fired Secretary of War Edwin Stanton. Congress responded by impeaching Johnson and came within a vote of removing him. The political result was congressional control over the spoils and, consequently, domination over the executive which lasted for decades.

Five years later, reformers seemed to win their first victory over the spoils. In reality, the incident foreshadowed the ambiguous political pattern of their successes. Reforms were supported by party leaders when they could turn the new rules to partisan advantage.

In 1871, the unexpected reform came from an unlikely source. President Ulysses S. Grant secured vague legislation that authorized him to "employ suitable persons" and "promote the efficiency of the civil service." He established a commission and appointed a prominent reformer to head it (George Curtis, succeeded by Dorman Eaton). The commission got down to business—publishing exhortations for further reform.[15] In fact, the most corrupt administration of the era was turning "the people's cause" to partisan advantage. Grant's Republicans, torn between "half-breed" (reform) and "stalwart" (conservative) factions, had lost fifteen seats in the House and five in the Senate at the midterm elections. The new commission helped avoid further political trouble. Grant's former critics now cheered him as a reformer; the Democrats lost the corruption issue, the party factions were reunited for the campaign, and Grant piled up a margin larger than any in the next thirty years. A short time after the election, the commission lost its funds, and Grant dropped the reforms it had instituted. The reformers' ideal served the politicians' need.

Rutherford B. Hayes succeeded Grant in 1877 after campaigning doggedly for civil service. Ironically, the reformer lost the election by some 265,000 votes (over 3 percent) and secured the presidency through the unabashedly partisan machination of party leaders. Though he made only limited progress toward civil service, that ideal framed some of the great conflicts of his administration.

Hayes launched a frontal assault on the greatest bastion of the spoils, the New York Customs House (the source of over 50 percent of federal revenues). The President forced a reduction of two hundred workers (about 20 percent) in the name of efficiency. He forbade the remainder to engage in politics. When Congress—the guardian of the spoilsmen—was recessed, Hayes sacked the collector of the port, Chester Arthur, and its naval officer, Alonzo Cornell. Hayes then demanded the application of civil service examinations.[16]

These were, however, limited victories. When the President tried to force the civil service rules onto all large customs houses and post offices, he was ignored. Civil service legislation made little progress in Congress. The next election left the erstwhile naval officer, Alonzo Cornell, governor of New York. Two years later, the deposed collector, Chester Arthur, was elected vice president. Indeed, for all the iniquity that had come to light about his administration, Ulysses Grant led the Republican convention for over thirty ballots (polling up to 312 of the needed 379 delegates) before giving way to James Garfield and Chester

Arthur. As Charles and Mary Beard put it, "Agitation for the spoils system went on making ripples . . . on the smooth surface of orthodox custom without alarming the politicians" or stirring the public.[17]

Then, in 1881, Garfield was assassinated by an office seeker. The murder gave the civil service reformers an effective political focus. "The men that did the business last fall are the ones to be remembered," the assassin had written. "No more revealing description of the spoils has ever been penned," crowed the reformers. *Puck* ran a cartoon in which the assassin demands of the President, "an office or your life." Lincoln's murder had been attributed to a Southern conspiracy; Garfield's could be blamed on the spoils. The Senate Committee on Civil Service reported darkly that "more than one President is believed to have lost his life" in the siege for office.[18] Newspapers began to clamor for reform; the ranks of the reform associations grew in earnest. The Mugwump call for public-sector virtue suddenly developed a large audience.

Civil service reform became a major issue during the 1882 midterm election. Republicans had controlled the White House and federal jobbing since Buchanan's administration twenty-eight years earlier. Now they were punished at the polls. The Republicans lost twenty-nine seats and control of the House. They lost the governorship of New York to the reform campaign of Grover Cleveland. The Democrats seemed poised to win the presidency. The prospect altered the political calculations. Republican party leaders grabbed civil service reform as a way to protect their officeholders (and their assessments) from the anticipated onslaught of the Democratic spoilsmen. "See the zeal of the new converts preaching that those who are in ought not be put out," reported the *New York Tribune*. Some Democrats suddenly thought it wiser to wait till after the 1884 presidential election (and their long-awaited crack at federal jobbing) before freezing administrators in place with a civil service reform. In early 1883, before the new Democratic majority took its seats in the House, Congress passed the Pendleton Act, a civil service reform bill. "A victory for the people, over the apparently hostile legislators such as begets fresh confidence in representative government" was the sanguine view. More sober observers, watching the spoilsmen push the reform through Congress, thought "the devil was sick and the devil a monk would be."[19]

The Pendleton Act required practical, competitive examinations for public posts; incumbents could not be assessed, put to political work, or rotated out of office. Among its concessions to practical politics, the bill allowed for a geographic distribution of the posts in Washington, gave preference to veterans of the Union army, and—critically—retained present incumbents in their posts. The merit exams would apply to new officials. Moreover, it was a partial system; only 11 percent of the federal posts (13,924) were "classified." The rest were still up for political grabs.[20]

The first hint of reform had come for unabashedly political reasons amid the corruption of the Grant administration. A decade later, the Pendleton Act was passed for similar reasons and signed by Chester Arthur, a politician who had spent his career enjoying the plum jobs of the spoils. The legislation itself was immediately put to political use, helping to hold together the party system it had been designed to destroy.

Arthur set the pattern in 1884. As predicted, his Republicans lost the presidency. Before relinquishing the White House, Arthur classified 1,200 additional offices, "blanketing in" the Republican party men who held them.[21] The new President, Grover Cleveland, had run as a reformer and pulled the Mugwumps to the Democratic party. No matter; after almost three decades out of office, the clamor for jobs was irresistible. Cleveland replaced 45,000 post officers. The "plunder and patronage" of party politics continued, with civil service adding the new political twist of massive "blanketing in" with each lost election. After losing in 1888, Cleveland extended civil service protection to 5,000 Democratic officeholders. His successor, Benjamin Harrison (who reputedly sacked a postmaster every three minutes of his term), blanketed in another 8,000 after losing the presidency back to Cleveland and the Democrats in 1892.[22] Cleveland, weary of the spoilsmen, urged him on. However, "the ones who did the work" continued to be remembered through Cleveland's second term. The President set an example for his followers by contributing ten thousand dollars to the party coffers.

The subordination of civil service to the scramble for jobs was dictated, in part, by the volatile politics of the era. Elections between the Grant (1868–76) and the McKinley administrations (1896–1901) were closer than in any period of American history: not one of the five winners received a majority of the popular vote; two actually lost it. At least one branch of Congress changed hands every election but two; the two chambers of Congress were split between the parties five out of ten sessions.[23] The jobbing at the start of each administration and the extension of civil service at the end provided leaders a measure of control over their chaotic, evenly divided followers.

Half a century before the Mugwumps, Jackson had subordinated American public administration to parties and politics. Now, brandishing the people as their beneficiaries and the Founding Fathers as their predecessors, reformers fought to free the administrative state from partisan conflict and establish a neutral, efficient civil service. In the end, the reform itself was subordinated to politics. Passed by a party facing defeat and repeatedly extended as a defensive political strategy, civil service reform became a device for keeping the parties patched together in a turbulent political era. Public administration continued to serve the nineteenth-century system of American political representation.

Finally, with the electoral realignment of 1896, the Republicans, under William McKinley and Theodore Roosevelt, seized control of national politics. Voter participation plummeted (see page 125).[24] As electoral politics grew stable, public officials had an opportunity to break with the Jacksonian system and remake executive administration along principles other than parties and patronage. By that time, thirty years after Grant had teased out the first administrative reforms, the Progressive movement was reaching its height, articulating a far broader reform agenda than the Mugwumps had contemplated. The Progressives won changes ranging from railroad regulation (1887) to women's suffrage (1920). In the process, they transformed American government, casting it into a recognizably modern form. The administrative changes were linked to reforms that promised to revitalize democracy and return power to the people.

PROGRESSIVE ASPIRATIONS

The Progressive Coalition

As the attack on the party state grew into the Progressive movement in the 1880s and 1890s, four political voices can be identified alongside the original Mugwumps. First, a diffuse populist impulse attacked not just political corruption but the economic and political oligarchies it fostered. Emerging corporations, most notoriously the railroads and utilities, flaunted their political accommodations. "I wanted the legislatures of four states," bragged the robber baron Jay Gould, "so I made them with my own money." Legislatures—state and national—seemed to be dominated by "the interests." "An increasing number are Senators because they are rich; a few are rich because they are Senators," wrote James Bryce. As the United States negotiated the transformation from bourgeois to corporate capital, the dislocations and inequity were, not implausibly, projected onto the bosses and the barons. "There were no beggars till Vanderbilts and . . . Goulds . . . and Fisks shaped the action of Congress and moulded the purposes of government. Then the few became fabulously rich, the many wretchedly poor."[25] This was, of course, the impulse at the center of the Populist crusade. It formed a significant strain of the Progressive tradition, especially in the Midwest.

A second call for reform focused on the inefficiency of the party state. As business and society grew more complex, local merchants became impatient with undelivered mail (especially the railroad mail), inefficiencies in the customs houses, and inadequate municipal services. The critics were urban merchants, not industrial capitalists. This sector of the business class became a major component of the Progressive movement. Their attack fused desire for efficiency to alarm over concentrations of economic power. Local chambers of commerce began to press for public institutions that more closely resembled the businessperson's image of their own organizations—comptrollers, city managers, nonpartisan elections. The New York postmaster Thomas James made the typical Progressive claim when he said he could accomplish more through "efficient postal service than by controlling primaries or dictating nominations." On the national level, an incessant flow of reports and commissions called for economy, efficiency, and the injection of what were called "business principles" into the "business of government."[26] The ambiguity of "the people" permitted optimistic classes trying to "get ahead" to combine with uneasy populists—a reflection of the coalitions of the 1830s described in the preceding chapter.

The businessmen found allies in the rising professional classes— lawyers, social workers, professors, physicians. Their public-sector ideal was shaped by the orderly systems that were defining (or redefining) their professions. Like the Mugwumps, the middle-class professionals were offended by corruption; like the merchants, they touted the gospel of government economy and efficiency.

Finally, the public executives themselves sought relief from the turbulent spoils. A neutral civil service promised to free the President from local party barons and their congressional allies. Without posts to distribute, the politicians would lose both their influence and their interest in the federal administration. For officers within the public service, reform would bring independence, status, and tenure. Their places would be secured from the quadrennial onslaught of party men. From "almoners . . . in danger of their lives," they would become "respected officers of state."[27] Eventually, even rank-and-file officials began to demand some independence, lobbying for the right to organize and petition Congress. In 1871, there were 51,000 federal employees; by 1901, 239,000.[28]* A growing, increasingly complex, functionally differentiated government set an interest in professional bureaucracy within the state itself.

Progressive Democracy: The Quest for the People

The Progressives faced a dilemma. They opposed the "bribing, bossing and thieving . . . of private interests." They sought to make it

---

*The Lloyd-LaFollette Act, passed in 1912, recognized the rights of federal workers to organize, codified procedures for demotion and dismissal, and permitted public employees, jointly or individually, to petition Congress or its members.[29]

"more difficult for the few and easier for the many" to control the state.[30] Yet the political order they assailed continued to mobilize the public. Voter turnout was reaching 80 percent for presidential elections, 60 percent at midterm. In 1896, 750,000 people (1 in 20 voters) traveled to Ohio to hear the Republican candidate, William McKinley, speak from his front porch.[31]

One response was to echo the Federalists and assail "King Demos": "An ignorant proletariat" following a "half-taught plutocracy." In New York, the Tilden Commission proposed restricting the franchise on tax matters.[32] However, such bald élitism receded as Mugwumps gave way to Progressives. By the turn of the century, reformist rhetoric and image had reconstructed the people into victims of oppression. The danger to the republic came from above at the expense of the classes below. The bosses ruled "with ideas . . . inherited from kings"; they perpetuated their power regardless of elections; they created courtiers by controlling jobs. Organization, power, and money subverted public interests. "Slowly men realized that they were not free." Misinformed and manipulated, they shared a "widespread but unconscious" yearning for democracy.[33] In a different time and place, reformers might have called it false consciousness and capitalist hegemony.

The Progressive diagnosis focused on the bias in political representation. The interest intermediaries, the channels between citizen and state, were corrupted. Indirect democracy in all its forms exacerbated the corruption and inequity by setting the people at a distance from their government. Progressives assailed the "impediments to popular rule." They attacked the entire panoply of party politics—party ballots and bosses, nominating conventions and newspapers. They incessantly proposed new ways to get the people more directly involved, "nearer the grub pile of government." The Progressives aimed, as Wisconsin's governor Robert M. LaFollette put it, to "return to the first principles of democracy," to "go back to the people" by permitting participation at every point in the political process.[34] The reformers would push beyond the corrupt mechanisms of representation and return to actual government.

The Progressives shared a diffuse hope that modernity and progress would bolster their democracy. The telephone, the telegraph, the proliferation of magazines, and the spread of education would all facilitate the new participation. The reformers championed one political contrivance after another, promising that each would more directly empower the public.[35] Consider, first, some of the devices, then the underlying vision of democracy that they imply.

For Andrew Jackson, nominating conventions empowered delegates "fresh from the people" over a closed congressional caucus. To the Progressives, the conventions now suffered the same oligarchic defects as the caucuses they had replaced. A Mugwump lament over the character of the party faithful—policemen, saloon keepers, former pugilists—was cast aside for the more democratic complaint that the people were manipulated by the "sharp practices" of party leaders, the popular choice regularly defeated by the politicians.[36] The Progressive solution was to pry the decision from the parties and place it directly before the public through primary elections. Some pushed the proposal to its logical conclusion, suggesting that voters rank-order their first three preferences to minimize the threat of brokered conventions.[37]

The short ballot was hailed with the same democratic reasoning that had cheered the Jacksonian long one. An overloaded ballot confused voters who could "make no proper choice" and were thrown back to the parties for guidance. Woodrow Wilson proclaimed it "the key to the whole problem of the restoration of popular democracy in this country." The National Short Ballot Association took up the cause in 1910.[38]

The Australian (or secret) ballot was introduced in Massachusetts in 1888; it proved so popular that most states instituted it within four years, all within eighteen.[39] The device promised to end intimidation and corruption at the polls. Straight-arm voting—in which floaters were lined up, paid, and marched to the voting box with a colorful party ballot held out in the ward heeler's view—was rendered impossible.

Like the revolutionaries and the Jacksonians, Progressives expanded the franchise, this time with voting rights for women. Wyoming entered the Union with equal suffrage in 1890; though three additional states shortly followed, the reform met widespread opposition, even ridicule. The Progressive party finally endorsed it in 1912; the Republicans in 1916 (though Woodrow Wilson refused, arguing for states rights and cognizant of Southern Democrats). While the more sweeping

Susan Anthony Amendment (resubmitted sixty years later as the Equal Rights Amendment) repeatedly failed, suffrage was secured with the Nineteenth Amendment in 1920. Its more sanguine supporters predicted that the feminine sensibility was less likely to be corrupted; electoral choices would be improved by the new participants.[40]

Progressives would also make legislatures more democratic. They lobbied for the direct election of senators so that candidates would stand before the people rather than the railroads and big business.[41] They attacked the elaborate rules that concentrated legislative power and managed to "overthrow" House Speaker Joseph Cannon in 1910. The powerful Speaker ("so conservative that had he been in on the creation he would have voted against the Lord for chaos") was stripped of control over committee appointments.[42] House procedures were liberalized. The Progressives also sought what would later be termed "sunshine reforms"; they insisted that committee hearings be opened to the public: "The only way to beat the boss . . . is to keep the people thoroughly informed. The whole tendency of democracy is towards more openess, more publicity." LaFollette claimed to spend "vast sums" reprinting the Congressional record and mailing it to his constituents.[43]

The Progressives would bypass legislatures as much as recapture them. Their "initiative" permitted the public to propose legislation; the referendum, to dispose of it. They lobbied, unsuccessfully, to reduce constitutional barriers to popular action: amendments would require only a majority vote in a majority of the states—a mark of the positive government they avowed as much as political institutions they distrusted.[44]

Even more nettlesome than the legislatures were the courts, great bastions of conservatism that repeatedly struck down Progressive legislation. Simplifying constitutional change was aimed at the Supreme Court as much as at Congress. In addition, reformers proposed a referendum on all Court decisions that struck down legislation, popular rulings on Supreme Court overrulings. They were more successful in winning the power to recall unpopular officials, especially justices who were not directly accountable to the public in any other way. Ten states instituted the recall between 1910 and 1914. When Arizona applied for statehood, President William Howard Taft vetoed its proposed constitution for including a provision permitting the recall of justices; Arizona deleted the offending passage, secured statehood, and promptly reinserted the Progressive device.[45]

In the end, Progressives' politics added up to a systematic and coherent vision of democratic participation. Their democratic reforms were all aimed at minimizing, even spurning, the role of the representational intermediaries that stood between the public and its government—parties, legislators, private interests, ultimately politics itself. Each change they sought—direct elections of senators, primaries, referenda, recall, initiative, constitutional amendments, public review of Court decisions—worked to bypass the institutions that had distorted public sentiment; each was designed to wrest control from the representatives and rest it more directly in the represented, in the people themselves.

The Progressive ideal renewed the colonists' search for actual government. The proposals read like an update of devices from the first American decade: open government deliberations (echo the galleries that the revolutionaries erected in some of their assemblies), referenda (the right of instruction), the recall (a substitute for annual elections), all kinds of mechanisms making elections more direct, an expansion of the franchise. Like the revolutionaries and the Jacksonians, the Progressives imagined a politics that, ultimately, pressed beyond representation altogether.

It was not a merely negative vision, restricted to razing the party state. Along with popular participation came the restoration of the classic republican constituency. Reformers would put Madison aside. They were weary of the pursuit of narrow self-interest promoted by the checks and balances of the Constitution and pursued through party conflict. In an era of skewed power and sweeping inequities, a fragmented state seemed to sap the sovereignty of the people. Political competition checked the mobilization of public power for national purposes; it reduced the public good into fractious partisan politics and politics into the pursuit of divisible benefits by local interests. Instead, the Progressives returned to a single, united, consensual people—beyond political competition, beyond politics itself. "I would not be a dredger Congressman or a farmer Congressman or a fresh-egg Congressman," reported Senator Beveridge in the keynote address to the 1912 Progressive convention. "I would like to be an American Congressman."[46]

There were competing definitions of the Progressive people. One variant—articulated by Herbert Croly,* Walter Lippmann, and the Bull Moose–era Theodore Roosevelt—embraced the great scale of twentieth-century America. Their constituency was a single national people, mobilized in opposition to the concentration of private power.[47] In the alternate, more populist vision of William Jennings Bryan, Robert LaFollette, and Woodrow Wilson, democracy resided in the "collective will" of small communities across America. The populist Progressives would destroy concentrations of power, public and private. Both views invoked a single undivided people—either across the nation or in each community—with a discernible common will that superseded narrow self-interested politics and the institutions that promoted them.[48]

The Progressives rested their vision on an imaginary republican people, rising above politics to proclaim an unequivocal public interest in a single voice. The nationalists who followed Croly and Roosevelt fused the idealized past to a utopian future. Precisely as the logic of capitalism split Americans into the classes Progressive historians would read into other historical episodes, American reformers rediscovered communitarian unity. They wished away the struggle between workers and owners. For example, when the protagonist of Edward Bellamy's hugely popular *Looking Backward* wakes up in the year 2000, his first question is "What solution, if any, have you found for the labor question? It was the Sphinx's riddle of the nineteenth century." A spokesman for the enlightened society of the future responds

> To speak by the book, it was not necessary for society to solve the riddle at all. It may be said to have solved itself. The solution came as the result of a process of evolution which could not have

---

*Croly's explicit marriage of Jeffersonian democracy and a Hamiltonian positive state (with the latter receiving a good deal more of the emphasis) is the classic expression of Nationalistic Progressivism, arguably the major work of the Progressive era.

terminated otherwise. All society had to do was to recognize and cooperate with the evolution.[49]

Bellamy's book became the best-selling novel in American history. One hundred fifty clubs organized to promote its vision. They imagined a new industrial era in which class conflict, economic need, and labor agitation quietly evaporated before industrial progress. The American Federation of Labor organized three years earlier, in 1886, articulating the same sanguine principle. As we have seen in the preceding chapters, it is precisely when powerful changes promote the most social turbulence that the ideal of unity seems most palpable.

However, the same implacable reality that frustrated their communitarian predecessors defeated both the nationalist and the populist Progressives. They were not able to root their unitary people in any concrete constituency. They were suspicious of the immigrants who gathered in the eastern cities, nervous of the farmers that flocked to the Populist party in the Midwest, unsympathetic to the blacks and poor whites in the South. Who were the people if not they?

The Progressives resolved their dilemma in a time-tested but untenable way. They looked wistfully to Jefferson and the "ideal civilization" of the New England town with two hundred inhabitants, "the best educational environment ever realized in history." They celebrated the "local solidarity" of a lost America and yearned for the politics that sprang from the "ideal hearth and fireplace of olden times."[50] The Progressives invoked the vanished frontier where, as Theodore Roosevelt put it, "real Americans might do something valuable."[51] In short, they embraced the democratic wish, seeking communal constituencies that were part memory and part myth.

Here, in sum, was every feature of the democratic impulse—the people, direct participation, public interest consensus, and idyllic community. To be sure, the image of "the people" had evolved. Jefferson insisted that they worked their own land; those who collected in the cities were "sores" and "canker[s]" on the body politic.[52] Jackson had celebrated the same frontier, log-cabin yeomen, but broadened "the people" to embrace the artisans and mechanics in the cities (and just in time for the nineteenth-century immigrations). Croly and the national Progressives moved the people off the land entirely and found a new republican promise in the industrialization of the twentieth century. Regardless of the age or the formulation, the powerful myth stirred the reforming imagination without offering a practicable guide to political action.

Unable to infuse real meaning into their political vision, the Progressives relied on the trusty American image of democracy—invoked with references to town meetings and frontiersmen—floating free of concrete constituencies or political realities. Like the colonists and the Jacksonians, the Progressives promised a return of unity and virtue if power was restored to the people. When their people failed to materialize, Progressive democracy was undone. In political practice, the Progressive devices repeatedly subverted their democratic purpose. Before analyzing the unanticipated consequences of Progressive democracy, I examine the quest for science, the second conception with which the Progressives would lift the polity above politics and self-interest.

Progressive Administration: The Quest for Science

The Progressives fashioned an administrative ideal that matched their democracy. Public decisions would be placed in the hands of skilled experts who could utilize their specialized knowledge to do what was correct. Once again, the centrifugal forces of self-interest and faction would be cast aside, replaced by objective facts employed for the good of an undivided people. There was, in the Progressive vision, no Democratic or Republican way to sweep a street or regulate a railroad or administer the state. Rather, there was a *best* way—precise, expert, scientific. The correct technique would yield the correct solution.

Scientific government, managed by trained administrators rather than partisan legislators, dominated the reforming imagination. Once the people were liberated "from the baleful superstition of partisan politics" as Samuel ("Golden Rule") Jones, the reform mayor of Toledo put it, they would be rewarded by the "progress . . . of scientific government." Across the political spectrum, leaders invoked science and its promise. Roosevelt hailed the "value . . . for humanity" of "applied science"; even Big Bill Haywood, the radical Wobbly, had "a dream that there will be no political government, but experts will come together."[53]

The notion that improved knowledge could solve national problems seemed plausible. American society was being transformed by technology. Reformers recalled when railroads like the Erie scrambled to find rolling stock while cars in perfect order stood idle for months. Now new administrative methodologies told management "the precise location of every car and engine . . . at any hour of the day."[54] The same progress could solve public problems.

In 1891, for instance, economist Richard Ely discovered that no records were kept of paupers in public institutions. No government agent, state or national, knew how many citizens were on the dole. If the railroads could be rationalized, so could the state.[55] The law could be built into "a science of justice," the analysis of politics transformed into political science, the study of society into social science. Social progress would follow from the marshaling of facts and the faithful application of correct technique. Solutions to the dilemmas of poverty and ill health, child welfare and fair labor, agricultural production and urban slums could all be found like the lost freight cars of the Erie road.[56]*

The advance would be led by a new kind of administrator, imbued with the scientific ethic. Public administration would reflect the new professions: Planners and managers would reshape the city. Agrostologists, geologists, hydrologists, and foresters would apply their sciences to the countryside. Efficiency experts and economists would improve working conditions, train more productive employees, and vanquish unemployment. A knot of experts gained national fame. Gifford Pinchot, Roosevelt's forester, relentlessly preached the gospel of efficiency. Ironically, when Taft seemed to falter from Roosevelt's Progressive ideals, Pinchot precipitated an old-fashioned political crisis between his congressional allies and the administration.[58] Frederick Taylor insisted

---

*The entire enterprise was embodied by LaFollette's "Wisconsin idea," symbolized by State Street (in Madison, Wisconsin): At one end of the street stood the State University, at the other end, the State Capitol. LaFollette and the Progressives regularly—almost ostentatiously—drew on the university community for assistance with public matters.[57]

that the efficiency his time and motion studies had brought to business could be applied to government. The "one best way" to perform any task could be measured, precisely defined, and implemented. Taylor's disciples lobbied to create a cabinet-level post for efficiency experts. As one New York comptroller sermonized, "The practical man knows how, the scientific man knows why, the expert knows how and why."[59]

Expert administrators required independence. They were set in executive agencies, apart from the corrosive politics and interest groups of the legislatures. Each agency would preside over a narrowly delineated functional area—railroad rates, food and drugs, banking, public health, commerce—so that specialized expertise might be brought to bear on public problems.

The new conception of administrative structure was timely. Through most of the nineteenth century, bureaucratic expansion had merely kept pace with national growth. Between 1816 and 1861, 80 percent of the new federal jobs were in the Post Office. Now, however, the state was assuming a multitude of new functions.[60] Many were delegated to new agencies structured to Progressive specifications. The Interstate Commerce Commission came first, legislated in 1887 and ostensibly strengthened in 1905.* Roosevelt won the Food and Drug Administration in 1906, brandishing Upton Sinclair's *The Jungle* at the opposition. Woodrow Wilson added, among other agencies, the Federal Reserve Board (1913), the Fair Trade Commission (1914), the Federal Farm Loan Board (1916), and commissions on shipping, the tariff, and federal employee compensation. Each was created independent of large cabinet departments; most regulated a narrowly deline-

---

*A large literature claims to illuminate the single source of railroad regulation—whether Western merchants, Eastern business, Pennsylvania oil interests, the Grange farmers, the railroads themselves. Edward Purcell[61] argues that it was a broad coalition of these groups, each pursuing its own interests, that won the formation of the ICC; in any event, the railroads quickly won its politics. In this and other cases, the dominance of the industries over the regulators seemed so pronounced that it became popular to argue that industry sought the regulations in the first place. This argument overlooks many recurring features of American political economy: the repeated cycle of business opposition to regulation which eventually works to its advantage; the reformers repeatedly winning political devices that, in practice, exacerbate the problems they were meant to address. As I suggest later in this chapter, corporate dominance came from the political dynamics of the agencies in operation, not a conspiracy at their formation.[62] Still, the revisionist literature includes some of the outstanding works on the period.[63]

ated portion of the economy. On the state and municipal levels, scores of similar commissions were granted jurisdiction over railroads, utilities, labor, agriculture, food processing, medicine, and so on.

The key to the entire Progressive apparatus lay in the smooth coordination of the different, functionally specific agencies. Incessantly, the Progressives urged rationalization, systemization, coordination, efficiency. They sponsored a centralized budget, a general accounting office, a bureau of efficiency, a commission on economy, a committee on department methods, and a bureau of centralized administration (analogous to the British Treasury, one of the few rationalizing devices they failed to win). "If there is lack of proper coordination among the parts," wrote Walter E. Weyl, "if there are jurisdictional disputes . . . between state and nation . . . between legislature and judiciary . . . then no true efficiency can be maintained."[64] A single people would be served by a coherent administrative state. The Progressive vision required experts impartially applying specialized knowledge in specialized fields, all of them fitting together into a rationalized, coordinated, governmental whole.

Note how Progressive administration fits neatly with the other features of the reforming mind-set. Clearly it assumed the triumph of a professional civil service over party fealty and the spoils. The Republicans were emerging from the incessant demands of party politics.* They enjoyed sixteen uninterrupted years of majority, both in Congress (beginning in 1895) and in the presidency (1897). The Progressives urged on the final conquest of Jackson's apparatus—the elimination of geographic qualifications and the classification of every administrative post below cabinet level.[65]

To be sure, the Progressives pushed democracy back on the people, then seemingly snatched it safely away to the expert. But their administration complemented their democracy. Each operated beyond poli-

---

*Though the spoils were unquestionably receding, their demise can be exaggerated. Roosevelt blanketed in fourth-class postmasters in the Northeast, where his Republicans were secure. Taft desperately blanketed in 52,236 posts in the South and West after his defeat. Wilson rolled back Taft's posts, changing the old rules by insisting that even the incumbents be subjected to merit exams. Wilson's secretary of state, William Jennings Bryan, was an avowed spoilsman in the Jacksonian tradition (the last presidential candidate explicitly to endorse spoils, in 1896). Bryan threw open his department to an old-fashioned Democratic party spoils rush. Nor was he the last of the unabashed spoilsmen, as we shall see when we consider the New Deal.

tics; each would dig below partisan claims and clashing interests for the objective public interest of a cohesive people. The new public administration would efficiently implement the public will articulated through the newly purified democratic mechanisms. Taken together, the two parts of Progressive reform comprised a coherent view of representation—eschewing subjective private interests for an objective public one, spurning a multitude of special constituencies for a single, universalistic people. Here, once again, was the classical republican faith, with scientific experts playing a role roughly like the one of natural leaders. It was no less a view of representation for its premise of an objective public interest, no less a reformist vision for its sweeping, unambiguous failure.

PROGRESSIVE FAILURES

The Progressive institutions were designed to accommodate the public-spirited people. Once in place, of course, they encountered the narrow clashing interests that had greeted their reforming predecessors. Consider the consequences: first, for Progressive administration; then, for its democracy.

Consequences of Administrative Science

From the start, the purportedly scientific agencies faced political obstacles. The cadre of experts who were to guide the administrative state failed to materialize. For every public-spirited reformer, there were scores of industry spokesmen; they were eager to staff the Progressive agencies if possible, willing to lobby them if necessary. The politicians who selected regulatory commissioners predictably accommodated powerful groups and industries. Theodore Roosevelt set the political pattern, conceding "gentlemen's agreements" over both the power and the personnel of new agencies. "I believe in the . . . next

119

step, not . . . the two hundredth step," he snapped at the purists while negotiating his compromises.[66]

Even agencies staffed in correct Progressive fashion immediately encountered political trouble. Consider, for instance, the most sustained Progressive effort at scientific administration: conservation policy. The conservationists disdained compromise with self-interested groups—a violation of the gospel of efficiency. However, they were swiftly mired in rural politics. Their precise, ostensibly scientific land-use plans infuriated local groups and property owners, who were not mollified by professionalism when it minimized their needs. The people stubbornly insisted on their admittedly narrow but undeniably concrete self-interests. Farmers were angered when they got less water so that distant industries might get more power; local developers fought river-basin plans that gave somebody else the dam.[67]

The grass-roots interests responded to the agrologists and geologists in the time-honored political way. They alternately sued the conservationists and scurried to sympathetic congressmen who oversaw administrative appropriations. In addition, local groups discovered a potent new political device. They began to form national organizations. Together, local groups and their national spokesmen pressed a pliant Congress for traditional boondoggles—irrigation works, flood control projects, river and harbor funds—regardless of the rationalists and their technical plans.

Worse, the scientific ideal failed to illuminate the difficult choices among competing values such as wilderness preservation, the development of rural industry, and support for agriculture. The Progressive conservationists had no technically correct response to the rural interests that challenged their goals. The ultimately political choices were inevitably made in political ways. Ironically, the policies of Progressive conservation were shaped, not by science beyond politics but by the National Water Users Association, the National Rivers and Harbors Congress, or the National Livestock Association.[68]

The conservationist's dilemma was emblematic. Everywhere the ineffective scientific ideal withered before political power. The Interstate Commerce Commission was not empowered to mete out sanctions but had to sue recalcitrant railroads; it lost fifteen out of the first sixteen cases it brought before the Supreme Court. The commission was eviscerated within a decade. When Roosevelt and the Progressives sought to restore it with "ironclad powers," congressional conservatives weakened their proposal (producing the Hepburn Act of 1905) before an unsympathetic Supreme Court weakened it further.[69] Similarly, a pitched battle over the Meat Packing Act ended in compromises that established regulatory principles but profited large meat packers over their small competitors. Antitrust policy met the same political fate; the Sherman Act was legislated in 1890 and enfeebled by the Court within six years. A decade later, Roosevelt played up his trust-busting image while sacrificing the systematic effort to restore competition to an untenable but politic distinction between good and bad trusts.[70] Repeatedly, the ideal of administrative science was undone by industrial power and the checks and balances of a hesitant state.

Even Taylor's time-and-motion studies, with their promise of efficiency and the one best way, were driven from the public workplace by employees. Public workers resented the intrusion on their new autonomy; they rejected the contention that precise measurements could replace bargaining over wages or working conditions.[71] When the studies were performed, they were done surreptitiously.[72]

Still, Progressive administration faced a far more profound dilemma than fragmented public institutions or aroused private interests. Their administrative technique itself was ineffectual. Scientific management offered no clear guide for discerning the public interest. There was, to be sure, enormous pressure for increasing government efficiency. The decline of the spoils and the proliferation of agencies broadly extended both the competence and the capacity of the American state. However, the Progressive faith that the correct method would inexorably deliver the correct solution was invariably disappointed.

For instance, the Interstate Commerce Commission had been designed to Progressive specifications, an independent commission with a broad, vague mandate. The commissioners were to ensure that railroads charged "just and reasonable rates." However, the principles of scientific management provided no guidance to the quickly bewildered commissioners, who lamented in their first annual report: "The question of reasonableness of rates is quite impossible to deal with on purely mathematical principles, or on any principles whatever. No conclusion which may be reached can . . . be shown to be absolutely correct."[73]

The perplexity of the ICC commissioners, declaring that they could not find "any principle whatsoever" to direct their independent judgments, was echoed throughout the new administrative establishment. On every level of government, officials found no formula for discerning the public good. The symbolic victories over railroads, or meat packers, or trusts were popular but evanescent; Progressive technique afforded the administrators no manifestly correct alternatives to the suasions of private power. Even "neutral" administrators remained obstinately attuned to the demands of their own personal and organizational interest.

Moreover, the independence and narrow scope of the agencies provided an advantage to interests who were less likely to clash with other groups seeking to exert influence in the same circumscribed political arena. The ICC was quickly dominated by the railroads, which used the agency to enforce essentially private agreements. On every level of the state, the narrowly delineated, independent agencies accommodated narrowly defined self-interested groups. Local business dominated tax decisions, developers shaped resource management, agricultural associations made farm policy, physicians controlled licensure boards. Administrative agents pursued their own equally narrow interests by promoting private client organizations, which could then lobby Congress on behalf of the agency and its services.

A half-century later, this "capture" or interest-group liberalism became the major premise of the popular "élite-pluralist" analysis of American politics. It, in turn, would be challenged by a state-centered approach that shifted the emphasis from the interest of private groups to the interest of the state officials themselves. In both cases, the analysis turns on narrow self-interest, either of private groups or of government agents. Both interpret the Progressive legacy in a similar fashion—a search for broad public interests which yielded, instead, a multitude of narrow ones. The result is a more diffuse system than its party predecessor, but hardly a more democratic one.[74]

Finally, the different parts of the Progressive state failed to cohere, much less function together in an efficient whole. The reformers left behind a broad array of independent agencies with no centripetal political force holding them together. Under unusual circumstances, a president might briefly impart some image of coordination among the many parts (as both Roosevelts sometimes managed to do). But even then, the inchoate, fragmented apparatus—routinely penetrated by private interests—mocked the Progressive ideal.

The Progressives transformed the American state. However, their aspirations were frustrated at every turn. They sought disinterested science and got interest group politics. They envisioned a rationalized, coherent administration and structured a fragmented, uncoordinated one. They promised to mobilize public power to a single national purpose and, instead, enhanced the exercise of private power by narrow, self-interested groups. The state was refitted to an industrial society; it was rendered far more flexible. But the Madisonian system that scattered public power was preserved and carried forward, its checks and balances renewed and multiplied. Congress, the courts, a newly empowered president, and a complex federalism were joined to a disorderly cumulation of administrative agencies on every level of government. The state remained difficult to mobilize for any sustained public purpose. Its multiplicity of uncoordinated parts remained vulnerable to private interests, which now reconstituted themselves into national associations.

Consequences of Progressive Democracy

The Progressives resolved the contradictions within their reform agenda by invoking an idealized people, united by a yearning for the public interest. Popular parties were attacked and scientific administration promoted in order to restore the imagined republican past. When the people failed to emerge, the reforms that had been predicated on them collapsed. The many devices designed to empower the people proved unwieldy in operation and élitist in effect. The reformers weakened existing links between the people and the state without offering practicable replacements. The result was a pervasive political bias that reinforced the outcomes of Progressive administrative reforms.

The Progressive electoral innovations, for example, eventually helped undermine the party bosses. The consequence was a diminution of popular political participation. Though the Australian ballot had seemed a benign effort to end intimidation and corruption at the polls, it stripped the parties of a major function—the printing of ballots. It weakened the command they held over their followers. And it served to disenfranchise illiterate voters, most conspicuously the black voters in the South.* Ironically, even the Progressives' central democratic achievement, women's suffrage, helped subvert the political influence of urban immigrants. Burnham argues that women in those communities were often reluctant to vote.[75] Suffrage diluted the ethnic vote and further weakened the party leaders who relied on it.

The nominating primaries had an analogous effect. Naturally, they eroded the influence of the bosses. In the process, parties lost their monopoly on political opposition, facilitating the rise of single party states. Loosening the boss grip on nominations did not empower the public. On the contrary, adding an additional election to each campaign enhanced the role of organization and money. As parties declined, both were increasingly provided by business corporations and interest groups.[76]

The other contrivances of Progressive democracy bore similar consequences. The people were swamped rather than strengthened by the referendum. In Oregon, for example, voters were asked to judge forty-one amendments and sixty-one laws in twelve years.[77] The ostensibly democratic device clearly favored educated voters who could fathom the complex questions being put to them. It took organization and money to organize referenda, launch an initiative, or circulate recall petitions.

The entire panoply of Progressive democracy worked with a consistent bias. Taken together, the reforms transformed the channels of influence between the people and the state. They attenuated the political parties at every turn. The forms of political representation that

---

*No Progressive failure was more wretched than the complicity in the almost complete disenfranchisement of southern blacks. Poll taxes, grandfather clauses, literacy tests, and a host of other devices were employed—all supported by a perversion of the Progressive's "scientific method," purporting to demonstrate inherent inequality between the races. I treat the issue at length in chapter 6.

replaced them did not convey the desires of the people speaking in a single public-spirited voice. Instead, Progressive democracy advantaged precisely the same organizations that were mobilized by Progressive administration—narrow organizations articulating the desires of powerful private interests.

In their fashion, the Jacksonian parties had aggregated the demands of many constituencies; interest groups broke them apart. Parties, organized by geography and empowered by numbers, sought out the immigrants, the uneducated, and the poor. Interest groups, organized by functional categories and operating on money and influence, did not need them. Voter participation plunged. In the seven presidential elections between 1876 and 1900, turnout averaged 80.8 percent. In the seven elections after 1900, the average was 60.5 percent.[78]

Progressive democracy mirrored Progressive administration. Each disaggregated American politics into a multiplicity of fragmented groups organized around private interests and their public-sector allies. The nineteenth-century party state was superseded by twentieth-century interest-group liberalism. A multiplicity of National Rivers and Harbors Congresses ascended as the Republicans and Democrats declined.

CONCLUSION

On its surface, the Progressive movement seems an inchoate (even contradictory) bundle of notions, stretching over almost five decades and embracing a wide variety of groups and causes. So diffuse a movement, argue some social scientists, is no movement at all and ought to be dispensed with as an analytic category. I have argued, on the contrary, that the Progressives manifest the recurring features of the democratic wish. Indeed, it is the political ambiguity of the American reforming philosophy that facilitates the development of such broad coalitions. Moreover, this movement traced a political pattern roughly similar to that of past reforming generations. Consider the four stages of the Progressive reformations:

First, accumulating demands for change faced an unyielding status quo. The struggle against the party state was, as Skowronek has shown, merely incorporated into party struggles. Decades of reformist maneuvering failed to produce fundamental change. When the reconstruction of American politics finally came, it was organized around a variation of the democratic impulse.

The second phase comes with the democratic ideology and the introduction of institutions designed to accommodate it. Progressive rhetoric was redolent with calls to the people. More important, Progressive proposals were organized around the unlikely neoclassical ideals. Reformers concocted their steady stream of protoparticipatory schemes, reflecting the notions of "actual" government—new constituencies, more direct citizen action, more open politics. Their reforms were designed around the assumption of a unitary, discernible public interest, stretching beyond factions and even politics itself. The effort echoes the classical republicans urging virtue: that is, the subordination of private interests to public good.

The multiple, often conflicting images of community the Progressives called on suggest the trouble they had in finding a concrete political constituency that could realistically anchor the notion of public-interested unity. I have argued, however, that it is precisely when social and political change seems most relentless that American reformers articulate their yearning for a unitary people beyond politics. As Americans reconstructed their state to the imperatives of a new corporate capitalism—with its raw class schisms—they imagined the underlying communal interest. It is that communal paradigm which makes the Progressive project coherent and consistent.

What I have referred to as the Progressive oxymoron—direct democracy with scientific administration—is a contradiction only when observed from liberal ground. If, instead of clashing interests, the people really did share an underlying communal good, then both methodologies served the same end. Primary elections and administrative science would tap the same public good. It is a faith that, in steadily evolving forms, organizes reformist thinking for each reconstruction of the American regime.

The third stage comes when the reformist institutions are won and implemented. The Progressive innovations might be made coherent by the assumption of communal consensus in the public interest; however, they failed precisely because the assumption was false. Instead, their reforms provided new arenas and new rules for distinctly self-interested political clashes. Like previous reformers, the Progressives both legitimated and limited political change.

The political limits are the more vivid results in this period. Repeatedly, the democratic aspirations were defeated by the imperatives or organization and power. Like the colonial attempt at legislative government and the Jacksonian parties and people's bureaucracy, the Progressives eventually delivered power into élite hands. The Federalist gentlemen commanded the first administrations; the bosses and barons captured Jacksonian democracy; narrow functional interests and (equally narrow) state agencies won Progressive government. Each democratic surge reconstructed the regime for a new era. None fulfilled the democratic yearning that helped negotiate the change.

Despite the defeat of its broadest democratic aspirations, each movement integrated new publics into American political life, each extended participation to previously suppressed groups. The Revolutionary generation won independence and articulated a new conception of popular sovereignty. The Jacksonians recruited workingmen into political action. The Progressives, for all their democratic shortcomings, won political rights for a still larger class when they finally secured the Nineteenth Amendment.

Finally, the political cycle ends with the transformation of American public administration. A new status quo is organized around new political rules, new state capacity, new public powers. The revolutionaries turned British colonial rule into the American constitutional regime. The Jacksonians radically revised the administration of the Federalists for a new era of emerging capitalism and mass immigration; they devised a rudimentary bureaucratic apparatus. The Progressives redesigned that rough bureaucracy and founded the contemporary American state. Their fragmented administration would persist and grow through the twentieth century.

There is one final, subtle continuity between the new administrative vision and its predecessor, between the Jacksonian and the Progressive bureaucracies. Delegates of the people, rotating in and out of office, share a striking characteristic with administrative experts applying scientific methods to achieve the single best policy. Each is founded on a mechanistic, self-equilibrating view of administration. Neither requires careful judgment or statesmanship. Instead, impersonal forces—elections, science—guide the polity. In a nation that insistently subordinates administration to democracy, the constant touchstone is bureaucracy without reflection; administration by inexorable, autonomous forces rather than the deliberation of leaders. The Progressives replaced the spoils, seeking good, even active government. However, they promised to do so without introducing public power that was self-conscious, that would think for itself. Despite the size of the Progressive establishment, the American dread of government remained.

4

Progressive Administration without the People: The New Deal

To some persons the New Deal is a program that will carry us into a new era of prosperity and a better civilization. To others, it is a scheme to destroy individual initiative, throttle our historic economic liberty and reduce us all to the dead level of a regimented people, ruled by a vast and tyrannical bureaucracy.

E. E. Lewis, 1935

The Great Depression briefly eclipsed the American wariness of government power. The Roosevelt administration, acting with unusual political latitude, broadly extended the administrative state.* However, the New Deal administrative inventions did not break sharply with the past. Roosevelt left behind a far greater government, but not one fundamentally different from the Progressive institutions that he found.

While the dread of government was in abeyance, the New Dealers did not call on the people to sanction their reforms. For the most part, Roosevelt did not need the democratic wish. As a result, the frenetic

*As an example of latitude, Roosevelt received $3 billion in discretionary funds in a two-year period for which the entire federal budget was $11.2 billion. Roughly similar powers over executive administration had been granted Wilson by the Overman Act during the First World War.[1]

state building of the mid-1930s differs from the episodes I have traced in previous chapters—a partial exception that illuminates the pattern.

By the late 1930s, however, the old dilemma had returned: How could Americans reconcile their expanded bureaucracy with their notions of democracy? The question itself testified that the old liberal boundaries were back in place, challenging extensions of public power and government programs.

In this chapter, I briefly investigate the dynamics of state building without the people, reflecting on both the roots and the legacy of New Deal bureaucracy. I turn to Roosevelt's democratic wish in part II (chapter 5) because the New Dealers called on the people to reconstruct a single policy area—albeit the crucial one of labor relations—rather than to transform the administrative state itself.

ADMINISTRATIVE SCIENCE BECOMES
INTEREST-GROUP LIBERALISM

The New Dealers rallied one another with the watchwords of Progressive administration. "It is expertise that is desperately needed," urged James M. Landis, the Harvard Law School professor who helped draft the Securities Exchange Bill. "Technology, science and expertise," echoed David Lilienthal, as he organized the Tennessee Valley Authority's power policy.[2] The nation's economic crisis could be overcome by trained specialists if they applied their disciplines to carefully delineated problems free of political interference. Congress was expected to acknowledge its "institutional incompetence," grant the agencies their mandates, and oversee them loosely. "It is easier to plot through a labyrinth of detail when it is done in the comparative quiet of the [administrator's] conference room than when it is attempted amid the turmoil of a legislative chamber."[3] The meddlesome courts would, it was hoped, also defer to expert administrative judgments.[4]

When New Dealers considered the Progressive failures, they attributed them—in correct Progressive fashion—to insufficient specialization. They contrasted the Progressive Federal Trade Commission, policing the entire economy, with the more focused New Deal agencies such as the Securities and Exchange Commission. Efficient administration required "the creation of more rather than less" administrative agencies.[5]

Roosevelt responded to the call. The New Deal was chaotic with experimentation. "Take a method and try it," said the President. "If it fails . . . try another. . . . Above all try something."[6] New tries produced new agencies. Administrative bureaus were created quickly— "more rapidly than causes could be isolated and problems defined." Roosevelt's penchant for new organizations appears, in some accounts, as an "addiction" or a "kind of nervous tic."[7] By 1935, sixty new— loosely organized, overlapping—agencies sprawled over the national executive, each with its alphabetic code name: Federal Emergency Relief Administration (FERA), Agriculture Adjustment Administration (AAA), Tennessee Valley Authority (TVA), National Recovery Administration (NRA), Civil Works Administration (CWA). After crushing the Republicans in 1936, Roosevelt reported that administrative chaos had been the greatest weakness of his first term and the issue on which he had felt the most vulnerable.[8]

The chaotic administrative structure was skillfully overseen by the President. He used uncertain agency jurisdictions to motivate and manipulate subordinates. The result, however, was conflict as much as creativity. Secretary of Interior Harold Ickes scrambled anxiously to wrest the Forest Service from the Department of Agriculture and annex it to his department. Agriculture Secretary Henry Wallace responded by helping to defeat legislation Ickes wanted. When the National Recovery Administration's director, Hugh Johnson, was denied control of public works, he bitterly denounced the jealousy of cabinet members; he declared himself "ruined" and later joined the opposition.[9] Repeatedly, the ostensible experts maneuvered and scrapped to gain advantage for themselves and their agencies.

Organizational self-interest produced a more vexing difficulty than clashing bureaucrats. With few exceptions, the fate of the New Deal agencies mirrored those of their Progressive predecessors. Once again, narrow public agencies mobilized narrow private interests. However, while the myth of expertise continued to be invoked, by the 1930s it had acquired a detached, academic tone which no longer stimulated the reforming imagination. The new agencies differed from the old largely in the eagerness with which they accommodated private interests. Agencies actively sought support clienteles and fostered constituencies for their services. They cultivated private interests that were keen to win their own institutional advocates within government. The Progressives had tried to render government neutral by ending special favors; if the New Dealers were neutral, it was because they seemed to endow favors on every organized group.[10] The New Deal ideal was the pursuit of the public interest by dispassionate experts; the widely acknowledged reality was constituency service: defining, even organizing, private interests that could be accommodated within the governing coalition. "It spreads like a grease stain," complained a contemporary. "Every group organized around a special and selfish interest demands . . . recognition. Our government has been the mere tossing of tubs to each whale as it . . . sticks its head out of the water."[11] The lament that opens E. Pendleton Herring's 1935 study of the new public administration underscores the New Deal's rhetorical break with past state-building episodes: "The voice of the people . . . sometimes suggests the squeal of pigs at the trough."[12]

For instance, the Progressive's Interstate Commerce Commission had been mandated to constrain the railroads, though it was soon catering to them. The New Deal's Civil Aeronautics Board was less ambiguous from the start. It was explicitly designed to promote the American aviation industry.[13]

Both eras stimulated rural organization. Progressive land-use plans prompted Western landowners to organize in defense of their interests. The New Deal's Agriculture Adjustment Administration was less oblique; it organized the farmers, helped them modernize, and paid them to grow less. The AAA had an additional bias. It profited wealthier, larger, more easily organized farmers. Small, poor farmers bore the burden of New Deal agricultural policy. They lost jobs when the large farms modernized; they were not eligible for many AAA benefits. "To him that hath, shall be given," summarized one observer.[14]

The same pattern dominated industrial politics. The Progressive search for economic competition through trust busting was replaced by cooperation under the aegis of national planning. The National Industrial Recovery Act, considered in detail in the following chapter, was loosely based on the planning experience of the First World War. Government facilitated industry negotiations over codes of business conduct. The codes would vitiate destructive competition and—it was hoped—restore profits. Corporations and trade associations dusted off agreements they had drafted during the Hoover administration, and happily promulgated them. "The plan is good enough . . . for the powerful," claimed Walter Lippmann, "but for the weak it is brutal." "The small proprietor . . . is ruined, but thank God his big competitor is thriving at the old stand," exaggerated Clarence Darrow.[15]

The New Deal was not as overtly class biased as these examples imply. Rather, it was driven by interest-group liberalism with its more subtle class bias toward the affluent and the organized (or easily organized). Thus, the National Recovery Administration embraced organized labor as well as industry, although doing so exceeded even the relaxed limits on legitimate action afforded the state in the 1930s. It was the unorganized worker in the marginal firm that suffered the brunt of New Deal liberalism.

The New Dealers invoked the Progressive idea while pursuing the politics Progressives had assailed. Most of the old Progressives in Congress opposed programs such as the NRA. They continued to conjure up their "qualified experts representing the nation as a whole"; they scorned the "boards composed of the bargaining representatives of various interests."[16] The irony is that precisely the same outcome repeatedly followed from the Progressive ideal, regardless of the era or the administration. The effort to empower independent experts over narrowly delineated arenas systematically turned politics away from a universalistic people; it advantaged narrow organized interests by organizing narrow functional political arenas. The New Dealers may have been willing, even eager, to achieve this philosophically unsatisfying but politically useful outcome. Nevertheless, the old Progressive reformers who denounced them did so without acknowledging that the narrowly focused agencies allied with private groups were the direct (if unexpected and unwanted) progeny of their own vision.*

VARIETIES OF NEW DEAL ADMINISTRATION

The rising new administration jumbled together all the past ideals of American public service. For a brief moment, fit characters, the party faithful, and civil service bureaucrats rubbed shoulders.

Perhaps the most celebrated group was Roosevelt's "brain trust." Professors "accustomed to the raspberries of sophomores in bare smelly schoolrooms," as H. L. Mencken put it, were now "thrown into power." They dominated the early New Deal, proposing one national experiment after another, while cautious politicians deferred to the new administration. The brain trust dimly reflected the Mugwump-Progressive ambition, the return to power of well-educated "fit characters." Intellectuals may have been more influential during Roosevelt's frantic "first hundred days" than they had been since the Federalist era. Their restoration was brief.[18]

Opposition to the brain trusters came, in part, from the federal bureaucracy. Rank-and-file administrators resented the "arrogant," "impractical" intellectuals who overran Washington. The civil service had once anchored the Mugwump-Progressive aspiration for good, efficient government; by the 1930s, the reality had long been conceded: "chosen dullards" plodded through a "long, uneventful, thoroughly secure working life."[19] As their numbers multiplied, the warning raised

---

*Richard Hofstadter takes the opposite view and interprets the New Deal as a break with Progressive philosophy. He notes both the absence of what I call the democratic wish and the profound discomfort of the old Progressives with the New Deal reform. He fails, however, to distinguish between reforming aspirations and political consequences across the two periods. Thus, he contrasts Progressive ideals (rationalization, coordination, and so on) with New Deal political reality (administrative fragmentation and constituency service) without acknowledging that the Progressives ended up in precisely the same political place as the New Dealers.[17]

by Orestes Brownson during Jackson's administration was voiced with increasing frequency. Senator William Borah of Idaho, who had once denounced the aristocrats of patronage, now fulminated over that "meddlesome, irritating, confusing, destructive thing called bureaucracy."[20] Fifty years after the Pendleton Act, the civil service appeared bureaucratic, stultifying, and—since they had controlled six of the last seven administrations—Republican.

A third group, the Democratic party regulars, were uneasy about both liberal brain trusters and Republican civil servants—though they exaggerated the influence of the former and the political sympathies of the latter. After twelve years out of office, the Democratic faithful clamored for posts. Roosevelt manipulated the jobbing with all the gusto of his predecessors in the party era. The politicians within the administration, led by Postmaster James Farley, helped Roosevelt preside over one of the last great spoils scrambles in American history. The "plum book of 1933" simplified the task for the job seekers by listing 100,000 federal positions that were up for political grabs (no examinations necessary). The pace of the first two Roosevelt years added another 100,000. Even so, there were twenty applicants for every post. While brain trusters crowded into some agencies, departments like War, Justice, and the Home Owners Loan Corporation distributed positions on the time-honored basis of party service. Paul Van Riper calls it the "most spectacular resurgence of the spoils in American history."[21] Unlike some of his nineteenth-century predecessors, however, Roosevelt was not able to use the jobbing to influence elections. "It's a bust," diagnosed Farley, even before the results of the 1938 midterm vote was in; Roosevelt's effort generated considerable enmity without influencing many races.[22]

In a sense, Franklin Roosevelt balanced the heirs of Federalist, Jacksonian, and Progressive administration. However, the brain trusters and party men were soon subordinated to the civil service. Roosevelt was widely criticized for threatening administrative neutrality. By 1940, he had folded most of the new posts into the civil service system (following Woodrow Wilson, the incumbents were required to pass exams). Stripped of the old promises about political purity and public interest, however, an expanding administrative apparatus raised the classic riddle: How were bureaucracy and democracy to be reconciled?

The inadequacy of nineteenth-century solutions was clear; the dilemma remained.

For a time, an academic reinterpretation became the prevailing solution, though it never mobilized reform or gained popular currency. The argument inverted the Progressive idea, neatly reconciling American thought with the threat of a positive state. The failure of scientific administration, it was argued, was not merely inevitable but good. Administrators properly resisted aloof, expert judgments that would have been skewed by the limitations of information and human judgment. Instead, they were instructed by the people through a sort of political market: A group or an interest that felt strongly about a matter would mobilize for political action, approach the relevant administrative body, and bargain out their differences with any other groups that might have mobilized over the issue. Public administrators assisted in the bargaining and ratified the results. In this way, the administrators' search for constituency was reinterpreted as a sort of democratic urge. Institutions that had been designed to be scientifically correct were celebrated for being sensitive to popular demands. The failed trustees were reinterpreted as delegates. The same impersonal character that had animated earlier theories of administration was rediscovered in the interest-group liberalism of the New Deal. Government administrators did not make calculated, self-conscious judgments; they simply responded, almost mechanically, to the forces of the political market.

In brief, American political thought mimicked two centuries of American political experience. It subordinated the administrative state to democratic politics. A sprawling bureaucracy pursuing its own self-interests in consort with private groups (pursuing theirs) was conjured into a vast democratic market responding to citizen wishes as they were articulated by organized groups.

The pluralist argument appeared early in the century, reappeared in the 1930s, and gained wide academic currency in the two decades following the Second World War. Perhaps its popularity grew as the threat of a large independent administrative apparatus penetrated public consciousness. In any case, popular recognition of that threat marked the end of the New Dealers' political autonomy. The renewal of the

American dread of government also explains one of the most bizarre political episodes of the New Deal.[23]

THE LIMITS OF LEGITIMACY

The demise of Roosevelt's own domestic agenda coincided with his effort to force coherence on the fragmented American state. The President attacked obstructions to the New Deal in each branch of government. In 1937, the maladroit Court-packing scheme would have permitted him to name a new Supreme Court justice every time an incumbent reached seventy and refused to step down. The plan was beaten, though Roosevelt ultimately got his way with the Court.[24] Second, during the 1938 midterm elections, the President unsuccessfully campaigned for a more ideologically sympathetic Congress. Finally, he proposed to rationalize the disorderly administrative apparatus. The first two ventures were politically risky, their failure no surprise. In contrast, the furor ignited by the apparently routine executive reorganization continues to puzzle observers.

Certainly the executive branch was chaotic with duplication and overlap. "The plain fact," reported Roosevelt, is that under "the present organization of the Executive . . . the government cannot be . . . effective."[25] In contrast to the judiciary machinations, administrative reorganization was carefully drafted by a genuinely distinguished committee (Charles Merriam, Louis Brownlow, and Luther Gulick).* Their recommendations were submitted in January 1938, as Roosevelt was losing the Court fight and (more or less) winning a minimum wage. On the surface, the plan appeared entirely unexceptional. It had several aims:

---

*Louis Brownlow was first a newspaper reporter, then a commissioner of the District of Columbia (beginning in 1915). Charles Merriam was both a political theorist and a Chicago politician; he taught Machiavelli by day and fought the ward bosses in the evening, comments Barry Karl.[26] Like Merriam, an academic, Luther Gulick focused his career more directly on the study of public administration.

1. Expansion of the White House staff.
2. Strengthening the managerial arm of the executive, especially the agencies concerned with budget, efficiency research, personnel, and planning.
3. Extension of the merit system "upward, outward, downward" to cover almost "all non policy determining posts." Most New Deal agencies would be placed within the civil service system.
4. Overhauling the roughly one hundred independent agencies, administrations, authorities, boards, and commissions by placing them within one of twelve cabinet agencies.
5. Restoration of complete responsibility for accounts to the executive and the introduction of a genuine post-audit of all fiscal transactions by an auditor general.[27]

At the end of the 1937 congressional session, the bill sailed through the House (283 to 75). The Senate did not reach it, and the reorganization plan came up again in the following year. This time, the dull administration reform was popularly designated the "dictator bill."

Senator David Walsh of Massachusetts declared that it "plunged a dagger into the very heart of democracy." One hundred Paul Reveres mounted horses and galloped to Washington, each carrying a banner that read "no one man rule." Committees to Uphold Constitutional Government sprang up around the country.[28] The *Washington Star* warned that the administrative reorganization would "pave the way to Sovietize the United States"; other columnists thought it more like "Hitlerism."[29] From the Republican politicians to organized labor (which had supported the President's Court bill), from the Catholic church to the Interstate Commerce Commission, organizations rushed to denounce the plan. Three hundred thirty thousand telegrams poured into Washington, overwhelmingly negative; the torrent was so great, lamented Harold Ickes, that telegraph offices set aside all other business.[30] As the criticism surged, Roosevelt released an extraordinary statement:

A. I have no inclination to be a dictator.

B. I have none of the qualifications that would make me a successful dictator.

138

C. I have too much historical background . . . to make me desire
any form of dictatorship . . . in the United States of America.

On 8 April 1938, the House narrowly defeated the President's bill
(204 to 196). As the tally was announced, the chambers broke into
"wild cheering."[31]*

Most scholars are frankly puzzled by the political defeat. Eighteen
months earlier, the President had won one of the great landslides in
American electoral history. Of all the sweeping New Deal plans—from
tinkering with the courts to the quasi-fascistic effort at national planning—why did this administrative plan provoke the outcry that required Roosevelt to declare, even facetiously, that he was not a dictator?
The broad historical context of the democratic wish and American
administration suggests an answer.

Narrow interests scrambled to protect their agency, commission, or
authority. The constituents of the new bureaucratic apparatus were
invested in the unwieldy status quo. Rationalizing public administration into a manageable number of coherent departments would threaten
the privileges of private interests and the autonomy of public officials.
In order to protect their institutional fragment of the state, private
interests and public officials mobilized the people. They successfully
evoked the venerable symbols of democracy usurped, the dread of government. Administrative "usurpations" have repeatedly set off the
American democratic furors. The Roosevelt administration faced the
old dread without the cover of democratic yearning: on the contrary,
it was its opponents who summoned the imagery of the people. In
this case, organized interests only briefly ignited the deep-set wariness
of administrative authority. However, the outcry signaled the end of
both the New Deal and the peacetime expansion of state authority.

The panic of the Depression and the exhilaration of "doing something" had worn off. Public hostility toward public power had returned, marked by all the melodrama of the "dictator bill." To be sure,
Roosevelt had tried to rationalize administrative powers that, by 1938,

---

*In the end, Franklin Roosevelt won some but not all of the Brownlow Commission report.
Weaker legislation passed quietly in 1939; it explicitly exempted twenty independent agencies
from administrative rationalization.

were already part of the national executive. However, in a slightly larger historical frame, the President had assumed broad new authority over a multitude of areas. The "dictator bill" briefly held the changes up to the public eye. Roosevelt would no longer extend the New Deal. On the contrary, he would have to fight to maintain it as Congress cut programs and slashed appropriations. True to ideological form, Americans marked the end of the New Deal not with a constitutional or economic crisis, but with a great conflict over a minor effort to consolidate administrative power.

CONCLUSION

The New Deal expanded the fragmented American administrative state. A cumulation of bureaus and agencies were piled onto the Progressive frame. The private interests that had perplexed the Progressives were often embraced by the New Dealers. Private constituents helped public officials pursue their own agendas. Ironically, it was Roosevelt's stab at imposing order that had "plunged the dagger into the heart of democracy."

As the New Deal public administration continued to evolve, it would draw on two contrasting American traditions. The Progressives left reformers the ideal of scientific management, computing the public good with quasi-scientific accuracy. Economists, policy analysts, and managers would, in time, populate the public service with increasingly sophisticated trustee administrators pursuing this rationalist vision. Those who resisted the Progressive faith drew on an alternate tradition of "actual government" championed by the Antifederalists and Jackson's populist bureaucracy. From this perspective, government officials were more properly delegates, mirroring popular sentiments. For a time, political scientists thought they saw, in American government, a series of referees, balancing the private interests that came forward and impartially responding to the forces of the political market. When pluralism finally fell out of favor, it was for celebrating a distorted reflection of the people.

In either tradition, the ideal was public administration as a mechanistic force rather than as independent judgment. As Margaret Weir and Theda Skocpol point out, New Deal Keynesianism relied on automatic formulas rather than discretionary "political" choices.[32] The impulse is deeply rooted in American political history. Across the generations of reform, we have seen the search for automatic politics and the suspicion of public officials who would think for themselves. Even after the New Deal had expanded the role of the state into every aspect of American life, the dread of ministers remained.

Of course, American administration would continue to evolve. The Second World War doubled the civilian employees of the federal government.* Both the 1960s and the 1980s brought new efforts to recast the scope and bias of the public sphere. However, the essential profile of the American state was set in place during the Progressive and the New Deal eras. The unwieldy system remains: checking the mobilization of public power to a single national end; breaking up policy into narrow, poorly coordinated arenas; preserving the inchoate public administration still marked by Madison's intricate checks and balances.

New reformers would operate within this context. In the 1960s, for example, another mass movement invoked democracy in a familiar way. It demanded participation, celebrated grass-roots community, proclaimed the consensus of the people, mobilized previously oppressed Americans, and won new political rules and institutions. For all their democratic aspirations, the activists of the 1960s did not reconstruct the administrative state. Reformers struggled within the fragmented apparatus that they found, winning changes in race relations or housing or health care. Analysis, prescriptions, even the reformers themselves, were caught up in the narrowly delineated functional arenas of American government. Those with a broader vision were swiftly frustrated. The Students for a Democratic Society began with the republican idyll of the Port Huron Statement (1962), championing par-

---

*In 1932 there had been 605,496 civilian employees of the federal government; by 1940—just before mobilization—there were 1,042,420. By 1945, the number rose to 3,816,310; then receded in the late 1940s, fluctuating around 2,100,000.[33]

ticipatory local politics (now tagged "decentralization" in proper bureaucratic argot); within seven years, they had fallen to the impotent window smashing of their "days of rage." In short, the fragmented, specialized, chaotic administration that was first devised by the Progressives and carried forward by the New Dealers would constrict both the process and the outcomes of the democratic wish.

The result is a polity still more powerfully biased toward the status quo. Throughout the twentieth century, public officials have been caught between the imperatives for change and the limits of American government. In part II, I suggest that they negotiated the challenge in the same way as their state-building predecessors. They called on the people.

If the democratic wish now serves more narrowly defined ends, the political pattern remains familiar. Public officials use the rhetoric of democracy to expand the state into uncertain new areas; they use the power of the people to frame new institutions; the new structures mobilize, focus, and—in some ways—co-opt populist movements. When the marches, strikes, and late-night meetings fade away, Americans are left with newly legitimated groups, new rules and institutions, and new forms of state authority.

In part II, I use the patterns of dread and yearning to reinterpret three great twentieth-century reforms: the reconstruction of working-class politics, the struggle of black Americans in northern cities, and the transformation of medical politics. Together they suggest the broad scope and continuing evolution of a political pattern that stretches back to the Revolution. The same politics that constructed the American state continue to reform it.

II

THE PEOPLE
AND REFORM:

*The Political
Reconstruction of Class,
Race, and Profession*

5

The Reconstruction of Working-Class Politics

The way to show that you are a part of this great army of the New Deal is to insist on {the Blue Eagle} symbol of solidarity. . . . This campaign is a frank dependence on the power and willingness of the American people to act together as one person in an hour of great danger. —Hugh Johnson, 1933

For over a century, the bias of American labor policy tilted, often violently, against working-class organization. Military force broke strikes while the legal code undermined unions. The restraints suppressed class-based movements and ultimately reshaped the patterns of representation and the political aspirations within the labor movement itself. Moreover, the union-bashing status quo was extremely hard to alter. Sympathetic state governments (inspired by the Populists) and national legislation (by the Progressives) were not enough. In this chapter, I argue that when change finally came, in the 1930s, it was negotiated by a variation of the democratic wish.

The broad latitude afforded the New Dealers by the Great Depression did not extend to meddling in the industrial sector. Even at the height of the New Deal, Roosevelt was not able to assert a definitive industrial policy. When the Democrats managed their National Industrial Recovery Act, its administrator frankly acknowledged that any

145

disaffected interest could topple the entire program. Roosevelt's response was to call on the people.

With rhetoric drawn from the American republican tradition, the New Dealers invoked the people, community, direct participation, cooperation. Shadowy malefactors who might be tempted to set private interest before public good—and competition before cooperation—were warned of the sanctions that would be imposed, not by the state but by the people, acting in unison.

The vague intimation of community offered working men and women an opportunity to mobilize. Quasi-governmental agencies, with only symbolic authority, gave their mobilization a focus. The old rhetoric and new institutions reframed American labor politics. In this context, the patterns of representation within the labor movement were reconfigured, the place of labor within the American government renegotiated, the bias of the state reconstructed.

At the same time, by offering workers an opportunity to struggle for legitimacy on the periphery of the American state, the New Deal took a potential revolution and transformed it into an interest-group battle. Once again, the search for community yielded conflicts; the nature of those conflicts both legitimated and limited a new class of political participants. Even by the late 1930s, American labor politics had begun to settle back into an equilibrium organized around a new status quo: working-class organization entered American politics; the state wielded new authority in labor relations; capital aquiesced in the new arrangements and, in many ways, turned them to its own advantage.

THE PATTERNS OF WORKING-CLASS POLITICS

Organized labor was weak before the stock market crashed in 1929. Union membership fell by a third in the 1920s, then dropped an additional 14 percent in the first four years of the Depression. By 1933, there were fewer than three million union members.* Three related forces had combined to wreck the American labor movement: employer opposition, government policy and the organization and attitude of labor itself.

The American employing class fought trade unions with what Lewis Lorwin described as exceptional persistence, vigor, costs, and conviction. Other observers are more direct: "The United States has the bloodiest and most violent labor history of any industrial nation."[3] The officers of the major steel corporations demonstrated the intensity of the antagonism at a routine meeting with Frances Perkins, Roosevelt's secretary of labor. Perkins had invited William Green, the timid president of the American Federation of Labor, to sit in on the conference. When the steel executives saw the labor leader, they scrambled to the other end of the conference room "like frightened boys." For forty-five minutes, they refused to risk meeting Green, lest word seep back to their steel industry towns. "It was the most embarrassing social experience of my life," reported Perkins.[4]

Industrialists interpreted unions as a challenge to property rights. As an alternative, many companies offered the paternalistic benefits of corporate welfare. The logic of these programs, which were widely introduced following the First World War, was articulated by George Baer, president of the Philadelphia and Reading Railroad: "The rights and interests of the laboring man will be . . . cared for—not by labor agitators, but by the Christian gentlemen to whom God has given control of the property rights of the country."[5] Corporate welfare fit easily in a long tradition of entrepreneurial paternalism that imputed natural order, hierarchy, and virtue to the organization of the workplace. Recall how the antebellum mill owners imagined that they were inculcating "punctuality, temperance, industriousness, steadiness, and obedience"[6] (see chapter 2, pages 77–8). The strategy, of course, justified corporate control; and by offering private programs, corporations fostered the illusion that the state was irrelevant to American industrial relations.

---

*Union membership dropped from 5,048,000 (1920) to 3,443,000 (1929) to 2,973,000 (1933).[1] The commentary of the late 1920s is full of judgments such as "the ten-year decline . . . has already gone too far to be rejuvenated by anyone."[2]

Capital also adopted a variety of more direct strategies to check worker organization and collective bargaining. The yellow-dog contract, for example, proscribed union membership as a condition of employment; workers who joined were fired for breach of contract. Companies circulated elaborate "blacklists" of labor agitators. Legal stipulations were buttressed by violence. An elaborate network of company spies, police, and armies began to flourish after the Civil War. The National Labor Relations Board estimated that, by 1936, American industry employed 40,000 to 50,000 anti-union spies. Over 200 private agencies offered union-busting services.[7]

One popular image about the balance of power in American labor relations was summed by the Interchurch Commission investigating a failed steel strike: "The United States Steel corporation was too big to be defeated by 300,000 working men."[8] In fact, corporate dominance was powerfully supported by the bias in American public policy.

On the political surface, the state backed private power with public violence. When company troops failed, local police and state militia were dispatched; if they were unwilling or unable to end strikes, federal forces were called. For instance, the Baltimore and Ohio Railroad strike of 1877 spread beyond the strike-breaking capacity of the railroad, the local police (who sympathized with the strikers in some places), and the state militia. The Hayes administration responded with federal troops who left 26 dead in Pittsburgh, 13 in Reading, 19 in Chicago. Such violence would typify public policy toward organized labor till the New Deal (and beyond, on the local level). Between 1902 and 1904 alone, government agents killed 198 people while suppressing strikes.[9]

In the company towns that characterized industries such as steel or coal, state authority and industry power were indistinguishable: the companies themselves held a monopoly on legitimate—or, at least, state-sanctioned—violence. South Carolina, Pennsylvania, and Maryland all formally invested company police with law-enforcement powers. In many other places, company agents were deputized (thereby becoming public officials) at the first sign of labor unrest. As Josephus Daniels, the Democratic politician and newspaper editor, would write to Franklin Roosevelt after a strike in North Carolina, the troops "might as well have been under the direction of the mill owners."[10]

More subtle, and ultimately more significant, was the bias of the legal system. The rules of the polity reinforced corporate dominance. Too narrow a focus on the violent pyrotechnics obscures the point that labor challenged capital in a system markedly pitched against working-class organization.

For example, till 1842, labor organization was, by legal definition, criminal conspiracy. Fifty years later, a bloody steel strike in Homestead, Pennsylvania, collapsed when its leaders were indicted for treason against Pennsylvania. (In this case, the men were eventually acquitted, but not before one of the strongest American unions had been "buried beneath bail bonds.")[11] The courts sustained yellow-dog contracts till 1932, essentially enjoining labor unions where they were widely used. In West Virginia, 316 coal companies obtained a court injunction that virtually barred the United Mine Workers from the state.[12]

Federal officials offered industry a potent new legal device during the Pullman strike of 1894. Workers struck after Pullman cut wages but not the cost of living in the company town (the workers, an investigation later showed, were $70,000 in arrears for rent alone). The strike spread to other companies and soon involved 125,000 workers. Grover Cleveland (overruling Illinois's Governor John Altgeld) dispatched federal troops, who promptly shot thirty people dead. When the strikers persisted, Attorney General Richard Olney devised a more effective strategy. Under his guidance, the railways sought an injunction on the basis of the Sherman Antitrust Act. The courts complied, enjoining "all persons whatsoever . . . from in any way or manner interfering with, hindering, obstructing or stopping" railroad business. Strikers were now in defiance of the courts. Labor leaders across the country were hastily indicted for conspiracy, and the strike collapsed.[13] In the following years, capital vigorously invoked antitrust law to break unions and strikes. Ironically, the antitrust regulation originally sought by labor, small businesses, and farmers was ceded to the corporations it had been designed to constrain.

The successful inversion of Progressive legislation illustrates an important principle. In a fragmented system full of checks and balances, it is difficult to alter the bias of the political status quo. Interests invested in existing arrangements can often find public-sector allies to help them block change.

Reformers managed to forbid the yellow-dog contract in sixteen states, only to have the courts strike the legislation down.[14] When Congress moved to strengthen the Sherman Act with the Clayton Act in 1914, it explicitly exempted unions. Samuel Gompers, the president of the American Federation of Labor, cheered Clayton as "labor's Magna Charta."[15] His verdict was premature. The courts read Clayton differently from its Progressive authors and continued to apply anti-trust statutes to organized labor.

In the case of labor, popular action could not easily shift the state's mobilization of bias. Victories in the states encountered opposition on the federal level; victories in Congress were undercut by the White House and the courts. As we shall see in the following chapter, the Supreme Court would be on the other side when it moved to end racial segregation in the 1950s and 1960s; the judiciary would be frustrated in its turn by the Senate, state governments, and local officials.

Perhaps the most powerful result of industry resistance and state bias was the influence they had on the labor movement itself. The resistance recast the definition of union workers, the shape of their unions, and the strategies they pursued. In the language of representation, the constituency, the representatives, and the authorities they petitioned all evolved in response to the opposition.

The union constituency moved sharply away from class-based politics. To be sure, workers had repeatedly tried to articulate a broad proletarian movement. The Knights of Labor, the International Workers of the World, and the Socialist Labor Alliance were among their well-known efforts. The American Federation of Labor, formed in 1886, was swiftly infused with Samuel Gompers's dim judgment about such working-class movements: "In every previous industrial crisis the trade unions were mowed down and swept out of existance."[16] In response, the AFL eschewed broad industrial unionism for a far narrower organization on the basis of crafts.

The AFL was divided into small organizations of skilled craftsmen— Carpenters and Joiners, Hod Carriers, Boilermakers and Machinists, Flint Glass Workers. Strategically placed tradesmen could wring concessions out of industry on the basis of their expertise. They ignored— indeed, they disdained—the unskilled industrial armies. Organized craftsmen sought advantages that employers would be loath to confer upon large numbers of more easily replaced workers.

The rejection of unskilled industrial masses was both a strategy for organizational survival and a reflection of ethnic prejudice. The crafts had long been dominated by specific ethnic groups: Irish in transportation, Italians in construction, Jews in the needle industries. Ethnic prejudice reinforced élitism. As Gompers had articulated the biased consequences of his organizing logic, "There are not many skilled mechanics among the colored workers of the South."[17] Unskilled groups posed a threat that exacerbated ethnic prejudices and antagonisms. Blacks formed only 2 percent of the AFL membership in 1928 and were accepted by only a handful of locals. "The rubbish," opined the Teamster Dan Tobin about the Italians, Slavs, blacks, and poor whites. "My wife can always tell from the smell of my clothes what breed of foreigners I have been hanging out with," commented Bill Collins when a group of Italians tried to join the New York Federation of Labor.[18]

Narrow worker constituencies were represented by narrowly defined union organizations. The AFL premised its politics on the autonomy of the member unions, each acting "as they think is just and proper in their own trades without the . . . let of any other body."[19] Even as the tumult of New Deal labor policy raged about them, one AFL convention spent its time adjudicating a dispute between carpenters and roofers who each claimed jurisdiction over the installation of metal trim.

A flood of new, unskilled workers could threaten both the craft union philosophy and the conservative union leaders. The oligarchs of the AFL preferred their small but stable baronies to the hazards of mass organization. They maintained their own power and pursued advantages for their craftsmen with a mode of organization that was manifestly irrelevant to the mass production industries that had swept the American economy by the turn of the century. The great industries at the heart of corporate capitalism were almost entirely unorganized.

Small wonder that the representatives of the working man appeared weak; as Grant McConnell put it, "they had no desire to be strong." The editors of *Fortune* happily announced that, by the 1920s, the AFL suffered "from pernicious anaemia, sociological myopia and hardening of the arteries."[20]

Finally, the craft unions turned away, not just from working-class politics, but from government altogether. They pursued a "voluntarist" strategy which rejected government intervention in industrial relations. The AFL would shun government and rely on its own economic power. Labor would win concessions directly from industry; the unions themselves offered worker benefits such as disability insurance. They wooed industry with promises of responsibility and efficiency. The AFL spurned collective bargaining legislation ("labor has never asked that it be gained by law").[21]

Even after the onset of the Great Depression, AFL leaders opposed a minimum wage or government unemployment insurance (which would "pull at our vitals and destroy our trade union structure" as Green put it). While the New Dealers were offering each organized group its spokesman within the government, the unions studiously ignored their cabinet agency. The Department of Labor was derisively nicknamed the "Department of Labor Statistics"—a neutral, largely irrelevant, cabinet office surrounded by bureaus that openly advocated client interests. Though Franklin Roosevelt was not particularly sympathetic to unions, he had to urge Perkins to be more of a secretary *for* labor—a stance she thought "unorthodox."[22]

On the face of it, here is a powerful testament to the American dread of government. The AFL appeared to be standing in a long American tradition which preferred the private struggle for rights over petitions to the state—that repository of coercion and tyranny. (Recall Madison's judgment that the American Constitution was "a charter of power granted by liberty" rather than the European "charter of liberty granted by power" [see introduction, pages 2–3].)

To be sure, American ideology played a role, but one that was a good deal less direct. American workers had not failed to petition their state. What they discovered was that its rules and institutions— perhaps indeed framed around a dread of public action—were not easily mobilized in new directions. Even labor's victories, such as the Clayton Antitrust Act, had been turned against workers. The AFL's strategy was forged by calculations drawn from past defeats.

The Roosevelt administration may have proclaimed a new deal, but the working men and women faced a daunting and complicated task. Industry continued to oppose them—and massive unemployment made jobs scarce and troublemaking workers expendable. Liberals may have won the White House, but the conservatives still sat in the courts. And, most troublesome, the terms of worker representation—the organization and strategies of the labor unions themselves—left little room for bold reforms in working-class politics.

NEW DEAL LABOR POLICY AS DEMOCRATIC WISH: FROM NRA TO THE WAGNER ACT

By 1933, one out of four workers—13,000,000 people—was unemployed.[23] Half of manufacturing units in America were shut. The value of industrial and railroad stock had declined 80 percent.[24] Full-time employment in the largest American industrial corporation, U.S. Steel, charted the economic fall: 225,000 in 1929, 54,000 in 1931, 19,000 in 1932, and none on 1 April 1933. Countless anecdotes chronicle the misery: children without pants or shoes in Philadelphia, 50 men fighting over a pail of garbage in Chicago, wages of four cents an hour in Detroit.[25]*

When the Roosevelt administration took power, at least four different solutions were on the political agenda. The rejected alternatives are as illuminating as the recovery program that finally emerged.

Perhaps the most popular answer was public works. Private construction spending had plummeted from $13 billion to $2.8 billion. Public works, it was argued, would boost the construction industry, put people to work, and stimulate demand. Even before Roosevelt was elected, the Hearst newspapers were campaigning for a $5.5-billion public program.[27]

Second, a lingering Progressive sentiment sought to inject the state more forcefully into the industrial sector. Resurrecting the new nation-

---

*It is commonly noted that even those who held jobs suffered a precipitate decline in wages—27 percent between 1929 and 1932. In real terms, however, the average decline in wages was only 4.2 percent—an average distributed extremely inequitably across the work force. Unorganized workers saw their wages fall 30 percent more than the organized.[26]

alism of Herbert Croly and the Bull Moose, advocates envisioned a neo-corporatist, public-private partnership. Private industry, represented by its trade associations, would operate under a national planning council firmly guided by the government. The state would keep private interests from acting selfishly; it would guide "the coordination between all parts of the economy."[28] Proponents of national planning invoked the memory of the First World War, when the government had virtually run the nation's railroads. As the Roosevelt recovery program finally began to lurch forward, its director would give Frances Perkins a copy of *The Corporate State*, a glowing account of Italian corporatism under Mussolini.[29]

Third, business leaders proposed suspending economic competition and antitrust policy. Competition—"that murderous doctrine of savage and wolfish individualism, looking to dog eat dog and devil take the hindmost"—was thought to be the root of the economic trouble.[30] Industry officials reasoned that they had been trapped on a competitive treadmill: competition led them to glut their markets by producing too much; they cut prices to maintain markets; they cut wages in order to lower prices; lower wages, in turn, reduced aggregate demand which exacerbated the market glut. Business would substitute cooperation and coordination for "destructive competition." Under the aegis of their trade associations, industry would set prices and production levels—essentially seeking stability by divvying up their markets. It was a corporate ideal that stretched back from nineteenth-century pools and trusts* to the medieval guilds. In the most depressed economic sectors—coal, oil, textiles—the ideal of industrial self-regulation had been championed throughout the 1920s. Model codes governing the industries had been designed, congressional hearings held. Now the National Association of Manufacturers, the Chamber of Commerce, and many trade associations pressed for industrial cooperation across the American economy.[32]

Finally, organized labor had its own solution to the economic crisis. Uncharacteristically, its was the first bill on the legislative docket. The

---

*John D. Rockefeller articulated the corporate quest for escape from competition: "All the fortune I have made has not served to compensate for the anxiety. . . . Work by day, worry by night, week in and week out, month after month."[31]

union doctrine of voluntary action had cracked somewhat under economic pressure. The railway workers had put it aside in 1922 when they sought congressional protection for union organization and collective bargaining.[33] A decade later, in November 1932, the AFL voted to sponsor federal legislation regulating length of the workweek. Senator Hugo Black of Alabama introduced its bill the following month. The Black bill rested on the popular notion that technology had permanently displaced a large mass of workers. If the remainder worked fewer hours at the same wages, there would be employment for everybody and a return to prosperity. In 1929, over 80 percent of the labor force had worked more than forty-nine hours a week.[34] With beguiling specificity, Black purported to show how a maximum workweek of thirty hours would restore full employment.

In short, the new administration faced a broad gamut of approaches to restoring the American economy—corporatist-style national planning, regulating the workweek, public works expenditure, and industrial self-government. The alternatives ranged from powerful state intervention in the economy to the wholesale vesting of state authority with organized industry. Within four months, the New Dealers had sifted through the options and emerged with a program that typified the American pattern of political change.

The Black bill was before the Senate when the Roosevelt administration arrived in Washington. The plan made the New Dealers distinctly uncomfortable. They were uneasy about the bald state intrusion into the economy. The thirty-hour limit seemed arbitrary. "What about the rhythm of the cow?" Roosevelt kept asking. On the other hand, administration officials were constrained by the popularity of Black's panacea.[35]

The administration negotiated its dilemma by modifying the bill. It added a sliding scale of hours, minimum wages, and support for collective bargaining by labor organizations. The changes helped cement a coalition hostile to Black's legislation. Though the Senate rejected the changes and passed the original measure, the House substituted the administration version.

Business leaders launched a concerted effort to defeat the legislation. AFL leaders turned against the revised proposal. Minimum wages might become industry-wide standards and vitiate the craftsmen's advantage;

moreover, the government was asserting too prominent a role in labor policy.[36] The administration, joining with business and labor, withdrew its tepid support for the Black bill; together they defeated the plan.

The National Industrial Recovery Act

With the wage bill safely dispatched, the Roosevelt administration proposed its own legislation. Its program, the National Industrial Recovery Act, appeared to be a vague mélange, drawing from all the sources that had come forward with a proposal—a combination, however, more apparent than real.

The plan included a public works proposal—but Roosevelt lodged the program in a peculiar place. Most accounts take his justifications at face value: he fretted about creating too many independent agencies; he did not wish to burden the administrator of the National Recovery Administration with too many tasks. Then, on what appeared to be the spur of the moment (and to the frank delight of the cabinet members who were jealous of the NRA), the President stuck the works program in the "organizationally appropriate" place—Harold Ickes's Department of the Interior. Roosevelt's stated reasons were odd. The President was hardly fastidious about organizational neatness. Nor, at the time, was he enthusiastic about public works. It is plausible that he fixed responsibility for public works precisely where they would grow most slowly—in the ultracautious, almost compulsive hands of Harold Ickes. If so, the delighted Ickes sounded just the right note when the President offered him control: "I think I have the negative and austere qualities that the handling of so much public money requires." The self-assessment proved accurate: it was years before Ickes began to spend the public works funds entrusted to him.* Roosevelt may have constrained public works precisely as he buried the Black bill—by the manner in which he embraced the popular proposal.[38]

The heart of the National Recovery Administration offered industry much of what it had lobbied for. Competition and antitrust policy were

---

*Ickes, in one of the countless illustrations of his fastidious character, complained a short time later of the "wanton waste of valuable film" as reporters snapped his picture "all day long."[37]

set aside for industrial cooperation. The program did not chart a definitive economic plan. Instead, each trade association was empowered to design codes of "fair competition." The codes were to have specified standard wages and hours for each industry; in practice, most included agreements over prices and production levels as well (568 out of 700 codes eventually set minimum prices). The vague legislation left public policy largely in private hands.

The NRA was not, however, simply a case of business dominating the state. The code negotiations that defined the program for each sector would include labor leaders as well as businessmen. The legislation included an enigmatic guarantee of the workers' right to organize and bargain collectively. The Senate strengthened the passage by forbidding employer "interference, restraint or coercion" over worker representation.

Industry had paid scant attention to the labor provisions contained in section 7(a). The passage was "constantly on the verge of being defined out of existence."[39] When the Senate began to strengthen 7(a), employer groups took notice. The National Association of Manufacturers decried the effort to "deprive Americans of their precious liberty to associate" and "disrupt existing satisfactory relations" between employer and employee. Senator Bennett Champ Clark of Missouri scribbled an addition to 7(a): "Nothing in this title shall be construed to compel change in existing satisfactory relations between employer and employee"—an affirmation of the status quo which negated the rest of the passage. The change won acceptance among some administration officials, then approval in the Senate, before being deleted.[40] Eventually most industry lobbyists grudgingly accepted the ambiguous labor provisions in exchange for industrial self-government. In its final form, section 7(a) asserted that employees "shall have the right to organize and bargain collectively through representatives of their own choosing, and shall be free from the interference, restraint or coercion of employers of labor."[41]

An "Emancipation Proclamation," thought the Mine Worker president, John L. Lewis. "Labor's Magna Charta," agreed William Green.[42] But like Gompers, who had hailed the Clayton Act with the same historical metaphor, Green's judgment was premature. To be sure, the NRA promised more than Clayton. But the entire act was shrouded in ambiguity, section 7(a) particularly so. How exactly were workers going to chose their representatives? Who would prevent employers from discriminating against those who did? What counted as "interference" or "restraint"? Program administrators signaled the contest ahead when they hastened to assure employers that the NRA was "not going to be used as a machine for unionizing any industry." The National Association of Manufacturers warned that it would "fight energetically against any encroachments by closed shop labor unions."[43] For workers, the NRA was more a vague possibility than a concrete entitlement. The state offered no sanctions to prod employers; employers frankly announced their intention to retain control over employees; and the labor unions showed no appetite for either signing up the workers or challenging their bosses.

On 16 June 1933, control of the NRA passed to General Hugh Johnson, a voluble, rambunctious, hard-drinking, opera-quoting, unpredictable volcano of a man. "It will be fire at first and dead cats afterwards," he announced at his first news conference.[44] Johnson and his NRA immediately faced a dilemma. The new program operated with limited power and dubious constitutionality. He set out to avoid challenges to the state's tenuous authority by unambiguously ceding it to the industrialists operating through their trade associations. "NRA is exactly what industry . . . makes it," he told an appreciative business group. "The NRA thinks that business should run itself under government supervision."[45] That supervision did not include administrative sanctions. The Progressive image of strong national planning had waned as the program took shape. The policy that emerged did not include significant public powers. On the contrary, it underscored state weakness in a dramatic way. Hugh Johnson was left to negotiate a complex recovery program while acknowledging that any disaffected interest could wreck it with a lawsuit.

Although the NRA may have emerged from complex negotiations involving a large number of political forces, the political outcomes are distinctly recognizable. Proposals for a recovery program had ranged from powerful public intervention in the economy to a privately dominated program. Even in the trough of the Great Depression, there was an inverse correlation between the level of government intervention in a proposal and how far the proposal got. State-centered economic planning was ignored. Legislation that stipulated specific economic regulations (the Black bill) was defeated. Spending on public works was buried in implementation for years. The NRA ceded control of the recovery program to industrial interests. The New Dealers rejected a concrete policy for a vague process and then conceded control over it to the private sector.

Even the weak program of the NRA stretched the limits of legitimate government action. It operated with dubious constitutional legitimacy. Administrators frankly conceded the fragility of their mandate. The hesitant American state selected the weakest alternative, in part, because even during an economic crisis it could not muster the legitimate power to undertake decisive collective action.

What is most striking about the political outcome is its fit with past reform. Every state-building revolt had sought to overcome the clash of narrow interests and secure the public interest of a unified and consensual people. The New Deals's economic remedy dimly reflected the old communal ideal: cooperation would replace competition. A united people shared a common interest, even in the sphere of economic competition. The improbable aspiration that every single interest in the nation might acquiesce (thus avoiding a constitutional challenge) has a lineage back to the first republicans and their belief that only "self-murderers" could have an interest contrary to the public good. Ultimately, the need for consensus flowed from the Americans' dread of government, the faith that consensus might actually be achieved from their democratic yearning.

Moreover, the same vague yearning for unanimity which turned the problem to the industrial community, defined the community broadly enough to include labor: the bias of the communal ideology favored section 7(a). The communal conception would soon be extended into its full traditional form and incorporate the entire "American people." The intimations of past reform implicit in the politics of the National Industrial Recovery Act were more explicitly articulated in the odd events that followed.

The Call to the People

Like past efforts to achieve consensus, the National Recovery Administration was quickly mired in conflict and stalemate. The textile industry had a code ready the day the law was passed. Six weeks later, no other industry had settled on a code. In many cases, the role of organized labor proved a divisive issue on which employers refused to compromise. With little formal power and only an ambiguous mandate, how could the NRA push industry into agreements? The solution was another invocation of the democratic wish.

Administration officials launched an extraordinary campaign. They sponsored speeches, parades, brass bands, mass meetings, and motorcades. The symbol of the movement was an Indian ideograph, the Blue Eagle, introduced around the nation as the emblem by which "those who cooperate with the program [will] know each other." (Just as "in the gloom of night attack," continued Roosevelt, "soldiers wear a bright badge on their shoulders to be sure that comrades do not fire upon comrades.")[46] Companies that abided by industry codes could fix the emblem on their products. Hugh Johnson stormed around the nation, whipping up support: "When every American housewife understands that the blue eagle on everything she permits into her home is a symbol of the restoration of security, may God have mercy on the man . . . who attempts to trifle with this bird."[47]

The public responded. Around the nation, the Blue Eagle became a focus of patriotism, an emblem of democracy. In the greatest single demonstration, a quarter of a million men and women paraded up New York's Fifth Avenue while another million and a half showered them with tickertape. Over two million employers, swept up in the excitement, "signed up" for the Blue Eagle; consumers—including Herbert Hoover—signed pledges of their own. Familiar rhetoric floated above the fervor: Johnson celebrated the "power of the American people," acting "together as one person." Donald Richberg, his deputy, excoriated "the slacker who palsies the national purpose with legalistic arguments."[48]

Almost immediately, industry negotiators began to settle on their codes. Some were concerned about the widespread price fixing, almost all were uneasy about section 7(a). However, amid the excitement of the Blue Eagle, 144 codes were signed in the last weeks of July; 546, in August.[49] Checked by the limits of their political institutions, politicians had turned to the most powerful symbols of American democracy. Despite the manifest illogic of their call, Johnson and Roosevelt mobilized the public with a bizarre variant of the democratic impulse. The people—"acting as one person"—would overcome the lure of selfish interests and the limits of state authority. The "American housewife"—not the government—would discipline violators of the economic recovery plan. States often stimulate patriotism; they rarely substitute it for public authority.

In sum, the American plan for industrial recovery was set in an avowedly American mold. An ambiguous, vaguely legislated program was launched with great aspirations and few formal powers. It operated outside the normal channels of government, stretching legitimate state authority by resorting to a cry for broad participation by the people. In this apparently uncontroversial context, new—unrecognized or previously illegitimate—groups came forward. For a time, there was an effort to focus the citizen impulse on consumer representation. The NRA had advisory committees for consumers as well as for business and labor. A "consumer movement" rose up, demanding a cabinet department of "consumer administration" and urging the organization and empowerment of a "consumer minded public."[50] The call for consumers found no organized constituency—"spears without shafts" was the braintruster Rexford Tugwell's often-repeated jibe—and soon faded from the political scene.[51]

Labor was another matter. Within a para-governmental program launched with the exaltation of the people, labor received its ambiguous invitation to participate in the American political economy. Before the NRA, industry leaders had bridled at the least hint of legitimacy accorded the union movement. But in the context of national crisis, with the invocation of the people and in the relative safety of a program that granted employers new powers without imposing state sanctions, they accepted section 7(a).

Interpretations of New Deal labor policy have generally acknowledged the peculiarity of the Blue Eagle while failing to understand its importance. Many scholars have tried to interpret the NRA's bias by tracing its origins; ultimately, these are inconclusive. A wide variety of political influences shaped the NRA: government liberals like Senator Robert Wagner of New York added section 7(a); business leaders acquiesced to 7(a) in order to secure industry codes; labor's mobilization would swell and change to fit the opportunity. However, all the political actions and reactions operated in a context shaped by the potent ideologies of dread and yearning. Liberals were not able to secure more forceful legislation; conservatives were hard pressed to reject a call for community, consensus, and the people. As with each prior invocation of the democratic impulse, this one legitimated previously repressed conflicts without determining their outcomes. The NRA established a political arena in which New Deal labor policy could be fought out; it simultaneously legitimated and—as we shall see—limited labor's demands. Moreover, it left scholars enough conflicting data to sustain the usual dispute: Was this revolt from below or manipulation from above? Any answer to the question of who the NRA was designed to benefit is inconclusive for precisely the same reason that the program was possible: it was ambiguous. The next stages of the political cycle—the policy conflicts and their outcomes—would be shaped by the political response. Where there was no sustained mobilization—as with "consumers"—the effort was largely symbolic; where previously suppressed interests mobilized, they were given a new political ground on which to challenge dominant élites and infuse an ambiguous program with meaning.

The Clashes over Representation

John L. Lewis, president of the United Mine Workers, grasped the implications first. "The bill will only help those who help themselves," admonished the *United Mine Workers Journal*. The UMW sent one hundred organizers into the mine fields. "The President wants you to organize," exaggerated their soundtrucks; their leaflets announced, "All workers are fully protected if they join a union." The response was staggering.[52]

Entire coal-mining regions seemed to rush the union. The NRA had been signed on 16 June 1933; within a week, one organizer reported that "all the substantial mines in Kentucky are organized." By the end of June, the UMW claimed 128,000 new members in Pennsylvania alone; in July, it claimed 90 percent of all the coal miners in Colorado and New Mexico. In two months, the United Mine Workers announced a fivefold increase in membership.[53] While Lewis sat in Washington, wrangling over the bituminous coal code, his constituency swelled.

A few other unions followed Lewis and the miners in seizing the opportunity of 7(a). The International Ladies Garment Workers Union, which had lost more than 60 percent of its membership in the preceding decade, jumped from 50,000 to 200,000 by 1934. The Amalgamated Clothing Workers, down to 7,000 workers in 1932, added 125,000 new members.[54] These organizations and their leaders—John L. Lewis, David Dubinsky, Sidney Hillman—built up their own organizations, then set out to reconstitute the labor movement.

Even where the established unions made no efforts to mobilize, workers flocked to join. The AFL executive council reported that "people held mass meetings and sent word that they wanted to be organized."[55]* The Oil Field Workers Union, whose 35,000 members had been beaten down to just 300 in the preceding decade, established 125 new locals within a year. There were similar responses throughout the industrial sector: 100,000 automobile workers mobbed the unions; so did 70,000 Akron rubber workers, 50,000 steel workers, and 300,000 textile workers.[57] Perkins judged the mobilization an "education," teaching Americans that workers wanted to join unions if they could do so without getting fired.[58] Still, the obstacles to unionization remained formidable.

For one thing, the aging oligarchs of the AFL had no intention of risking their own power by disrupting the status quo. The mobs demanding membership were destabilizing and spoiling for confrontation. "Now, John, let's take it easy," implored the AFL's President

---

*One often-told story captures some of the ebullience of the early rush to unions. Employees of a Philco plant in Philadelphia were refused a contract and sent representatives off to Washington in two old automobiles. There, they prowled the hallways of the Commerce building, using an old newspaper photo to identify General Johnson. When they found him, they argued him into signing a declaration that announced, "The law is on our side." Philco, so the story goes, promptly agreed to a contract. While the worker exuberance was widespread, the easy acquiescence of the employer was distinctly uncharacteristic of labor relations in 1933.[56]

Green while Lewis was whipping the mine workers into unions. Green—"the all-American mushmouth" was one of his more polite nicknames—resisted every break with the craft traditions of the AFL.[59]

The AFL bewildered the Akron rubber workers by parceling them into the nineteen separate craft unions that held jurisdiction over rubber. When workers came to meetings of the wrong local, they were turned away. When one group called for a national rubber union, local AFL officials branded them secessionists and commanded them to disband. Though the order was overruled, the rubber workers began to melt away. The 70,000 who had flocked to the union quickly fell to a demoralized 22,000 under the tutelage of AFL organizers.[60]

Other locals in other industries repeated the cycle—spontaneous outbursts repressed by a frightened leadership. In steel, Michael "Grandmother" Tighe managed to reduce the 50,000 workers who had rushed his organization to a manageable 5,000. By 1935, the seventy-six-year-old leader had a stable membership of 8,600 members in his Iron Steel and Tin Workers Union.[61] In automobiles, the unions successfully repelled 90 percent of the new members by blunting the demands they tried to make of industry.[62]

The union leaders clung tenaciously to the old forms, denouncing even brief departures from union tradition. Local leaders complained when the AFL chartered temporary "federal" unions prior to dividing the surging workers by crafts. "This will completely demoralize, if not actually destroy, the various international unions," thought the metal workers in 1933. In addition to internal stability, the rigid hierarchy insisted on the traditional qualifications and mores. They turned away unskilled workers: "We don't want . . . the riff-raff." They insisted on braking worker militancy: "I never voted for a strike in my life"; "we do not want the men today if they are going to go on strike tomorrow."[63] (The often-quoted grumpiness came from Daniel Tobin, president of the Teamsters, and Bill Collins, who organized the automobile industry for the AFL.)

In sum, section 7(a) fostered a crisis of representation within the labor movement. Workers thronged to the unions. Organizations like the United Mine Workers and the needle unions embraced them. For the most part, however, instability and confrontation threatened organized labor. Within the movement, the revolt from below was resisted from above.

While organized labor was thrashing out a response to its constituency, industry mobilized to contain the threat of 7(a). Employers who accepted the wage-and-hour provisions in the industry codes "would be hanged if they would meet with a committee of workers." They were infuriated when "men who had been working for them for ten years came in and demanded collective bargaining." Henry Ford flatly rejected any code that mentioned collective bargaining; steel executives expressed their preference for jail.[64] The National Association of Manufacturers took the lead. Like Lewis, it pounced on the ambiguity of 7(a). Around the nation, factory bulletin boards sprouted the NAM's message: "The NRA does not attempt to describe the kind of organization, if any, with which employees should affiliate." The industrialists proposed company unions, a device refined by U.S. Steel. For years, employers had formed their own unions as an alternative to outside agitation; now company plans were organized to meet the requirements of 7(a). The NAM distributed model constitutions—actual kits for launching a captive union. In most cases, "management conceived the idea, developed the plan and initiated the organization." Four hundred company unions were organized in the first five months of the recovery program.[65]

Workers charged that these "employee representation plans" were "fake representation." They were elaborately staged negotiations between employees and their bosses under rules imposed by management.[66] Some employers offered inducements for joining union plans. Generally they used benefits like life insurance, though the mine operators infelicitously handed out popsicles, prompting the UMW mine workers to scorn the "popsicle men" who attended company rallies. Industry contended that its company unions satisfied the requirements of 7(a); workers countered that they were "economic blackmail" and a violation of the law. The W. J. Burns Detective Agency noted in an interoffice memo, "There is a great field for furnishing guards to those organizations which are having labor troubles."[67]

A wave of strikes swept across the nation: 137 broke out in June, 240 in July, 246 more in August. One distinctive feature of the unrest was the issue at stake. In 1932, fewer than one out of five strikes had been about the right to organize into unions; by 1934, the figure was almost half; in 1937, 51 percent.[68] The American workers were not emphasizing substantive benefits such as wages, hours, or improved working conditions; instead, they struck over representation, over voice. The NRA not only stirred up the American workers; it shaped the nature of their demands.

In the summer of 1934, one year after the National Recovery Administration had begun, national attention turned to a series of spectacular confrontations. In San Francisco, the longshoremen struck, demanding union recognition and joint control of the hiring halls (an effective end to the blacklist). The owners, eager to crush the union, refused. When the Industrial Association tried to open the port by force, they set off a day of bloody fighting. Two workers died; many were injured. As the National Guard restored order, the Teamsters joined the strike. Four days later, so did everybody else in the city. The first general strike in fifteen years rattled the nation. Frances Perkins convinced a panicky cabinet not to recall the President from a cruise, lest the crisis be exaggerated. General Johnson blundered into San Francisco and, articulating the bourgeois fear, proclaimed "it is civil war." The *San Francisco Chronicle* echoed his judgment, announcing "war in San Francisco." Having stopped the city and stunned the nation, the strikers were unsure what to do next. Four days later, their strike collapsed. In the end, both the longshoremen and the owners accepted arbitration; the union won most of its demands, including recognition by employers.[69]

In Minneapolis, the Teamsters organized; the employers moved to smash them. A broad and well-coordinated strike repeatedly erupted into violence. The "Battle of Deputies Run," a wild melee involving some ten thousand people, left two industry deputies dead. Later, police fired into a crowd of workers, killing two and injuring sixty-seven. Eric Sevareid (then a reporter for the *Minneapolis Star*, later a television news commentator) was told, "This is revolution." The governor, Floyd Olson, declared martial law to restore order but refused to break the strike. After four months of violence, the business coalition capitulated. The Teamsters Union had won the right to bargain for the truckers.[70]

Despite spectacular worker victories in Minneapolis, San Francisco, and Toledo, most strikes failed. For instance, textile workers suffered a series of stinging defeats. Their strike spread across the southern and New England states and involved 375,000 workers. The National Guard was repeatedly summoned; it left one dead in Alabama, six in South Carolina, fifteen in Georgia. In Rhode Island, workers fought the troops in the streets. "A few hundred funerals will have a quieting influence," sniggered the trade journal, *Fibre and Fabric*. Within a month, both the strike and the textile union had been broken. In all, fifteen strikers had been killed in 1933, forty in 1934.[71]

In the end, Lewis had been exactly right. The hazy section 7(a) offered no more than vague possibilities to be worked out in political practice. Workers, unions, and owners were pitched into an extended, often violent battle over the representation of workers. None of the representational categories were delineated in advance. How were workers' constituencies to be defined—by company (as the companies insisted), by craft (according to the AFL unions), or by industrial sector (as the beleaguered workers in Akron had proposed)? Once they were defined, how would constituencies choose their representatives? How many different groups were the companies required to negotiate with? All the complex issues of worker representation had been raised by a program that disavowed the authority of the state.

These questions of representation were thrashed out in practice. Workers mobilized, demanding independent unions. Organized labor occasionally seized the opportunity but more often shrank from the threat. Even industrialists who were willing to accept worker organizations were often baffled by the bedlam. Local groups came forward to speak for labor, sometimes quarreling among themselves. Established unions denounced them, denying their authority to speak for the workers. Unorganized employees remained silent. Like new political participants in the past, labor was disorganized, disruptive, and confused.

Most companies sought to impose their own representational mechanisms on employees. Companies formed unions and declared that they had met the requirements of 7(a). The company unions stood alongside the different workers' organizations, further scrambling the disputes about representation.

The weak and ambiguous NRA had stimulated both a labor uprising and a corporate backlash. At the same time, it powerfully bounded their fight. The bloodshed in San Francisco or Minneapolis demonstrates the narrow scope of the conflict by hinting at broader possibilities. Hugh Johnson and Eric Sevareid notwithstanding, the struggle of American labor rarely approximated class conflict. Despite the misery of the Great Depression, the fight never spread into a broader contest between labor and capital or rich and poor; nor did the workers focus their fight on such substantive grievances as wages, working conditions, the distribution of wealth, or the control of the means of production. Except for the briefest historical moments—like the four days in San Francisco—the struggle of American labor fixed largely on the forms of representation—both in the workplace and in the recovery program. The Americans transformed their potential class struggle precisely the same way they had shaped their state-building conflicts: they turned it into a battle over representation.

The Wagner Act

The administration was jolted by the labor turmoil. Worker days lost in strikes had not exceeded 603,000 for any month in the first half of 1933. With the passage of the NRA, there were 1,375,000 in July and 2,378,000 in August.[72] The conflict gradually forced the Roosevelt administration to devise a more definitive stance toward labor. As workers, unions, and industry fought for control of the NRA, the New Dealers' policy began to evolve.

General Johnson's first reaction was "vacillation punctuated by melodrama."[73] He dashed about the country trying to avert strikes that might threaten economic recovery, siding alternately with management and workers. In August, with the Mine Workers teetering on the edge of a strike (in part because the owners were reluctant to sign a code), the government took its first tentative step toward rationalizing a new labor policy. An ad-hoc labor mediation board was established within the NRA.

The National Labor Board hastily formulated a strategy. Strikes would be terminated, strikers reinstated, and secret elections held under NLB auspices. Workers would choose their own representatives for collective bargaining. The policy was devised with all the trappings of American democracy triumphant. As Perkins recalled the meeting, a German hosiery mill operater who "looked like a Nazi" claimed his workers opposed the unions that were "horning in" on the plant. Gerald Swope, a General Electric executive on the board, suggested, "We'll have a free election by secret ballot and every employee of yours can vote. . . . Then we'll know . . . whether he wants to be represented by the union." "Vy," returned the mill operator, in his thick foreign accent, "vy should they vote?" "Because," he was told, "this is America and that's the way we do things here." Over the objections of the operator, elections were held, first in that hosiery mill, then across the nation. For a time, the board successfully evoked the symbolic powers of the free elections and secret ballots, the "American way" to settle differences. It successfully intervened in a series of strikes—silk mills in New Jersey, tool and die shops in Michigan, soft-coal fields in Illinois.[74]

However, the NLB faced a perplexing issue. Workers and employers were embroiled in a basic question of representation—majority rule versus proportional representation. Industry spokesmen pressed for the latter. Each worker should be represented by the union he or she voted for; brandishing their own arguments about liberty, employers insisted that an organized majority "should not be permitted to deny the rest of our employees from having the representatives of their own choosing." Workers retorted that it was too easy for employers to favor the company unions and destroy the independent ones where both existed. The NLB eventually embraced labor's majoritarian principle. The representatives who won election negotiated for all the workers.[75]

The battle over the majority principle was complicated by the board's weakness. Like the rest of the NRA, it did not have the authority to enforce its decisions. The only sanction at the NLB's disposal was the stripping of the Blue Eagle, an emblem whose significance swiftly receded as the excitement of the summer demonstrations waned. General Johnson was extremely reluctant to permit even this symbolic disapproval lest his bird be lost in labor disputes.

By November 1933, employers began to defy the NLB. Weirton Steel was struck, called in the NLB, signed a mediation agreement, and got the workers back to their jobs. As the election approached, the company president, Ernest Weir, announced that the workers would vote only for officers in a company union. Outside "racketeers" would not be permitted on the ballot. Weir claimed the company would lose its customers if it recognized an outside union. Hugh Johnson called Weir's bluff: "In my opinion you are about to commit a serious violation of federal laws." Weir ignored him. The case was remanded to the U.S. attorney general who pursued it unsuccessfully. Other companies followed Weir's lead.[76]

Program administrators, led by Hugh Johnson, were struggling to maintain the NRA and its tenuous mandate. Anxious for the credibility of their program, they broke with their labor board and called for proportional representation in the worker elections. The NLB, widely identified with its majoritarian position, refused to yield. The issue came to a head when auto workers threatened a strike. The manufacturers, frank in their opinion that 7(a) had been a mistake, rejected outside labor organizations. Nervous AFL leaders managed to put off a strike pending Roosevelt's personal intervention. "You have a wonderful man down there in Washington," Bill Collins told the reluctant workers. The auto companies, minus Ford, which refused to be involved, went to the White House conference in a position of strength. The industry was leading a mild economic recovery: "Don't cut the patient's throat," warned the *Detroit News*. In separate meetings—management would not meet directly with labor leaders—the industry made concessions on every issue but proportional representation, which it insisted on and won. "The governments only duty is to secure the absolute, uninfluenced freedom of choice," declared the settlement.[77]

The labor board's majority principle was cast aside in the auto industry. Company unions would bargain for the workers who selected them. To institutionalize the agreement, an Automobile Labor Board would supersede the NLB. "All's well that ends well," concluded Alfred Sloan, president of General Motors. For a time, the AFL's president, William Green, defended the settlement; as worker criticism mounted, he changed his mind. The *New York Times* was more direct: "Labor's drive for a greater equality of bargaining power . . . has been nullified." Both the principle of majority representation and the National Labor Board, which had promoted it, swiftly declined.[78]

Within the government, Senator Robert Wagner of New York was labor's strongest advocate. Wagner had shepherded 7(a) through its legislative vicissitudes; he had chaired the National Labor Board and held it to the majoritarian position. In the spring of 1934, Wagner set out to replace the gutted NLB with stronger legislation. He proposed a new commission with broad powers to authorize elections, prohibit acts of coercion, and force business to negotiate with representatives elected by a majority of their workers. The Chamber of Commerce, the NAM, the auto industry executives, and scores of others denounced the new bill for "its injustice, its invalidity, and its impolity."[79] The legislation was weakened in the Senate. Even the milder version was unlikely to pass. However, while the businessmen expressed horror and indignation in Washington, workers were striking across the country. Roosevelt cut a middle course; he requested congressional authority to establish labor boards which would hold worker elections, but without the powers Wagner had proposed. In June 1934, the administration formed the National Labor Relations Board, a compromise that briefly stayed more definitive action.

The new board was slightly more powerful than its predecessor. For instance, it could subpoena company payrolls in order to oversee elections. Nevertheless, the NLRB was quickly entangled in the same dispute over worker representation (it, too, opted for majority rule) and undone by the same inability to force compliance on recalcitrant employers. It was unable to mobilize even the weak sanctions at the government's disposal. NRA administrators remained reluctant to withdraw Blue Eagles; the Justice Department refused to pursue violations in the courts. The NLRB simply reiterated its predecessor's life cycle—controversy over representation, outright industry defiance, and political defeat. The NLRB announced a return to the majority principle in November; the Houde Engineering Corporation, egged on by the NAM, immediately defied it. When the already shaky NLRB sought to reinstate a union member who had been fired by a newspaper, Roosevelt referred the case to the industry-dominated code authority. Just as the NLB had been stripped of jurisdiction over autos, the NLRB was forced out of cases where other labor relations mechanisms existed. Since the NRA sanctioned boards across the American economy, the NLRB was consigned to irrelevance.

The NLRB had been formed in June 1934. The great wave of violent strikes—San Francisco, Minneapolis, Toledo, textiles—crested that summer. By the fall, the labor board was impotent. In November, the New Dealers won their enormous midterm congressional victory. In the new political setting, Wagner reintroduced the labor legislation Roosevelt had set aside eight months earlier.

The state had cautiously edged toward recognizing organized labor— from the amorphous 7(a), to the majoritarian ideal asserted by the powerless NLB, to the slightly stronger NLRB mandate to conduct employee elections. Gradually the principles of worker representation and collective bargaining had been established. Now Wagner proposed the final step: a labor board, modeled on the Federal Trade Commission, with full enforcement powers of its own. The board would be authorized to hold elections, prohibit coercive employer tactics, and require collective bargaining with representatives selected by a majority of the workers. There were no new principles of industrial relations, only new powers to enforce those that had been timidly articulated. After three tries, the American state was prepared to establish an authoritative labor policy.

Wagner introduced his bill "as the next step in man's eternal quest for freedom." The business community countered with the same trusty emblems of democracy: the legislation "would out STALIN Stalin, out SOVIET the Russian Soviets"; it would arm unions with "the most dangerous weapons of social coercion" and "end the fine spirit of cooperation . . . which has been growing through employee representation plans." Al Smith (former New York governor and the 1928 Democratic nominee for president) now captured both sides: "It is all right with me if they want to disguise themselves as Norman Thomas or Karl Marx or Lenin . . . but what I won't stand for is allowing them to march under the banner of Jefferson [and] Jackson."[80] It was the labor leaders who articulated a more thoughtful defense of capital. Lewis warned that since American workers had embraced the promise of representation, "denial will breed revolt." Lloyd Garrison, a University of Wisconsin law professor who had chaired the NLRB, called organized labor "our chief bulwark against communism and other revolutionary movements." The American Communist party echoed Lewis and Garrison by attacking the Wagner proposal. The more radical possibilities seemed, however, only brief rhetorical flourishes, lost in the bombast over "man's eternal quest for freedom." American labor continued its struggle with industry over the terms of representation, each largely oblivious to more profound kinds of industrial change.[81]

Most observers were surprised by the ease with which Wagner's bill passed. While the Roosevelt administration remained ambiguously silent, the act swept through the Senate, 63 to 12. Roosevelt finally endorsed the measure, assuring a thumping victory in the House. "No one, then or later, fully understood why Congress passed so radical a bill with so little opposition and by such an overwhelming margin," comments William Leuchtenburg.[82] The politics of the democratic wish provides at least a partial answer.

Economic crisis had prompted a wide variety of proposals. The limited American state was able to muster only a weak program, rooted in the American reforming tradition of cooperation, consensus, and community. When even that stretched the limits of legitimate public power, the NRA was promoted by an unabashedly symbolic appeal: the Roosevelt administration put its recovery program into place on the force of "the people," "acting as a single person." The familiar political cycle followed: vague promises of representation triggered the mobilization of a previously suppressed group and focused their demands on an undeniably legitimate issue. Ultimately, labor struggled with capital over the proper interpretation of a statutory provision designed to ensure free representation.

At the time, the conflicts appeared to throw American industry into turmoil. However, by turning class struggle into a dispute over representation, the NRA transformed the labor issue into the kind of political change the American state most easily digests. Driven by the massive mobilization their policies had legitimated, American leaders gradually responded to worker unrest with a cautious, incremental series of bureaucratic steps, each introduced and carried forward as "the American way": from the amorphous 7(a), to the weak NRB, to the slightly stronger NLRB, to the Wagner Act. By 1935, as the final step was being debated, Lewis, Garrison, and the American Communists all articulated a conclusion that was slowly dawning on American industrialists: organized labor, as it had reconstructed itself to secure the promises of the NRA, was scarcely a threat to capitalism or property rights. On the contrary, in the face of the turmoil—provoked, in part, by New Deal policy—it served as a distinctly pacific influence on the American workers. The Wagner Act passed so easily because its innovations had already been introduced and played out in a political context that did not violate the symbols of democracy or threaten the reluctant capitalists. Labor won its legitimacy in semipublic agencies dominated by private (hence, noncoercive) interests adjudicating disputes about representation without formal (again, coercive) public powers.

A LEGITIMATE WORKERS' MOVEMENT

Roosevelt signed the Wagner Act on 5 July 1935. If American labor ever had a Magna Charta, this was it. To be sure, there were battles ahead. The American Liberty League published a brief signed by fifty-eight lawyers declaring the Wagner Act unconstitutional. The Supreme Court gave their judgment verisimilitude when it struck down most of NRA while the Wagner Act was still before Congress. A new wave of violent strikes would soon sweep across the country. However, the state had shifted the bias of its labor policy; administrative rules now tilted away from employers fighting independent unions. Hazy possibilities within the the NRA had evolved into authoritative policies with the Wagner Act. Traditional union-busting procedures were less effective in the new legal context. As Charles Beard noted a short time later, "Companies did not hire finks . . . for the purpose of beating up . . . the men and women who came . . . in the name of federal authority."[83] The Supreme Court completed the transformation of state policy two years later; facing Roosevelt's Court-packing threat, Justices Charles Evans Hughes and Owen Roberts made their celebrated switch and gave the Wagner Act a six-to-three majority.[84] As Roosevelt signed the Wagner Act, organized labor had yet to seize its new opportunities. But the subsequent battles were played out in the context of a state that had altered the mobilization of bias in the rules and agencies governing labor relations.

Four months later, in November 1935, the labor movement began to reconstitute itself. With characteristic bombast ("Heed this cry from Macedonia ... organize the unorganized") and the most celebrated punch in labor history (decking Bill Hutcheson of the Carpenters as an entire labor convention goggled),[85] John Lewis bolted the craft-bound AFL. Along with Hillman, Dubinsky, and a handful of others, he founded the Committee (later Congress) of Industrial Organizations; the new trade union rejected the restrictive craft union philosophy and started organizing the industrial workers.

Industry resisted. The counsel to Weirton Steel announced, "I feel perfectly free to advise a client not to be bound by a law that I consider unconstitutional."[86] Once again, newly legislated worker rights met an employer backlash and triggered a wave of strikes—2,014 in 1935, 2,172 in 1936, 4,740 in 1937.* This time, however, the political alignments were different. In 1933, the AFL had struggled against worker militancy; by 1936, the CIO was scrambling to organize it. The NRA was an amorphous law that set out vague rights unprotected by state power; the Wagner Act staked out an authoritative national policy which protected worker organizations and collective bargaining. Even before the courts sanctioned the shift, the new policy bias began to tell.

The first major clash broke out in Akron in February 1936. The NRA had originally sent the Goodyear rubber workers rushing to the unions; they were quickly repulsed by the byzantine craft rules of the AFL. In 1934, a declining NLRB had ordered union elections; the rubber companies brushed them aside with a court order. Seven months after Roosevelt signed the Wagner Act, the company laid off 137 workers without giving notice. While AFL leaders counseled moderation, 10,000 rubber workers struck.

In below-zero temperatures, pickets walked the eleven-mile perimeter of the Goodyear plant. The CIO sent in organizers and donated money. The workers hit upon a new tactic, the sitdown strike: by occupying the factories, the sitdown prevented employers from replacing the strikers and resuming production. When sheriffs, "sluggers," and deputies from the James and Braddock Detective Agency threatened to attack,

---

*As percentage of workers employed, the significant rise was in 1937. The figure went from 5.2 percent in 1935 to 3.1 percent in 1936, 7.2 percent in 1937, and 2.8 percent in 1938.[87]

union leaders massed thousands of armed workers at the entrance to the plant. Government officials stayed neutral. The governor of Ohio refused to use the state militia to clear the factory. The assistant secretary of labor arrived, negotiated, recommended that the employees return to work, called for arbitration, and left town to the jeering of four thousand workers. After four weeks, Goodyear more or less capitulated, recognized the union shop committees, reinstated the fired workers, and reduced the workweek. The workers had won a significant battle, but Goodyear would not actually sign a contract with the United Rubber Workers until 1941.[88]

The next major engagement was against General Motors. It broke out in Atlanta, spread to Kansas City and Cleveland, and then centered on a sitdown strike in Flint, Michigan, in December 1936. Though CIO leaders had targeted steel, they followed the rank and file and turned their resources to the auto industry. For six weeks, negotiations alternated with armed struggle: in the "Battle of Running Bulls," workers repulsed company forces by playing fire hoses on them. Finally, an apparent settlement led to the evacuation of the occupied building. However, word circulated that General Motors intended to engage in collective bargaining with an organization of Flint businessmen rather than the union. Workers feigned an attack on one assembly plant and—as a brawl developed outside it—slipped into another. The sitdown was on again. Michigan's governor Frank Murphy ordered GM not to shut off heat, lights, or, ironically, water in the occupied building. On 2 February, a court ordered the factory cleared. As the deadline approached, workers flocked in from surrounding areas. Rubber workers came from Akron; auto workers from Toledo, Lansing, and Detroit. A women's "emergency brigade" came waving an American flag; thousands of supporters gathered between the police and the strikers inside the plant. Local authorities and company deputies decided not to enforce the court order with a direct assault. Finally, pressed by Roosevelt and Perkins, auto executives met—this time, directly—with the CIO and automobile union leaders. In February 1937, the United Auto Workers were granted what amounted to six months of exclusive recognition for the seventeen plants that had been struck. Within a year, the UAW, now affiliated with the CIO, claimed 350,000 members. The new union had won another victory.[89] Note the strikers' prize: a franchise monopoly over the right to organize automobiles. The clearest victor was the UAW.

Sitdowns quickly swept the country. There were 48 in 1936; roughly 500 in 1937. Between September 1936 and the following May, almost half a million workers used the tactic. "The phone would ring," reported a union official, "and the voice would say . . . I'm a soda clerk at Liggett's; we've thrown the manager out and we've got the keys. What do we do now?"[90] Local police were turned loose on just a handful of the sitdowns (about 2.5 percent).[91]

The press from below extended the transformation of the labor movement itself. Even "Grandmother" Tighe stopped fighting the steel workers. While Green urged him to hew to the craft traditions ("This business about steel workers clamoring to get into unions is nonsense"), Tighe reluctantly accepted both the tactics and the assistance of John Lewis and the CIO. In June 1936, an ad-hoc Steel Workers Organizing Committee was established and soon had 500 organizers working the steel mills.[92]

The most significant union victory came six months later. The United States Steel Corporation had battled organized labor as furiously as any company in America. Its chairman, Myron Taylor, was one of the men who had run from William Green during the infamous nonmeeting in Perkins's office. U.S. Steel had developed and publicized the company union as a response to 7(a). By the end of 1936, however, the corporation's attitude was changing. Profits were rising; so were the costs of repressing unions, as the conflict in Flint was demonstrating. Lewis and SWOC were more formidable opponents than "Grandmother" Tighe and the AFL. The state was withdrawing as a union-busting ally. Most important, Taylor and U.S. Steel had learned the unexpected lesson of the NRA. Reluctantly, the corporation had negotiated with Lewis and the United Mine Workers over the NRA coal code. (The steel companies owned "captive" coal mines.) In the safely biased setting of industry-dominated codes which would not be enforced, the steel executives discovered that negotiating with the UMW was far more efficient than fighting disgruntled, disorganized miners. The code agreements promoted industrial peace in the captive mines. In January 1937, U.S. Steel surprised most observers by announcing that it would enter into collective bargaining without a fight. Two months later, Myron Taylor signed an agreement with SWOC—later dubbed, with some hyperbole, "the most important single document in American labor history."[93] Significantly, the new agreement incorporated many of the principles of worker representation that had been hammered out three years earlier in the NRA coal code negotiations.

The CIO victories threatened the AFL. AFL leaders had insisted on their cautious approach largely to maintain their own institutional authority. Now the CIO organizers around the nation had reversed the imperatives of institutional power. The old union threw off its repressive traditions and set out to counter the successes of its upstart rival. During the last four months of 1936, the AFL had spent $82,000 on organizing; for the same period in 1937, it spent $466,000. The union abandoned the craft barriers on which it had been founded. Locals began to search out new members. "I couldn't see much future in just working meatcutters," explained an official in the butcher's union, "so I started on the creamery, poultry and egg houses."[94] The Carpenters began to accept the lumbermen they had previously shunned (even fighting bloody naval battles with the CIO organizers in the Pacific Northwest); the Teamsters took warehousemen; the Electricians signed up utility workers. In the two years following the Wagner Act, the AFL lost 38,000 members. In the next two years, they claimed 698,000 new ones, then 1,300,000 more in 1940 and 1941.[95]

As the state slowly elaborated its authority over labor policy, industrialists discovered the advantages of negotiating with organized labor unions. In 1933, the NRA had stretched the boundaries of legitimate public authority. In the context of its code negotiations, Lloyd Garrison, John Lewis, Myron Taylor, and the Communist party all saw the American trade unions exert a stabilizing influence on the industrial workers. The Wagner Act codified the political balance that had been negotiated in political practice. By the end of the decade, the independent unions had become legitimate players in a political economy that had repressed them for more than a century. To be sure, there was violence and oppression in the decades that followed. Many employers would continue to resist, sometimes backed by the local authorities. For instance, the tactics of the Little Steel companies (Republic, Bethlehem, Inland, and Youngstown) and the Chicago police were so vicious that the newsreels in the late 1930s were censored to avoid riots in other cities. Defeated in the streets, the workers outflanked the steel companies in administrative arenas and courtrooms—precisely reversing the long historical experience.

CONCLUSION

For over a century, American government and business suppressed trade unions with a singular intensity. Workers were prosecuted for treason, conspiracy, abrogating their work contracts, and—in a bizarre legal turn—violating the antitrust laws. By the 1920s, the dominant American unions were responding timidly; the AFL rejected collective action, government assistance, and most industrial workers. The Depression and the New Deal scrambled all these patterns. It is commonplace to observe that sweeping changes occurred suddenly. What is less well understood is how the transformation of labor policy was typical of structural reforms in America. Drawing out the continuities illuminates how and why the changes occurred.

In many ways, the Depression relaxed the traditional limits on American public action. Roosevelt flaunted the extraordinary circumstances and called for "unprecedented" powers from start to finish.[96] The profusion of proposals for coping with the industrial crisis appear to demonstrate the point; however, each suggested alternative ran its course with the dull predictability of normal American politics. The less governmental intrusion into the economy, the more successful the proposal. State-centered national planning was ignored, national wage-and-hours regulation defeated, public works delayed. The National Recovery Administration is usually interpreted as a typical instance of interest-group liberalism—the granting of public authority to private interests for their own advantage.

The recovery plan was a process without substance which ceded public authority to private industry. It was designed by trade associations, promoted by the National Chamber of Commerce, and offered industry the opportunity to collude on everything from wages to pro-

179

duction levels. In the classic tradition of interest-group liberalism, even
the weakest mobilized interest was tossed symbolic benefits. The legislation conferred vague promises of legitimacy on organized labor,
quickly retracted in the public speeches of program administrators:
"The NRA is not going to be used as a machine for unionizing labor";
"The NRA is exactly what industry . . . makes it."[97]

Furthermore, the limits of public authority were manifest. Any interest that was crossed could bring down the program by turning to
the courts. Hugh Johnson may have thought Mussolini's corporatism
a model for the NRA, but the comparison merely set the American
effort (with its Blue Eagle histrionics) in an ironic comparative context.
The American variant of tripartite corporatist bargaining was dominated by business, only vaguely invited labor, and practically excluded
the state from the negotiating table. Even in the great moment of economic crisis, legitimate public action within the industrial sector was
narrowly constricted.

Still, the interest-group model offers an incomplete analysis of the
NRA. Of all the approaches to economic recovery, why this one?
Knowing that industry supported the plan does not explain why it did
so or how it was able to sell it to the administration. Moreover, it is
not obvious why industry would permit the government to raise the
sorest question of American industrial relations. Section 7(a) might
have been enigmatic, but it almost scuttled the program in many industrial sectors. And how to explain the patriotic hysteria provoked by
the Blue Eagle? Or Johnson's odd scramble for consensus? The democratic wish fills out the analysis.

Facing economic crisis, aroused interests, widespread public attention, and the blunt limits of their own authority, the New Dealers
transported the classic democratic pattern of American political change
into the economic sector. They pursued the communitarian ideal in
which cooperation eclipses competition, community replaces state authority, and the image of broad and direct public participation sup-
plants decision making by established government officials. At first, the
communities were defined functionally rather than geographically. Each
industry was conceived as a political constituency which could come
together and work out its own recovery: business, labor, and consumers—the whole industrial community—would be represented. Despite

the inclusion of sharp antagonists, consensus was assumed. Indeed, the survival of the program was predicated on it. The assumption of unanimity appears fatuous in the Madisonian rubric of clashing interests; it is, however, a central feature of the communal politics that lay implicit in the effort.

These traces of the American reforming pattern were more vividly underscored by the Blue Eagle drama. When the negotiations which were to define the NRA broke down (precisely because the industrial community had been defined too broadly, because labor had been included), the democratic reflex was to appeal to a still more general community. State authority was eschewed for a call to the people. The most distinctive feature of the outburst that followed was the constant repetition of an old republican theme: the Americans as one people, enforcing a single public will on any miscreant who might obstruct the national recovery for some selfish purpose. It was the "American housewife" and Americans "acting as a single person" who would enforce the New Deal recovery program.

The American reforming pattern also framed the politics that followed. The usual analyses of New Deal labor politics turn on inconclusive debates about which came first, the labor uprising or the labor programs.[98] I have argued that labor politics was an extended dialectic between worker rebellion and state response, profoundly shaped by the Americans' democratic iconography. In a polity so suspicious of public power that even the New Dealers were not permitted an authoritative industrial policy, the Americans sought popular consensus and the people. The NRA gave workers a mobilizing focus; the next moments in the conflict were forced by workers demanding the representation that had been vaguely promised by the National Industrial Recovery Act. As they had done many times in the past, Americans took a potentially revolutionary dispute (redolent with threats of class conflict and the mobilization of collective power) and transformed it into a dispute about representation.

When the "American people" acting "as a single person" proved insufficient, a labor board was formed and promoted an electoral solution "because this is America and that's the way we do things here." Employers countered with their own representational forms. They unwittingly staked out a position rooted in John Stuart Mill and proclaimed themselves champions of minority rights. Workers responded in kind. They denounced the "fake representation" and insisted on majority rule. Labor's position was temporarily muscled aside with the proclamation that the states' duty was "to secure the absolute, uninfluenced freedom of choice." Liberals eventually countered with the Wagner Act; it was introduced "as the next step in man's eternal quest for freedom" and attacked, with allusions to Joseph Stalin, as "the most dangerous weapon of social coercion."[99] All the rhetorical flourishes point up the content and scope of New Deal labor policy. It was introduced, disputed, and settled as a question of representation. The redefinition of the issue simultaneously legitimated and biased the debate. It did not, of course, determine the outcome. American labor policy was hammered out through the clash of groups and individuals—in and out of government—pressing their own interests within the context of the redefined issue. What is perhaps most striking is how all the influential political actors—workers, public officials, and business leaders—accepted the redefinition of the labor question and formulated their demands within its framework.

First, consider the workers' response. The hints of legitimacy offered by section 7(a) set off a worker uprising. The NRA simultaneously triggered their revolt and focused their demands. From the exuberant Philco employees—roaming the bureaucracy in search of General Johnson—to the strikers in Flint, workers fought for the right to join unions. The deeper issues of wealth and power were only intermittently raised and never sustained. Rather than revolting for wage policies, economic equity, or control over the means of production, workers struck for the representation and due process ambiguously promised by 7(a).

The union élite reconstituted their organizations around the worker mobilization. The same logic that had shaped traditional AFL strategies—maintaining authority over the rank and file—now prompted the rise of the UMW, the revolt of the CIO, the reconstruction of the AFL, and, by the end of the decade, the restoration of a conservative labor hierarchy. After winning legitimacy and power, a new labor leadership soon reverted to the old union preoccupations—protecting their considerable gains and maintaining institutional power. Even the United Mine Workers would collaborate in the wholesale abandonment of coal mines throughout the Appalachian valley: the strategy protected the coal industry along with UMW authority. As Grant McConnell put it, the owners praised the union, 300,00 Appalachian miners cursed it.[100] Like Americans who rebelled for representation in the past, the workers progressed from disorganized rebels to stalwart supporters of the status quo. As the New Deal coalition began to come apart in the 1970s and 1980s, labor leaders began to return all the way back to voluntarism—at least claiming to consider support for the repeal of all labor legislation.

The evolution of the federal government's role in the battle for representation is more subtle. Social scientists are often tempted to explain conservative outcomes by imputing intent to state officials. After all, New Deal labor policy protected the stubborn capitalists (and the state officials themselves) from more radical rebellion, perhaps even class struggle. And by empowering labor, the Democrats cemented a coalition that would exercise power for three decades. However, a careful look does not sustain the view that political leaders consciously manipulated the workers' rebellion. Different government officials responded to events, pressing their own institutional advantages within the limits of their legitimacy and power.

The democratic trappings of the NRA were a response to the constraints on public authority. For all his bluster, Hugh Johnson pushed industry only till it resisted. With the threat of defiance, litigation, or even a diminution of his agency's prestige, Johnson and his subordinates relented. The NRA administrators focused almost entirely on fostering the consensus necessary to maintain their program. (In fact, their timidity helped reduce the program from a patriotic movement to an object of scorn: "National Run Around," "No Recovery Allowed," and "Negroes Ruined Again" were among the popular jibes.)[101]

At the same time, the program aroused a worker constituency that made demands and offered support. Labor's mobilization slowly expanded the boundary of legitimate public action; the administration was pressed to respond to the worker's crusade it had prompted. The New Dealers reacted in standard bureaucratic fashion: they created administrative boards. The NLB and the NLRB incrementaly expanded public authority over labor relations. More important, they shifted the constellation of institutional interests within the state itself. The labor boards developed organizational interests that differed from those of the NRA or the Roosevelt administration; the boards' bureaucratic interest lay in carving out a distinctive policy role for themselves. The industry position, proportional representation in worker elections, did not require independent agencies: the code authorities would have cheerfully overseen it. Naturally, the board members pursued their own ideologies; perhaps they responded to pressure from workers as well. In either case, their choices were congruent with the requirements of enhancing their organizations. Indeed, both labor boards were rendered irrelevant as soon as Roosevelt overruled their majoritarian policy: they lost their institutional purpose along with their policy preference. However, once the NLB was formed, it altered public-sector politics by institutionalizing the workers' view of representation within the government. Each time a labor board was undermined, its members and their clients were organized to clamor for a more powerful successor.

In short, the Roosevelt administration negotiated the call for industrial action and the constraints on its own authority with the democratic wish. The program that resulted from the ideals of community and cooperation simultaneously provoked the workers and limited their rebellion. The workers, in turn, restructured the labor movement and put new demands for representation on the political agenda. Once the process was set into motion, labor policy evolved in an incremental, bureaucratic fashion. In the process, public power was withdrawn from busting unions and invested in protecting them.

Capital underwent a cycle that matched the changes in both labor and government. At the start of the New Deal, industrialists had recoiled at the prospect of shaking a labor leader's hand. The American quest for community created a safe arena in which they could do so. In a para-governmental program dominated by industry and void of sanctions, employers learned the advantages of negotiating with labor. The workers may have been loud, clumsy, disorganized, overreaching, and inefficient. However, industry soon discovered that even the aggressive unions exerted a pacifying influence by controlling the rank and file. After years of bloodshed, American capitalists learned that negotiating with organized labor yielded more stability than fighting it.

It is currently fashionable to criticize the process and its ultimate consequences. The Right resented the end of industrial hegemony and

184

scorned the self-interested distributive compact that evolved between industry and labor. It was frankly titillated when the early Reagan administration invoked the union-busting symbols of the nineteenth century. For example, the administration's aggressive posture toward an ill-fated air traffic controllers (PATCO) strike provoked precisely this conservative satisfaction: the union was broken along with the strike. More generally, the absolute number of union members began to decline for the first time since the 1930s. The 1920s' talk of irrelevant unions could be heard again.[102] On the other side, the Left laments the failure to sustain a spontaneous, participatory workers' movement. It decries the reassertion of conservative union oligarchy. The workers' rebellion might, in its view, have focused on more profound economic arrangements or won more enduring changes in American industrial relations.

The transformation of labor policy reflects the persistent patterns of American reform. The quest for participation and the people has repeatedly provided a framework in which public and private organizations can work out new accommodations. The democratic promises that fire the reforming imagination merely serve to relax the constraints on change within American public administration. The cycle has been repeated so regularly precisely because the promise of a new democracy is so widely taken at face value. The political outcomes—a newly legitimated group, an incremental growth of public authority, an adjustment of the political rules—seem a wan reflection of the democratic hopes that facilitate them.

Measured by the standards of American labor history, the early New Deal fashioned an extraordinary transformation in the rights of working men and women. Contrasted to the prospects of more profound social change, however, the workers' outburst ended in a political whimper that typifies the contemporary reforming pattern: newly legitimated labor organizations struggle for marginal gains, their own stability, and the preservation of the new institutional status quo.

6

The Reconstruction of
Racial Politics

Night is an African juju man
Weaving a wish and a weariness together
* to make two wings*
O fly away home fly away
Do you remember Africa?
O cleave the air fly away home
— Robert Hayden, "O Daedalus, Fly Away Home"

In 1954, the Supreme Court ruled against racial segregation in public schools. The struggle that followed vividly illustrates the incoherence of the American regime. The state simultaneously articulated new rights and unleashed dogs on black citizens who exercised them. The Court's decision (in *Brown* v. *Board of Education*) did not end segregation; by altering the political rules, however, it prompted a citizens' movement which ultimately transformed American racial politics.

The black struggle occurred in two stages. First came an effort to win basic citizenship rights in the South. Though Southern segregationists violently resisted racial change, the civil rights movement had the advantage of struggling for plain ends (like the right to vote) with clear tactics (nonviolent passive resistance). In its broadest terms, the conflict was an elaborate dialectic between black citizens and an ambivalent state biased against the redistribution of power. With each wave of protest, the government conceded some of the citizenship rights that had been formally promised by the courts.

Second, after a decade of slow progress in the South, racial conflict spread to the northern cities. There, the effort to win political and economic rights was more complicated because the mechanisms of discrimination were more obscure: black Americans already voted in the North. Stripped of clear goals and frustrated by the lack of progress in the South, the movement turned violent. By the mid-1960s, the Johnson administration faced a racial crisis marked by urban riots, revolutionary rhetoric, and sharp limits on the legitimacy of government intervention. The policy response, the "War on Poverty," met the problem with an invocation of the democratic wish. Echoing the labor legislation of the 1930s, the War on Poverty tried to replace racial conflict with communal consensus and public power with citizen participation. The race problem was redefined as a class issue and worked out as question of representation on para-governmental boards legitimated by the Jeffersonian ideal. In the process, the program channeled the political energy of the civil rights movement into mainstream American politics.

In this chapter, I sketch the American racial setting; review the Southern civil rights movement with its clear—though violently contested—invocation of traditional democratic values; and then suggest how a variation of the democratic wish negotiated the more complex civil rights dilemmas of the northern cities. Ultimately, as I argue in this chapter, the tensions of the 1950s and 1960s were negotiated so as to transform racial politics without resolving the underlying dilemmas of American racial relations. Once again, Americans underwent a polical, but not an economic, revolution.

THE PEOPLE AND REFORM

RACE POLITICS BEFORE *BROWN*

Black Americans faced legal segregation in the South, political and economic inequity throughout the nation. Measures of their oppression are easy to find: More than sixteen hundred blacks were lynched between 1900 and 1930; fifty-seven more in the first three years of the New Deal.* The Senate repeatedly spurned black pleas for protective legislation as undue "interference with the police powers of the state[s]."[1] The Federal Housing Authority actively promoted segregation till the 1940s (to "retain neighborhood stability"), then continued to underwrite it through loan policies into the 1960s.[2] The military was segregated till 1949; the public bathrooms in Washington, D.C., till the mid-1950s. Black unemployment in the 1950s stood 70 percent higher than white; black median family income was 49 percent lower; black life expectancy eight years less (the differential had been 11.1 years in 1940). One out of three black Americans lived in poverty—three times the rate of white Americans.[3]

Patterns of Discrimination

In the South, the repression was codified by an elaborate network of Jim Crow laws. Black Americans could not attend white schools, seek care in decent hospitals, live in (indeed, visit) the better neighborhoods, play in public parks, or buy a cup of coffee at a Woolworth's counter. "Segregation is so complete," reported Gunnar Myrdal in 1944, "that the white Southerner never sees a Negro except as his servant and in other standardized and formalized caste situations. . . . Today, the average Southerner of middle or upper class status seems . . . to judge all Negroes by his cook."[4]

The white establishment maintained supremacy by rigidly excluding blacks from politics. It relied on political tactics elaborated in the three

*The Census Bureau puts the figure at 1,620; Tuskegee Institute at 1,886. The vast majority, 1,489, took place in seven southern states.

decades following the Civil War: violence, race hatred, and legal machination. Violence had come first. Secret societies such as the Knights
of the White Camelia and the Ku Klux Klan tried to intimidate black
voters. These societies were given free rein in 1877 when Rutherford B. Hayes removed Northern troops (and attention) from the South.
Southern Democrats also played on both racial animosity and postwar
xenophobia. White Republicans in the South were denounced as "scal-
awags," grasping traitors under the influence of Northern "carpetbag-
gers." Their "nefarious design" was depicted—in crude racist terms—
as the "lapse of Caucasian civilization into African barbarism" or the
"degradation of the Caucasian race as the inferior of the Negro."
Southern Progressives mixed race hatred with "goo-goo" moralizing,
casting Reconstruction politics as a kind of Southern Tammany: "This
travesty of an American government . . . voted themselves champagne,
gold watches . . . and other incredible things. . . . The White South
could not be expected to submit supinely to be ruled and plundered
by its former slaves." Driving black men (and their Republican allies)
out of politics was rationalized as a battle against the familiar specter
of corruption.[5]

Though the Bourbon Democrats quickly recaptured control, bloodshed and race hatred were not enough to provide them a secure hold.
In 1880, after the departure of federal troops, 70 percent of the black
citizenry voted in most southern states, over 50 percent in almost all.[6]
A decade later, Southern Populists forged a coalition between white
dirt farmers and black citizens ("they are in the ditch, just like we
are"). The new threat galvanized the Democratic establishment to find
more effective disenfranchisement devices.[7]

The white-supremacist solution was an intricate legal sophistry that
effectively gutted the Fifteenth Amendment. The "crowning achievement," as V. O. Key termed it, was the literacy test: the test required
voters to read or understand (a loophole for illiterate whites) "any
section of the constitution of the state." Other techniques included poll
taxes (Georgia adopted a $1 tariff in 1877, when three quarters of the
southern population had an average income of $55.16), grandfather
clauses, education qualifications, extended residency requirements, and
the fiction that the unchallenged Democratic party was a private or-

ganization entitled to set its own discriminatory rules (like white primaries). All were backed by the usual forms of suasion.[8]*

By the turn of the century, Southern blacks had been forced out of the political system. In Louisiana, 130,000 black voters were reduced to 1,300 in eight years (between 1896 and 1904). By 1954, when the *Brown* decision was announced, a decade of voter registration drives had not shaken the segregationist grip. Black registration was 5 percent in Mississippi, 11 percent in Alabama, 19 percent in Virginia, no higher than 39 percent anywhere in the South. In the "black belt," where white rule was vulnerable, the suppression was most severe: in one Mississippi county, 13,000 blacks mustered 6 registrations; in Selma, the black majority formed less than 1 percent of the electorate as late as 1965.[10]

When Southern white supremacy faced its next challenge in the 1950s, the response was already set. Political leaders would reflexively muster up the Reconstruction-era strategies: violence, the inflammation of racial (and xenophobic) sentiment, and legal manipulation.

The difficulties outside the South were more subtle. At the turn of the century, blacks began moving north in large numbers. More than half a million migrated between 1910 and 1920, three times as many in the 1950s. By 1957, 40 percent of the black population lived in the North.[11] Though free of the Jim Crow strictures, blacks still faced poverty, exclusion, and animosity. They could apply for jobs, but employers hired them only when necessary—during strikes or wars, for instance. There may have been fewer statutes mandating segregation, but blacks were still pressed into ghettos. They could vote, yet remained excluded from the political system.

There were no black mayors and few black elected officials on any level. Blacks almost never held appointive office. They were confined largely to menial public jobs. A handful represented overwhelmingly black districts, but they were exceptions operating within a white po-

---

*Not all of them were violent, as V. O. Key illustrates:

"One of the gentler techniques is illustrated by the . . . registrar of a county with over 13,000 Negroes 21 and over, six of whom were registered in 1947. The registrar registers any qualified person, black or white, if he insists. When a Negro applies, however, she tells him that he will be registered if he insists, but she gives him a quiet maternal talk to the effect that the time has not yet come for Negroes to register in the county. The people are not ready for it now and it would only cause trouble. Things move slowly, she tells the applicant, but the day will come."[9]

litical establishment. Even cities with large minority populations were governed by white men. For example, by the mid-1950s, Detroit was one third black; all nine city councilmen were white. Newark was approaching a black majority, but its power structure, too, was completely white.[12]

Worse, as blacks arrived in the North, they found relatively stable (often ethnic) political coalitions. Government agencies served organized vocal constituencies. The allocation of public services—sanitation, education, city jobs—had already been set. As urban resources contracted after the Second World War, established groups were not willing to sacrifice city services or jobs to the growing black populations which were not organized to demand them. On the contrary, public policies often benefited white constituencies in ways that victimized black populations. For example, the solution to downtown blight was urban renewal, aptly tagged "Negro removal." Substandard housing was demolished in the effort to reduce crime and revitalize business districts with no concern over where the former residents, characteristically black, would live. On the other hand, city governments often rejected federal funds for low-income housing rather than battle the white residents who mobilized to "protect" their neighborhoods.[13]

The legacy of past reforms reinforced the political exclusion. Civil service restricted patronage and complicated the task of building a local political base, especially among the poor. At-large elections, nonpartisan campaigns, city managers, and the demise of political parties all aggravated the difficulty, shutting off the passages of mobility used by previous generations of newcomers. The rise of unions added another barrier, for the labor organizations rejected the black threat to white jobs.[14]

As the issue of racial equality entered the political agenda in the 1950s, *Newsweek* queried, "Could the migrants turn the Northern cities into predominantly colored communities run by colored officials?" At the time, the verdict was, "not in the foreseeable future" (though in its relentlessly qualified style, *Newsweek* allowed that "their influence would grow steadily").[15] Racial reformers faced a daunting set of tasks: in the South, overt segregation, physical oppression, and the denial of the most basic citizenship rights; in the North, a more complicated pattern of political and economic exclusion.

191

Traditions of Black Politics

Twentieth-century black Americans articulated at least three different strategies to cope with the denial of citizenship rights. Each would define their struggle at different historical moments and in different political settings.

First, beginning in the 1890s, Booker T. Washington preached a bourgeois gospel of accommodation and hard work: "Agitation on questions of social equality is extremest folly. . . . The best course to pursue in regard to civil rights is to let it alone, let it alone." Instead, Washington urged his people to impress white America with hard work and self-respect: "It is at the bottom we must begin. . . . We shall prosper as we learn to dignify and glorify common labor." "Be patient, do good work, give no occasion against us." In this way, black people would pull themselves up; it is a universal and eternal law, he promised, that "merit is in the long run, recognized and rewarded." Washington urged white Southerners: "Cast down your buckets among the eight million Negroes whose habits you know, whose fidelity and love you have tested. People who have, *without strikes and labor wars*, tilled your fields, cleared your forests, builded your railroads."[16]

The strategy of conciliation and self-help echoed labor's retreat from confrontation under the American Federation of Labor. Both were strategies predicated on political weakness and shaped by the violence of the opposition. Washington's vision dominated black politics till the 1950s (though it is often said that the audience who most appreciated this message was white).[17] Black leaders were avowedly moderate, their tactics cautious. For example, though the often-segregationist AFL had rejected an antidiscrimination clause in the Wagner Act, the National Urban League warned black workers against "jubilantly rushing towards" the presumably leftist CIO. When black riots erupted during the Second World War, black leaders rushed to organize a "good conduct" campaign. When more aggressive civil rights leaders called for mass protests against Jim Crow (both during and after the war), they were widely condemned by black leaders and the black press. Most civil rights leaders renounced all activity that might have given white America "cause against us." Even when civil rights leaders broke with Washington's precepts and sponsored political action, both their objectives and their tactics were guided by his philosophy: a campaign against lynching, voter registration drives.[18]

Though Washington and many of the civil rights leaders who followed him were people of enormous dignity, the philosophy of conciliation did not prove any more effective for black people than it had for industrial workers. Decades of moderation did little to crack white political and economic hegemony.

Beginning in the early 1900s, a major alternative was pressed by W. E. B. Du Bois, the distinguished Harvard-trained sociologist:

> The South ought to be led, by candid and honest criticism, to assert her better self and do her full duty to the race she has cruelly wronged. The North—her copartner in guilt—cannot salve her conscience by plastering it with gold. We cannot settle this problem by diplomacy and suaveness. . . . Can the moral fiber of this country survive the slow throttling and murder of nine millions of men?[19]

Du Bois spurned subordination and submission. He would cast aside Washington's "apologies for injustice" and take up direct confrontation, anchoring resistance in the pride of black heritage. Du Bois's strategy turned on three broad racial reforms: the right to vote, civic equality, and a proper education for black youth. It was an explicitly élite strategy, based on the training of an intellectual vanguard ("the talented tenth") which would assert organization and leadership. Du Bois's search for élite leadership led to the formation of the National Association for Colored People in 1911, though he would eventually repudiate the organization.[20]

Du Bois's calls for action—he was one of the leaders who sought to puncture "good conduct" with the protests against Jim Crow—were generally resisted till the 1950s. However, one break from the politics of conciliation clearly foreshadowed the future direction of the civil rights movement. As the United States mobilized for the Second World War, both the armaments industry and the state clung to their traditional racial discrimination. In most firms, "the hiring of Negroes was against company policy." Roosevelt refused to act against federal contractors who rejected black workers; the administration's National Defense Training Act, designed to prepare Americans for defense work, accepted fewer than 5,000 blacks among its 175,000 trainees.[21] Privately, Interior Secretary Ickes described the bias (with remarkable candor):

> When we are supposed to be making our maximum efforts, here are ten percent of our people who are not even considered for defense jobs while, at the same time, the color line is pretty rigidly drawn in the Army. I do not see what enthusiasm the Negroes could be expected to show in helping us defend ourselves from Hitler. Of course, Hitler has drawn the color line openly and boldly, notwithstanding which I doubt if the Negroes would fare much worse under him than under us.[22]

In response, A. Phillip Randolph, president of the Brotherhood of Sleeping Car Porters, organized a black people's march on Washington, D.C., set for July 1941. Turning away white liberal assistance, Randolph predicted 100,000 black marchers. Over 50,000 contributed to the March on Washington campaign. Black rallies were held across the nation. After trying to dissuade Randolph, the President reluctantly bargained with him. Randolph called off the march in exchange for the first executive order on civil rights since Reconstruction. The largely symbolic action prohibited discrimination by companies engaged in defense-related work and established the Fair Employment Practice Committee to monitor compliance. Clearly, the threat of mass mobilization brought results that good behavior did not; Roosevelt would not make even symbolic gestures supporting the NAACP's campaign to secure legislation against lynching.

A third vision, only intermittently asserted, was championed by men like Marcus Garvey. Garvey arrived in the United States in 1916 and bluntly attributed the black American condition to white racism. He denounced interracial solutions of any sort, called on blacks to arm themselves, and celebrated what he labeled "black power": "It will be a terrible day when Blacks draw the sword to fight for their liberty." His solution was mass emigration and the founding of a pan-African empire. With great panache and drama, Garvey celebrated black heritage and nationalism: "Up, up you mighty race, you can accomplish what you will." He became the voice of the poorest black Americans, especially those in the northern ghettos. Thousands poured their savings into his black enterprises (such as the Black Star Line). Hundreds of women joined his Black Cross nurses; men joined his paramilitary guard. At the time, Du Bois assailed his "revenge" and "hate," dismissing Garvey as "either a lunatic or a traitor." (Garvey, in turn, thought the NAACP "worse than the Ku Klux Klan.") Inevitably, Garvey's movement collapsed (he himself was deported).[23] The exhilaration of emigration and empire was myth, projecting power on the powerless; in the words of an old black fable, it wove "a wish and a weariness together to make two wings and fly away home."[24] Even so, the images of black nationalism and black power, somehow divorced from a tyrannical white polity, would recur, playing an important role in the racial politics of the 1960s.

The three traditions of black politics can be conceptualized as loyalty (Washington), voice (Du Bois), and exit (Garvey).[25] Taken together, these visions of representation and American society are striking both for what they include and what they omit. Voice and loyalty are traditional political reactions. However, the popularity of Garvey's black nationalism points to the uneasy black place within the American regime. Garvey was not proposing traditional revolution but, literally, departure. A return to Africa was the precise reverse of the Western frontier. Garvey rejected a central image of the American republican myth; instead, he would go east, returning to the Old World and its memory of empire. The civil rights movement would repeatedly have to balance two incompatible visions: on the one hand, the rhetoric and tactics of traditional American democracy with its emphasis on the direct popular participation and its promises of freedom; on the other, the language and imagery of separation, of exit from a hostile polity whose founders were slave owners. The Democratic wish—the imagery of Jefferson and Jackson and LaFollette—would not fit easily into American racial politics.

The missing tactic has been a sustained effort to transform racial issues into class politics. Washington appealed to the dominant white class; Du Bois would ally educated blacks with liberal whites; Garvey addressed the black urban poor and linked them with black people in other nations. However, the classic revolutionary formula, an alliance of the have-nots against the haves, was rarely articulated or effectively pursued. The Southern populist movement briefly promised this powerful coalition just before the turn of the century, but it quickly collapsed into racial hatred. On the contrary, we shall see that when Kennedy and Johnson tried to manage the racial crisis of the 1960s, they would seek to redefine the issue from race to class. It is a mark of both the depth of America's racial cleavage and the evanescence of its class politics that black mobilization has so rarely found an alliance based on class. Instead, black politics has repeatedly balanced loyalty, voice, and exit.[26]

Civil Rights in a Fragmented Regime

While black Americans contended over the definition of their movement, political élites struggled to frame a response. By the 1950s, the political patterns and institutional biases were well established.

Postwar American images of international politics set the context. As blacks mobilized for civil rights, the African nations were throwing off colonial rule. Ghana sent diplomatic delegations to New York and Washington in 1957; by 1963, two dozen new nations had won their independence in sub-Saharan Africa. They were the objects of an ideological struggle between the United States and the Soviet Union. Each moment of the civil rights campaign in America was measured for its cold war consequences. The issue was ubiquitous in the commentaries of the period. A commission appointed by President Harry Truman framed the issue in the following fashion:

> We cannot escape the fact that our civil rights record has been an issue in world politics. The world's press and radio are full of it. . . . Those with competing philosophies . . . have tried to prove our democracy an empty fraud and our nation a consistent oppressor of underprivileged people. This may seem ludicrous to Americans but . . . the United States is not so strong, the final

triumph of the democratic ideal is not so inevitable that we can ignore what the world thinks of our record.[27]

Truman drew the cold war conclusion: "In a world that is half colored, the top dog . . . ought to clean his own house." The State Department tossed in, with the specificity of bureaucrats, "Fifty percent of the Soviet propaganda against the United States focuses on the race issue."[28] The purported audience institutionalized an interest in reform, however tenuous, within the foreign policy establishment. By raising the issue in American minds, foreign observers may have also helped transform the racial struggle that followed into a test of American democracy, especially to the growing number of young liberal activists.*

The international context was misleading, however, insofar as it implied a single national interest. Granting full citizenship rights to black Americans would shift the balance of political and economic power in many places. Political leaders and entrenched interests, North and South, would not relinquish power without a struggle. The checks and balances of the American political system made it extremely difficult to force their hand. The bias against collective action structured into American political institutions enabled even relatively small minorities to frustrate reform. They could rely on a profusion of institutional veto points. Though the Supreme Court would formally assert black citizenship rights in 1954, the fragmented American state was not able to secure them in practice.

The Court bound itself to the enfeebling principle of unanimity. The National Recovery Administration had sought consensus within entire industries to avoid a constitutional challenge. Similarly, the Warren Court permitted its most reluctant members to set the pace of implementing the constitutional changes that it articulated.

Congress was bound by its own powerful consensual bias. Majorities

---

*Almost every commentary of the period was concerned with the rising black states in Africa.[29] Even the cold warriors' proudest moment was linked to the issue. Schlesinger filed the liberal report: "As the delegate from Upper Volta put it to the United Nations . . . 'for one small Negro to go to school, the United States threatens Governors . . . with prison.' " Three months later, African leaders "were prepared to deny refueling facilities to Soviet planes bound for Cuba during the missile crisis."[30]

favoring civil rights legislation were repeatedly frustrated by filibusters. The parliamentary device effectively raised the number of Senate votes needed for racial reforms from a simple majority to the two thirds required for cloture. Even members who professed sympathy for proposed legislation often refused to vote cloture as a matter of institutional principle. As a consequence, the Senate failed to break a single filibuster between 1927 and 1963. Instead, Congress repeatedly substituted symbolic bills for substantive benefits.

The presidents varied in their commitment to black Americans. From Roosevelt to Kennedy, however, all were outspoken about the limits of their authority. In a governmental system characterized by weak political parties, forceful action in a controversial area was often sacrificed to maintain coalitions necessary for other victories. Till the mid-1960s, no Democratic administration would risk offending its Southern allies. The one Republican administration was more interested in fostering a political realignment in the Democratic South than in forcing racial reform on it.

The checks on political action in Washington were magnified by those structured into American federalism. Southern leaders threatened by civil rights repeated all the tactics of post-Reconstruction politics. They disinterred the nineteenth-century fossils of states' rights, concocted byzantine legal strategies, whipped up a segregationist frenzy among their constituents, and played on Southern xenophobia.

When the black threat to established power relations spread north, political leaders fought to protect the status quo by trying to manage the demand for civil rights. Public officials were willing to distribute benefits, but insisted that the (white) institutions they controlled should do so.

In sum, the civil rights movement involved two simultaneous conflicts. The black constituency struggled to define the nature of its challenge: in one decade, it moved from "good conduct" through peaceful confrontation to black nationalism. Second, whatever the tactics, reform had to be won from the inchoate array of public and private institutions that govern the United States. In its most general terms, the civil rights movement progressed through a series of confrontations in which mobilized black Americans prodded a state biased against the redistribution of political and economic power—exactly the pattern set by Randolph's confrontation with Roosevelt.

THE CIVIL RIGHTS MOVEMENT: 1954–63

"All Deliberate Speed": Brown *v.* Board of Education

The moderate black leaders were most successful in the federal courts. Through the 1940s and early 1950s, the NAACP mounted a careful assault on Jim Crow. Led by Thurgood Marshall, it won a series of victories around the edges of Southern discrimination, then turned on segregation itself. The NAACP successfully challenged the white primary in 1944 when the Court reversed itself and ruled against Southern evasions like construing the Democratic party as a private club.[31] The Court forbade housing covenants that proscribed selling to blacks (1948), struck down laws requiring segregation on interstate bus lines (1946), and threw out the partitions that segregated railway dining cars (1950).[32] Finally, the NAACP turned on the patent inequality of "separate but equal" education.[33] It began with higher education: states were required to provide a separate graduate training, even if few blacks applied. A separate black law school, hastily flung up in Texas, did not meet the test of equality (1950). Where separate institutions were not provided, universities were forbidden from segregating classrooms, cafeterias, or libraries (1950).[34]

In December 1952, the court held oral arguments on five cases, consolidated into *Oliver Brown* v. *Board of Education of Topeka, Kansas.* Chief Justice Fred Vinson, who was resisting a bold departure, died suddenly that summer. Earl Warren, the former governor of California (and 1948 vice-presidential candidate), replaced him. Briefs were resubmitted the following December. Observers predicted a historic ruling. Yet the Court remained silent. Two justices opposed the majority; Warren judged that so explosive an issue required unanimity. Two years later, a bargain was struck, and Warren announced the celebrated decision: "In the field of public education the doctrine of separate but equal has no place."[35]

A year later, the price of unanimity became clear. The implementation order, announced in May 1955, followed the approach advocated by the Southern attorney generals (and opposed by the NAACP). School desegregation was to proceed "with all deliberate speed." However, deferring to the minority of two, the Court specified no dates and left the details in the hands of local school authorities and federal judges.[36]

For a brief moment, there was relative calm ("the calm of incredulity," Alexander Bickel called it).[37] The border states quietly began to desegregate their schools. The *Nashville Tennessean* commented, "Given a reasonable amount of time" Southern people "of both races can learn to live with this." However, Lieutenant Governor Ernest Vandiver of Georgia pointed to the ambivalence of both the ruling and the state apparatus charged with implementation: "A reasonable amount of time can be construed as one year or two hundred. Thank God we've got the federal judges."[38]

Although the Supreme Court had altered the legal framework of American race relations, its cautious implementation strategy meant that new citizenship rights still had to be negotiated through the political system. The decision was as much a potential vehicle for social change as a definitive state policy. The rhetoric that greeted the decision staked out the contours of the political debate. Both sides invoked the traditional democratic images, placing them in the cold war context.

"This is democracy's finest hour. This is communism's greatest defeat," exulted Adam Clayton Powell, the black congressman from Harlem. Jubilant black leaders hailed "a second Emancipation Proclamation"—precisely what the Progressives had thought of Pendleton and John Lewis of the Wagner Act.[39]

Southerners inverted the imagery: "Communists . . . have been trying since 1936 to destroy the South." "The communist masses of Russia and China must have howled with glee on black Monday." One columnist scored integration as worse than socialized medicine. Senator James Eastland of Mississippi defended segregation: "Free men have a right to send their children to schools of their own choosing, free from governmental interference and to build up their own culture free from governmental interference."[40]

Almost the entire southern congressional delegation (101 members including every senator but Estes Kefauver, Albert Gore, and Lyndon Johnson) issued the Southern Manifesto. The Founding Fathers, they proclaimed, "gave us a Constitution of checks and balances because they realized . . . no group . . . can be safely entrusted with unlimited power." The senators condemned "the clear abuse of judicial power"—indeed, the substitution of "naked power over judicial law." Facing an unsympathetic Court and unable to muster a majority in Congress, they looked elsewhere among the Founding Fathers' checks and balances: they called on the states and—inevitably—"the people . . . to resist."[41] Senator Harry Byrd of Virginia pressed home the states' rights theme, denouncing the decision as the "most serious blow . . . struck against the rights of the states"; he championed "massive resistance."[42]

The Supreme Court was threatening the social and political order that the white élite had erected after the Civil War. Southern leaders quickly reverted to the old tactics. Long-dormant constitutional arguments were dredged up. Virginia announced its power of "interposition," the state's right to protect its citizens from federal transgressions of the Constitution. The device had originally been proposed by Jefferson and Madison as a challenge to the Alien and Sedition Acts—the short-lived Federalist effort to create the kind of one-party state the segregationists were struggling to maintain. Five other states adopted some variant, all trumpeting their authority to declare the Court's decision "null, void, and to no effect." In three months, forty-two segregationist measures were passed in just five states; in the months that followed, more than four hundred additional laws and resolutions were designed to frustrate the *Brown* decision. Segregation was mandated, integration declared a crime, the NAACP outlawed and harassed. Southerners dreamed up bureaucratic regulations to foil desegregation—complicated procedures for student placement, the decentralization of authority to the lowest administrative levels. "The decision tortured the Constitution," chortled John Temple Graves of Alabama. "Now the South will torture the decision."[43]

Southern leaders insisted that "the Negro is not oppressed," that the federal government was "disrupting racial harmony" and that "black southerners did not want integration any more than whites." Demonstrations were invariably blamed on outside agitators. The theme of contented black people stirred up by outsiders was replayed in every community when protests first broke out. The denial of dissatisfaction precisely mirrors the owners' reaction to labor in the 1930s—as in Champ Clark's proposal that nothing in the NRA should alter "satisfactory labor relations," or management's repeated insistence that only outside agitators trying to "hone in" on local plants favored independent unions.

The leaders helped provoke a violent racism. Politicians scrambled to avoid being—in the vicious phrase of Alabama's gubernatorial candidate George Wallace—"outniggered." Eight black men were lynched in 1955, more than in the previous eight years combined. Black leaders trying to register voters were publicly murdered; often arrests were not made.[44] White supremacy organizations flourished. The Ku Klux Klan drew the lower middle class; the White Citizens Councils spoke for the bourgeoisie.

The violent reaction was an ironic parody of the American democratic impulse. All the traditional elements were present: charges that a tyrannical state had usurped citizen rights, demands for the traditional liberty of free men, calls for the people to resist, invocations of Madison and Jefferson. Indeed, the outburst (as well as years of vigilante repression that preceded it) illustrated the Madisonian critique of Jeffersonian orthodoxy—tyrannical passions can grip local populations. Still, the persistence of Jeffersonian sentiment left liberal commentators wavering because, as one legal scholar put it, "mobs of our people do not generally gather to oppose good laws."[45]

Desegregation and American Federalism

American racial policy evolved through a series of dramatic, often violent, clashes. One of the first took place in Little Rock, Arkansas, an unlikely setting for racial confrontation. The governor, Orville Faubus, had been a moderate. Desegregation was not expected to be difficult. The day before schools opened in 1957, however, the governor made an unexpected television address. He announced that order could

202

not be maintained if the schools were desegregated; then he mobilized the National Guard. The perplexed school board went before the federal district court, which ordered it to follow the desegregation plan. The next day a screaming mob and 250 soldiers greeted 9 terrified black high school students. The troops turned the black teenagers away. After two years of posturing, resolutions, and rhetoric, a governor was using his militia to defy the courts.[46]

As the crisis grew, President Eisenhower stayed aloof. Privately he lamented that *Brown* "had set back progress in the South at least fifteen years." Publicly he repeated, "You can't change men's hearts through legislation and force," infelicitously adding as a comment on Little Rock that white Southerners feared "the mongrelization of the race, as they call it."[47] The President refused black pleas for a national television address on desegregation, a Washington conference to mobilize Southern moderates, or federal intervention to enforce the *Brown* decision. Instead, he met with Faubus, and both made politic statements. The militia was withdrawn. The NAACP and the Justice Department took the case to court. Two weeks later, the courts granted an injunction against Faubus and sent the teenagers back to school.

The following day, the national media and what the *New York Times* called "a mob of belligerent, shrieking hysterical demonstrators" were on hand. Members of the crowd had come from communities "two hundred miles distant"; agents of the governor were widely reported to be stirring them up. The adults faced their enemy: "two, three, a half dozen scrubbed, starched, scared, and incredibly brave colored children." The hysteria grew as the students entered the school. White parents called their own children out of Central High, "away from the niggers." By noon, the mayor had sneaked the black students out a side door.[48]

The direct challenge to federal authority led Eisenhower to respond. He dispatched a thousand paratroopers to Little Rock and placed the local militia in federal service, action he had previously rejected as "unimaginable." As Eisenhower explained on national television,

Our personal opinions about the [*Brown*] decision have no bearing on the matter of enforcement; the responsibility and authority of the Supreme Court to interpret the Constitution are clear. . . . It [is] necessary for the Executive Branch of the Federal Government to use its powers and authority to uphold Federal Courts.

Having defined his action entirely in terms of institutional maintenance, Eisenhower explained the "tremendous disservice that has been done in Arkansas."

At a time when we face grave situations abroad because of the hatred that Communism bears toward a system of government based on human rights, it would be difficult to exaggerate the harm that is being done to the prestige, and influence . . . of our nation. . . .

Our enemies are gloating over this incident, and using it everywhere to misrepresent our whole nation.[49]

The Little Rock incident was a conflict within the American state. The issue at stake was the authority of competing public institutions as much as civil rights for black Americans. A governor created the event; he stirred up local mobs to keep it going. He was opposed by federal courts and the Justice Department. Eisenhower resisted expanding the scope of political conflict—refusing to mobilize moderate sentiment as liberals urged him to do. When he finally acted, it was—by his own account—in order to preserve the authority of his office from the dual challenge of states' rights and communist propaganda.

Though federal troops enforced the court order at Central High, the larger conflict within American federalism continued. In Arkansas, Faubus won the role of a local hero. He would be returned to office for an unprecedented third term by a record-breaking count. The following year, he sidestepped the courts by shutting down the Little Rock public schools. Other school systems followed Arkansas's lead. Three cities in Virginia closed their schools to avoid integration; white children were shifted to segregated private schools at public expense.[50]

While public officials fought to maintain personal and institutional power, black Americans themselves began to mobilize. They put aside

Booker T. Washington's "patience" and "good conduct" and took up Du Bois's politics of confrontation. Ironically, the transformation began in Montgomery, Alabama, "the cradle of the confederacy."

Desegregation and the Movement

In December 1955, a forty-three-year-old seamstress riding home from work, sat in the first row of the black section of the bus. When the front filled with whites, their section was extended backward in the segregationist fashion. This time, Rosa Parks demurred. "Somewhere in the universe," the black nationalist Eldridge Cleaver would later muse, "a gear in the machinery had shifted."[51] Parks was quietly arrested. Bail was posted by the local president of the NAACP, a protegé of A. Phillip Randolph; it was time, they decided, to return to the tactics of his mentor.

About 65 percent of Montgomery's bus passengers were black. They hastily organized a boycott and placed a twenty-six-year-old minister in charge. That night Martin Luther King, Jr., electrified the thousand supporters who overflowed the Holt Street Baptist church: "Let no man pull you so low," he urged, "as to make you hate him."[52] The politics of confrontation began with a quotation from Booker T. Washington.

The strike spread swiftly. Four days later, as Parks received her ten-dollar fine, 90 percent of Montgomery's black bus riders had joined the boycott. An elaborate car pool provided transportation. Downtown merchants claimed to lose a million dollars in the first two months. The bus company raised its rates and reduced its routes. At first, the strikers asked only to keep their seats in the back. However, when city officials refused concessions, the strikers extended their demands—open seating, the hiring of black drivers—and sued.

As the strike wore on, derision turned to apprehension within a white establishment long accustomed to the black policies of deference and good conduct. The mayor and his commissioners ostentatiously joined the supremacist White Citizens Council. He warned his white constituents that the blacks were "after the destruction of our social fabric."[53] King was arrested for speeding. A bomb shattered the front of his house. The strike leaders were arrested for violating an obscure statute forbidding the hindrance of business. (King was convicted and got the choice of a $1,000 fine or 385 days in jail.) The state legislature tossed in, outlawing the NAACP and fining it $100,000. City officials indicted the strikers for operating their car pool "business" without a license. As King made his way back to court, news broke that the Supreme Court had ruled in favor of the strikers.[54] After 381 days, the boycotters had won.[55]

The *Brown* decision set a new framework within which black Americans could pursue their citizenship rights. Southern officials resisted the decision and struggled to preserve the racial status quo. In Montgomery, black Southerners took advantage of the shifting legal bias and began to mobilize a mass movement. The *Brown* decision may have been as significant for the transformation of black politics as it was for the concrete entitlements it formally conferred on black people (precisely the effect of the NRA on labor).

Officials in Washington responded cautiously to Little Rock and Montgomery. The Supreme Court continued to strike down segregation—in schools, parks, theaters, beaches, and golf courses.[56] Neither the Eisenhower administration nor Congress moved to assure the rights that the Court had asserted. Jim Crow strictures remained throughout the South; the civil rights movement had not touched the North. The government's role in ending segregation remained up for political grabs.

As the 1958 elections approached, both parties groped for an expedient racial policy. The Democratic coalition was shaky: Eisenhower had carried four states in the increasingly less solid South in 1952, five in 1956. Many blacks—including the Democratic congressman from New York, Adam Clayton Powell—had gone Republican; they were angered by both the thumping segregationism of Southern Democrats and the timidity with which Northern Democrats responded. In 1958, the Democratic strategy was to avoid offending anyone. Democrats in Congress collaborated with the Eisenhower administration to produce predictably weak civil rights legislation in good time for the midterm campaigns. The bill they produced dodged the tumult over desegregation and sponsored a moderate affirmation of suffrage. The legislation was further weakened in the Senate. The sanctions in the bill—empowering the attorney general to seek injunctions on behalf of individuals whose constitutional rights had been violated—were struck. What remained was largely symbolic. "A modest step," judged one legislator. "A sham," suggested another.[57] Neither Congress nor the administration were ready to follow the courts and protect constitutional rights ranging from suffrage to school integration. Firmer public action awaited fuller political mobilization.

In early 1960, after a brief lull marked by scattered boycotts and protests, the mobilization of Southern black citizens began to grow. The pace of peaceful confrontation would accelerate for four years before changing character.

In February 1960, four black college students sat down at a Woolworth's counter in Greensboro, North Carolina. Naturally, they were not served—but they returned, day after day. The tactic caught the imagination of people across the South. The sitdowns spread, despite the white supremacists who stood behind the protestors and jeered or held lighters to the women's hair. Within a year, some 70,000 people, black and white, had participated; almost 4,000 were jailed in six months.[58] Workers had spontaneously seized on the sitdown during their legitimation conflict in the 1930s; the sit-in was the civil rights equivalent, dreamed up by four freshmen who took the national organizations—Congress of Racial Equality, NAACP—by surprise. The sit-ins became a broad participatory protest campaign marked by spontaneous local action action throughout the South.

Slowly—the original demonstration in Greensboro lasted six months—lunch counters began to desegregate. In over a hundred communities, at least one eating place yielded in a year.[59] From lunch counters, the sit-ins spread to movie theaters, parks, pools, art galleries, libraries, churches, courtrooms. In 1961, civil rights activists hit upon another tactic—"freedom rides." (Unlike the sit-ins, the freedom rides were a strategy designed by the leadership, specifically James Farmer at CORE.) Blacks and whites rode through the South to test the segregation of transportation facilities. Riders were beaten in Birmingham, Alabama; a bus burned (with the apparent sympathy of the local police) in Anniston; a representative of the attorney general was knocked unconscious in Montgomery, where a thousand people armed with pipes and clubs attacked the freedom riders.[60]

Throughout, Martin Luther King continued to articulate the movement's leitmotiv: "We will soon wear you down by our capacity to suffer, and in winning our freedom we will so appeal to your heart and conscience that we will win you in the process."[61] King was mistaken. While overt segregation receded in the border states and the occasional lunch counter integrated, the deep South remained violent and implacable. The direct action stirred an increasingly violent resistance, marked by a series of highly publicized confrontations.

In 1962, James Meredith, an eleven-year Air Force veteran, won a court order permitting him to enter the University of Mississippi. (Again, the NAACP handled the litigation.) The governor, Ross Barnett, blocked the door. The saga of Central High was replayed at Ol' Miss. University officials were cited for contempt and relented. Barnett remained adamant. The governor brandished all the segregationist symbols: he railed against the "evil and illegal forces of tyranny." He announced that the Mississippi courts were "as high as any other court and a lot more capable." He invoked interposition. The students sang "glory, glory segregation." Having whipped up white resistance, Barnett found it difficult to retreat in the face of federal intervention. At the last moment, he tried to concoct wild deals with the attorney general: Meredith could register, for instance, if the state guard were confronted by a larger federal army (with its guns drawn) and forced to surrender.[62]

It was too late. The white supremacists were inflamed. Major General Edwin Walker, who had commanded the federal troops at Little Rock, now retired and penitent, exhorted the mob: "Rally to the cause of freedom. . . . Bring your flags, your tents, and your skillets."[63] When federal marshals arrived to execute the court order, they found thousands ready to engage them. A battle raged all day on the campus at Oxford, Mississippi. Two were killed, 375 hurt (166 of the injured were marshals, 29 by gunshots). Meredith matriculated to the racist jibes of classmates ("Was it worth two lives, nigger?"). Three hundred federal troops remained till he graduated, two years later.[64]

Throughout the South, the racist reaction grew with the civil rights movement. When black students sought to enter the University of Alabama in May 1963, the entire drama was replayed. Governor George Wallace echoed Barnett's imposturous rhetoric of aggrieved democracy: "I draw the line in the dust and toss the gauntlet before the feet of tyranny and I say, segregation today, segregation tomorrow, segregation forever."[65]

As Southern political leaders resisted a surging civil rights movement, the federal government continued its struggle to define a racial policy. Congress remained divided. A civil rights bill introduced in 1959 provoked a long Southern filibuster; its toughest sections were struck. The weak bill that finally emerged established criminal penalties for throwing bombs and ineffective protections for black voters. In 1962, liberals tried again, introducing a constitutional amendment designed to secure voting rights. Once again, a long filibuster gutted the measure. The Twenty-fourth Amendment outlaws the poll tax, a marginally significant device used in only five states; it makes no mention of literacy tests, then still the linchpin of disenfranchisement.

A new Democratic administration appeared to signal change in the executive branch. John F. Kennedy had stumped hard for the black vote and got 70 percent of it—an increase large enough to be credited for his victory.

Theodore White commented,

The most precise result of response to [campaign] strategy lay . . . in the Negro vote. Almost all dissections agree that seven out of ten Negroes voted for Kennedy for president. . . . It is difficult to see how Illinois, New Jersey, Michigan, South Carolina, or Delaware (with 74 electoral votes) could have been won had the Republican Democratic split of the Negro wards and precincts remained as it was, unchanged from the Eisenhower charm of 1956.[66]

And as the Students for a Democratic Society put it in their Port Huron Statement, "President Kennedy leaped ahead of the Eisenhower record when he made his second reference to the racial problem."[67]

Through most of his administration, however, Kennedy sacrificed civil rights to his fragile coalition with the Southern Democrats. He repeatedly refused to submit legislation; even trying, he argued, would wreck his entire legislative agenda. Instead, he asked congressional allies to put aside civil rights and work for the Democrats' tax cut.[68] Kennedy insisted that executive action would be more effective than legislation; but he put off reforms even on matters under his control. Federal policies ranging from the administration of veterans' benefits to federally secured mortgages retained their segregationist bias. For more than two years, the administration resisted the executive action—"the stroke of the pen," as it was widely called—that would end housing discrimination sponsored by the federal government itself. The President was "cool" on mass protesting and, like Eisenhower, reluctant to intervene.

When the administration acted, it was in response to the protesters. The freedom riders galvanized the Interstate Commerce Commission into forbidding segregation in bus terminals. The highly publicized battle in Oxford over James Meredith's enrollment prompted the long-awaited housing order. Even so, the Kennedy administration often failed to enforce the ruling. And, at the same time, segregationists in Albany, Georgia, broke a year-long civil disobedience campaign. The white establishment refused to conform to the law but, by maintaining calm, managed to avert federal reaction on behalf of black people demanding legal rights (such as voting or desegregated lunch counters).[69]

The stalemate of national policy was finally broken after the Birmingham campaign in the spring and summer of 1963. The city, nicknamed "the American Johannesburg" and "Bombingham," was fiercely segregationist. Its baseball club folded rather than play integrated teams; its parks, playgrounds, and golf courses were closed when a court ordered them integrated. Eighteen racial bombings and scores of Ku Klux Klan cross burnings had been reported in the preceding five years.[70] The police commissioner, Bull Connor, was a perfect foil for the movement, a jowly unrepentant white supremacist who had just lost a run at the mayoralty. In early April, a small group of marchers, many of them children, were arrested. The following day, police broke up a larger demonstration. Throughout the month, demonstrations grew, the police acted with less restraint, the media attention intensified. Martin Luther King led the defiance on Easter Sunday with a kneel-in—the tactic for protesting segregated churches. King was arrested, for the thirteenth time, and jailed for five days (which he spent writing his classic "Letter from Birmingham City Jail").[71]

By the beginning of May, Birmingham was the focus of national attention. On 2 May, five hundred blacks, many of them young, were arrested. White bystanders threw bricks. The police, trapping the freedom marchers in a park, played firehoses and released dogs. The media vividly portrayed the state's violence: television captured the force of the firehoses stripping the bark off palm trees; newspapers around the world ran the photo of a police dog leaping at a terrified marcher.

The President reported that it made him "sick," but there was nothing he could "constitutionally do."[72] Instead, Kennedy prodded industrial leaders to pressure their Birmingham counterparts. A desegregation agreement was hashed out through these private channels and the U.S. attorney general's office. The demonstrations would be suspended in exchange for concessions from the city. Even before it was publicized, the compromise was brushed aside by Governor Wallace, who announced he would "not be a party to any compromise on the issue of segregation."[73]

The next night, after a Ku Klux Klan rally, explosions ripped both the house of King's younger brother and the black headquarters at the Gaston Motel. Black people poured into the streets and began to riot. The younger King sought to calm them, responding to the bombing with "forgive them for they know not what they do." The mayor took a less tolerant view: "I hope that every drop of blood that's spilled he [the attorney general, Robert Kennedy] tastes in his throat."[74]

Birmingham appeared to be one more demonstration combining the usual elements of the 1960s civil rights struggle: large-scale peaceful demonstrations for basic citizenship rights which had already been affirmed by the courts; a violent segregationist reaction stirred up by local leaders clinging to political power; a President who felt there was nothing he could "constitutionally do." However, the violence, and publicity of this episode had three consequences that helped restructure the politics of black entitlement in the South.

First, Birmingham triggered a massive reaction that brought the Southern civil rights movement to its high point. Protests spread across the region. The Justice Department counted 758 separate demonstrations—and over 14,000 arrests—in the ten weeks that followed Birmingham; there were more than 1,400 in three months.[75] From Philadelphia to Florida, black citizens joined marches, boycotts, demonstrations, prayer-ins, kneel-ins, sit-ins, and other forms of peaceful civil disobedience. The widespread protests capped a decade of black struggle within what Kennedy termed the "highest traditions of American democracy."[76]

Second, the Kennedy administration abandoned its politically ineffective effort to maintain the old coalition, cast off the Southern Democrats, and allied itself with the civil rights movement. In June, Kennedy withdrew a weak proposal he had submitted to Congress the previous February and replaced it with a strong bill. As Arthur Schlesinger put it, Kennedy "did not call for change in advance of the movement. . . . Birmingham and the Negroes had given him the nation's ear."[77] Kennedy announced the new alliance in a blunt and passionate speech. Citing the events in Birmingham, he addressed the "moral issue . . . as old as the scriptures and as clear as the American Constitution."[78]

Finally, as the nonviolent movement reached its high point in the South, "frustration and discord" began to spread north. As it did so, the black political constituency would shift its style and tactics yet again. In Montgomery, the tradition of conciliation and good behavior had been transformed into direct challenge and nonviolent protest. As the President finally endorsed the change, noting its roots in the American democratic past, the next phase of the protests were beginning. After Birmingham, the third, radical, tradition of black politics would manifest itself with increasing regularity.

By the summer of 1963, more people were protesting; the President had declared himself their ally. However, relatively little else had changed. A decade after the *Brown* decision, the constitutional checks and balances invoked by the Southern Manifesto continued to bedevil the search for black entitlement. In the old Confederate states, a tiny handful of black children—one sixth of 1 percent—were in schools with white children. Over two thousand school districts were still entirely segregated. While lunch counters may have started to serve black customers, the vote—"the central front," King called it—was widely denied.[79] For all the activity of the preceding ten years, black registration in Mississippi was 6.6 percent; Alabama, 18.7 percent; Virginia, 24.8 percent. No southern state had more than half its black voters registered; in contrast, over 60 percent of the white voters were registered in every southern state.[80] Even Kennedy's new civil rights bill, which promised real advances, faced the same Southern filibuster that had wrecked every previous civil rights effort.

The New Racial Crisis

In order to help secure the civil rights bill, black leaders organized a March on Washington for Jobs and Freedom. The different reactions—liberal, reactionary, radical—dramatized the shifting politics of black entitlement.

From the liberal perspective, it was a stirring interracial triumph that marked the new alliance between the Kennedy administration and black Americans. Once again, the civil rights movement initiated the action. A. Phillip Randolph—who had pressed Roosevelt with a similar idea—now proposed the march to a leery Kennedy. Once again, a nervous President tried to dissuade Randolph. What if Congress were offended? What if the demonstration turned violent? What if the organizers could not deliver the 100,000 marchers they predicted? With great dignity—Schlesinger, then a presidential adviser, called it the best meeting he attended in his years at the White House—the civil rights leaders are said to have persuaded the President.[81]

On 28 August 1963, over 250,000 people, black and white, marched on Washington; the *New York Times* called it "the greatest assembly for the redress of a grievance that the capital has ever seen." Liberals viewed the demonstration as a rally of "deep fervor and quiet dignity," perhaps the movement's final moment of unabashed hope. The marchers gathered before the great statue of Lincoln; they linked arms, sang spirituals, and dreamed the eloquent, moving dreams of Martin Luther King. It was, in Russell Baker's view, "a national high watermark" in "sweetness, patience, and mass-decency."[82]

The Right responded differently. Southern segregationists denounced Kennedy's attempt "to whitewash the question of communist involvement in these Negro demonstrations." The Republican press carped throughout the summer: "Misguided pressure . . . capped by climactic idiocy" (*Washington Star*), "The March Should Be Stopped" (*New York Herald Tribune*), there could be "catastrophic outbreaks of violence, bloodshed, and property damage" (Agnes Meyer, *Newsweek*'s owner).

Nor did the event itself convert the conservative skeptics. "All this probably hasn't changed any votes on the Civil Rights Bill," conceded Senator Hubert Humphrey of Minnesota on the day of the demonstration; Senator John Stennis of Mississippi disagreed, predicting it was "going to help defeat" the measure.[83]

What is more, legal maneuvers and racial demagoguery were increasingly giving way to violence in the deep South. For example, James Farmer had missed the march. He was in Plaquemine, Louisiana, where state troopers on horseback were using cattle prods and clubs to rout black demonstrators; as Farmer recounted the event, he had been forced to hide while state troopers screamed, "Come on out, Farmer. . . . When we catch that goddam nigger Farmer we're going to kill him."[84] Eighteen days after the Washington demonstration, a bomb exploded in a Birmingham Sunday school, killing four black girls (as they changed out of choir robes, it was plaintively reported). By one count, it was the fifty-first racial bombing in Birmingham without a conviction.[85] As black mobs protested, police killed a black teenager, and white youths shot a thirteen-year-old riding a bicycle. A year later, a voter-registration drive (known as the Mississippi Summer Project) in Mississippi provoked eighty beatings, at least six murders, thirty bombings, thirty-five church burnings, and one thousand arrests.[86]

The Southern reaction in the 1950s and 1960s reversed the post-Reconstruction disenfranchisement process. This time, it began with legal machinations, progressed to the manipulation of racist and xenophobic sentiment, and ended in open violence. Once again, the first proved most effective; violence tended to mobilize the political bystanders against the white supremacists. Where the Southern political establishment discriminated quietly, it usually avoided a federal response. The increasingly violent alliance between local public officials and racial extremists helped tip the political balance in Washington. By 1963, the President had joined the courts in pressing desegregation; Congress would do so in the following year.*

---

*In his civil rights address of 11 June 1963, Kennedy laid out the problems facing black Americans in blunt detail: "The Negro baby born in America today has about . . . one seventh as much chance of earning $10,000 a year, a life expectancy which is seven years shorter, and the prospects of earning only half as much . . . as a white baby born . . . on the same day."[87]

A third reaction to the March on Washington came from the black Left. King's eloquent nonviolence was attacked as irrelevant and naïve: "I don't see any American dream," responded Malcolm X, "I see an American nightmare."[88]

While Schlesinger was impressed by the "dignity" of the meeting between Randolph and Kennedy, the Left saw an alliance between frightened white politicians and increasingly irrelevant black leaders. As Randolph himself had told Kennedy, "If the civil rights leadership were to call the Negroes off the streets, it is problematic whether they would come."[89] Malcolm X crystallized the emerging new perspective:

That was black revolution . . . out there in the street. It scared the white power structure in Washington to death. When they found out that this Black steamroller was going to come down on the capital, they called in these national Negro leaders . . . and told them "Call it off." And old Tom said, "Boss I can't stop it because I didn't start it." . . .

But the White man . . . became the march. They took it over. . . . And as they took it over, it lost its militancy. It ceased to be angry, it ceased to be hot, it ceased to be uncompromising. Why it even ceased to be a march. It became a picnic, a circus. It was a sellout, a takeover. . . . They controlled it so tight, they told those Negroes what time to hit town, how to come, where to stop, what signs to carry, what song to sing, what speech they could make, what speech they couldn't make and then told them to get out of town by sundown.[90]

The Left's analysis followed Malcolm X's. The march was a grave blunder; the visible alliance with a political establishment that had long temporized over black rights stripped the movement of independence. In this view, the mainstream black leaders appeared frightened of their own mobilized constituents. Uncertain of their own followers, they permitted themselves to be co-opted by the liberal white élite. "For the first time since Montgomery" wrote Louis Lomax in 1962, "criticism of Dr. King is now appearing in print."[91] The march, commented a more recent observer, "probably did more to divide and retard the

Black Freedom Movement than any other single mobilization between 1960 and 1966."[92]

In some ways, the progress of the black Left echoed the evolution of labor sentiment in the early 1930s: A broadly participatory movement invoked democratic ideals and mobilized a populist challenge to the political establishment. Like the AFL, the black leaders chose stability over rebellion; both groups allied with ambivalent liberal officials in Washington (recall how labor officials tried to cool the auto strike in Flint by talking up FDR). In both cases, the moderate strategy prompted challenges to the movement's leadership (the CIO in the 1930s, black nationalists in the 1960s). Of course, the analogy is a partial one: black nationalists like Malcolm X and Stokely Carmichael articulated an entirely different version (of both politics and America) than the one the labor rebels like John Lewis and David Dubinsky had pursued in the 1930s.

As the struggle for civil rights began to spread from the South, the third tradition of black politics—hostile, often violent, rejection of the white establishment—began to replace the liberal tactics of peaceful protest. A decade of nonviolence had scarcely raised the issues that confronted Northern black people. They already voted and sat in the front of the bus. Marches and prayer-ins might dramatize disenfranchisement or desegregate a church. What could they do about inferior education, substandard housing, the high infant mortality rate, or "the prospect of earning half as much" as whites? These problems had obscure causes and unclear solutions; opponents of political and economic redistribution were already mobilized. Ten years of demonstrations had affected little in the North except what King had termed the Zeitgeist:* black people everywhere could measure the nonprogress of nonviolence against the swaggering Southern resistance. By

---

*Originally a comment about Rosa Parks and why she wouldn't move ("She had been tracked down by the Zeitgeist"). Later, in his "Letter from Birmingham City Jail," King refers to the entire race: "Consciously or unconsciously, he has been caught up by the Zeitgeist and with his black brothers of Africa . . . the United States Negro is moving with a sense of great urgency towards the promised land of racial justice." Radicals later returned to the learned phrase to suggest that King—and by inference, his strategy of nonviolence—was overly intellectual and irrelevant.[93]

mid-1963, peaceful marches had begun to give way to more angry demonstrations.

Malcolm X resurrected Garvey's separatism and found a similar following in the northern ghettos: "We all have a common enemy—blue eyes, blond hair, pale skin." Stokely Carmichael would soon articulate the new motif: "This is the twenty-seventh time I've been arrested, and I'm not going to jail no more." Books like *The Fire Next Time*, *Black Power, Negroes with Guns*, and *Look Out, Whitey! Black Power's Gon' Get Your Mama!* distilled the new philosophy. Groups like the Black Panthers and the (post-1964) Student Non-Violent Coordinating Committee set out to mobilize it.[94]

The ideal, eventually framed as "black power," was as difficult and ambiguous as the oppressions it confronted. Stripped of the obvious goals and plain methods of the Southern campaign, ends and means grew murky. In the spring of 1964, demonstrators blocked New York City's Triborough Bridge and littered it with rubbish. In Cleveland, protesters chained themselves to a segregated construction site till one minister was crushed by a bulldozer. In San Francisco, four hundred were arrested in a night of violence that followed "the siege" of the Sheraton Hotel. Protesters drowned out President Lyndon Johnson as he opened the New York World's Fair. White liberals who had applauded the black effort in Montgomery and Birmingham now grew frightened and hostile. (A poll of white New Yorkers discovered that Martin Luther King and Malcolm X were the two most highly recognized national black leaders: 85 percent approved of King; 2 percent of Malcolm.)[95] Then, in the summer of 1964, the urban riots began: Harlem, Bedford Stuyvesant, Rochester, Jersey City, Paterson, Elizabeth, Chicago, Philadelphia.

A violent new racial crisis confronted the Johnson administration. The state had strained the limits of its authority merely to extend suffrage. How would it address the more perplexing difficulties faced by black Americans? The American state was caught, once again, between an imperative for action and political institutions biased against undertaking it.

THE WAR ON POVERTY AS DEMOCRATIC WISH

Eleven years after *Brown* v. *Board of Education*, the Senate broke an eighty-seven-day filibuster and ratified the Civil Rights Act. In 1965, it would pass a second measure, the Voting Rights Act. By the time the legislation was secured, however, it no longer met the political need. The Johnson administration faced an increasingly violent racial crisis (as well as an election). It responded with a variation of the democratic wish.

Race Becomes Class

The racial crisis of the mid-1960s perplexed the political establishment partially because it overran the normal boundaries of American political discourse. The movement in the South had clung to the democratic traditions, brandishing familiar aspirations and rhetoric. In contrast, the new militant leaders scorned "the American dream": they were suspicious of the liberal and republican traditions that had guided previous American reform movements. They were not even traditional revolutionaries for they did not claim to act for—indeed, they rejected—the majority of the nation. In short, the racial crisis of the 1960s was marked by a kind of ideological exit from American society: black power operated beyond the usual values, traditions, ideals, and rules.

Daniel Bell articulated the establishment's discomfort. Writing in *Time* magazine—that is, for the middle-class mainstream—Bell virtually pleaded with the black community to transform itself, somehow, into a proper New Deal interest group:

There are two preconditions for successful political bargaining in the American system: one is that the Negro community has to choose its political spokesmen in a responsible way (in the way farm groups have done); the other is that the Negro community has to specify its priorities and demands, so that we know what to bargain about. In short there has to be a consensus about the ends desired—and such a consensus is not simply a list of slogans . . . [or] the single abstraction of "integration" with little heed to plan or method.[96]

The Kennedy and Johnson administrations negotiated the black threat to New Deal politics (and American liberalism) in a remarkable fashion: they converted the racial crisis into a class issue. Complaints about racial oppression were answered with programs designed to ameliorate poverty.

The redefinition of the racial issue was not a conscious strategy. In part, it was an administrative reflex known as the "garbage-can model" of organizational choice: rather than puzzling out solutions to the new problem, policy makers simply applied existing solutions to old ones. Poverty had already been "discovered," largely as a white problem. Michael Harrington's widely publicized 1962 book, *The Other America*, depicted poverty in "the valleys of Pennsylvania" as much as "the segregation of the slum."[97] Kennedy grew interested in the issue after campaigning in West Virginia. The stereotypical juvenile delinquent was a member of a white youth gang. Accordingly, most of the social programs of the early Kennedy administration—manpower training, Appalachian development, juvenile delinquency—were targeted to white populations.[98] As the urban riots pressed the complex problems of Northern black people onto the political agenda, existing poverty policies were hastily converted into racial ones. The issue—even the meaning of the word—was reconstructed: "While we see the poverty problem today as almost coal black, it was [earlier] at most light gray."[99] For the next decade, *poverty* became an ironic political euphemism for *black*. In public documents and political rhetoric, *poor* meant *black*, regardless of income.*

Administrative reflexes aside, the redefinition of the racial problem

---

*John Strange, after an exhaustive review of the literature, makes a similar comment: "Though the official documents referred to poor, poor was often interpreted to mean black or Puerto Rican or Indian without regard to income."[100]

   Although my interpretation of the War on Poverty focuses on black Americans, a similar argument can be made about other minority groups, particularly Spanish-speaking Americans.[101]

was politically useful. Class politics was far less trouble. In 1963, Kennedy had wondered out loud why the American poor were not "angrier and more politically demanding."[102] Moreover, poverty programs skirted the American racial cleavage. They did not mobilize Southerners protecting segregation, urban élites defending their own power relations, or militant black leaders demanding "the abstraction of integration." Poverty programs could be passed without marches or filibusters.

Substituting poverty for race restored the traditional framework of American political discourse. For conservatives, debating the dole reintroduced such trusty themes as Lockean individualism, merit, and hard work. Senator Barry Goldwater of Arizona demonstrated how political capital could safely be made in this arena by bashing welfare chiselers when Newburgh, New York, illegally restricted its rolls.[103] For the liberal Left, poverty introduced the familiar New Deal matter of needs that could be measured and met.

In contrast to the problems of race, the related problem of poverty seemed, in the mid-1960s, to have clear answers solidly rooted in the classic patterns of American political reform. The social welfare establishment—respectable professionals with university degrees—had been analyzing the issue for a decade. Three theories—each analyzing the difficulty and proposing a solution—were especially influential. All three were associated with prestigious institutions: the Ford Foundation, a presidential commission, Columbia University.

The Return to Community

The Ford Foundation diagnosed the trouble as a failure to coordinate. The fractured American policy apparatus could make progress against poverty by fashioning a more coherent response to it. The Ford solution was to bring together the many institutions, public and private, that served the poor. The watchword was coordination. Ford Foundation analysts had been frustrated by the political stalemate of the Eisenhower era ("Our won't power is growing faster than our will power").[104] Predictably, their definition of the problem did not require a bold new government response so much as the rationalization of existing programs: the strategy could be pursued on the local level by public and private officials who were already in place.

The Ford prescription unwittingly revived an old Progressive ideal. Recall Walter Weyls's warning: "No true efficiency can be maintained, if the system as a whole is ill geared, . . . if there is a lack of coordination among the parts" (see chapter 3). True to Weyl and the Progressives, the Ford Foundation called on professionals, public and private, to take action where the politicians had failed.[105] Ford's most influential public-sector ally was the Bureau of the Budget, itself a product of Progressive efforts to impose coordination. The ideal had resurfaced briefly during the framing of the National Industrial Recovery Act, when public-private coordination was to replace "wolfish" competition and restore prosperity. However, by the 1960s, the failure of past efforts to force coherence on American policy were long forgotten. The old reform seemed fresh and timely.

A second approach was sponsored by the Kennedy administration's President's Commission on Juvenile Delinquency and Street Crime (PCJD). Whereas the Ford Foundation reflected the liberal frustration of the Eisenhower era, the President's Commission exuded the faith in rationalization and innovation that fairly permeated the Kennedy Camelot. The President's Commission also promoted coordinated planning, but gave it a different conceptual twist. Rather than emphasize coordination, it "almost obsessively" insisted on rationality and technique.[106] The commission's whiz kids were entirely committed to their comprehensive, intellectually coherent plans. They were willing to delay—some thought, abjure—action in their search for technical precision.

The President's Commission's faith was also steeped in American reforming history. Scientific planning was, of course, the mainstay of Progressive administration. The ideal also briefly penetrated the NRA debates with the call for vigorous state-directed national planning. Scientific planning was even less suited to the problems of race and poverty than it had been to Pinchot's land policy. Once again, the emphasis on pristine technical plans would be run over by political activists pursuing their interests.

The Ford and PCJD solutions focused entirely on the organization of social services. The causes of poverty, the desires of poor (never mind black) populations, or broad expansions of social services were all subordinated to the rationalization of the existing welfare establishment.

Two sociologists from Columbia University, Richard Cloward and Lloyd Ohlin, promoted a third, less élite-centered argument: Troubles like juvenile delinquency were communal rather than personal. They were rational individual responses to the community "illness" of oppressive poverty. Programs that did not focus on the entire community—the individualistic emphasis of traditional relief, for instance—would inevitably fail.[107]

The term *community* was, as we shall see, rich with reassuring symbolic connotations. The layers of meaning often obscured the details of Cloward and Ohlin's solution: reform would be designed to help poor and black communities shake off their powerlessness; it would rouse them to assert their own interests. A small group of young administrators, the self-styled bureaucratic guerrillas, promoted community participation. (The guerrillas lived off the administrative countryside, "hitting" the foundations and big departments, then disappearing into the bureaucracy.) Clearly, their ideal was redolent with implicit threat to established power relations and full of promise to the black communities that were struggling for a way to break into them.[108]

The solutions did not fit together. Élite coordination and technical planning were in tension with community participation—precisely the contradiction within Progressive reforms. Moreover, they were oblique approaches to the dilemmas of poverty and race. More direct approaches—massive job creation, a crash program designed to end illiteracy, a substantial redistribution of income—were either rejected or not proposed. These would be budget busters; even at the start of the Great Society, Johnson was not willing to undertake—and by most accounts could not have secured—such direct solutions.[109]

The three less costly ideals—coordination, technical planning, and community—were bundled into one program, the administration's response to the race crisis. The *New York Times* caught the spirit of both the era and the enterprise by labeling it an "anti-riot" bill.[110] The President, seeking something more grandiloquent, termed it the "War on Poverty." In any case, it appeared to be more modest than the rhetoric that surrounded it—a collection of unremarkable old programs coupled to a national network of vaguely defined new agencies with large aspirations and small budgets.

At the fringe of the War on Poverty was a pork barrel of small programs with little focus beyond the ambiguous idea of "opportunity." A Youth Employment program for dropouts, already before the House, was renamed the Job Corps and included. A Work-Study program to assist needy college students was borrowed from a pending education bill. Funding for demonstrations that trained and employed welfare recipients had been authorized since 1962. A National Service Corps, modeled on the Peace Corps, had already passed through the Senate; it was renamed VISTA (Volunteers in Service to America) and drafted into the "war." A small loan program for rural businessmen and marginal farmers was added at the behest of the Department of Agriculture. A Work Experience Program for young people was placed within the Department of Labor.

The Office of Economic Opportunity was established to administer the war. The agency was placed directly in the executive office of the President, independent of established bureaucracies. Lyndon Johnson articulated the organizational logic: "This thing can't survive less'n everybody knows when they're hitting it, they're hitting me."[111] Presumably, too, independence would facilitate planning and coordination among existing programs.

The smattering of minor programs promptly exposed the myth of coordination. Existing agencies scrambled for a share; the new programs' director, Sargent Shriver, was denounced for a czar and spent his time furiously negotiating with other federal officials, all fretfully defending their bureaucratic turf. In the end, the Office of Education (in the Department of Health, Education and Welfare), the Welfare Administration, the Department of Labor, the Department of Agriculture, and even the Small Business Administration all won a piece of the War on Poverty.[112] In all, $447.5 million out of a $962.5-million total was controlled by other departments. (The turf grabbing did not end with the legislation: by 1968, eight programs had been spun off, including the Job Corps and Head Start.)[113]

At the heart of the program were the Community Action Agencies. These local agencies were to assemble the leaders of each community and chart the assault on poverty. Plans would be written, existing programs coordinated, new initiatives designed and launched. None of the then-current antipoverty notions—coordination, planning, community—was overlooked; but there was scarcely a hint about priorities. The details were left obscure, repeated the program sponsors, so that local communities could gauge their own antipoverty needs. In the general spirit of community, the program's beneficiaries were expected to participate to the "maximum feasible" extent. The CAAs would be new, organized specifically to direct a war on poverty. Their relationship to existing public and private agencies—to the local political establishment—was also left to the communities (except for the vague exhortations to "coordinate"). The local agencies would be approved ("designated") and overseen by the Office of Economic Opportunity in Washington.

Lyndon Johnson launched the War on Poverty in 1964: "I propose a program which relies on the traditional American methods of organized local community action." A program administrator was slightly more detailed, brushing past the familiar political pitfalls before trying his own uncertain definition: "The program is not job creation, . . . not economic development, . . . not social work, . . . not the dole." Instead, it "is designed to assist communities to mobilize their own local resources to improve the capacities of the poor in their midst." As if they were reciting a too-familiar litany, officials propounded the obscure rationale of the program by repeating the reassuring term *community*. Nobody involved in the War on Poverty missed an opportunity to celebrate American communities. All the ambiguities and contradictions of the effort were obscured by the belief that local communities would define the program for themselves. Consensus was universally assumed.[114]*

But what did it mean? What exactly did it mean to "rely on the time tested American methods of community"? Or, to "assist communities to mobilize their own resources to improve the capacities of the poor"? What indeed, did they mean by "the community"? Or by "maximum feasible participation"?

The answer is simple. They meant very little. Daniel Moynihan would

---

*As one of the architects of the program later put it, no one had anticipated major conflicts, even "in a community as sensitive to the problems of . . . power as Washington."[115]

scoff that the phrase mandating maximum feasible participation was just a rhetorical fillip to the Jeffersonian tradition.[116] He was precisely correct. The images that defined this program were invocations of the idealized American constituency—"the people." The War on Poverty's "community" conjured up the same reassuring vision as Jefferson's "chosen people of God" or Jackson's "common man" or LaFollette's "the people." Like every previous stirring of "the people," this one was grounded in a republican image of local citizens coming together to work out the common good. Once again, community consensus would displace the clash of selfish interests. Citizens rather than politicians—the people rather than the state—would solve the problems of race and poverty.

Faced with a profound crisis and checked at every point by political limits, Johnson pursued the path of least political resistance. Precisely the same spirit had moved the New Dealers to turn the economic crisis back to the people—pledges and rallies and tickertape parades had substituted for definitive state action in the 1930s. The Johnson administration took a distinctly similar course. If the racial crisis was ominous and the state weak, community action—the people—was popular and legitimate.

This traditional political reflex was not available as a direct response to the racial crisis. Unlike the leaders of past American movements, militant black leaders disavowed the American democratic tradition; the realities of black ghettos and race riots made it difficult to imagine communal consensus. However, once the issue had been recast as poverty, the Jeffersonian imagery could safely be applied. Indeed, since writers like Harrington and Ohlin and Cloward had defined poverty as a communal problem, the images seemed particularly apt. A great "war" to vanquish poverty was well suited to the rhetoric and imagery of the American republican tradition. Like many leaders before him, Johnson reconciled the need for action with the many checks in the political apparatus by creating a program that relied on the people coming together in local communities and working out their own problems with minimal government interference (read "coercion"). The Democrats turned the racial crisis into a poverty problem, then sent it back to the local communities.

For good measure, the War on Poverty was brimming with other reformist themes, such as "coordination" and "scientific planning." Like "community," these were devices that promised, somehow, to soothe an angry racial crisis without the trauma of redistributing power.

Critics would soon lash the War on Poverty for its ambiguities and internal contradictions. It was, however, exactly those ambiguities, shrouded by the most revered emblems of American democracy, that made the program possible in the first place. It passed easily, supported by most of the potential critics. Five mayors testified in its favor. Even the Southern Democrats acquiesced (after punishing a whiz kid and protecting their flanks).* The Republicans were hard pressed to oppose a war on poverty directed by the American people—though the Democrats, shortsightedly grabbing a sure bet in an election year, rudely excluded them from the legislation's markup.

Oddly, the analytical question most often asked about the program is not what became of it but how it came to be. Popular interpretations include: Leftist administrators snookered Congress. The power establishment set out to manage the black revolt by co-opting it. Policy élites like those at the Ford Foundation blundered into it after a decade of experimentation. I offer a different answer: the Johnson administration overcame the many checks to action by invoking the powerful myths of the American democratic wish.

Still, even symbols have concrete particulars. The legislation passed because of its images: "community," "participation." The specific program that resulted—the concrete manifestation of the democratic wish—actually facilitated new forms of "community" and "participation." By doing so, the War on Poverty launched the next stage of the democratic political pattern. Black Americans were mobilized and aroused. The new program gave them a focus within the state itself. Rather than struggling for such apparently threatening vagaries as "shared power," "freedom," or—recalling Bell's admonition—"integration," black Americans were offered the opportunity to contend

---

*Adam Yarmolinsky of the Ford Foundation, one of the key framers of the War on Poverty, was slated to be deputy director of the program, under Shriver. The Southerners, however, rudely cut him out as the price for support. The bill of particulars against Yarmolinsky: "abrasive," "intellectual," "leftist," "whiz kid."[117] The Southerners sought protection in a governors' veto, employed mainly by Wallace and Reagan. It was reduced to a merely symbolic power in the following year.[118]

over the terms of their participation in the War on Poverty boards. It was precisely the alternative offered labor by section 7(a)—a contest over participation and representation on para-governmental boards infused with great expectations and little authority. The program itself may have seemed weak, even trivial; the struggle over it would have profound implications. In a sense, it focused the amorphous Northern civil rights movement onto the same issue that had provided the "central front" in the South—political representation.

Battles over Representation

The emphasis on community and coordination neatly fit the Johnson administration's requirements. It promised a program that appeared significant, did not cost much, and did not overtly offend anybody important. At the same time, the program solved a problem for black groups and leaders. Their movement had floundered for a focus in the North. The poverty boards provided it. Community organizers, seizing on the vague promise of participation, roused black citizens to demand their places. To many observers, the loose organization and participatory ethos of the program reflected the style of the civil rights movement from the start. Further, it had no established white constituency mobilized to fight off black insurgency. Many of the barriers to black participation in local politics were removed in this one program.[119]

The participatory promises of the War on Poverty were not immediately apparent. From August 1964 (when the bill was passed) to November (when the first agencies were to be designated), the cities dutifully prepared their programs. Mayors filled the poverty boards with prominent locals. Together they hastily designed new agencies to receive the proffered federal funds (the money was 90 percent federal). When officials in the Office of Economic Opportunity inquired whether the poor had participated, the answer was invariably the same: "Not very much but as much as feasible. We need to move fast." In the early days of the program, it was rarely clear who spoke for black people or how they could be involved. National groups had coalesced around winning civil rights in the South; there was little political organization within the Northern black communities. More important, city officials treated this program like any other. Helping the poor minorities had never meant involving them. One study found that in a sample of twenty cities, not one had actively worked with minorities (or poor people) in designing the local agency.[120]

After several months, the protests began. The Office of Economic Opportunity began to receive critical telegrams and letters. At first, local offices of moderate national organizations—the NAACP, the Urban League—complained that they had not been consulted. The allegations did not shock anybody. Mayors rarely consulted black organizations. Few had paid much attention to the ambiguous call for maximum feasible participation buried in the legislation. When the issue was raised, local political officials shrugged it off. The mayor of Nashville had not included black representatives because they were "unqualified"; Atlanta was proud of its one black representative, Martin Luther King's father.[121]

Moderate complaints were followed by angrier ones. They came from entirely new groups, often organized specifically to claim representation on the Community Action Agencies.[122] As implementation progressed, the poverty boards became the center of the civil rights struggle across the country. Mayors, many of them old pragmatic liberals, suddenly came under fire for ignoring black constituents.

In San Francisco, for example, the program had the conventional liberal credentials. Mayor John Shelley appointed a board of business and labor leaders in September 1964. The program was targeted to poor blacks. Various neighborhood advisory committees were set up. A black stockbroker was appointed executive director. The mayor, of course, expected to oversee the program. To his surprise, a group of young activists, fresh from the civil rights movement, organized (Citizens United Against Poverty) and challenged him. Neighborhood residents, they claimed, should review and approve any poverty proposals submitted to the federal government. The mayor ignored them. The young men escalated their attack. Media coverage grew. Before long, Mayor Shelley was pitted in a jarring conflict over control of the poverty board. The fight soon spread into a broad struggle for political power.[123]

In Newark, Mayor Hugh Adonizzio had a poverty proposal ready before Congress enacted the program. The agency was organized by public officials and civic leaders. The mayor viewed it as an opportunity to dispense federal patronage to Newark's growing black majority. Cyril Tyson, a black man, was named executive director. Tyson upset the mayor's calculations by organizing widespread grass-roots participation. Once involved, the black community demanded more authority over its program. Then, agency members began "speaking out for the black community" on a broad set of issues: they attacked unpopular urban renewal projects, agitated for citizen influence over the Board of Education, criticized city services from street lights to police. From the mayor's perspective, a minor patronage program was getting out of hand.[124]

Around the nation, city governments plunged into conflict with their aroused black constituents over the new agencies. As the mirage of community consensus evaporated, it exposed all the hard questions about the representation of conflicting interests. Who should be represented? How should their representatives be selected? How much authority should they get? The communal idyll had obscured the difficulties of designing institutions resilient enough to frame sharp conflicts; now these difficulties were thrust onto the program.

The mayors' expectations were clear. They sought to control the poverty program. Established city institutions would formulate policy. Representatives of the poor and black communities would be advisers in many places, "sub-professional participants" (read, "beneficiaries of patronage") in some. Your job, Hugh Adonizzio told the first meeting of the Newark Board, "is to act as the eyes and ears of the antipoverty program . . . advising on what is needed. If the [agency] begins to think of itself as a political weight, it will fail."[125] Across the country, Mayor Richard Daley, even less moved by the spirit of shared power, offered patronage in the old Chicago style: "Many depressed citizens are ready for sub-leadership roles. But Chicago believes their energies would be best utilized in salaried sub-professional roles rather than . . . advisory roles . . . that lead to nonproductive protest activities."[126]

Within the rubric of traditional city politics, the mayors could have imposed their preferences on the quiescent black community. The mayors' offices, the city councils, and the school boards were established powers with their own constituents and rules. Suddenly, however, the minority communities were aroused by the promise of a role in the new agencies. The obscure language of the act promised them whatever participation they could muster in the political battles that defined what was "feasible." And, crucially, the final arbiters of the conflict were not the mayors or the local establishment but the Office of Economic Opportunity in Washington.

At first gingerly, then with growing vigor, OEO officials in Washington sided with local groups claiming more participation. An early task force announced that maximum feasible participation meant "at least one representative" from each neighborhood served by the agency.[127] As the bewildered mayors applied for their grants, they were badgered to include black participants. By Spring 1965, the requisite number had expanded to "roughly one third" of the agency's governing board, chosen by "democratic techniques."[128] The guidelines remained vague and negotiable, a lever with which OEO prodded reluctant city officials when black participants pressed their claims. In some places, black leaders began to demand outright control over the local Community Action Agency. In some cities—about twenty—they succeeded, usually with glaring media coverage. Adam Clayton Powell held congressional hearings that further publicized the newly organized local groups. Powell grabbed headlines himself by espousing their cause and roasting local officials in New York, Los Angeles, Chicago, and other cities.[129] In some places where minorities failed to capture the board, they dominated the agency's staff. In many other locations, they took control of the organizations formed by the CAAs—neighborhood councils, Head Start programs, advisory boards.

The conflict for control of the agencies focused on the selection of the board members. Clearly, who they ultimately stood for would be determined by who nominated them and how. The OEO injunction to employ "democratic technique" covered a multitude of possibilities. The fight for power in the CAAs was fought as a conflict over the mechanics of political representation.

At the start, the mayors or their subordinates chose CAA board members. As the conflict warmed, few were able to maintain the prerogative. (Chicago was one of the only places where—after considerable conflict—mayoral selection met the OEO test of a "democratic technique"; the Daley machine unseated two OEO regional officials in its campaign for control.) Numerous alternative mechanisms were hashed out, each with its own political bias.

In some places, minority groups wrested direct control over appointments. In New York, for instance, minority organizations won the selection process. Where more than one group claimed to speak for an area, spirited elections between them aroused intense local interest and participation.

However, neither city hall nor its adversaries were often successful in staking an indisputable claim over the poverty board. Most cities settled on some middle ground. After losing direct control, many mayors found special elections the least threatening alternative. Critics howled with derision as 2.7 percent of the eligible population voted in Philadelphia, 2.4 percent in Boston, 4.2 percent in Cleveland, 0.7 percent in Los Angeles.[130] In reality, the elections reflected a political stalemate. Public officials had lost control over the selection process; by setting up special elections, however, they kept selection out of the hands of black organizations. Individual candidates for the CAA did not have the resources to wage election campaigns, much less mobilize widespread support within the black community.

Once the small turnouts were publicized, OEO forbade the device. A wide number of other selection mechanisms were negotiated, including screening committees, town meetings, and neighborhood corporations. Each mechanism had its own political implications; each placed the agencies either more or less firmly within the control of local black communities.[131]

Federal officials in the Office of Economic Opportunity were the key to the "headlong . . . plunge into grassroots democracy."[132] Local groups who challenged city authorities had powerful allies in Washington. Maximum feasible participation quickly rose out of obscurity and eclipsed the forgettable ideals of planning and coordination.

The Office of Economic Opportunity embraced participation for at least three reasons. First, many officials were personally committed to it. Shriver repeatedly compared the War on Poverty to the Wagner Act, establishing "the principles of representation, full participation and fair bargaining."[133] The metaphor was surely not lost on Jack Conway, the director of the Community Action Program (within OEO), for he had been there the first time, organizing auto workers for the CIO (Conway left thirty years of union organizing to join the War on Poverty). The "guerrillas" were receptive to any tactic that promoted social change.

Furthermore, by embracing the demands for participation, OEO officials attached their program to the most powerful impulse in the nation, the civil rights movement. It gave them a large and vocal constituency. It turned an overpromised, meagerly funded program into one with the potential to promote significant social change. Though events would demonstrate flaws in the strategy, sponsoring "the Northern branch of the civil rights movement" held more promise than compiling even masterful planning documents or overseeing Job Corps programs. In short, sponsoring participation appeared to be in their institutional interest.

Finally, the matter was not entirely in their hands. The civil rights movement was sweeping the nation, mobilizing the black population. The War on Poverty was an obvious focus for its attention. The forerunners to the CAAs—funded by Ford and the President's Commission on Juvenile Delinquency—did not invoke participation or community. Yet they, too, had been attacked for excluding black citizens. Political analysts have made a great deal of the mandate to achieve "maximum feasible participation"; as one widely quoted commentary put it, "because of this single phrase . . . the 1960s will most likely be remembered as the decade of participation." It is more likely the other way round: the phrase is remembered because the 1960s were a decade of participation. Black citizens might well have placed demands for participation on anything that purported to be an "anti-riot" program, regardless of the fine legislative print. And the War on Poverty could not be a credible civil rights effort if it were scorned by the black population.[134]

In sum, "maximum feasible participation," an obscure mandate in a vague statute, thrust the racial issue onto local politics. Rising black groups, still struggling to organize, demanded it. Officials in Washington championed their cause. In a program where *poor* meant "minority," "maximum feasible participation" signified anything that could be won in the local scramble for control. The contest was played out as a dispute over the mechanics of representation within the new agencies.

The sheer fact of the conflict, however, signaled a more profound development—an incipient black mobilization for power in local American politics. The War on Poverty mediated the civil rights movement with the urban political setting by providing a framework in which previously excluded black communities could organize their demands for political inclusion. Focusing black demands on the mechanics of participation and representation gave them legitimacy. Still, beneath conflicts over representation lie disputes about power.

Poverty Warriors Challenge the System

Everywhere the new organizations seemed to jolt the local political establishment. Their vague charge—"to improve the capacity of the poor in their midst"—produced an extraordinary range of activities—often creative, sometimes controversial, at times manifestly radical.

In Syracuse, a black majority captured control and shocked everyone with their pranks. Federal funds for training organizers were used to prepare what the *Wall Street Journal* called "agents provocateurs." A remedial reading test preached "no ends are accomplished without the use of force." When the local NAACP cautioned about materials "geared to rioting," the agency stopped assailing the Republican mayor long enough to denounce the NAACP.[135]

In Newark, staff members used the CAA mimeograph equipment to publicize a protest rally against police brutality. The rally ignited the Newark riots. A national advisory commission later revealed that the agency staff members had vainly tried to calm the violence; nevertheless, they were widely blamed for starting it. Their frankly unapologetic tone reinforced the suspicion.[136]

In New Mexico, War on Poverty activists were outspoken in their support for a radical Spanish American leader, Tijerna. Tijerna "arrested" forest rangers and "attacked" court houses in his efforts to publicize government violations of old Spanish land grants. Agency personnel were widely charged with helping him evade the police.[137]

Everywhere, similar images of radical misbehavior were trumpeted in the press. One agency director suggested that "negroes arm themselves with guns." Another ominously ordered telescopic sights for high-powered rifles (inexpensive microscopes, he said). The largest gang on the South Side of Chicago, the Blackstone Rangers, won a grant. So did the avowedly radical Harlem Dance Troupe. And everywhere CAA mimeograph equipment seemed to promote agitation and protest.[138]

Egregious cases like Syracuse may have been rare exceptions among some thousand local agencies. But there were more than enough angry confrontations to make the exaggerations plausible. Black people challenged white political authorities across the nation. Reports quickly followed one another about incidents in New York, Los Angeles, San Francisco, Newark, Oakland, Mingo County, Durham, and West Point, Mississippi.

Moreover, like new political participants back to the colonial era, the Poverty Warriors were rough and crude. Robert Kennedy's description of one meeting, though it did not involve a Community Action Agency, caught their unschooled political style: "it was all emotion and hysteria. They stood up and orated. They cursed. Some of them wept and walked out of the room. . . . You can't talk with them as you can with Roy Wilkins [NAACP executive director] or Martin Luther King."[139] At times, the hostility seemed indiscriminate, directed at allies as much as enemies. Sargent Shriver was screamed off the podium at one convention. At another, every aspect of the program was mocked except one—"it gave our organizers some bread." (The *New York Times* reported the incident, stodgily explaining that "in leftist slang, bread means money.")[140] Moynihan articulated the distaste felt by established political officials: "They are going to get hold of a lower level of . . . genuine leaders who are—what?—inarticulate? irresponsible? unsuccessful? I am sorry . . . these are not the principles on which Tammany Hall, the International Longshoreman's Association or the New York Yankees recruited indigenous leadership."[141]

Inexperience had more damaging consequences than injudicious attacks and inflated rhetoric. The War on Poverty was beset with allegations of fraud and financial mismanagement. Haphazard bookkeeping and a general indifference to formal rules and regulations exacerbated the problem. Impossible organizational design made matters worse. Agencies struggled to cope with governing boards of more than one hundred members (both Philadelphia and Newark tried); the boards continued to grow till Congress finally set limits in 1967. The participatory tone of the civil rights movement biased the new poverty activists against structure, hierarchy, and exclusion.

However, the backlash against the agencies had little to do with boisterous rhetoric, bad management, or fraud. There is a rich tradition of such peccadillos in American local politics. Moynihan was exactly wrong about both Tammany and the Longshoremen: both provoked precisely the same Tory reaction he himself articulated. Recall, for example, the "Adamsite" fury when the Jacksonians smashed the White House furniture, marched their floaters to the polls, or filled their raucous nominating conventions with "former pugilists" (see chapters 2 and 3). Rather, the high dudgeon provoked by the CAAs came from a more profound menace—the danger that they might succeed. By organizing black populations for politics, the CAAs threatened to upset the political balance in cities around the country.

Consider the Newark agency. It repeatedly violated the norms of polite behavior. But city officials who blamed the CAA for starting the riot were making different calculations. Newark was 52 percent black, 10 percent Spanish-speaking. The political establishment was overwhelmingly white. The Board of Education had two black members (out of nine); so did the city council. And these were the public agencies with the highest percentage of minority members.[142] Suddenly the Community Action Agency boasted a black majority. Worse, its members insisted on holding the rest of the political establishment to account in the name of their black constituents. They fought for black appointments on the school board, police department, and other agencies; they organized local opposition to urban renewal projects, housing conditions, and police behavior. Entirely regardless of telescopic sights or the use of mimeograph machines, by mobilizing the black majority for politics the agency posed a profound threat to the dominant white minority.

Mississippi saw an even more dramatic case. As the Community Action program was put in place, Shriver pushed "national demonstration projects" onto the local CAA agendas; the most popular was

Operation Head Start, preschool education for poor children. White civil rights activists from the North joined with black Mississippians to form the Child Development Group of Mississippi. In the summer of 1964, six thousand black children were taught in eighty-four centers, often by civil rights activists. The program grew rapidly, although meeting places were firebombed, and the first director was discreetly replaced. Most observers thought it a rousing success. Children were given "education, medical care, social welfare services, . . . even clothes . . . the likes of which they had never seen before." In addition, blacks were hired in large numbers. CDGM leaders understood the political potential of their federal funds; a core of black Mississippi activists were winning financial independence from the white establishment.[143]

Precisely those successes made Senator Stennis and the rest of the Mississippi congressional delegation dizzy with segregationist ire. Just one year after George Wallace had "drawn the line in the dust" at school desegregation, a federal program was casually bypassing the segregated mechanisms of social control. Senators Stennis and Eastland denounced OEO for funding thinly veiled civil rights agitation.[144] They brandished instances of haphazard administration and mismanagement. OEO leaders wilted before the powerful Democrats and quickly sponsored another agency; the capitulation so incensed the OEO staff, however, that a meeting was held to quiet them. In the end, liberal pressures led to the restoration of some CDGM funds, though the program was cut back from twenty-eight counties to fourteen. Once again, it was the threat of change—of political success—that inspired the charges of mismanagement and fraud.

Most cases were less sensational. But around the nation, the CAAs roused their black constituents. They used an enormous variety of strategies, stretching from the political mainstream to the edges of legality. The agencies sponsored police review boards; organized rent strikes; threw themselves into the politics of local education; ignited controversies over previously unquestioned zoning regulations; challenged the procedures and priorities at county hospitals; picketed for increases in school lunch appropriations. They confronted transit authorities on bus routes, sanitation departments over garbage collection, park administrations about their priorities. In Durham, North Carolina, the Community Action Agency harassed landlords by repeatedly calling out city inspectors about code violations in the ghetto. In Mingo County, West Virginia, the CAA formed a fair elections committee to challenge voting irregularities. In many places (Houston, Palm Beach, Durham), the agencies launched voter registration drives—like the old spoilsmen, using their government offices to get out the vote.[145] In one city after another, CAAs protested urban renewal projects. In San Francisco, Mayor Shelley charged the agency with triggering "a chain reaction of unrest . . . that has left its mark on every major civil improvement project attempted here."[146]

The myth of coordination had evaporated as swiftly as the ideal of communal consensus. The War on Poverty, like most agents of bureaucratic coordination, had neither the power nor the incentives to adjudicate the turf struggles of the American welfare establishment. Nevertheless, the CAAs had a profound impact on the scope and style of the entire social services bureaucracy.[147]

First, the CAAs pressured other government agencies to increase their services. They hired local citizens as part-time caseworkers; these "subprofessionals" were often poor and usually black. They went out into poor communities and directed citizens to government services. In this fashion, insulated bureaucracies were linked to black citizens who had been suspicious of (or uninformed about) them.

Second, the Poverty Warriors sponsored Neighborhood Legal Services, another national demonstration project and their most effective mechanism for forcing social change. In one year, 1.5 million poor people received free counsel. More important, the lawyers formed a powerful advocacy instrument, winning class-action suits on a wide variety of topics. They overturned welfare restrictions in eighteen states by successfully challenging the "man in the house rule," the termination of benefits to single mothers who "consorted" with men. Other welfare restrictions, such as denying benefits to employed mothers, were struck down as a violation of equal protection. (A federal court in Atlanta ruled that the restrictions were used more frequently against black women.) Legal Aid lawyers fought for Filipino housing in San Francisco, successfully contested Medicaid regulations in California, constrained landlord practices in Durham, and cut down residency requirements for welfare everywhere.[148]

The outreach workers helped overcome social and racial barriers to public services. The poverty lawyers struck down legal restrictions. As a consequence, the demand for government services began to soar. Even liberal public officials opposed the new entitlements the War on Poverty was unexpectedly committing them to. The chief counsel for the OEO noted the political conundrum of success:

> I'll never forget the day in 1967 when the Supreme Court struck down state residency requirements for welfare eligibility. . . . Many of our best friends on the Hill, in Governors' mansions, the Mayors' offices—they were all mad at us. This would cost them millions. They might have to raise taxes. Yet here was a decision that did more to alleviate poverty than almost anything else we had done. And that was always our quandary: How could we alleviate poverty without hurting the people whose support we needed to alleviate poverty?[149]

In effect, the agencies used the Neighborhood Legal Services to form a coalition with the courts. The politics of federalism were shaping the War on Poverty in roughly the same ways (though with less intense conflict) that they had influenced the Southern civil rights movement. Once again, the judiciary—now allied with a national network of federally funded agencies—sponsored reforms despite opposition from congressmen and local officials. Once again, the innovations threatened to disrupt stable relations between elected white officials and their constituents—new spending (and taxing) obligations threatened Northern politicians just as new black voters threatened their counterparts in the South. By the late 1960s, a good deal of the conflict over black rights was being waged within the public sector, between competing institutions of the American state.

Moreover, the CAAs pushed other agencies to change their operating styles and include black communities in their policy deliberations. The pressure helped force school boards to decentralize and relinquish some power to community groups in Los Angeles, Detroit, New York, St. Louis, and other cities.[150] Labor departments, welfare bureaus, and police departments made often grudging concessions to the participation of black citizens. The participatory ideal was pressed from public programs to private institutions—colleges, hospitals, YMCAs, charity organizations like the United Way. Everywhere, the lax, barely organized, participatory CAA style seemed to jolt the bureaucratic establishment. One sympathetic official explained the differences:

> If we in public welfare want to try something new, we first have to examine the law, then we have to examine the manuals, then we have to look at the bureaucracy to see who can be pushed, then we have to see if the legislative leadership is with us or against us. . . . But when OEO was established, there were no state laws, no local traditions, no bureaucracy, no need for the state legislature to get involved. As a result, OEO has been the biggest damn goosing tool anybody ever created.[151]

The Community Action Agencies never pursued their formal, largely symbolical tasks. They certainly did not defeat poverty: they did not even win much progress in the fight against it. They did not coordinate other agencies (as the Ford Foundation had hoped) or utilize sophisticated methodologies to design needs-assessment plans (as the Commission on Juvenile Delinquency would have had it). In many places, the poverty agencies were inert. Poor whites often shunned them because, as one executive director complained, "it has always been thought of as a program for Negroes."[152] In other places, poor people submissively went through the participatory paces at the prodding of professional staff members.[153] However, in communities with a significant minority population and at least some legacy of civil rights activity, the CAAs arrived on the local political scene with a bang. They forced new services on the social welfare establishment—the more direct response to poverty that the Ford Foundation, the President's Commission on Juvenile Delinquency, and the Johnson administration had all overlooked. They picketed, protested, marched, lobbied, and sued. They took the excluded minority populations and thrust them into local politics. Public and private institutions that had long ignored black Americans were suddenly called on to work with them. However, the CAAs most profound impact may have been on the black constituency itself. As we shall see, the act of mobilizing to win concessions proved more significant than the concessions themselves.

Poverty Warriors Become Bureaucrats

The political establishment fought back. In 1964, the Conference of Mayors had cheered the proposed War on Poverty. By June 1965, their annual meeting reverberated with condemnation. Mayors Sam Yorty (Los Angeles) and John Shelley (San Francisco) sponsored a resolution that accused OEO of "fostering class struggle."[154] Beleaguered William Walsh (Syracuse) bluntly announced that "if we cannot have control of the program, we do not want it."[155] Repeatedly, the mayors charged Washington with endangering "the integrity of our governments." Pointedly, they named one colleague who had won control over the local CAA board, Richard Daley, to chair an antipoverty committee. Daley snubbed Shriver and the OEO officials and complained directly to the vice president; Hubert Humphrey immediately promised relief. Two months later, at a meeting of the League of Cities, Humphrey told the mayors, "I'm your built in Special Agent to make sure you are represented in this program twenty four hours a day, 365 days a year."[156]

The mayors were joined by the Southern segregationists. Efforts such as the Mississippi Head Start program or the Durham voter registration drive had vividly demonstrated the War on Poverty's challenge to both white supremacy and, more generally, established political relations. Local officials inevitably blamed "outside agitators" for stirring up "contented" blacks.[157] Congressmen struck a more high-minded pose and denounced mismanagement. Senator Strom Thurmond of South Carolina fulminated, "This program has been in operation for a year, and its history provides a catalog of futility, abuses, political partisanship, wastefulness, slipshod administration and scandal."[158]

Worse, by excluding the Republicans, program sponsors had turned potential allies into eager critics. Senator Hugh Scott of Pennsylvania, a moderate, echoed Thurmond: "The War on Poverty has degenerated into a nightmare of bureaucratic bungling, overly paid administrators, poorly organized field workers and partisan politics."[159]

The Johnson administration itself began to back away, starting with the Bureau of the Budget. The bureau had never been comfortable with "maximum feasible participation"; bureau officials had imagined a more technical try at coordinating services. In November 1965, the BOB joined other critics of the program by leaking their definition of maximum feasible participation to the *New York Times*: "It means . . . using the poor to carry out the program, not to design it."[160] The redefinition (which closely echoed Daley and Adonizzio) challenged the black demands for control which OEO had been endorsing. The bureau was the first agency in the executive branch to begin "hitting" at Shriver's program; the President did not respond as though they were hitting him. The political context had begun to change. Important Democrats were complaining, the civil rights movement was cooling off, the war in Southeast Asia was heating up. By the summer of 1966, one presidential aid noted, "It would have been hard to pass the Emancipation Proclamation in the . . . prevailing . . . atmosphere."[161] An increasingly unsympathetic Johnson asked Shriver, "Is OEO being run by a bunch of kooks, communists and queers?"[162] The program did not have the security of a niche within an established bureaucracy. The withdrawal of presidential approval further opened the way for its critics.

Shriver juggled the competing demands and constituencies. He insisted on participation by the poor, but cut deals with powerful mayors. OEO would not take on Daley. It permitted a board that underrepresented blacks in Atlanta. It terminated the Syracuse grant. At the same time, officials indulged challenges like the ones in Newark and San Francisco. Before long, however, all the attacks on city hall were being reined in. By 1966, many mayors had won a veto over Community Action projects within their jurisdiction. Shriver, struggling to rekindle the lost magic of "community," retreated from maximum participation: "We have no intention, of course, of letting any one group, even the poor themselves, 'run the jobs' or 'run the programs.' That's not COMMUNITY action . . . by all segments of the community."[163]

For a time, liberal activists rallied around the program. When some congressmen moved to cut it in 1966, they were astonished by the protest. The plan was hastily dropped and denied. Instead, the representational procedures established by OEO were formally codified: at least one third of each CAA government board was required to represent program beneficiaries.

The reprieve was short. In the midterm elections, Republicans gained forty-seven House seats, mostly at the expense of liberal Democrats. (The Democrats also lost four Senate seats.)[164] The program's allies could not longer muster a majority. The new Congress promptly signaled its intentions by excluding OEO staff members from a general pay increase. In December 1967, the coalition of urban officials and Southern segregationists—"the Bosses and Boll Weevils"—won the Green amendments (after the Oregon congresswoman Ethel Green) to the Economic Opportunity Act; mayors were permitted to take control over the Community Action Agencies.

To the surprise of many observers, few mayors took over the local poverty board. After six months, only about twenty-five (less than 3 percent) had taken advantage of the Green amendments; roughly two dozen others had previously managed to take control. The rest of the poverty boards—the vast majority—remained independent. In searching for an explanation, most analysts focused on the calculations made in city halls. Mayors were afraid to ignite protests or they had found other mechanisms of control.* A more penetrating answer lies within the agencies themselves. All administrative agencies are thought to experience a bureaucratic life cycle—from crusading young idealism to cautious rule-bound maturity. The poverty agencies appear to have run their cycle at a manic pace: three years after the start of the program, they had already begun to enter "bureaucratic middle age."[166]

For one thing, the Washington office was transmitting entirely different signals. More conservative staffers were replacing the "kooks and bongos"—the liberal activists—in the Office of Economic Opportunity. The leaders at OEO tossed in with the conservative con-

---

*Another explanation of the continued independence of most CAAs was that the Green amendments also limited the number of poor representatives to one third of the board. Still other observers propose precisely the opposite. The mayors were afraid to upset whatever equilibrium they had managed to strike. In places where there was a great deal of agitation, swallowing the CAA would only provoke more—and destroy a useful outlet. These interpretations are both compatible with the one I suggest.[165]

gressional drift and issued regulations prohibiting "partisan political activity" and the employment of "subversive organizations."[167] The entire program hung in a more precarious congressional balance each year. And funds that were once unrestricted so that each community could judge its own needs were now carefully earmarked: the national demonstrations got a growing share; funding for "local projects" began to vanish.[168]

Still, the most important change was not in Congress or the OEO but in the Community Action Agencies themselves. Strikingly, they internalized the imperatives of organizational maintenance passed to them from Washington. As one activist lamented, "A CAP [Community Action Program] agency director has to decide at some point whether he wants to do his job—or keep it." More and more, the local agencies, volunteer board members as well as paid staff, struggled to keep their jobs as much as they did to reform city institutions.[169]

In the heady days of mobilization at the start of the program, the details of administration had been brushed aside. Both professional staff and board members had thrown themselves into political activism—arousing a constituency, framing demands, sponsoring protests. Long meetings full of unprecedented controversies with previously unchallenged authorities had electrified many communities. It was impossible to sustain such activity and maintain the organizations. With each CAA slip, opponents launched into new denunciations of "futility, wastefulness, slipshod administration and scandal."

Advocates found it necessary to pay more careful attention to their organizations and how they were run. The details were a good deal less exciting than the politics of confrontation. Radical behavior was ground down under the inevitable concomitants of bureaucracy: "a sea of documents, a maze of deadlines, a constant redefinition [of regulations]."[170] The dull chore of complying with the prescribed procedures—budgetary, planning, personnel—transformed the agencies. Ultimately, the CAAs were restrained by their own administrative processes. "In the space of three short years," summarized the director of the Harlem agency, the process "has been overwhelmed by its own complexities and its own bureaucracy."[171]

The bureaucratic process was exacerbated in some places by the effort to maintain control over constituents. A few agencies began to exclude new groups and members, reflecting the behavior they had once ferociously attacked.

In sum, even the most radical War on Poverty agencies began to lose imagination and verve as they struggled to maintain themselves and their achievements.[172] In the process, they became less threatening to established public officials. They became more like the urban institutions they had once assaulted. By 1968, just three years after the start of the program, few mayors found it necessary to take the control Congress offered them. To be sure, the CAAs still spoke for black constituents; some were still capable of an occasional protest. But for the most part, organizational maintenance replaced ideological fervor. The Community Action Agencies entered the same phase that signaled the end of every prior revolt for democracy—the evolution from mass participation to administrative consolidation. Despite their quiet demise—or more accurately, partially as a consequence—the CAAs made a profound contribution, both to the civil rights revolt and to the governance of American cities.

The New Political Legitimacy

The Community Action Agencies were the first public institutions to invite—indeed, to admit—black participation. The informal requirement that one third of the board be minority was unprecedented; of course, it was not put so baldly: "residents of the target area" was the formal circumlocution. Nonetheless, it opened one agency of the state to black Americans, redefining them as a legitimate group within the constellation of American interests.

The new agencies brought new resources into minority and poor communities. The most important was organization. The CAA governing boards gave activists a plausible new focus around which to mobilize black residents and frame demands of the white establishment. In addition, the CAAs founded a network of affiliated agencies: program advisory committees, civic associations, neighborhood boards, area councils, parents' groups (for Head Start). Independent organizations sprang up to serve as CAA subcontractors, managing programs like Community Outreach, Neighborhood Health Centers, and Head Start.[173]

Across the country, CAAs developed thousands of affiliated organizations. One sample of 18 poverty agencies counted 190 affiliates; they were dominated by minorities (on average, 67 percent of the members were black or Spanish-speaking) and almost entirely new (only 13 percent existed prior to 1965).[174] The Community Action Agencies often provided staff, allocated funds, and buffered the new participants from hostile mayors or probing congressmen. In time, many of these organizations began to spin off from their founders, sometimes preserving the militancy that faded in the CAAs themselves.

The new network meant new jobs. It formed the first systematic patronage source open to black Americans. For black professionals, the program provided an unprecedented opportunity. In addition, there were a great many more part-time "subprofessional" positions in the agencies; at one point, the *New York Times* counted 180,000 (half of them filled by people who had been "poor on welfare").[175] Together, the Community Action Agencies and their affiliates formed a new structure of opportunity and independence. Minorities were recruited and paid often to implement ideals civil rights activists were marching for. Stennis and Eastland immediately grasped the political implications when they denounced the Head Start program in Mississippi. A black political infrastructure was being constructed with federal funds.

There was, of course, the standard goo-goo criticism. In most American cities, reformers had vastly reduced the number of patronage jobs. Observers were shocked at their sudden resurgence. Even in less reform-oriented cities, there was widespread consternation at seeing the old practice in new hands.[176]

The War on Poverty agencies played precisely the same functions that political parties and their ward heelers once played for Irish and Italian immigrants. They were the intermediaries between dispossessed citizens and an impersonal state. Rising black officials dispensed subprofessional posts to cement their new constituencies (regardless of civil service regulations). The job recipients, often outreach workers, combed through the poor neighborhoods, seeking out complaints and advertising public services—welfare, housing, employment bureaus, legal aid. As the mayors blasted the Community Action Agencies, they were surely aware that the new institutions were performing old political functions that their own organizations might profitably have undertaken.

In addition to jobs, the new organizations introduced a profusion of resources into the ghettos. All the complaining over the abuse of War on Poverty mimeograph equipment is an ironic testimony to the effectiveness with which it filled a local need. Community organizers now had stationery, telephones, offices, office staff, newsletters, a place to meet, access to legal and professional advice—in short, all the means of contemporary organization.

The Community Action Agencies took on the energy and aspirations of the civil rights movement, refocused it, and gave it an entrée into the urban political system. The CAAs offered black Americans jobs, organization, resources, authority over public programs and—however ambiguously—the sanction of the state.[177] They frightened local political authorities by setting out an independent power base. They harassed even the most torpid federal bureaucracies with the "biggest damn goosing tool anybody ever created."

As the CAAs began to decline, they were often replaced as neighborhood spokesmen by the organizations they had formed. For example, when the Model Cities program was legislated in 1966 (displacing the Community Action Program at the center of Johnson's urban policy), its framers painstakingly placed it under the aegis of the mayors. Participation was to be included, but carefully controlled. However, minority neighborhoods were now organized and primed for political action. The same cycle of challenge was repeated at a much faster pace. City halls were condemned; minority groups demanded more authority over the Models Cities agencies. Often it was the organizations spun off by the CAAs that coordinated the calls for more participation in the new programs. They led the black demand for a political say into a wide variety of new places.[178]

The Community Action Agencies left a more significant legacy. Thousands of black Americans (along with members of other minority groups) got an opportunity to participate in local politics. They received an apprenticeship that "even Tammany at its best . . . would have envied."[179] Citizens campaigned for the poverty boards, developed constituencies, articulated a reform agenda, and learned to manage an (often beleaguered) organization. They learned to cope with a leery white establishment—with landlords, welfare agencies, and police commissioners. They organized, lobbied, litigated, delivered speeches, and chaired meetings.

As the agencies began their struggle to survive, the new political activists turned from confrontation to cooperation and developed a different set of skills. They wrote budgets, applied for grants, met deadlines, made contacts, learned their way around the courts. In short, they learned to work the local political system.

The threatened white establishment slowly yielded. The conflict was somewhat constrained by the political field. The new political participants did not immediately disrupt old patterns of distributing government jobs or services. They contended over "their" program—a war on poverty with no authority over established agencies and a national budget only one third the size of the one allocated to New York City's schools. The conflict was waged in the legitimating terms of representation and participation. Once again, a group was integrated into American politics fighting about representation in the safety of a vaguely defined, almost meaningless program. The white urban power structures learned the same lesson that had been forced on capital in the 1930s: the insurgents were less disruptive and unpredictable once they were inside the political system. The hostile white establishment learned to work with black citizens. Black citizens, in turn, were socialized—and, as we shall see, co-opted—into the incremental bargaining of mainstream American politics—precisely the transformation of black politics Daniel Bell had called for in 1964.

In this fashion, a new generation of American leaders entered a political process that had violently shunned them. A Senate investigation put it succinctly: "The Office of Opportunity programs have produced a cadre of citizen leadership heretofore neither seen nor heard in the community arena." They have brought "to the fore a sizeable cadre, for the first time in the Negro community, of young energetic and striving leadership."[180] That "cadre of striving" leaders and the political bases they developed are the most important contribution of the War on Poverty. Black Americans moved from the Community Action Program into local American politics.

The Newark agency confirmed the fears of the white opponents when its vice president, Kenneth Gibson, entered the 1968 primary for mayor. Two years later, in large part as a result of the CAA infrastructure, Gibson won.[181] In Detroit, one of nine city councilmen had been black when the War on Poverty was declared. Four years later, in 1969, the chairman of the CAA subcommittee on participation, Richard Austin, became the first black person to force a run-off in a mayoralty campaign. One critic complained about the confluence of civil rights and War on Poverty: "The major civil rights groups in Detroit have well established channels of influence over the CAA—so well established, in fact, that the CAA may also have . . . informal authority over the civil rights groups."[182] Austin lost. But the same political infrastructure rooted in the CAA provided much of the organization for Coleman Young's victory in the next election. The chairman of the Oakland Community Action Agency, Lionel Wilson, united the black community which had been split between militants and moderates; in 1967, he was elected the city's first black mayor. Similarly, the agencies were instrumental in electing black mayors in Atlanta (Maynard Jackson), Gary (Richard Hatcher), Cincinnati (Theodore Berry), and Los Angeles (Tom Bradley).[183]

When the War on Poverty was declared, ten years after *Brown* v. *Board of Education*, there had been no black mayors in America and only 70 elected black officials at any level of government. Five years later there were almost 1,500. By 1981, there would be 5,014, including mayors in 170 cities. Four of the nation's 6 largest cities would be governed by black men.[184] The Community Action Agencies were the vehicle through which black Americans were integrated into the political system. The jobs, organizational networks, and political experience provided them their foothold into the local political system.

Not that white hegemony could have been perpetuated indefinitely, whatever the policies of the Johnson administration. But the Community Action Agencies were the agents of integration. They were not designed as such; on the contrary, they were designed primarily to be uncontroversial. Following the path of least political resistance, the Johnson administration created a national network of agencies in which Americans could, once again, replay their old dialectic of political reform.

CONCLUSION

The civil rights politics in the 1960s strikingly reiterated the themes played out by labor in the 1930s. In both cases, state authority perpetuated overt oppression. One branch of the federal government tentatively signaled a change in policy—a change it was unable to enforce. The shift, however, aroused an organized but previously quiescent constituency and provided them a new political framework in which to pursue their rights. In both cases, the new participants met with resentment and brutality. The fragmented American state, marked by competing institutions with conflicting agendas, was caught between increasingly urgent demands and the limits of its own authority (and capacity and will). In each case, the tensions were resolved by a vague statute that established extragovernmental agencies with obscure powers. They were mandated to coordinate and plan, drawing their authority not from the state but from the people. Both the Recovery Act and the Poverty program were mobbed by a previously excluded group. In each case, its fight for political power and legitimacy was played out as a contest for representation within the new program. Each insurgent interest denounced the "fake representation" by which established powers sought to retain control. Each had federal allies who were willing to support its claims about representation. Each revolt ran the same cycle—from apparently radical to "responsibly" bureaucratic. In each case, the new group entered mainstream politics through a quasi-governmental program marked by the participation of the people, legitimated by the democratic wish. And in both cases—in each instance of the democratic wish, back to the Founding—the newly legitimated participants came to be swept up with consolidating their new powers; the requirements of organizational maintenance eventually supplanted the fervor of revolt.

In its broadest terms, the state mediated the tension between the need for action and its inability to undertake it by organizing a program grounded in a potent myth. In both cases, the republican imagery of communal consensus structured a framework that permitted intense conflicts to be played out as battles for representation on the political periphery. In each case, an insurgent group simultaneously won political legitimacy and, in the process, grew politically moderate.

Early commentators were frankly puzzled by the War on Poverty because it failed to evince the interest-group lobbying that supposedly characterized American public policy formation. Moynihan blazed onto the scene by seizing just that characteristic and attacking it. The program was a mess, argued Moynihan, because it deviated from the traditional patterns of interest-group politics. Social scientists in and out of government had designed a program around their academic theories of "community" and essentially took in the politicians. Congress never intended maximum feasible participation as anything more than a rhetorical flourish. A coalition of naïve theorists and bureaucratic fellow travelers seized the phrase and caused the trouble. Moynihan's thesis, however, ignores the stubborn fact that Congress not only approved but strengthened the participatory requirements in 1966. The argument that responsible leaders were bamboozled, then somehow went along, explains little about the implications of this extraordinary program for American politics and institutions.

Piven and Cloward, on the other hand, argue that the national Democratic coalition was crumbling, and that Democrats in Washington sought to replace defecting Southerners by forcing excluded blacks into the party structure over the objections of local party hegemons. The strategy would simultaneously restructure the Democratic coalition and quiet black rebellion through standard political co-optation. Piven and Cloward have generally been read as arguing that the Democrats in Washington self-consciously designed this "managerial strategy."* It is difficult, however, to sustain the argument that this was in any way planned in advance. Put bluntly, there is no evidence for a conspiracy. Political élites were neither as foolish as Moynihan proposes nor as far-sighted and effective as Piven and Cloward sometimes imply.

Ultimately, the images of democracy mattered. Pursuing them altered the political framework in the cities; the effort to restore com-

---

*The authors themselves are ambiguous on the point, alternately portraying it as carefully planned strategy and as fumbling incrementalism (for example, "Federal officials felt their way, step by step, as they evolved an approach to deal with the political troubles in the cities").[185] In any case, the consequence was similar to what they describe: the CAA turned black leaders from protest to working within the system.

munity restructured political arenas in a way that permitted the civil rights rebellion and the power establishment to confront one another. Still, Piven and Cloward raise the crucial question implicit in the issue of co-optation: in the end, after their two decades of struggle, were black Americans made better off?

Black Americans won a significant place within the political system. They dismantled the most egregious forms of racial oppression and became active participants in the Democratic party coalition (though as the quadrennial squirming over Jessie Jackson's candidacy illustrates, they get plenty of the blame as the coalition comes unstuck). And there are undeniable stories of economic success: black Americans who complete college, marry another wage earner, live in the North or West, and hold a white-collar job actually make more than their white counterparts.

Still, in the United States it is not easy to mobilize political power for righting economic wrongs. Economic indicators continue to tell a dismal story about race in America. Most demographic categories show slight improvement in the 1960s and 1970s, followed by a leveling off or decline in the late 1970s and 1980s. Black illiteracy, for example, declined from 10 percent (in the late 1940s) to 2 percent in the late 1970s (exactly the white figure, incidentally, in the late 1940s). Black men without a high school education earned 67 percent as much as similar whites in 1967, 74 percent in 1978. By the mid-1980s, however, black family income was 55 percent the level of white family income—almost precisely the figure of three decades earlier, down 5 percent from the mid-1960s. Twice as many blacks are unemployed— again a figure that has not changed. Even after transfer payments, almost one in three black Americans still live in poverty (31.3 percent in 1985); more than half the black children less than three years old are poor; and as a group, those children are born with a lower life expectancy than the citizens of twenty-nine other countries (and almost all of the industrialized world).[186]

Dismantling overt segregation has permitted individual successes and a rising black middle class. Yet even these accomplishments cause political complications. The visible success of some blacks has revived the politics of Booker T. Washington. As a result, there is little agitation or political mobilization for the many black Americans who remain impoverished. As Ira Katznelson sums it up, on the subject of racial progress in the American economy, "the realist must remain a pessimist."[187]

Although the legacy of the struggle for black rights is, at best, mixed, its accomplishments should not be minimized. Black Americans have won a significant and growing role in a political system that violently excluded them two decades ago. Perhaps the most dramatic symbol of change sits in the mayor's office of Birmingham, Alabama. Twenty years after Bull Connor released his dogs on men and women peacefully marching for civil rights, the Democratic candidates for President dutifully courted the mayor, Richard Arrington. He is, of course, a black man. In what is surely one of the great transformations of recent American history, Arrington's political organization delivered a primary in which his father would not have been permitted to vote.

7

The Reconstruction of Medical Politics

A. You can't win.
B. You can't break even.
C. You can't leave the game.
—Mark Kleiman (on citizen participation), 1981

The reconstruction of medical politics in the 1970s appears to share little with the political legitimation of workers in the 1930s or black Americans in the 1960s. The politics of class and race involved the most traditional of political patterns—oppressed citizens mobilized to win rights that élites were reluctant to concede. While the political task facing the Old Left (in the 1930s) and the New Left (1960s) was difficult, the egalitarian conceptions guiding their efforts were simple. In contrast, health policy involved the most prestigious and lucrative profession in America. The issue was not empowering an oppressed group but subordinating a dominant one. The task was analytically complex. The health case raised such matters as the control and management of valued expertise, the sources of inflation in the American service sector, and the proper boundary between political authority and economic markets in the allocation of a semipublic, semiprivate good. The crises of race and class triggered classic distributive and redistributive politics; the crisis in health care raised what Daniel Bell calls the "counterintuitive" issues of postindustrial society.[1]

And yet, for all the differences in task, setting, and constituency, the changes were negotiated in a similar fashion. The politics that empowered labor subordinated the doctors. Once again, the American state faced pressure for change without the authority to achieve it—a long stalemate eventually broken by the invocation of the democratic wish. The medical profession's domination of medical politics was ended, not by authoritative state action but by a vague program that promised communal consensus, public participation, and better coordination while shunning significant authority. The promise of the people triggered the same reactions as those described in the preceding chapters. In the process it transformed American medical politics.

THE AUTONOMY OF THE MEDICAL PROFESSION

A single pattern dominated American health care politics for most of the twentieth century: public power was ceded to the medical profession. Health care providers acted as trustees of health care policy. Legislation they opposed was defeated; programs that were legislated were placed in their hands. In many ways, the profession's power constituted an exaggerated case of interest-group liberalism—government authority wielded by an industry, generally for the benefit of its members.

Physicians exercised three different kinds of authority, each resting on a different source. At bottom lay their politically uncomplicated claim to professionalism: physicians act on the basis of technical expertise acquired through prescribed training, guided by internalized norms, and accurately evaluated only by colleagues. Medicine's link with scientific progress made its claim to professional authority particularly persuasive; physicians, not their patients, were the best judges of appropriate therapy. Through most of the twentieth century, pro-

fessional authority over the practice of medicine seemed beyond challenge.[2]

Second, professional command over the content of medical treatment
was extended to state-supported control over the health care industry.
Almost every business—from barbers to egg checkers—has used the
cover of professional expertise to seek government limits on potential
rivals. Medicine enjoyed what might have been the paradigmatic case
for self-regulation. Physicians were well constituted to meet the Progressive regulatory ideal of relying on skilled professionals to protect
the public from abusive practices. In the first two decades of the twentieth century, physicians appropriated public authority to take charge
of the health care field. They defined the content, organization, and
even financing of acceptable medical practice. By the end of the First
World War, physicians had consolidated their domination over a wide
array of potential rivals—osteopaths, chiropractors, midwives, homeo-
paths. Boards of medical examiners controlled professional licensure
and disciplined unprofessional conduct. The boards were comprised of
physicians usually chosen by private medical societies: sixteen states
legally limited selection to candidates nominated by the medical societies. Furthermore, membership in the medical societies themselves
constituted an additional, de facto, form of professional licensure. In
theory, the private power of the associations was used to extirpate
unethical practitioners such as alcoholics, charlatans, or abortionists.
In practice, sanctions were extended to any perceived threat to professional dominance. Southern societies barred black physicians; throughout the country, rebels who introduced new forms of medical
organization or financing were punished. In one celebrated case, an
Oklahoma physician organized a prepaid medical co-op among local
farmers; the medical society, fearing a legal challenge for directly ex-
pelling the renegade, disbanded, then reconstituted itself without him.[3]

Defying the medical societies became "professional suicide." The
politics of licensure protected the profession from alternative styles of
medical practice, from incursions by giant capital, or from the threat
of new organizational forms. The ideal of professional autonomy—free
from controls originating outside the profession—was won and forcefully maintained. The American Medical Association and its constituent state societies used both public and private power to extend the

primacy of medical judgment into a professional hegemony over the American health care system.[4]

Third, physicians sought to control health care politics. Government programs that enhanced their professional authority were frequently won; those that threatened their autonomy were, until the 1960s, generally defeated. For example, almost every industrial nation eventually sponsored a national health care system. In the United States, the reform was repudiated whenever it was proposed. The political outcomes are usually ascribed to raw interest-group muscle. By the 1920s, the American Medical Association had developed a reputation for political influence that would grow steadily for almost fifty years. The association was unhampered by serious internal schisms, well organized, and richly financed. The *New York Times* judged it perhaps "the most powerful [lobby] in the country," explaining in unabashedly pluralistic terms: "The American Medical Association is the only organization in the country that could marshall 140 votes in Congress between sundown Friday night and noon on Monday."[5]

Although the AMA's ability to mobilize on short notice was undeniable, simply ascribing medical dominance to interest-group power is to miss the underlying structure of American politics. The state's right to take on new tasks is always open to question. Moreover, through much of the twentieth century, political institutions—Congress and the presidency—were divided over social programs. The political pattern rarely varied: public officials (usually Northern Democrats) proposed a program like national health insurance; reformers cheered; as public opinion polls came into fashion (in the late 1940s), they generally indicated that the public concurred.[6] However, other public officials (Southern Democrats, Republicans) opposed the extension of government authority. Health care reforms were sacrificed for other programs and the maintenance of political coalitions—a victim of the American system of checks and balances as much as of the dreaded AMA. A political structure with stable political coalitions between executive and legislature would likely have won the reform many times over.

The shrill character of AMA politics can be reinterpreted within the framework of a weak state. Each encroachment on professional dominance triggered not debates about policy but uproars about tyranny. In 1918, the AMA house of delegates denounced "compulsory" social insurance as a "dangerous device . . . announced by the German emperor from the throne the same year he started plotting to conquer the world." Over the next five decades, the rhetoric remained unchanged, except for its growing stridency. Even before Roosevelt took office, the AMA warned the nation of the "forces representing . . . public health officialdom, social theory, even socialism and communism—inciting to revolution." By the 1960s, national health insurance had evolved into Lenin's "keystone to the arch of socialism."[7] The relentlessness of the theme, which has alternately baffled and amused political analysts, is clear in the context of a weak state: the AMA responded to the threat of public incursions into the physician's domain by underscoring the limits of governmental legitimacy.

The AMA's political influence derived both from its ability to provoke a deep-seated American dread—to politicize the boundaries of legitimate public power—and from its willingness to sponsor alternatives. Politicians eager to legislate popular health care programs were provided uncontroversial options that reinforced the power and autonomy of the profession. The result made it easy to ascribe power to the industry and its lobbyists. Even a cursory history of American health care policy demonstrates the repetition of a political pattern: the ceding of public authority to the medical profession.

PUBLIC POWER AND THE DOCTORS: 1933–66

The Progressives led the first charge for national health legislation, a typically Progressive blend of moralism, economic efficiency, public-spirited idealism, and politically naïve blundering.[8] The reform vanished (along with the Progressives) following the First World War, then returned with the neo-Progressive New Dealers. Though national health insurance was a decidedly minor aspect of the deliberations over social security in the mid-1930s, even subordinated to old age pensions and unemployment insurance, it was still political dynamite. As soon as the Committee on Economic Security announced a subcommittee to study health insurance, "the telegraphic protests poured in upon the President." Edmund Witte, who chaired the committee, complained about "vilification and misrepresentation"; sympathetic physicians faced professional boycotts. The social security bill that was ultimately submitted to Congress included just one reference to public health insurance, the usually safe exhortation for further study. As administration officials saw it, however, "that little line was responsible for so many letters to the members of Congress that the entire Social Security program seemed endangered." The Ways and Means Committee unanimously struck the passage, burying the idea for a decade.[9]

Though muted in the early New Deal, questions about governmental legitimacy were never far below the political surface. ("Won't you agree that there is just a teeny-weeny bit of socialism in your plan?" Perkins was taunted when she testified at the congressional hearings on social security.) As we have seen, issues ranging from the recognition of labor to the rationalization of the bureaucracy turned on what the government could legitimately (and constitutionally) do. The New Dealers were always chary when confronted by the matter. When the medical profession raised it over national health insurance, the administration quickly retreated. Roosevelt followed Perkins's advice and never even released the health policy recommendations of the Committee on Economic Security.[10]

Postwar Health Policy: Hill-Burton

A decade later, Truman revived the liberal ideal. He campaigned hard to "remove the financial barrier to medical care." His proposal—introduced by James Murray, Robert Wagner, and John Dingell (in 1945, 1947, and 1949)—offered federal funds but, typically, left the details of organization and finance to the physicians. The proposal provoked the usual uproar, conducted along the usual lines. The AMA decried "the final irrevocable step toward state socialism." It pictured the threat of lay supervision and the reduction of physicians to slavery. Senator Robert Taft of Ohio pitched in by denouncing the plan as "the Moscow party line," torn "straight out of the Soviet Constitution."[11] Private insurance was the preferred alternative, "the voluntary American way." The AMA financed its campaign by taxing each member $25 and amassing a "war chest" for the fight against socialized medicine. Though analysts have made much of the AMA mobilization, which was highly sophisticated by the standards of the era, AMA politics was political theater as much as genuine power brokering.[12] Truman's entire domestic agenda (packaged as the Fair Deal) met congressional opposition. National health insurance was one more Fair Deal proposal that never came close to passing. Instead it offered Truman a popular campaign issue with which to tar a do-nothing Congress. When the President championed national health insurance, he was fighting for re-election as much as reform.

The medical industry offered an alternative. Rather than directly financing medical services, the government could build up the medical establishment—a health care strategy known, for some reason, as "the Argentina Model." Following the Second World War, the American Hospital Association proposed that the federal government fund hospital construction. Relieved politicians immediately justified the plan with arguments that might easily have been applied to national health insurance (had that debate been less focused on "socialism" and "slavery"). Forty percent of our young men, claimed Senator Lister Hill (a Democrat from Alabama), were found physically unfit for military duty; the maldistribution of medical services caused "hundreds of thousands of preventable illnesses" and "thousands of premature deaths."[13] Hill joined Senator Harold Burton (Republican from Ohio) in sponsoring the Hospital Construction Act of 1946, popularly known as "Hill-Burton." The legislation was emblematic of postwar health policy. The state financed the industry's workshops and laboratories, while it studiously avoided meddling with professional decisions. The federal government did what it does best: it distributed funds to organized claimants; choices about where and how to build were left largely to industry.

Hill-Burton was a model of restrained public power, full of checks to bureaucratic incursion. Federal regulation of hospital policy was explicitly forbidden. The statute was only nine pages long, but there was space in it to invite disgruntled local administrators to appeal to the courts if the surgeon general rejected their project. Not that federal bureaucrats were permitted any discretion: a fixed formula determined the allocation of funds by state. A council of industry experts and lay advisers was formed to keep an eye on the administrators. The legislation's one intrusive stipulation was a requirement that grantee hospitals provide "a reasonable volume of . . . services to persons unable to pay." Congress immediately appended a loophole by adding "unless such a requirement is not feasible from a financial standpoint."[14] The implementing bureaucracy simplified matters for the grantees by never writing the regulations or monitoring compliance of the indigent care provisions. More than twenty-five years later, the courts denied standing to indigent consumers who sued for free care in Hill-Burton hospitals; the regulations were still unwritten.* Government meddling in medical business violated the spirit of the enterprise.

Hill-Burton was an immediate political hit, a do-good boondoggle. In less than two years, the Public Health Service provided funds for 347 construction projects in forty-two states. Over the next thirty-five years, the program disbursed $3.7 billion on the federal level, drew $9 billion more in state and local matching funds, and contributed to almost a third of the hospital construction projects in America.[16] When a hospital wished to expand, it applied for federal funds with the assistance of state officials (who freely amended state planning documents to help local hospitals qualify for grants). Federal money poured into the medical sector with no strings attached. The state provided funds while ceding authority over the program to the profession, which used the money to build up a sophisticated (and lucrative) institutional infrastructure for the private practice of medicine.

The same pattern marked national funding for medical research. Every facet of the research programs were controlled by the medical and scientific communities. Scientists chose their own projects; panels of private professional peers made the funding decisions. Crusades against cancer or heart disease financed professionals to continue doing their research, regardless of its link to policy goals.[17] Highly publicized "potential breakthroughs" became a regular feature of the budget cycle. Funding for health and mental health research grew steadily. (The former rose from $3 million in 1941 to $76 million a decade later.) Again, there were no federal strings attached: for example, training

---

*The regulations were finally written in the Carter years after considerable judicial prodding.[15]

residents in mental health could take government stipends, then practice wherever they wished. Like Hill-Burton, the research programs permitted political officials to demonstrate concern for health without mobilizing the public power that would be required to win national health insurance. The faith in professional autonomy appeared to be rewarded when dread diseases such as polio were cured in the early 1950s.[18]

In this fashion, the state funded the medical profession without seeking to control it. Medical care for the poor, national health insurance, a systematic approach to chronic physician shortages in rural communities, or wide-scale public health projects were repudiated. All would have required the use of significant public power and a break with health policy practice. Instead, the government built up professional capacity without violating professional autonomy. Hill-Burton, the National Institutes for Health, the National Institute for Mental Health, and a host of smaller programs all continued in the traditions established by the Progressive licensure statutes: they permitted the profession to determine the shape and character of the industry.

Medicare and Medicaid: The State Articulates an Interest

Although liberals fought long and hard for national health insurance, they never challenged the model of professional dominance. Instead, the liberal slogan—"removing the financial barriers to medical care"— cast the reform as, somehow, outside the scope of actual medical practice.[19] Reformers would pose no threat to professional autonomy or power; they would simply deliver the patients to the physician's door. Medical leaders perceived—quite accurately, it turned out—that massive federal funding would give the government powerful incentives for managing their sector.

The most important victim of the industry's opposition was the reformers' ideal itself. Liberals slowly whittled away Truman's plan in a vain effort to win political support: from comprehensive national health insurance to national insurance for the elderly to a partial hospital plan for the elderly. Despite the backpedaling, the terms of the debate never varied. Throughout the 1950s and early 1960s, the industry continued to question the legitimacy and the capacity of American government to implement the reform, regardless of how the liberals defined it. The AMA tirelessly evoked the twin specters of galloping socialism (that is, illegitimacy) and a medical system dominated by Kafkaesque bureaucracies (incapacity).

The debate quickened when the Democrats recaptured the Senate in 1958, and rose to its peak after Kennedy's election. It was an astonishingly exaggerated, almost hysterical dispute.[20] In perhaps its most delicious moment, the AMA sent every physician's spouse a recording with which to persuade friends and neighbors to write Congress opposing Medicare. The final words of the exhortation crystallized the antistatist imagery of the day:

Write those letters now; call your friends and tell them to write them. If you don't, this program, I promise you, will pass just as surely as the sun will come up tomorrow. And behind it will come other federal programs that will invade every area of freedom as we have known it in this country. Until one day . . . we will awake to find that we have socialism. And if you don't do this, and I don't do it, one of these days you and I are going to spend our sunset years telling our children and our children's children what it was like in America when men were free.

The voice, clearly recognizable twenty-five years later, was Ronald Reagan's, casting in against big government in 1962.[21]

The great, generally overlooked, irony is that the rhetorical pyrotechnics did not matter. A dispute about the legitimacy of governmental action turned almost entirely on the preferences of public officials. The debate dragged on with little variation for decades. The actual reform awaited a confluence of political will in Congress and the presidency. Throughout the Truman, Eisenhower, and Kennedy administrations, at least one branch rejected the proposals. Naturally, institutional biases complicated the task. For example, during the Kennedy years, a congressional minority was able to defeat reformers. In civil rights, they did so through filibusters; in health care, they relied on control of key congressional committees. When Lyndon Johnson was elected in 1964 with the largest Democratic majority since 1934, the public-sector stalemate was broken, and passage was assured—"the politics of legislative certainty," as Marmor calls it.[22]

In the new political setting, the AMA put aside antigovernmental rhetoric and proposed an alternative to Medicare, a welfare bill that would be administered by the states. Led by Wilbur Mills, chairman of the Ways and Means Committee, Congress promptly passed both: Medicare for the elderly; Medicaid for indigents who fit into the American patchwork of public assistance categories.*

The liberals' long-sought triumph did not alter the traditional contours of American health care politics. Authority over the new programs was promptly ceded to the industry. The statute itself broke with legislative tradition: rather than promising everything to everybody, this law began by promising to change nothing. Its first three sections all denied the charges of government intrusion that had been repeated for five decades: "Nothing in this title shall be construed to authorize any federal official or employee to exercise any supervision or control over the practice of medicine." The next five passages embellished the theme, forbidding state control over medical personnel or compensation or organization or administration or choice of provider or selection of insurer.[23] The implementing details were all of a piece, reflecting the unorthodox protests that introduced the legislation.

The method for paying health care providers was set loosely. Shunning payment schedules or other controls, Medicare reimbursed providers their "reasonable costs"—essentially, whatever they charged. In order to avoid the stigma of government bureaucracy, private insurance companies would process the payments; hospitals were permitted to select their own fiscal intermediaries, a potent guarantee against overzealous scrutiny of reimbursement claims. In addition, industry lobbyists demanded that depreciation costs be included in reimbursements, an unusual procedure for nonprofit institutions (many of them built with Hill-Burton funds in the first place); moreover, they insisted on reckoning depreciation on the basis not of original value but of

---

*The AMA had originally proposed an "eldercare" bill as a counter to the Johnson administration's Medicare proposal. Mills, a long-time Medicare opponent, took both parties by surprise when he proposed passing both (along with a third alternative sponsored by House Republicans). The administration bill became Medicare (Part A); the AMA bill, Medicaid.

current replacement costs. Implementing officials acquiesced, adding 2 percent to all reimbursements to cover the costs of capital. The program was lodged within the Social Security Administration, an agency geared to swift claims processing rather than meddlesome regulation. The tone of the new program was set by one of its advisory councils, established to advise Medicare officials; of the sixteen members, just one was to represent "the general public." Clearly, the expectation was that medical professionals would guide the Medicare program, defining "reasonable" reimbursement levels, monitoring the quality of health care provided, advising public officials on needed regulations.[24]

The usual deference to providers may have been exaggerated by the sheer burden of implementation. Sixteen million elderly would be eligible for benefits within a year (Johnson called it the largest organizational challenge since the invasion of Normandy).[25] Provider cooperation was uncertain. However, the unconditional surrender with which the liberals followed up their Medicare victory had far deeper roots than implementation timetables or physician boycotts. Public and private officials, liberals and conservatives, all shared in the same biases. Their approach to medical politics—even the conceptual categories with which they perceived it—was shaped by six decades of deference to the medical profession.

The continuation of professional dominance was reflected in two medical programs legislated in 1965—Medicaid and Neighborhood Health Centers. Though Medicaid varied across states and suffered from the stigma of "welfare medicine," it did not disrupt prevailing patterns of medical practice. After all, the program had been proposed by the AMA as a counter to Medicare; implementers were generally solicitous of the profession. For instance, rather than developing general fee schedules, most states gave each physician his or her own, an arrangement that begged for a jump in "customary" charges. Indeed, Medicaid relieved the industry of much of its charity care, paying for indigents who had previously been able to pay little or nothing. In general, Medicaid paid the profession to continue doing what it had done in the past.[26]

In contrast, the Office of Economic Opportunity launched its own health program, a rough equivalent to storefront legal services. A national network of Community Health Centers opened in poor neighborhoods. The clinics were efforts to overcome discrimination and the shortage of services in ghettos and rural communities. True to the War on Poverty ideals, the Community Health Centers emphasized comprehensive services regardless of professional turf or institutional boundaries. They employed low-income (especially minority) residents, promoted citizen participation, and scorned the professionalism of conventional medicine. When one clinic was criticized for distributing food staples through its pharmacy, the director responded with a Poverty Warrior's panache: "Last time I looked in the book, the specific therapy for malnutrition was food." The program was conceived as companion to Medicaid, growing at roughly the same rate. Officials imagined one thousand facilities serving twenty-five million poor people by 1973.[27]

Medicaid promised only to overcome the financial barriers to traditional medicine; the Community Health Centers, to overcome other barriers by rethinking service delivery. Medicaid grew quickly; the Community Centers quickly faded. Providers assailed the local clinics for drawing off paying customers and soon won congressional limits on the number of paying patients permitted the Community Centers. (Ironically, Medicaid's effort to make indigent Americans more financially desirable to physicians made the clinics a greater threat.) In the end, the Community Health Centers proved too radical a break in a system that had still not produced regulations defining "a reasonable volume" of indigent care in private hospitals constructed by the state. As Medicare and Medicaid were implemented and began to grow, the traditional model of medical politics remained intact: public authority continued to be ceded to the profession itself.

HEALTH POLICY AS DEMOCRATIC WISH: COSTS, CRISIS, AND CONSUMERS

The state had helped finance a technologically sophisticated medical system, then assumed the responsibility for those least able to afford the rising costs. Payments without controls sent health prices soaring. In 1954, the health sector claimed 4.4 percent of the gross national product, a figure that had held roughly steady for a decade. The health care system grew to 5.3 percent of GNP by 1960, 5.9 percent in 1965, and—with the implementation of Medicare and Medicaid—reached 7.3 percent by 1970.[28] Rising prices radically redefined the health policy agenda.

The discovery of a "cost crisis" followed fast on the implementation of Medicare and Medicaid. President Nixon declared "a massive crisis in this area" in 1969. *Business Week* ran a cover story on the $60-billion crisis. *Fortune* judged American medicine "on the brink of chaos."[29] For the next decade, the crisis of rising costs became the major issue of American health care policy. Corporations, insurance companies, labor unions, and consumer groups joined the politicians in calling for solutions. Even a cursory look at the health policy journals of the late 1960s and 1970s demonstrates both the unwavering focus on costs and the English language's wealth of synonyms for *rising*.

The usual interpretation is a simple one: the government passed Medicare and Medicaid; costs exploded; both public and private sectors scrambled to frame a response. The political reality was more complex. It can be interpreted only by considering the dynamics of problem definition in American politics. The cost crisis trumpeted by Richard Nixon, *Business Week*, and almost everybody else was not an uncomplicated reflection of some objective economic reality that followed Medicare. Prices had already been rising for a decade. In the five years that preceded the program, total health costs jumped 13 percent as a portion of GNP; in the five crisis years that followed, 20 percent. To be sure, the inflationary pace quickened, and there was a cumulative effect. More important, however, the national government had suddenly socialized a large percentage of the costs. Federal health care outlays rose steadily: from $9.5 billion (1965) to $25.4 billion (1970) and then to $41.5 billion (1975).[30] By nationalizing a large portion of the bill, Medicare made health care inflation a public-sector problem and placed it on the policy agenda. Shifting the uncontrolled spending from private pockets to the public tax system is what suddenly made a crisis out of rising costs.

For six decades, medical politics had turned on spreading the undisputed benefits of medicine to more Americans. When the issue was recast as one of constraining costs, professional expertise was no longer the critical skill. The redefinition of the issue turned professional judgment from the solution to the source of the problem. The AMA's anti-Medicare campaign made it easy to cast the profession as mean and narrowly self-interested, as just another self-seeking group. All the celebrated features of American medicine could be reinterpreted in the new political context. The system was said to be too technical, emphasizing sophisticated (and expensive) tertiary care over (inexpensive) prevention and health maintenance: the former was cold and unfeeling; the latter, humane and ultimately more effective. Medical treatment was provided in a haphazard pastiche of institutions (hospitals, high-tech nursing homes, long-term low-tech nursing homes, physicians' offices) with no logical flow from one to the next. "The American way" of financing care was now perceived as an irrational patchwork of public and private programs, often stitched together in a way that left families vulnerable to ruinous bills. At the same time, by covering most people most of the time, public and private health insurance encouraged inflationary overuse of medical services. The entire health care "empire" concentrated itself in urban areas, leaving many American with inadequate coverage.

Even the sources of medical professionalism were challenged. Consumers demanded an accounting, inverting the traditional norm of responding to professional peers rather than to clients. Previously subordinated providers challenged physicians: midwives, osteopaths, acupuncture specialists, and a host of others staked their own claims to professionalism in a more sustained fashion than they had done since the Progressive era. On the fringes, popular books claimed that the profession did more harm than good; they marked the resurgence of what Paul Starr termed "therapeutic nihilism," an antiprofessional sentiment that had been dormant since the nineteenth century. Suddenly, more was less in medical practice.[31]

In short, the new crisis challenged every level of professional authority: the physicians' trusteeship over public policy, their control over the health care industry and even the professional definition of proper medical practice. And yet the new skepticism did not lead to new politics. Instead, the widely perceived crisis produced political stalemate. The next decade would demonstrate once more how difficult it is for American institutions to strip power they have ceded to small minorities, even to win benefits for broad majorities. The old pattern of health politics, ceding authority to the medical industry, proved extremely difficult to undo. The legitimacy of professional authority may have come under fire; it did not follow that the American state enjoyed a new legitimacy of its own.

The programs that followed the discovery of crisis were bounded by the limits placed on the American public sector. Each sought a source of legitimacy outside the government—reverting to the old patterns of professional dominance, looking to free economic markets, redefining the problem. More direct solutions than any that the Americans tried can easily be imagined. Indeed, the Canadians faced with the same crisis in the same period nationalized their hospital financing and promptly solved the problem. Within a decade, Canadian health care would consume 2 percent less of their GNP, though they had started at the same point as the Americans.[32] The Canadian solution was not seriously considered by the Americans, for it involved unabashed state power over the hospital sector. Instead, the United States, caught between a widely perceived crisis and an inability to mobilize public power, ticked through the standard reform repertoire of American liberalism, then turned to the democratic wish.

Painless Prescriptions

The first responses to the cost problem operated within the established rubric of provider dominance. The uncontroversial Comprehensive Health Planning Program, passed in November 1966, funded voluntary planning agencies. Community leaders were brought together to chart local health needs, then coordinate "public, voluntary, and private resources" to meet them. The haphazard network of informal planning boards was generally organized and run by hospital administrators and physicians. They looked distinctly like the Ford Foundation programs that preceded the War on Poverty. Both were public-private partnerships dominated by private-sector élites pursuing the mirage of social progress through better coordination of existing efforts. Each sought to organize away profound American dilemmas without the use of systematic state power. A series of amendments (in 1967, 1970, 1972) tried to sharpen the focus of the health agencies on containing costs; however, health care providers had neither the incentives nor the power to limit the expansion of their industry.[33]

An only slightly bolder step followed in 1972. Legislation mandated Physician Standard Review Organizations to monitor the utilization and quality of local medical services, ostensibly with an eye to unnecessarily costly treatment patterns. The agencies were organized locally, then designated and overseen by federal officials. The cost-cutting effort, however, remained firmly in professional hands. The legislation—after some agitation in Congress—forbade anybody but physicians to participate in PSRO decisions, banned the promulgation of national norms, and refused to permit federal officials to claim data generated by local agencies. Like past health programs such as Hill-Burton, the PSROs carefully proscribed bureaucratic intrusion over medical authority. In fact, local groups of physicians were far more likely to dwell on the inflationary matter of promoting quality than to take on the controversial task of criticizing professional peers for "inappropriate utilization." Nevertheless, physician leaders bitterly resented the legislation; "the most dangerous government intrusion into medical practice in American history," judged one AMA leader.[34] He was not far wrong. Though physicians had captured the regulatory effort, some members of Congress had been seeking to promote lay judgments about essentially professional choices. Still, the first responses to the new problem did not break with the old political logic: the federal cost-cutting programs—CHPs, PSROs—ceded public authority to local medical élites in the hope that they would solve the problem. Predictably, the approach had been better suited to the industry's expansion than to its retrenchment.

A third political reflex was to redefine the problem. The Nixon administration, along with many congressional leaders, tried to dislodge the difficult new issue of rising costs and restore the old one of insuring adequate medical coverage. Rather than grappling with an inflationary industry, they would protect individuals from catastrophic costs. Socializing the expenses of the most severe cases would only exacerbate overall medical costs (and the state's fiscal obligation). However, it returned public officials to comfortable political ground—removing financial barriers without meddling in the profession itself. Furthermore, the proposal offered members of Congress their political ideal, providing concrete benefits to identifiable constituents. Ultimately, state officials were trying to return to a debate they had already won; rather than grapple with the limits on state power, they would pass Medicare again. In distinct contrast to what the Canadians had done, the leading American proposals expanded financing without asserting cost controls. The Senate Finance Committee approved the legislation, the National Association of Governors endorsed it; the opposition came from liberals who wanted to legislate a still more comprehensive national health insurance program. In the end, the proposal collapsed amid the political wreckage of the Watergate scandal. By the time the Democrats recaptured the White House in 1977, three more years of medical inflation intimidated them from pursuing the political redefinition. The reform was put off till the next scandal-plagued Republican administration reintroduced a modified version in 1987.

A fourth approach invoked an entirely different source of legitimacy. If state authority was suspect and professional autonomy caused difficulties, free-market competition offered an alternative solution. Certainly it appealed to the antistatist American ideology. Furthermore, the providers themselves had inadvertently promoted the approach by cloaking their long struggle for autonomy as a defense of capitalism and "the American way" against incursions from government bureaucracy and state socialism. The Nixon administration embraced the powerful market symbolism (as would the Ford, Carter, and Reagan administrations, each in a slightly different fashion). In 1973, a program promoting Health Maintenance Organizations (HMOs) was enacted. HMOs are prepaid group health plans, widely touted as a way of disciplining the profession by injecting market forces into the health care sector. The government role would be to stimulate and protect the markets in a manner roughly analogous to antitrust; competition would do the rest, vitiating the crisis through the inexorable forces of supply and demand. The potency of the symbol led some Nixon administration officials to make wildly extravagant claims: 90 percent of the nation would be enrolled in competitive health plans by 1990 (a prediction that would fall short by a factor of 6). Whatever the merits of the market claim—and they have been fiercely debated for twenty years—the HMO legislation briefly staggered the HMO industry, leaving it one of the most heavily regulated elements of the health sector till adjustments were made. Fifteen years of growth in prepaid group plans would show few of the promises that attracted four consecutive administrations. The market ideal always promised results for some distant future; the pressure of medical inflation on government budgets impelled political actors to search for more concrete and immediate results.[35]

In short, the traditional patterns of American health policy did not square with the new definition of the problem. Yet policy makers found it difficult to create a new approach. American public officials were, once again, caught between pressures for action and the lack of authority to undertake it. Their first responses carefully avoided governmental meddling in professional judgments. Public officials sought to turn the problem back to the profession. They tried to avoid government altogether and framed a policy based on the symbols of free-market competition. They sought to restore the old definition of the problem and extend publicly sponsored insurance, a form of action whose legitimacy they had already won. (Predictably, the direct government action was the only alternative that failed to win approval.) And, *mutatis mutandis*, they legislated a democratic wish.

Regulation by Communal Consensus

Hill-Burton was back on the congressional docket in 1974 when its authorization expired. The program had lost its status as the pork-barrel ideal. The era of state-financed expansion was over; Hill-Burton's popular distributive politics had given way to redistributive conflicts over who deserved how much free care from which hospitals. Congress combined the program with two smaller ones (including the voluntary planning agencies, the CHPs) and folded them into the National Health Planning and Resources Development Act of 1974. The Planning Act pressed together what seemed to most observers an odd amalgamation of ideas. It mixed minute specificity with vague generalities and was marked by colloquies in Congress that flatly contradicted passages in

271

the bill. Immediately prior to the vote, Republican Senator Pete Dominick of Colorado rose to declare, "I for one am confused."[36]

In the context of my analysis however, almost every feature of the program is familiar, for each had an analogue in the National Recovery Administration and the Community Action Program. The Planning Act established a national network of agencies (about 205, known as Health Systems Agencies or HSAs)* which were called on to better coordinate existing public and private resources. When the incoherent American state faces vexing problems, it reflexively musters up this hope of rationalization without fundamental change. The Planning Act's mandate to coordinate can be traced back to Walter Weyl and the Progressives (passed down the reforming generations from the industrial codes of the NRA, through the Ford Foundation's plan for the CAAs, and the hospital councils organized as CHPs).

The local agencies were required to devise voluminous health-planning documents (three-year plans, annual plans, and so on). Like coordination, planning is an abstraction Americans have found politically easy to legislate. The local health agencies, like the Poverty Warriors before them, were not given much guidance about what to plan for. The legislation proposed every health system desideratum its authors could imagine. For example, planners were encouraged to foster better care for more people at lower prices (respectively "quality," "access," and "costs" in health policy argot); overcome "geographic, architectural and transportation barriers"; improve competition; upgrade hospital management; help develop multi-institutional systems; and educate the public about its health habits.[37]

Proponents deflected criticism about the vagueness of the planning goals with another Progressive nostrum: science. They distinguished this planning effort from the failed CHPs, not by claiming to avoid industry dominance, but by promising the benefits of the latest planning technique.[38] Ten technical assistance centers were to be established; each local agency would be staffed by planning professionals. The failure of the whiz kids (on the Presidents' Commission) in their war on poverty, less than a decade earlier, was forgotten. Scientific planning—a phrase endlessly repeated—would discern the public in-

---

*The number of local agencies fluctuated as agencies merged, split, or lost their funding.

terest that had eluded health policy officials making narrowly political calculations.

The images of consensus, coordination, planning, and science all surrounded a more controversial task—the regulation of capital expenditures in hospitals and nursing homes. Construction or expansion of health care facilities had to be certified as necessary by the planning agency regardless of who was paying. The agency, presumably measuring proposals by its scientifically derived health plans, would approve or deny a certificate of need. The underlying logic was known a "Roemer's law": "A bed built is a bed used." After all, reasoned the reformers, health care professionals make the decisions about health care consumption: physicians order tests and fill hospital beds. An expansion in health care facilities would be followed by an increase in the demand for them.[39] The Planning Act left plenty of loopholes. Physicians' offices were not included; nor were existing facilities or anybody's operating expenses. The new regulation addressed only the institutional supply side of the future. In a real sense, the law turned Hill-Burton on its head. The state had been funding the expansion of American hospitals without asking any questions; now it began to question their expansion regardless of who was doing the funding.

The key to the entire health-planning effort lay in direct community participation. In distinct contrast to the generalities about planning and regulation, citizen participation was specified in painstaking detail. All meetings were to be open to the community, advertised (in at least two newspapers, forty-eight hours in advance), and designed to allow plenty of opportunity for public comment. Planning documents were to be placed in local libraries for citizens who wanted to do their homework. More important, the HSA governing boards were organized to further reflect the community. In a sharp break with past American health policy, providers were limited to a minority of the seats; the rest were to be filled by consumers of health care, "broadly representative of the social, economic, linguistic, [and] racial . . . populations of the area."[40]

In the original conception of the program, members of local government were explicitly excluded from the governing boards; the program's sponsors were seeking "non-partisan and non-political" community agencies: politicians would disrupt the consensus. Though local governments ultimately won an ambiguous role, the agencies were largely private nonprofit corporations funded by the federal government and, at least formally, independent of local political control.[41] Roughly 5 percent of the agencies were formally affiliated with local government, more or less the same proportion as the Community Action Agencies.

Just seven years earlier, Moynihan had prefaced his account of the Community Action Agencies with *"donna nobis pacem"* (grant us peace).[42] Yet here was a program organized along precisely the same lines (even the requirement for "broad participation"—apparently inadvertently—repeated the language of an old War on Poverty memo), promising nonpartisan consensus. The imagery of community was powerful enough to deaden the memory of recent efforts to achieve it.

True to its republican form, the program offered the community agencies no real power. Liberals tried hard to invest the program with "teeth," significant regulatory authority. "Health planning without regulation to enforce it just doesn't work," insisted Democratic Congressman William Roy, a physician from Kansas. Senator Edward Kennedy (Democrat, Massachusetts) would have had the citizen boards decertifying hospitals they ruled redundant. Many members of Congress viewed the HSAs as the infrastructure for national health insurance.[43] However, the program eventually emerged from Congress with virtually all of its "teeth" missing: most HSA decisions were reduced to recommendations to be passed along to more conventional authorities. In a larger political context, the weakness of the program is predictable. The NRA officials turned to Blue Eagle participation instead of authoritative state action for the same reason: it is the stalemate of public action that leads political officials to invoke the images of community.

When the state finally tried to vest health policy in nonprofessional hands, it did so with a program that reflected every aspect of the democratic wish: direct citizen participation in local community agencies where—with the assistance of scientific technique—the people would form a consensus about the public interest without resorting to narrow power politics (or politicians). Health care élites opposed the programs, still struggling to maintain a trusteeship grounded in professional skill. "Consumers who insist on flying airplanes are called hijackers," said Russell Roth, an AMA vice president; "a dangerous intrusion of the federal government into the practice of medicine," added Richard Palmer, chairman of the AMA Board of Trustees.[44] Still, if public officials were not able to challenge professional dominance with significant state powers, conservatives were hard pressed to turn back a program that invoked the democratic wish. The Health Planning Act was legislated with broad support. Even the professionals were muted in their criticism; the AMA urged physicians to become involved. At the same time, the program prompted the participation of tens of thousands of community activists. Once again, the vague outlines of the democratic wish proved acceptable to entrenched élites without appearing trivial to their challengers.

A Fragmented Policy

Facing a cost crisis, public officials legislated a regulatory program legitimated by the democratic wish. The pattern of ceding public authority directly to the medical profession was finally broken, at least in a formal sense. However, like their republican predecessors in the 1930s and 1960s, the HSAs operated in a fragmented policy environment, surrounded by hostile private and public institutions. They had almost no real power; and they were hobbled by the implausible organizational design that came from trying to regulate via community consensus.

Social scientists were not impressed by the prospects for change in health care policy: "Impossibly flawed." "A fatuously implausible construct." "We designed it backwards," judged one official. "Upside down" corrected a critic. "The awesome list of goals . . . strained the limits of credibility."[45] One political scientist exposed the troubles simply by specifying the cost-cutting logic of the program.

If the community representatives picked economy from among the many regulatory goals; and they planned in a way that restricted expansion (forgoing the obvious benefits of more local facilities); and they said "no" to local institutions whose expansion did not fit the plans; and the state agency accepted the negative recommendations; and it all summed to less construction; then (assuming that less construction would lower costs) some diminution in costs might occur.[46]

Of course, if public officials could have designed a more coherent policy they would not have needed to resort to the neo-Jeffersonian wish. The American state was once again articulating a policy that it was not powerful enough to achieve. The citizen boards faced a multitude of checks to any regulation they might try.

First, the HSAs were immediately plunged into the tumult of American federalism. The program alarmed state, county, and local officials. They feared that HSAs might become health care power brokers within their jurisdictions, but beyond their political reach. The governors won considerable control over the agencies as the program was being implemented. For instance, they secured the power to draw the HSA boundaries. In addition, they won the right to review HSA decisions—effectively reducing the agencies to advisory bodies. Finally, Congress tried to induce the states to legislate the authority for certificate-of-need regulation. Some flatly refused (at the cost of losing federal funds); most, lobbied hard by the medical industry, drafted weaker laws than Congress had intended. By 1978, only eight states had secured legislation that met the standards set in Washington. In typically American fashion, cost-cutting intentions in Washington were immediately diffused amid the cross-cutting cleavages of local politics.[47]

The clashes over local political turf were matched by conflicts in the Washington bureaucracy. A new unit in the Department of Health Education and Welfare (the Bureau of Health Planning and Resource Development) was formed to oversee the program. The bureau merged the staffs of the programs superseded by the Planning Act. The predictable organizational confusion—murky lines of authority, more personnel than formally approved slots—was compounded by the different ethos of the new program. The procedures and outlook of programs such as Hill-Burton were cast avowedly in the classic mold of deferring to the profession and encouraging expansion wherever it saw fit. Partially as a result, the directors of the new bureau repeatedly complained about subordinates who were "not very capable." "I don't have 11 people [out of 2,000] I can really count on," lamented one.[48]

The Justice Department tossed in its own challenge. Officials in that department circulated a memorandum questioning whether the HSAs constituted a violation of antitrust laws. Though Justice never pursued the matter, the episode further confused the local agencies as they struggled to organize themselves.

Furthermore, by moving into areas that had previously lain beyond the scope of federal authority, the planning program provoked even more than the usual rush of litigation. The AMA contended that the act violated state sovereignty (citing the Tenth Amendment), due process, and equal protection (the Fourteenth). The National Association of Regional Councils, the National League of Cities, and various individual states and counties filed challenges of their own. When officials began to delineate the boundaries of local HSAs, the politics of gerrymandering triggered another set of suits. Some local officials sought to split metropolitan areas; others wanted to incorporate distant counties. Longstanding local disputes were fought out over the health-planning boundaries. In the end, roughly one third of the local agencies operated with special waivers from the guidelines in the Planning Act. Naturally, when the program began to make regulatory choices, a third batch of suits was filed by local institutions that were denied expansion or aggrieved by the plans or disgruntled by the process. The National Health Planning and Resources Development Act resulted in the National Resources to Develop Health Lawyers Program, giggled the wags.*

In short, health care élites were offered a profusion of institutional opportunities to protect themselves from the program. They lobbied federal officials about regulations (one proposal elicited more than 50,000 complaints), state legislatures over the certificate-of-need laws, governors and local officials about the agencies' boundaries, the HSAs themselves about specific projects, the state health authorities (and governors and legislatures) over adverse decisions by the HSAs. Those who exhausted these sources of appeal turned to the courts. Most observers

---

*Paul Starr discovered that "in health reform, a little known law of nature seems to require that every move toward regulation be followed by an opposite move to litigation."[49]

agreed, however, that the weakest link in the chain of public authority lay in the HSAs themselves.*

First, the health professionals constituted a large minority of the governing boards (between 41 percent and 49 percent). Although mandating a consumer majority was a clear break with past policy, it seemed a recipe for the usual provider dominance. Here was the most elementary failure to distinguish between regulator and regulated. If long-established independent regulatory agencies were often captured by the industry they monitored, what hope could there be for the HSAs? Worse, the experts from the industry would be balanced by inexpert citizens. Few observers disputed the AMA when it scoffed that "two physicians on a 30-man board [would be enough to] sway the decision." Early reports from the field echoed the low expectations. "We're still looking for page numbers while they're heavy into the technical jargon," testified one board member.[50]

Second, local consumer interests did not seem to clash with those of the health professionals in any politically significant way. What could possibly induce HSA board members to fight against the expansion of medical services in their neighborhoods? Communities generally seek more facilities rather than less. Certainly, rising costs were a problem. However, Blue Cross premiums and Social Security taxes were set by distant bureaucrats; they were not obviously connected to any decisions a local board might make. The entire bias of the HSA enterprise seemed distinctly distributive. Local agencies were not allocating benefits from a fixed allotment. Instead, when they wrote plans, they imagined future health systems arrangements. When they regulated, they judged proposals from individual hospitals whose funding had already been arranged; and they did so one case at a time, so that different proposals did not directly compete with one another. Surely this was the essence

---

*The most widely reported political troubles followed the publication of proposed planning guidelines. HEW officials proposed goals such as a limit of four hospital beds for every thousand residents and a minimum number of two hundred operations for coronary bypass units (because the rate of success rose dramatically in units that performed more surgeries). Here was the first sustained effort by nonprofessionals to impose norms on the medical profession; the doctors responded with a deluge of protests. Though complaints were partially a result of a well-orchestrated campaign in several states, the sheer magnitude of the response rattled administrators and reinforced the widespread expectation that the providers were primed to dominate the Health Planning Act.

of pork-barrel politics—highly individualized choices about distributing benefits, each made without reference to any other, none of them taxing any fixed budget. Consumers, it was widely believed, would share the providers' interest in encouraging the expansion of local institutions.[51]

Finally, even if citizens could overcome the limitations of ignorance and apparent self-interest, they still faced the lobbying of the professionals. Consumer board members were being asked to apply impartially preformulated rules (for instance, no new hospital beds where there were already more than four per thousand citizens) despite enormous political pressure: local institutions would mix technical data and emotional appeals to demonstrate the necessity of the project; they would make theatrical predictions about increased mortality if the board voted a rejection; they would introduce grateful former patients who could testify to the importance of the institution's work (usually thanking God that no HSA had been around to say no before he or she needed treatment). Lawrence Brown vividly pictures the details of the regulatory process:

> Many hours of negotiation; the recurrent cycle of justification and critique; the charges of lay ignorance on the one side and provider dominance on another; the endless fiddling with formulas and ratios no one understands; the contrived public hearings at which a hospital displays its audio-visual aids to testify to the urgent needs of a venerated community institution; the community in attendance (three fourths of it employed by . . . the hospital) rises in long-winded support; the 4–3 vote finally taken at one A.M. in committee; the endless buttonholding and handholding; the threat of appeal and legal redress; all of this . . . raises the personal and organizational costs of nay saying very high.[52]

It would take confidence, knowledge, perhaps even courage to turn down local projects. But what were the incentives to do so? In legislating the Health Planning Act, Congress set out a long list of goals for the HSAs to pursue. Most observers expected consumers and providers to find plenty they could agree on.

Like the NRA and the War on Poverty, the Health Planning Act signaled a change in policy that the state was too weak to assert definitively. Most observers predicted that the HSAs would scarcely constitute a policy change of any sort. However, by legitimating the effort with the trappings of communal democracy, Congress subordinated disputes about political control to debates about representation within the program. The actual behavior of the health care boards would be shaped, at least in part, by who they answered to, by who selected representatives and how. Across the country, local agencies struggled to determine who qualified as a "consumer" of health care "broadly representative" of the community and how they ought to be chosen.

The Battles for Representation

The next stage of the cycle was predictable. Political reform had been propelled forward by an image of the people, of communal consensus. In political practice, the community turned out to be comprised of many conflicting interests; legislation that invoked consensus offered no obvious principles by which to sort out the different claims for representation. However, the health care case turned out to be more complicated than those described in the preceding chapters. There was no clear constituency, like labor or black Americans, to come forward and redefine the program. What, after all, was a health care consumer? The law and its implementing regulations seemed, at first blush, to offer little help: a health care consumer was not a health care provider (or paid by a health care institution or married to someone who was).

Across the nation, HSAs struggled to fill the governing boards with consumer representatives who would satisfy the federal funders in HEW. The only guide was the legislation's requirement that consumers be "broadly representative of the social, economic, linguistic . . . racial and geographic . . . populations of the area." (The implementing regulations simply repeated the phrase.) Congresswoman Ethel Green had struck a similar phrase from the War on Poverty for being unduly vague.[53] Now the HSAs scrambled to meet the hazy ideal of "broad" representation.

The phrase was no more than a legislative circumlocution for "the people." The unarticulated assumption was that somehow the entire community could be mirrored by the demographic characteristics of the twenty of so consumers selected for the governing board (or the executive committee, when governing boards began to run to a hundred or more members). Agencies developed extensive checklists of demographic types—religion, sex, education, age, income, and so on. Any group that sued or lobbied for a place would be added to the list. "There's one slot left," a staff member in central Illinois is reported to have said, "if we can find a retired, Black, Roman Catholic nun, we'll have [complete] representation."[54] Clearly, chasing after examples of social groups—representations rather than representatives—was an inadequate model of consumer representation. The vagueness of the mandate gave standing to a large number of groups who claimed they merited representation under the formula. Indeed, who did not? Suits were entered across the country. Left-handed Lithuanians never mobilized. But within the rubric of the legislation, they could have made a case. And they would probably have won.

Though several years of often confusing and sometimes bitter conflicts followed from the apparent ambiguity, the legislation had, in fact, defined exactly what public officials were seeking. Health providers had dominated health policy throughout the twentieth century. This law, responding to new pressures on the health care system, sought to break the pattern. The ideal of broad representation, of community, replaced the health professionals with a symbolic constituency whose legitimacy was beyond question. What officials in Washington were struggling to define was a new constituency for health policy programs. For all the apparent ambiguities packed into "broadly representative consumers," Congress had defined precisely what it wanted: consumers were not providers. Beneath the philosophic confusion lay political simplicity.

Within this broad political rubric, many interests staked a claim for representation. They understood that the key was not merely winning an ally on the board but controlling the mechanisms of representation: winning the right to make selections. A broad range of interests competed for control of the boards within the context of fighting over representation. Each had its own political agenda. Underlying the disputes about who should be represented was a debate about what the agencies ought to do.

In many places, black Americans mobilized for a place in the program. The promises of participation sounded like a revival of the War on Poverty. After all, black neighborhoods suffered from dreadful health problems. For example, the infant mortality rates in the inner cities approximated those of the Third World (the infant mortality rate for black Americans would rank thirtieth in the world—right behind the Sultanate of Brunei; for white Americans, the rate is half as high, the international ranking a more plausible tenth).[55] Here, said the civil rights challengers, was the health crisis HSAs should be addressing. Passages in the ambiguous Planning Act could be cited to support their claim that the program should focus on racial inequity and better access to health care.

Young liberal idealists joined the minority groups, seeking to define the HSAs as "social planning agencies" that happened to focus on health. Scarcely a day passes, wrote Barry Checkoway, the most prolific advocate of citizen representation in health care, "that the media fails to report . . . action by citizens to strengthen their participation in the decisions that affect their lives." The HSAs offered "an opportunity for health care to 'catch up' . . . with . . . participation movements."[56] Ultimately, the community activists were challenging professional dominance with a vague, ambitious, populist ideal. They would redesign health institutions to make them more accountable to the people.

Other groups came forward. Representatives of handicapped people made a sustained case across the nation. When the program began, they had been almost entirely overlooked; as word of successful claims on individual HSAs began to spread, the number of places where handicapped people demanded representation multiplied. When congressional amendments were added in 1979, they had become powerful enough to win a place in the legislative requirements (alongside "social," "linguistic," and "racial" groups). Spokespeople for the mentally ill, native Americans, migrant farmers, and other groups staked a claim for representation on many HSAs. In some places, rival social groups fought bitter conflicts: the Los Angeles agency was decertified when the clash of minority groups grew too intense for federal officials.

Far more quietly, an entirely different type of interest mobilized: corporate financial officers, union officials, insurance company representatives (the latter trumpeted their HSA participation in their national advertising campaigns), and Blue Cross officials. They defined their claim to participation under both the vague aegis of "community service" and the more concrete claim to be major purchasers of health care. Of all the groups that came forward, their political object was closest to the problem that had been defined in Washington—the control of medical inflation.

City officials played the same role they had played in the Community Action Agencies. They feared an independent health authority on their political turf. Though the conflicts were more muted (after all, the threat was smaller), the outcomes were the same. A small number of cities (Minneapolis, Chicago) won control of the governing boards; most did not. Predictably, the winners tended to be the same cities that controlled the earlier agencies (though Chicago lost its authority over the local HSA as the powerful Daley regime gave way to Michael Bilandic's ineffectual administration).

Finally, many provider associations assumed at the start of the program that they would recruit the consumer representatives, just as they had recruited board members for the CHPs. The implicit model they operated with was the hospital board of trustees—community notables who would help the industry grow without interfering in professional judgments. However, as the program developed, federal officials tightly restricted the industry's ability to nominate consumer board members.

The different claims for representation were adjudicated by officials in Washington. They followed the same pattern as had their predecessors in the National Recovery Administration and the War on Poverty. They forced the local agencies to embrace a wide range of mobilized interests. In contrast to the earlier programs, however, there was no single populist constituency that mobilized across the nation. Many groups came forward; different interests dominated local agencies in different places. Yet none was large enough to dominate the program or define a national political agenda. The various interests shared only a single significant trait: they were not providers.

The conflicts over representation were central to the definition of individual HSAs. For a time, the different agencies took off in different programmatic directions, depending on the profile of the board members and the pressures of the local political environment. The HSAs did not immediately set a distinctive national pattern. It was the next step in the reforming cycle that did. After the invocation of the wish, the mobilization of previously quiescent groups into a new policy arena, and the conflicts over representation comes organizational retrenchment. For the HSAs, this final phase defined the program's agenda and its overlooked political legacy.

DECLINE OF DOCTORS' POWER

The competing claims over the HSA agenda were ultimately settled by the demands officials in Washington made on the local agencies. With growing insistence throughout the 1970s, the HEW bureaucrats pressured the HSAs to control health care costs. Though the agencies were, of course, not well organized to do so, they were the only national policy instrument available to federal officials increasingly consumed with the issue. HEW cajoled, threatened, regulated, and lobbied the agencies into emphasizing certificate-of-need regulation at the expense of other program alternatives. The federal officials wielded a power over the HSAs that no other interest could match: organizational survival. The fate of the programs that preceded the Health Planning Act, the occasionally defunded agency, the accumulation of criticisms made by the agencies' many enemies, and the regular congressional calls for ending the program, all granted verisimilitude to HEW's constantly reiterated threat: either the HSAs cut costs, or they would be terminated.

Across the nation, the HSAs responded to the incentive. Other goals—like infant mortality in black neighborhoods—were organized out of the process. Consumer representatives responded the same way as their predecessors in the Community Action Agencies. Regardless of their political constituencies or personal ideologies, they struggled to maintain the organizations they volunteered their time to. Everywhere, they tried to control health care costs through certificate-of-need regulation.

Prior analyses of the HSAs all focus on the same question. Did they cut costs? The answer is clear: no. It is, however, the wrong question. The actual outcome of all those agonizing sessions where 4-to-3 votes were cast at one A.M. were irrelevant. For in those late-night disputes, the medical profession lost its trusteeship over American medicine. In every community, groups of lay people were making judgments on proposals submitted by the medical professionals. In so doing, they were transforming the way Americans think about health care policy. The hospitals may have won the 4-to-3 vote (or the appeal to the governing board, or the state agency, or the courts)—but in the process, in having to appeal at all, they lost their hegemony over medical policy.

The democratic wish had once again redefined the constituency of a disputed policy area. The state, in the mid-1970s, did not have the legitimacy to disrupt the patterns of professional autonomy. "The people" did. The principle of lay intrusion over professional judgment was established in the HSAs, driven by the imperatives of organizational maintenance as they were defined by federal officials. Just as the NRA legitimated labor and the CAAs black Americans, the HSAs invoked communal ideals to subordinate health professionals. In effect, they repealed the first sections of Medicare. Once the precedent had been set, lay managers would begin to take control over health policy in a wide variety of settings. A host of new programs—public and private, state and national—would explicitly assert controls on the profession, even to the point of seeking to alter patterns of medical practice.

In the next section, I zoom in on five agencies, in five very different political settings: Atlanta and the surrounding area of Georgia; Idaho; the greater Philadelphia area; the Detroit area; and the Twin Cities. All five agencies were driven by the pressures of organizational maintenance from a set of widely disparate political agendas to the same (almost exclusive) preoccupation with health care costs.

SNAPSHOTS OF FIVE COMMUNITIES

Atlanta

Atlanta, Georgia, is "a business man's town," long dominated by a small, stable, interconnected élite. Business leaders "set the line" on city policy; political leaders respond. Even pluralist skeptics acknowledge Atlanta's power élite.[57] As Mayor Ivan White described it, "You could pick up the phone and dial the Mayor at his office or his home or his club—your club—or his friend's house—your friend's house—and you could get your business done right there, on a first name basis."[58]

A dozen major commercial and financial enterprises constituted the power base of the city's élite; perhaps three dozen smaller businesses a second tier. The power strata—Floyd Hunter identified four levels—cut across business, social, and political life. Partially because there was little heavy manufacturing, industrial workers and unions never challenged the dominant economic class. Atlanta generally followed the standards and ethos of reform-style government favored by business—at-large elections, nonpartisan voting, a weak mayor system, and a largely nonconflictual style.[59]

The large black population constituted a second political interest—a silent, stable voting block, allied with the ruling élite since the 1940s. By Southern standards, it was well organized and politically sophisticated. Black Atlanta politics included a tradition of active community organizing—Martin Luther King formed the Southern Christian Leadership Conference in Atlanta (in 1957). However, the dominant black strategy self-consciously followed Booker T. Washington's ideals of moderation and conciliation. (Fittingly, his view was most clearly articulated in an address celebrating the Atlanta exposition.) The affluent white-black voter majority checked a third political force—the lower middle class, frankly racist, fundamentalists who dominated many Southern cities. Lester Maddox, who challenged civil rights protesters with an ax handle, was trounced (both in 1957 and 1961) running for mayor of Atlanta before being elected governor of Georgia.[60]

The ruling élite struggled to protect the status quo from racial activists, black or white. Racial moderation aside, black citizens derived largely symbolic benefits for their support: those employed by the city were addressed as Mr. or Mrs. just like white people. However, when urban renewal programs set out to reconstruct the business district, one out of seven black residents was dislocated (90 percent of the displaced citizens were black). As the black population grew, white counties were annexed, explicitly to blunt the threat to the political establishment. "Unless we get Buckhead and some other predominantly White sections in the city," warned Mayor William Hartsfield in the 1950s, "the Blacks will take over this city . . . we might even have a Black mayor some day." Later, ward-based elections were reintroduced for the same reason.[61]

The politics of geography and gerrymander failed to check black political development. In 1973, Maynard Jackson won the mayor's office. Jackson actively courted the business establishment. He risked relations with black activists to lead Chamber of Commerce trade delegations; he regularly appeared at business forums with bankers and executives. As Clarence Stone has argued, despite considerable tumult the essential patterns of Atlanta politics did not change with black electoral ascendancy.[62]

The health-planning effort reflected Atlanta politics from the start. Two applicants competed for designation as the local HSA; each was an established agency operating under a program being superseded by the Health Planning Act. Beneath the politics of organizational survival lay the clash of two local political traditions, each with a very different definition of community, representation, and the health needs of the area.

The Regional Medical Program was the spokesman for the profession. It was backed by the Georgia medical profession. Its executive director had been on the legal staff of the American Medical Association. Leaders of the medical community recruited the consumer representatives; they sought out influential business executives, veterans of charitable boards and committees. This was a board built up of the second and third rank of the Atlanta élite—vice presidents, operating officers of middle-size corporations, newspaper columnists, prestigious medical professionals. They were highly sympathetic to Atlanta's medical industry and distrustful of regulatory intervention or broad public participation.

The competing applicant was the Atlanta Regional Council, the local Comprehensive Health Planning Agency. The council reflected the politics of civil rights and community organizing. It placed a high premium on social change, racial progress, and the participation of black and poor citizens. The council was, as one opponent scoffed, "always speachifying about blacks" and "liberal, even socialist, in philosophy."* The activists would not have disputed the charge. Their political agenda included an attack on discrimination against black patients, expansion of the state Medicaid program, the creation of alternative medical centers (like outpatient clinics and Community Health Centers), the organization of poor people to demand new rights and services, and as much public participation as they could muster. They chilled the mainstream providers by calling for a moratorium on all hospital construction. Atlanta already had enough mainstream medicine; no new beds or nursing homes were necessary. If the Regional Medical Program sought out the powerful in the community, the CHP sought community power.

The bitter fight may have violated the traditional tone of Atlanta politics, but it was settled in a familiar fashion. The mainstream providers outflanked their rivals in precisely the same way that Mayor Hartsfield had once excluded their liberal predecessors—through creative political geography. The activist CHP was centered in the metropolitan area; the establishment RMP had covered twenty-four counties that stretched deep into rural Georgia. The latter lobbied state officials into drawing HSA boundaries that coincided with their own ("more conducive to regional planning," they said). When the state swiftly acquiesced, the establishment group became the logical choice for designation as the area's Health Systems Agency.

The new HSA had its organizational roots in a program designed to spread the benefits of medical technology. Its board was comprised of community influentials; its staff dominated by former industry officials—three staff members were former hospital administrators. After

---

*All unidentified quotations in this section are taken from interviews conducted during site visits. Because respondents were promised anonymity, I will not identify them any further. Site visits to the five agencies described in this section were conducted in 1979–80. The visits generally lasted two weeks each and included extensive, open-ended interviews as well as sitting in on meetings and collecting documents.

the first year, a study of Southern HSAs concluded that this one was "dominated by the providers."[63] The board members viewed many facets of the Health Planning Act as federal threats to a medical status quo they had no desire to disrupt.

At first, the agency rejected the unorthodox mandate to restrict the expansion of the industry. To be sure, all the health-planning indices suggested a metropolitan area saturated with hospital facilities. The average occupancy rate in Atlanta was 57.2 percent (the federal guideline was 80 percent); there were 8.7 hospital beds for every 1,000 citizens (the guideline was 4). Three hospitals were operating at below 30-percent occupancy, simply passing on the higher costs to the smaller number of patients (and illuminating the limits of Roemer's law on which the entire bed-cutting exercise was based). At the same time, the far-flung rural counties suffered from the opposite problem, with 1.8 (Meriwether County), 1.6 (Forsyth), and 2.2 (Butts) beds per 1,000 people.[64] Forgetting about the glut in Atlanta and focusing on the lack of facilities in the outlying counties was less politically complicated, neatly fit the mandate of the HSA's predecessor, and responded to much of the fine print in the health-planning legislation.

The major conflict facing the HSA came from its original rival. Former staff members of the Atlanta Regional Council formed an advocacy group and continued the fight. The participatory features of the planning program simplified their task. They pressed for more "community input," circulated newsletters denouncing the agency as "rigid and defensive," commented on every aspect of the agency documents (submitting almost half the public comments on the HSA's first health plan), and sued the agency for underrepresenting low-income, handicapped, and female constituencies.[65]

The litigation in Georgia (along with similar suits around the country) progressed slowly through the courts. However, HEW and Congress both pressed the HSAs to incorporate the challengers. Exactly repeating the cycle of the War on Poverty, federal administrators forced local agencies to accommodate rebellious interests; new constituents won both a place on the board and the right to select them by "democratic means." Officials in Washington stripped medical leaders of the power simply to seek out community notables as consumer representatives. By the late 1970s, handicapped, poor, minority, and senior citizen groups had won the right to select their own representatives in Atlanta. Some of the most outspoken critics of the Atlanta HSA eventually won a place on its governing board.

By the time the opponents joined forces, the differences between them were irrelevant to the agency. The HSA had discovered cost control and embraced its new mission with a vigor that bewildered local observers. An HSA subcommittee called for a moratorium on all new construction—precisely the heretical position advanced by the CHP from the start. The voluminous three-volume health plan was full of uncontroversial calls for coordination, scientific planning, and more health care facilities in the rural counties. However, they were all ignored while the agency entered furious disputes over certificate-of-need denials guided by the moratorium on new construction. Public hearings about the health plans were held in empty auditoriums; regulatory decisions drew large crowds, newspapers, and all the controversy. The HSA staff grew increasingly outspoken about medical inflation. The board—poverty lawyers who had once sued the agency, and hospital administrators who had denounced them as socialists—internalized the new goals. They focused on inflation and the certificate-of-need debates. They agonized over each new proposal and, after a time, began to turn them down.

Both sides abandoned the health system ideology with which they had entered the process, and began to focus on cost control. Both defended their conversion in the same terms, repeating the same phrase as if it were the motto of the agency: "We bite the cost-cutting bullet or we're gone." Their Washington funders were interested in a single issue—inflation. The HSA was created partially out of defunded health-planning predecessors (national networks of both Community Health Planning Boards and Regional Medical Boards were replaced by the HSAs); the memory of the old agencies cast an aura of institutional fragility onto the new one. Consumers, providers, and staff responded to the exigencies of organizational survival.

Agency members were not naïve about the limits of their power. They resorted to the standard reflex of Atlanta politics: they tried to mobilize the business community into the fight against medical costs. The HSA actively courted the Chamber of Commerce; they made formal presentations and informal connections. The business community was leery of the highly public conflicts that had marked the HSA. The chamber eventually formed a task force to study the problem. Its investigation, in effect an informal poll of members, was unambiguous: Atlanta business, perhaps conditioned by years of hospital philanthropy, was neither concerned with nor interested in controlling medical costs. The health agency set itself to the task of "educating" the business community.

The HSA process began to affect local medical politics. Providers had originally rejected any intrusion on their autonomy. But as the certificate-of-need hearings wore on, they tossed aside their solidarity and began to scramble for advantage. Hospitals that had recently expanded began to understand how regulation might help restrict competitors. The agency had been formed as a booster for the industry as a whole; it rapidly pushed providers to reconsider government regulation as a possible strategy in the growing conflict over market position.

The Atlanta-area Health Systems Agency continued its struggle with certificate-of-need regulation. It often relented before active provider lobbying, always to the fury of at least some of the board and most of the staff. When Grady Hospital, a large overcrowded hospital which served a largely black population, sought expansion, the public meeting was packed with black Atlantans who completely encircled the governing board. In the style of Atlanta politics, the arguments were made softly, the crowd was quiet. The governing board, also quietly, made an exception to its bed-cutting schemes. In another case, the board voted down a nursing home application after long hours of lobbying and deliberation; the state agency swiftly reversed the decision, giving no direct explanation for the overrule. In other cases, equipment denied to hospitals was placed in adjacent physician offices, a glaring loophole in the certificate-of-need program.

The striking fact about the Atlanta agency is not the paltry regulatory authority with which it tried to constrain costs, but that a board of health providers, community leaders, and consumer advocates overlooked the health needs they originally set out to pursue (all of them legitimated by the health-planning legislation) in favor of an unlikely, unpopular regulatory quest. They continued to court the Chamber of

Commerce, understanding it as a precondition for any real success. But the chamber's reluctance only underscores how the HSA had transformed itself into the most active regulatory force in the local health policy environment. Repeating, "We bite the bullet or we're gone," they lobbied the chamber hard enough to win a task force on the subject; they wrote angry letters to state officials still operating within the old pattern of deference to the profession; they helped break the political solidarity of health care institutions already feeling the pressure of competition with one another. In short, they began to reconstitute the local constituency of health care politics in Atlanta.

Idaho

A single Health Systems Agency does the community health-planning for the entire state of Idaho. The agency's stationery is pointedly inscribed, "health planning by Idaho, for Idaho"—an explicit denial of the link to Washington. An agency associated with federal bureaucrats is unlikely to carry much local credibility or support. Both the political setting and the local agency are fiercely antifederal, antibureaucratic, and antiregulatory. "In Oregon, they like government," reported one consumer representative; "in Idaho we do not."

The formation of the agency was guided by a direct political purpose—subordination to the political establishment. Providers, the local Comprehensive Health Planning Agency (CHP), the Council of Governments, and assorted minor interests all fought to defend their political jurisdictions. They designed competing proposals with seven Idaho HSAs (there are seven health and welfare regions in the state), six (planning areas, each with its own council of governments), and three (the distinct areas of the state). The governor would have none of it. The governors had won authority over agency boundaries when the Health Planning Act was being framed. Fearing a new federal presence within his jurisdiction, he designated a single agency centered in Boise. The governor sacrificed institutional logic (this "community" stretches 83,537 square miles) for political control.

The HSA frames its policies, then sends them across town to the Idaho Department of Health—which jealously shares precisely the same jurisdiction and functions—for final disposition. As a further safeguard against unorthodox health politics, most of the consumer board members are selected by local public officials. Provider organizations select their representatives directly.

The dominant political force in Idaho health politics is the health industry. It is powerful, well organized, and fiercely antagonistic to any governmental intervention. Throughout the 1970s, The Idaho Hospital Association and the Idaho Medical Association were unchallenged arbiters of health policy. No other interests in the health arena could match their social legitimacy, their political savvy, or their well-financed lobbying. When the National Health Planning Act prodded state officials to introduce certificate-of-need legislation, the hospital association fought it with an effective mass media campaign. Television commercials luridly asked: Will the federal government stop Idaho ambulances or close Idaho hospitals? Legislators declared the proposal "violated the American principles of life, liberty and the pursuit of happiness." They rejected it, six years in a row.

There might have been, by the late 1970s, a plausible competing view. The state Medicaid budget constantly teetered on the edge of financial crisis. The major Boise newspaper declared it "one of the state's most serious problems." Unlike Medicare, Medicaid is partially funded out of state general revenues. A burgeoning nursing-home industry "put the squeeze on taxpayers." Indeed, in 1979, the Democratic governor was forced to call the Republican legislature into an emergency session to allocate additional Medicaid funds. The legislature flatly refused and returned home.[66]

Even so, there were no cutbacks. Idaho's Medicaid, like that in many western states, is a middle-class program, largely dedicated to funding nursing-home care for the aged. The medical industry supports it, lustily resisting cuts in funding. Medicaid budget crises were repeatedly resolved, not with politically unpopular cutbacks but by creative accounting: the state "borrowed" from the following year's budget.

In this antiregulatory context, the Health Systems Agency struggled to define its role. It confronted a skeptical political establishment. Its members described themselves as "rural conservative Reagan Republicans" who shared the legislature's rightist orthodoxy. They were openly hostile to HEW supervisors, scornful of "welfare programs" such as health care services for migrant farmers, and sympathetic to the travail of private industries in the hands of bureaucratic regulators. In addition, the board members took an unabashedly local perspective: their loyalty went to their communities and local HSA sub-area councils, not to HSA central in Boise. The agency staff by 1980 was enormously deferential; they provided technical advice, not policy guidance.

The antiregulatory ideology matched the health care needs. Unlike the urban centers discussed in this chapter, Idaho suffers from a serious shortage of medical facilities. Its hospital beds fell far below the federal guidelines (2.5 beds per 1,000 people); despite the complaints of Medicaid cost crisis, nursing-home beds are in short supply; the real health care crisis was thought to be a nursing shortage ("The ladies make more money driving trucks these days," was one analysis). The agency's board was clear about constituent needs: more medical institutions and health professionals to staff them. The first goal, listed in the agency's plan is, somehow, to produce more emergency rooms for the state.

Even more than the provider-dominated agency that won designation in Atlanta, the Idaho board appeared set to pursue the less regulatory aspects in the planning program. Ideology, health care needs, and political environment all appeared congruent. If ever there was an agency ready to address the "geographic, architectural, and transportation barriers" to "quality health services," it met in Boise.

And yet, to the astonishment of local observers, the Idaho HSA picked a very different fight. It struggled to cut health costs. It sponsored a business-labor conference on health care costs (wrecked, in the end, by a labor dispute that broke out at an inopportune moment). Even without a dominant staff to press it forward, regulatory reviews began to dominate the agency. After several years of struggle, the HSA surprised everyone by rejecting proposals for expansion that did not meet all the appropriate guidelines. A nursing-home proposal—in an area that needed more nursing-home beds—was rejected: it was not "the most cost-effective alternative." Observers commented, with only slight hyperbole, "that was the first time anybody ever said 'no' to a provider in Idaho political history." A short time later, a second nursing-home application was turned down. The state agency rushed to overturn the decisions, not even waiting to receive formal notification from the HSA. The rural, conservative, antiregulators on the governing board were infuriated by the "political" calculations that prompted the swift overrulings. Even board members who had supported the applications denounced the subsequent rejection of an agency decision ("Worst case of round heels in the state"). Quietly the agency considered—but did not pursue—legal action against the Department of Health.

More striking yet, the agency threw itself into a battle for certification of need. Even though the proposal had been rejected repeatedly in the past, the HSA took on the powerful provider associations. The HSA officers, provider and consumer, testified in favor of the proposed bill. One adamantly conservative physician—still leery of Medicare and Medicaid as government intervention—paid high professional costs among his peers to support the bill. When asked why he had done so, his answer was straightforward: "What's the point of an HSA if there's no Certificate of Need Law to back it up?" Personal ideology was subordinated to the agency's administrative needs.

Predictably, the health agency made little progress in its unlikely effort to regulate costs. The community ideal was manifestly irrelevant to the boundaries the governor had drawn; it left the amateur officials struggling just to define a proper administrative process. Four years after the agency had been formed, the by-laws committee was still reporting: "A definition of a full term [on the governing board] cannot be found in the by laws or in board policy." Procedures were defined and redefined with every issue. All the usual complications of direct citizen participation were aggravated in an agency that demanded three days travel time for a meeting.[67]

The citizen representatives faced a hostile state agency with the same jurisdiction; an indifferent governor who viewed the agency as little more than a potential source of trouble; a critical state legislature; and a well-organized, powerful provider community ready to blunt any progress toward public intervention within the industry. The agency was able to mobilize local support just once: when HEW considered revoking its designation. For a fight with the feds, everyone supported them. And yet, despite the ideology of its board members, the incontestable health needs of the area, and every bias in the local political environment, the Idaho Health Systems Agency cast in with HEW in its effort to fight health care costs through the regulation of capital expenditures.

Philadelphia

Philadelphia politics is schizophrenic, split between high-minded, well-born, neo-Progressive reformers on the one hand and brawling, ethnic, patronage-based, party politics on the other. Black citizens have shifted their political allegiance between the two groups. Philadelphia is a Northern city with a Southern political style. Its stable social and economic élite is highly active in public affairs; in contrast, poor and minority citizens have traditionally been politically quiescent by Northern standards. Republicans dominated city politics through the Roosevelt era and into the late 1940s (and were finally defeated by a split in their ranks rather than by demands for social welfare policies).[68]

The first tradition is led by a long-established, almost aristocratic, élite and includes the usual constituencies of American reform politics—the upper middle class, the universities, the newspapers, the Chamber of Commerce business leaders (substantially less influential than in places like Atlanta), and a group of urban planners (who are substantially more so). Together they promote the typical universalistic good government policies in the typical nonconflictual style. Even by neo-Progressive standards, they have traditionally placed an especially strong emphasis on comprehensive planning.[69]

Party politics has survived alongside reform in Philadelphia politics. It draws support from the lower middle class (especially Irish and Italian ethnics), the labor movement, and rank-and-file municipal employees (including schoolteachers).

Finally, Philadelphia's black community has shifted between the two groups, alternately driven out of first one camp, then the other. It has often made for a crucial swing vote between reformers and party politicians.

For many years, an uneasy truce was maintained between machine leaders and the dominant economic class. The social élite financed the

Republican party which kept corruption within acceptable limits. When the coalition broke down in the late 1940s, the blue bloods turned to the Democrats, formed an exclusive political club (the Greater Philadelphia Movement, which had thirty-one members and $225,000 in 1951), and won a new city charter full of reformist changes: at-large elections (for seven of the seventeen councilmen), bureaucratic autonomy, a city managing director, a planning commission, and so on. Black leaders supported the reformers. Untypically, the extension of civil service rules helped middle-class black citizens enter public employment by breaking the grip of the white, lower-middle-class, party faithful.[70]

Reform mayors, Richardson Dilworth and Joseph Clark, held office through the 1950s. The men were, in Edward Banfield and James Q. Wilson's description, "throwbacks to the Mugwump ideal"—blue-ribbon "statesmen" from the best families who cultivated an image of good government and nonpartisanship.[71] Modern-day Mugwumps tend to be followed by a resurgence of party politics; in 1962, Jim Tate restored the Democratic party (and Philadelphia) to the party regulars who were itching for jobs after two reform administrations. Tate forged new links between the Democratic party and labor, between white ethnics and black minorities. Tate served his two terms (the limit imposed by the 1951 charter); in 1971, he handed the mayoralty and his Democratic coalition to the successor of his choice, Frank Rizzo. Rizzo was a beat cop who had risen through the ranks. A coarse, almost violent public official, he scrambled after any patronage opportunity afforded by federal programs. His often nasty law-and-order rhetoric appealed to some party constituents but humiliated others. Blacks and other minorities were fairly driven from the party coalition. The tough guy, blue-collar tone that was the essence of the Rizzo style can be illustrated by his sexist gay-bashing view of gender discrimination on the police force: "Who really wants broads on the police force? You want some bull dyke come chargin' on your property all ready with a swift kick in the Lasagnas? Not while I'm mayor."[72]

It worked for a time. However, the Rizzo politics drove the black population—which had overwhelmingly supported Jim Tate—back into a coalition with the reformers. They delivered the mayoralty to William Green in 1979 and to Wilson Goode, Philadelphia's first black mayor, in 1983. For a time, Goode was especially successful at reconstructing the reformist-minority coalition. Goode sported most of the correct neo-Progressive credentials: an Ivy League degree (from the Wharton School), experience as the Philadelphia city manager (the post that best exemplifies the city's tradition of scientific reform), and the appropriate low-key political style.

As the Philadelphia Health System Agency struggled to form itself, Rizzo was still mayor, though the strains in his political constituency were already showing. The conflict between patronage and reform politics had risen, once again, to the surface of Philadelphia politics. Community participation in health planning quickly reflected the fight.

A small group of civic leaders met in the courtyard of a local hospital to create the new agency. They were mostly board members of the old Comprehensive Health Plannning Council, a mix of medical and community élites very much in the Philadelphia reform tradition. They envisioned an agency that improved coordination through sophisticated planning methodologies—a neo-Progressive ideal that posed little threat to the health policy traditions of professional autonomy. The group retained the old CHP boundaries, an area that encompassed Philadelphia and four adjacent counties.

The Rizzo administration saw more potential for jobbing if Philadelphia won an HSA of its own and was leery of an agency that extended beyond its jurisdiction (and control). The politicians were joined by much of the medical community. The powerful county medical society and the hospital association (the Delaware Valley Hospital Council) enjoyed a stable relationship with the city administration. A Philadelphia agency was more likely to be pliant one. Typically, the local hospital workers' union aligned with the party leaders. Together, the coalition began to lobby for three health agencies: its own in Philadelphia, one for the two counties north of the city, one for the two to its south. Political officials and medical societies in the four counties also seized the opportunity to enhance their own health-planning role and supported the Rizzo administration's plan.

Finally, civil rights organizers and young liberal activists joined forces with the politicians in lobbying for a Philadelphia HSA. A decade earlier, black leaders had muscled their way into the War on Poverty (as well as into a Ford Foundation project), successfully challenging both the Tate administration and the élite reformers for control of the Community Action Agency. The CAA had a black executive director; 40 percent of the board represented the black and poor neighborhoods, which won the right to elect their representatives without meddling from the mayor (though the quiescent style of Philadelphia's racial politics somewhat diffused the threat to the political establishment). The Model Cities program set off precisely the same conflict between the same players.[73] Now, black leaders along with white community organizers recognized the opportunity in the health-planning mandate to "broadly represent" social, economic, and racial groups. They envisioned an HSA dominated by community activists in decentralized neighborhood sub-agency boards. Their ideal was firmly rooted in the memory of recent experiences with federally mandated citizen participation.

In short, the three traditions of Philadelphia politics immediately answered the call for community participation in the predictable manner: they fought bitterly for control of the new agency. Underlying each interest was a different health-planning ideal: coordination and planning through scientific technique; patronage and the continued expansion of the industry wherever the health professionals saw fit; and new efforts by the poor and minorities to win more control over and access to health care institutions. There was not a regulator in sight.

The conflict was fought out on several levels. City officials "called in all their political chips" in lobbying Governor Richard Shapp to create three health-planning areas. (It was widely believed that Rizzo's allies were calling from as far away as Florida.) Shapp complied. Federal officials supported his decision. The courts, however, found a procedural violation and ruled in favor of the single agency. After additional litigation and long rounds of negotiation, the original five-county HSA prevailed. All three factions promptly reappeared on the governing board.

Élite community leaders on the governing board (one came to meetings in a helicopter) pursued the traditional Philadelphia reformist agenda, stressing the importance, almost the sanctity, of the planning process. Planning technique took on a good government value of its own. In classic neo-Progressive fashion, this faction sought to address the problems of the health system by dreaming up more sophisticated ("pro-active") models and drawing multicolor charts. Solutions lay in better scientific method and less political bargaining. Predictably, the élite reformers formed a close alliance with the professional staff experts who aggressively promoted the planning ideal.

The major opposition came from the coalition of representatives from municipal government, county government, unions, and health institutions. Insofar as they had a leader, it was the vigorous provider peak associations—the hospital association and county medical societies, which opposed any moves to restrict the medical community. As the Philadelphia comptroller put it during one acrimonious debate: "I rise to speak in favor of the continued eminence of medicine in the city of Philadelphia."

The third group, the community activists, were not comfortable in either camp. They sided with the politicians and providers at the start, then switched allegiance to the planners and reformers—precisely mirroring the larger pattern of black politics in the city. However, they never became a major force on the HSA. The War on Poverty had mobilized widespread civil rights agitation. The protracted conflicts in distant arenas (Harrisburg, Washington, the courts) at the start of the planning program blunted any similar community mobilization for health planning. The community activists on the board struggled to pursue the more innovative mandates of the planning legislation (alternative health services, sweeping new forms of citizen participation); they tried to drum up support for a more activist stance on controversial issues (abortion, banning handguns). Their HSA partners voted them down; HEW officials discouraged them; Congress eventually forbade explicit lobbying. In the absence of broad constituent mobilization like the one that marked the War on Poverty, health planning in Philadelphia was a clash among the contending city élites.

The Philadelphia agency was characterized, most vividly, by a profusion of centrifugal forces. The deep-set political cleavages were exacerbated by organizational incoherence. The agency was unbearably unwieldy. The governing board had sixty-seven members representing thirty-six specified constituencies, selected according to at least a dozen different procedures. For instance, in Philadelphia, some consumer representatives were elected by district area councils (DACs) to the sub-area council (SACs) which elected representatives to the HSA governing board; at the same time, the Teamsters local directly named a representative to the governing board; one physician was elected from each area; local governments named their own representatives; and so on. The net effect was to enhance some organized constituencies, diminish others, and confuse everybody. On a deeper level, it reflected the American politics of fragmentation and stalemate: the organization was structured against action.*

Furthermore, the agency had few political allies. The political turbulence at the start isolated the agency. State officials, like their counterparts in Philadelphia, were not much interested in fighting local providers. By the late 1970s, no certificate-of-need law had been passed.

And yet, despite all the centrifugal forces—deep political fissures, a lack of organizational allies, a byzantine agency process, and a strong coalition of advocates for traditional provider-dominated health politics—the HSA began to cohere into a process marked by increasingly serious capital regulation. (Since Pennsylvania had not passed a certificate-of-need law, the agency regulated under the much weaker mandate of the 1972 amendments to the Social Security Act.) Despite all the incentives simply to accept applications for institutional expansion, the agency began to turn them down.

The major HSA activity eventually became the narrow processing of applications for capital expansion. Even the highly valued planning process was subordinated to the regulatory decisions that crowded in on the agency. The HSA members eventually found themselves overwhelmed by this bias within their work flow, laid out by federal overseers, tended by the agency staff and—particularly—their good-government allies on the governing board. As one consumer activist lamented, "There is a constant cycle of agency documents, each with its own deadline. First this deadline, then that due date become overriding considerations. There is constant pressure. And the reason for the process gets lost in the bureaucracy of it."

The sheer force of the bureaucratic process—the documents and

---

*The bias was exacerbated by the usual confusion over agency process. To take just one instance, the Education Committee reported "that there continues to be a lack of direction and guidance from DHEW and the Executive Committee regarding the . . . charges to the Education Committee and its functions."[74]

details and deadlines—pressed on the agency by HEW, began to dominate the agency itself. It began to focus the members on a common set of activities; it created a centripetal force among the clashing factions and alliances on the board.

For example, when two hospitals applied for new diagnostic equipment (CAT scanners), they were both rejected. When they reapplied, they were refused again. When they bought the machines anyway, they were censured by the governing board; the agency went further, successfully lobbying Blue Cross to join Medicare and Medicaid in refusing to reimburse capital costs connected with the machines. (The entire issue demonstrated the weakness of the HSA process; for all the trouble, the HSA secured a merely symbolic outcome and a marginal economic advantage for Blue Cross—the hospitals could easily recoup the costs by shifting them to the commercial insurers.) Board members justified their futile fight by assuring one another that they had "sent a signal to the medical community."

They sent a more dramatic signal in late November 1979. Pennsylvania Hospital sought a major expansion. The hospital was founded by Ben Franklin; it is the oldest hospital in America and one of the most prestigious in the state. The committee responsible for the case denied the application—the quintessential 4-to-3 vote taken at one A.M. The hospital lobbied the volunteers with extraordinary intensity. One governing board member received letters from six congressmen on behalf of the hospital. In the end, a block vote by the entire city delegation got the proposal through the governing board by a single vote.

What is most striking is not the final disposition of the case but how closely it was contested. The volunteer board had little to gain in the battle to deny a prestigious medical center the authority to expand. And yet, with increasingly frequency, it began to eschew pork-barrel politics and take a tough regulatory stance. Despite all the organizational limits and political incentives—the agency structure, its political isolation, the lack of sanctions with which to enforce its decision, and the agenda of every faction on the governing board—the agency began to develop the same identity as the other Health Systems Agencies I have described. The simple logrolling for "more" facilities, along with the many other politically attractive alternatives suggested by the planning legislation, was put aside

for the effort to exercise the shreds of cost-containment regulation provided to the agency. It is not a result that could be predicted by analyzing
Philadelphia's parallelogram of political forces.

Detroit

The approaches to Detroit along Interstate 90 are dominated by an
enormous billboard that ticks off an up-to-the-second count of the cars
manufactured in the United States during the current year. It is the
essential symbol of the Detroit political economy. America's sixth largest city is a one-industry town. Over one in five workers are directly
employed by the automobile industry; within the manufacturing sector,
42 percent of the jobs are in motor vehicle production, 37 percent
more in auto-related work.[75] Everything in Detroit, from urban renewal
to health policy, reflects the fortunes of the car makers.

This economic structure produces political alignments atypical of
American liberalism. The usual policy stalemate of narrow interests is
eclipsed by a broad class consciousness that is more comparable to
Western European countries than to other American cities. Both labor
and capital have a clear identity; their interests are articulated by powerful, hierarchical organizations—the big three auto makers, the United
Auto Workers. The dominance of these institutions permits a kind of
corporatist political bargaining—negotiations over public policies by
large organizations which exercise a monopoly over the representation
of their constituencies.[76]

The influence of the industry has been enhanced by a more recognizable feature of the American urban scene: weak local political institutions. A Progressive reform charter, introduced after the First World
War, stripped elected officials of much of their power. The mayor lost
patronage opportunities; the bureaucracy grew independent, entrenched and impermeable; the city council was reduced from forty-
two aldermen, each representing a ward, to nine members all elected
at large; nonpartisan elections undermined party influence over both
campaigns and public policy.

Auto influence has filled the power vacuum left behind by the reformers. The United Auto Workers provides the stable infrastructure for the Democratic party on both local and state levels. It won control of the state party by 1950 and the Detroit mayoralty by 1957. Still, Jerome Cavanaugh induced black voters to break with the UAW in the 1960s; and even though Coleman Young had been a UAW organizer, the organization opposed him in his first primary attempt in 1973.[77]

Coleman Young has managed to consolidate power in the mayor's office more effectively than any of his recent predecessors. He won a new city charter, built a stable electoral base (Young has been in office since 1974, as long as his three predecessors combined), gained some control over his bureaucracy, and led a downtown redevelopment.[78] Still, the mayor is not bashful about the power of the industry or the his reliance on it. Shortly after his election, he appointed Douglas Fraser, the UAW vice president, to chair a new police commission (a racially sensitive position in the early 1970s). About Henry Ford, Young commented, "I'm impressed. . . . He's big, he's rich and he doesn't stand on ceremony. I can reach him easier than I can reach Tom Turner" (the black president of the AFL-CIO Council). As the *Detroit Free Press* summed up their relationship, "The Mayor needs Ford's influence with the money men."[79]

The necessary alliances have been unambiguous. Young scrambled to satisfy the auto makers, especially Chrysler, which manufactures in town. Tax abatements were liberally allotted. Chrysler got a 50-percent abatement by threatening to move a plant out of Detroit. The riverfront development, wishfully called the Renaissance Center, won a similar tax subsidy, worth $7 million over twelve years. A large area in Hamtramck was cleared (over the protests of many residents) and turned over to Chrysler for an assembly plant.[80] At the same time, in the mid-1970s, the automobile economy slipped into a deep recession, forcing the politics of austerity on the city. The budget allocated to social consumption services (mass transportation, sanitation, health) were held stable or cut back.

The same political forces that dominate the city shaped the health-planning program. The key interests were the auto makers and labor unions: no other group—consumer, government, or provider—challenged them for control. They set an undisputed agenda, influenced largely by the weak business climate and the new social austerity; they worked to contain health care costs. In contrast to the agencies in the previous three cases, the one in Detroit never wrangled over the issues of representation, programmatic purpose, or political style.

With the passage of the National Health Planning Act, the old CHP agency simply redefined itself as an HSA. There were whispers that the mayor would have liked to assert control, but he never made a move. Nor did the providers offer opposition. The Detroit Hospital Council, for example, had been reviewing the proposed capital development projects of its members for Blue Cross reimbursement—a vestige of the old health policy pattern of ceding authority to the industry. The new HSA stripped the council of its capital-review function. The *Detroit News* called it "a bitter pill" for the Hospital Council, but the council did not fight back.[81] Nor did it seek to protect hospitals from the HSA. On the contrary, the council struggled to maintain itself by groping for the same constituency that controlled the HSA. It transformed itself from a hospital lobbyist to a management consultant, analyzing its former clients for the financiers.

The Detroit HSA did not fuss with complicated representation procedures. The auto makers and the UAW selected their members directly onto the agency. In many cases, the "consumer volunteers" from the industry participated in the agency as part of their jobs. A UAW lawyer, for example, allocated half her time to HSA activities. The influence of the industry could be seen in a multitude of ways: The HSA president was a benefits manager for General Motors. Six out of fifteen consumer members on the executive committee, the real decision maker within the agency, were representatives selected by the industry; in contrast, only one was a hospital administrator. The executive committee met, roughly, one morning a week. The industry representatives had the time and the incentives to become the dominant players.

Nor did they have to struggle against opposing interests within the agency. In one way or another, automobiles touched the lives of most board members. For example, the most active representative of the poor and minority interests on the executive committee was a retired woman who had spent most of her life as a UAW organizer. Indeed, the only sustained internal conflict came from the professional staff members who shared the board's policy preferences but fretted that the board did not leave them significant responsibilities.

The automobile industry's perspective was shaped by its role as a major purchaser of health care. General Motors, as policy analysts were fond of repeating in the 1970s, spent more on health care benefits than on steel. Unions found health care inflation eroding the benefits they had negotiated; while many local unions fought for the jobs created by hospital construction, the UAW sought to cut the costs associated with manufacturing automobiles. The virtual monopsony position of the auto makers in Detroit's health markets overturned the usual balance of health policy. The concentrated interest was not the health care providers but that of its buyers.

The HSA pursued its cost-control agenda with single-minded purpose. In one sixth-month period, for instance, it rejected almost 90 percent of dollars requested for new hospital beds and eight of the nineteen CAT scanners. Together with Blue Cross and the UAW, it sponsored state legislation to eliminate "excess" hospital beds: 2,400 beds were scheduled for elimination in the Detroit area. Further, the agency was planning to close or merge all the small hospitals (under 200 beds) within its jurisdiction ("inefficient," it said). Naturally, the opposition to actually closing hospitals was vociferous.[82]

The HSA claimed its plans would save the health system up to $300 million a year. But the debate was rarely framed in terms of science or planning. This agency was not infatuated with the planning process. In the United States, the celebration of rationality is often a substitute for political authority. The Detroit agency did not need it. Both board members and staff viewed their role in bluntly political terms. As the *Detroit Free Press* put it, "the [HSA] is the arena where health care technology meets health care politics."[83] At the end of one meeting, the president of the agency quipped, to general laughter, "Maybe there's more to all this than . . . scientific criteria."

Still, there were clear limits to the agency's authority. The most prestigious hospital within its jurisdiction, the University of Michigan Hospital, decided to replace its aging plant. The HSA judged the plan too costly and tried to reduce the $254-million project about 20 percent. The university was adamant. The HSA unanimously rejected the proposed expansion. Every politician in the state scrambled to stand behind the Big Blue. The university was lionized by state legislators; the decision overturned by state administrators. One board member, a former Detroit City Council president, announced on his weekly radio commentary that "regional health care planning has been dealt a body blow." The HSA kept fighting. By casting the battle as a reflection on their own legitimacy, the HSA members boxed themselves into an unpopular fight against an institution far more powerful than they. The struggle over the University of Michigan hospital lasted almost two years. Though the university won, the time and effort expended fighting the health agency complicated the financing (a bond referendum) and raised the hospital's costs.[84]

In contrast to the agencies in Atlanta, Philadelphia, and Idaho, the HSA in Detroit did not have to struggle to define its constituencies or their health policy agenda. The dominant powers in the area, the auto makers, were committed to cutting health care costs. Their political hegemony overcame the fragmented political apparatus that enabled providers elsewhere to struggle to maintain some of their authority over medical politics. The Detroit agency began roughly where most of the others ended up. Still, for all the differences, by the late 1970s the Detroit agency found itself in precisely the same role as every other agency I have described—struggling to say no despite the opposition of almost everybody in the political environment.

Minneapolis–St. Paul

Nowhere did the ideals of municipal reform triumph more completely than in the Twin Cities. In Minneapolis, the overt pursuit of narrow self-interest—the guiding assumption of most American politics—is treated almost as a violation of the rules of play. The approved alternative is the businesslike search for the public good. If the Progressive ideal does not always guide political action, it has profoundly shaped the political style. Alan Altshuler describes it as the Twin City ethos of "economy, efficiency, and the elimination of sin."[85]

The resulting emphasis on clean politics is, in comparative American urban terms, fantastic. Consider the grand jury indictments handed down on Elsa Carpenter, after her race for State Senate in 1980. One of the three counts alleged "improper campaign inducements." Carpenter had dished out free coffee, tea, and rolls at a coffee klatch—a gross misdemeanor, punishable by up to year in prison and a $1,000 fine. Worse, some of her literature urged voters to elect her "the first woman to represent Minneapolis in the State Senate"—a second gross misdemeanor for false campaign statements (another woman had been elected in 1979 to finish her husband's term). Needless to report, the grand jury was not playing politics; it indicted Carpenter's opponent, too.[86]

The story is not exceptional. In 1977, Governor Rudy Perpich was involved in a scandal. He had recommended two men for state jobs (at $16,558 and 14,700); an official in the manpower office alleged that, in his opinion, more qualified people were available. "The system is debased when government starts to become an employment agency for friends and friends of friends," thought the *Minneapolis Star*. Perpich appointed a three-member panel to investigate and, just to be sure, submitted all the employees in the office to merit exams. (By way of contrast, the Chicago alderman Fred B. Roti had sixteen relatives on the city payroll at a combined salary of $350,992.)[87]

The Twin City's social structure supports the good-government ethos. The traditional constituents of machine politics—immigrants from Ireland, Italy, and Eastern Europe in the nineteenth century, from the rural South in the twentieth—did not settle in the area in large numbers. In 1978, the unemployment rate was 3.1 percent (the national average was 6.5 percent). Minorities comprised less than 3 percent of the population. The major employers were large, white-collar, service-sector firms. In short, it is a white, middle-class area with a Scandinavian cultural heritage—in many ways, a city closer to Stockholm than to Chicago.*

Politics are nonpartisan, universalistic, and merit-based (in the 1970s, the mayor of Minneapolis appointed two subordinates). Incumbents are rarely punished for not accomplishing enough; "the few who

---

*The generalization about ethnicity is truer for Minneapolis than for St. Paul, which has Italian and Polish communities. In 1980, the Twin Cities Metropolitan Area was 95 percent white: the largest single ancestry groups were German (13.5 percent) and Swedish-Norwegian (8.6 percent); the next largest was Irish (2.7 percent). The ethnic mix is often cited by residents as a major factor in the political ethos of the area.[88]

lost were those who acted too much."[89] Predictably, the area has an exceptionally well-developed tradition of regional planning. The usual American tangle of competing bureaucratic authorities violates good-government rationality; in the Twin Cities, a powerful regional planning board (the Metropolitan Planning Council) wields jurisdiction over parks, sewage, airports, transportation, waste disposal, and other regional concerns. (However, rural "outstate" politicians who feared the centralization of political power blocked its formation for several years in a baldly political manner.) When the National Health Planning Act mandated HSAs, an existing health-planning board, which had been conducting certificate-of-need reviews under state authority since 1971, was adjusted to conform to the federal requirements and attached to the Metropolitan Council.[90]

The twenty-five HSA (or Metropolitan Health Board) members were selected in an orderly fashion. The governor appointed officials to the Metropolitan Council; each council member named one person to the Metropolitan Health Board. No demands for more democratic means were voiced in the Twin Cities.

The process produced community leaders who defined their role as trustees of the health care system. They rejected the notion that they represented competing interests or specific constituencies. Their authority derived from the data generated by the planning process rather than from their status as representatives of the community. Ironically, the same model of professional decision making that had always dominated medicine now guided the health-planning agency: the health care professionals had simply been replaced by the planners. The Metropolitan Health Board reflected the Twin City's political style: community leaders volunteered their time to search for nonpartisan solutions to local problems.*

The agency was clear about its mission. Highly polished, quantitative, planning documents defined the priorities; regulatory judgments followed from the data. The volunteer planners defined their tasks in good-government style, pursued them in a good-government setting, and were supported by the usual good-government allies: local news-

---

*Members on the governing board acknowledged just one split: gender. Women appeared to set the agency's tone of universalistic systems thinking. "Women build programs, not edifices," reported one leader. Even this was, however, a subtle fissure.

papers, the regional planning council, and a public interest research group (predictably affiliated with local business).

The local hospital occupancy rate stood at 68.4 percent; the federal guidelines were 80 percent. The data were, in the minds of the health board, unambiguous: the area had 2,115 excess beds. The agency gathered the hospital trustees of the Minneapolis and St. Paul areas, showed them the findings, and suggested that they make the painful choices. In what appeared to be a dramatic change in hospital politics, one of the trustee groups asked reluctant hospital administrators to leave the room, then began to chart the necessary cuts.[91]

A powerful new interest, it seemed, had been mobilized to a new public interest. Hospital boards were dominated by businesspeople. Though they were used to viewing the Twin Cities' health needs from the perspective of their own hospitals, they were more likely to judge the new data in a disinterested fashion than were the hospital administrators themselves. The community leaders on the HSA appeared to have persuaded their counterparts on the hospital boards to put aside narrow institutional interests for a broader public interest in rationalizing the health care system.

However, all the good will of the public interest triumphant was based on a complex set of arbitrary assumptions: Was 4 beds per 1,000 people really an appropriate target? How about the 80 percent occupancy rate? Would achieving either really cut health care costs? When the trustees agreed to reduce their own hospital capacity, they turned to a painless solution which underscored the arbitrary nature of the enterprise: roughly 900 of the excess beds did not exist, hospitals having been licensed for more beds than they operated. The trustees agreed to cut many of those phantom beds. For a time, the ideal of rational planning could be squared with institutional self-interest. The painful regulatory choices were put off to the future; the appearance of progress toward the public interest was maintained.

When the Veterans Administration proposed a new 845-bed facility for the Twin Cities in 1979, the board countered that a 649-bed hospital would be more efficient. The difference could be made up by sharing services with nearby hospitals. Predictable conflicts followed. Veterans' groups mobilized to tell of their sacrifices to the nation. The board, which had no formal jurisdiction over the VA system, turned to its political connections in pursuit of the rational ideal. One of its officers had served as treasurer of Congressman Carl Sabo's re-election committee; the congressman persuaded the House Appropriations Committee to fund the smaller hospital. It is interesting to speculate how Sabo's congressional colleagues must have viewed his effort to cut back a popular pork-barrel project for his district in the name of the hazy (the precision of the numbers notwithstanding) universalistic ideal implicit in shutting down 2,115 local hospital beds. In any case, in 1980 the health planners triumphed over the veterans and moved on to larger conflicts.

The prestigious Fairview Hospital Corporation proposed closing one facility in Minneapolis, remodeling another, and opening a new hospital complex in Burnsville, a growing Twin Cities suburb. The case generated enormous acrimony. Burnsville residents packed meetings, launched petition drives, and lobbied public officials to support the facility. Fairview retained legal counsel—a clear violation of the rational ideal that offended most of the board members. Eight smaller hospitals joined the fight against expansion. Clearly, both sides were jockeying for future position in the growing suburban market. However, in good Twin Cities style, they waved reams of numbers and planning ideals at one another. The health board was unmoved by the tumult. The proposal did not comply with the Health System Plan (though all acknowledged that the suburb would eventually require a hospital). In vivid contrast to similar HSA battles across the country, the state agency never considered overturning the decision: after all, the health board had the data.

By national health-planning standards, the Minnesota agency was remarkably successful. Nevertheless, its rational ideal was being eroded by the fractious politics necessary to pursue it. As long as its planning vision involved minor institutional adjustments or the adjudication of disputes between competing interests, the board was able to maintain its authority. Prodding hospital trustees to share the largely symbolic sacrifice of paper beds, recruiting a local congressman to scale back a large Veterans Administration project in the name of cost control, or siding with eight nervous hospitals against an expansive chain, all resulted in winners as well as losers, in political compromises that could be construed as victories for the public interest.

However, the hospitals were mobilized, aroused, and frightened. And with the election of Ronald Reagan in 1980, the political environment changed dramatically. Popular support for regulation seemed, on the political surface, to be over. And the Health Systems Agencies had few allies: it was clear that even the best of them did not have the tools with which to restrain medical inflation. In this shifting political environment, the Metropolitan Health Board took on one fight too many.

By its calculations, there was still 1,000 beds too many in the Twin Cities. The HSA detailed nine ways to achieve the cuts. Once again, the data seemed clear: several area hospitals were superfluous. One of the most cost-effective plans would be to shut them down.

One of the endangered hospitals, Mount Sinai, mobilized. The studies had overlooked a crucial political fact: Mount Sinai was the "only Jewish hospital in the upper Midwest." It had been founded, three decades earlier, in response to anti-Semitism. Still pursuing its antidiscriminatory mission, Mount Sinai claimed to care for more black people than any other hospital in the Twin Cities.[92]

The political cause was irresistible. Jewish groups were furious. The media took their side. "The Health Board's draft report," editorialized the *Star*, "is long on numbers and short on concern with people." The *Tribune* added, "The health board must . . . explain with more than statistics why some institutions are left to stay open while others are urged to shut their doors."[93]

Republican politicians happily seized their opportunity. Congressman Bill Frenzel urged, "bury the proposal as soon as possible so our hospitals can turn their attention to caring for the sick rather than . . . defending themselves against bureaucrats." Senator David Durenberger's staff issued a statement suggesting government "has no place limiting our choices unnecessarily. . . . We don't go around closing restaurants or small businesses that we feel aren't doing a good job." Senator Rudy Boschwitz and Governor Albert Quie joined in. Several bills materialized in the Minnesota legislature: they proposed reining in and, in one case, shutting down the Health Systems Agency. As a local reporter noted, "criticizing the report is a safe issue on which politicians could appeal to many voters. . . . It pits small hospitals against the bureaucracy."[94]

The health board had committed the classic "goo-goo" blunder: it believed the self-evident rightness of its rational plans for the public good. Eventually, threatened institutions were able to mobilize opposition by invoking more powerful political symbols than the reformers had at their disposal—racial justice, faith in the market, and hostility to government bureaucrats. As the politically motivated criticism mounted, the board retreated. It voted unanimously to drop its findings. Then, in a further effort to calm the protest, it abandoned its regulatory mission altogether. Like countless politicians before, the agency discovered the promise of market competition. The market would eventually weed out the unnecessary beds—precisely the logic that the HSA's past efforts had assumed wrong. Henceforth, the mission of the Metropolitan Health Board would be to help structure a properly functioning market which might reduce costs without inhibiting quality. (As it turned out, the new emphasis on completion would accelerate the rise in costs.)[95]

Few HSAs in the nation had pursued the rational planning ideal with more skill or self-assurance than the Metropolitan Health Board. Yet, when the imperatives of organizational survival shifted, so did the agency. After a decade of regulatory fervor, it turned on a dime and became an advocate of competition. The transformation was precisely the same one that had impelled the conservatives in Idaho or the providers in Atlanta to turn themselves into regulators in the 1970s.

The political legacy was also the same. The HSA had, in the universalistic Twin Cities style, accomplished precisely what the other HSAs accomplished, each in the political fashion of its area. It had taken a largely independent, highly prestigious industry and subordinated it to public authority. Like the earlier manifestations of the democratic wish, the HSAs were swept to the political periphery within the decade (and, finally, defunded in 1986). However, before fading into irrelevance, they had transformed the American politics of health care.

CONCLUSION

The five agencies I have sketched operated in different political settings, recruited different kinds of board members (using different mechanisms of representation), pursued different goals, and fought completely different political fights. At the start, each reflected the local political scene. The Planning Act (read naïvely) appeared to sanction their diversity. However, providers in Atlanta, rural conservatives in Idaho, politicians and planners locked in an old Philadelphia conflict, corporate politics in Detroit, and the Progressive ideal in the Twin Cities all produced the same outcome. In every case—regardless of ideology, apparent self-interest, or the bias of organizational design— the HSAs confounded all predictions and became the most forceful regulator in the region.

Moreover, these were typical cases. Despite almost universal expectations of provider domination, HSAs across the country asserted their independence and struggled to control the health care industry. By the late 1970s, the media had discovered "the planners' new muscle" in Honolulu, Dayton, San Francisco, Pittsburgh, northern Indiana, and many other places. Two studies of the New England HSAs found almost all of them engaged in regulatory conflicts. An analysis of certificates of need concluded that the program had a small but measurable nationwide effect on capital expenditures.[96]

Most social scientists are puzzled by the entire episode. Their analyses generally focus on the economic results: since medical inflation persisted, health planning failed—a predictable consequence for such an oddly designed program. The few observers who have pursued the matter further have generally sought analytic refuge in two trusty political models—interest-group pluralism and bureaucratic process.

The neopluralists simply chart the private interests that surrounded the agencies. At the start of the program, their analysis was widely repeated. Since local providers would generally have the most concentrated interest and the greatest resources—the will and the skill—they would set the HSAs' political agenda. When the agencies unexpectedly became regulators, the pluralists concluded that the industry must have changed its mind and sponsored the change. The conclusion fits their interpretation of regulatory programs as benefits to the industry. After all, well-placed institutions could use certificates of need to fend off new market challenges. If the regulators were tough enough, they could confer a virtual franchise monopoly on existing providers.

In this case at least, the interest-group model confuses cause and consequence. Health providers spent most of the century fighting for professional autonomy. When HSAs were organized in local communities, they generally continued that fight (amid exhortations to do so from national associations like the AMA). In every one of the cases examined here, the push for regulation came from some other source. In most cases, the provider groups resisted for a time; in some—Idaho, Pennsylvania—they did so throughout the 1970s. The HSAs focused on saying no even where providers disputed their legitimacy to do so. It was only after the regulatory process had been imposed that local health care institutions (in some places) sought its advantages. Providers responded to a process that was set into motion despite their efforts to check it.

Precisely the same cycle characterizes many new forms of political regulation—initial industry opposition followed by unanticipated benefits to some of its members. For example, at the dawn of national regulation, the railroads fought the Progressives, then so profited from the Interstate Commerce Commission that popular accounts picture railroad barons manipulating reformers into thrusting the reform on an apparently reluctant industry. As we have seen, a similar argument suggests that enlightened conservatives protected established élites (over their apparent objections) by manipulating labor into the NRA and black Americans into CAAs. In the health care case, the conspiracy theory has not been fully articulated. The historical details offer little support for it. It is, however, precisely the model implicit in the pluralist's interpretation of continued provider dominance: somehow the providers manipulated consumers into forcing regulation on them despite their protests.[97]

The bureaucratic model shifts the focus onto the agency staff. Congress mandated "scientific planning." Consequently every HSA had the services of professional staffers often steeped in the latest planning technique. If health care providers constituted a concentrated, intensely interested political force, they were matched and trumped by the HSA

315

staff. The latter, too, had relevant expertise and a livelihood at stake. The planners' internalized skill ideology turned on precisely the rationalized idealism that chases after abstract criteria (like the infamous 4 beds per 1,000 people) regardless of political obstacles. Staff members always exert substantial influence on volunteer organizations. In this model, they lobbied, indoctrinated, dominated, or bullied HSA board members into planning and regulating despite the board's obvious interest in more local health care services.

The bureaucratic model explains some of the events in some of the agencies. But it leaves many gaps. First, in many places the staff was not committed to the rational ideal. Some staff members were drawn from the industry itself (as in Atlanta). Often the staff of a new agency was made up of the same men and women who had come from the weaker, deferential predecessors, the CHPs. And the revolving door to the local hospital industry was madly swinging throughout the health-planning program. Other staff members (especially in the early years of the program) were community organizers interested in re-creating the political conditions of the War on Poverty; they were far more committed to social change than scientific criteria. Second, the staff failed to win the agenda that rational planners were most likely to choose—rational planning. The ideal of careful scientific planning was thrown aside along with many other goals in the bluntly political regulatory battles that occupied the HSAs. In the final analysis, the staff as well as the board members abandoned their original conceptions of HSA policy for a single-minded pursuit of health care cost containment.

In this chapter, I have elaborated a fuller interpretation, one that accounts for both the extraordinary continuities and the occasional contrasts with prior democratic politics. The peculiarities of the National Health Planning Act can be explained by the political forces that prompted it. Federal officials confronted a difficult new problem—uncontrolled growth in health care costs—without the political authority to assert an effective solution. The state had ceded its authority over health care politics to the health care professionals. Both the strength of the Americans' antistatist ideology and the weakness of their political institutions make it extremely difficult to strip control from private interests and place them in government hands. The cross-national experience suggests that national health insurance or a tough cost-containment program might have solved (or ameliorated) the problem. Such programs were repeatedly introduced and repudiated amid fears of governmental illegitimacy and incompetence. Partially as a consequence, the United States experiences the highest rate of medical inflation in the world.*

The National Industrial Recovery Act (which enacted the NRA) and the War on Poverty (which sponsored the Office of Economic Opportunity) frustrated reformers seeking more powerful solutions; similarly, the weakness of the Planning Act disappointed liberal activists in the 1970s. The state once again overcame the checks it faced by abjuring public power and calling instead on the people. The program that followed had all the trappings of the democratic wish: community, participation, a consensual public interest (to be derived by a combination of representation and science), all coupled with weak authority and an ill-defined mission. The participatory reflex was not a conscious strategy; liberals sought far stronger legislation. However, the invocation of community without any real power was all they could negotiate through the American shibboleths of dread and yearning.

Once the program was won, it underwent the recognizable cycle with a single important difference. Many groups mobilized, demanding representation. Local communities were plunged into conflicts unprecedented in the health care sector. But, in contrast to the efforts described in the preceding chapters, no single interest was powerful enough to dominate and define the health-planning program. On the contrary, the legislation had been driven by the pressures, not to empower a suppressed constituency but to subordinate a dominant one. Beneath all the legislative hand waving about "broad representation," Congress defined the people as citizens who were "not providers."

In this context, local agencies struggled to define the agenda Congress had failed to specify. A great many political forces pushed them in different policy directions. The HSAs operated in a fragile political equilibrium; they faced hostile providers, jealous local governments, suspicious state officials, and a steady barrage of litigation. (All five

---

*Uwe Reinhardt argues that "Americans spend about three percent of their GNP for the luxury of not having national health insurance."[98] The 3-percent figure derives from the differences that have developed between Canada and the United States since the early 1970s—when Canada took action and the United States deferred it.

agencies described, for instance, were sued, some repeatedly.) National organizations like the AMA lobbied Congress for an end to the experiment in medical-sector democracy. The agencies enjoyed little support once the exuberance of community representation melted into the inevitable conflicts and obvious inefficiencies of broad participation. Still, the medical inflation that had prompted the effort persisted. Federal officials had no better programmatic levers with which to address their most pressing health care problem. They hounded the agencies to be "tough," to regulate. They organized the health-planning process in a way that rendered all its other goals irrelevant. The agencies could not miss the signals. Their utility to the federal funders turned on a single issue: as the members of the Atlanta agency put it, "we bite the cost-cutting bullet or we're gone." Across the nation, the HSA volunteers internalized the message. The agencies—consumers, providers, and staff—threw themselves into the cost-cutting task. Regardless of ideology, background, or professed health care interest, they worked the unlikely regulatory apparatus. They did so because organization maintenance—organizational survival—hung in the cost-cutting balance.

Perhaps the most striking symbol of the HSA experience was a provider representative in Idaho. He was conservative; he disliked government interference; he joined the agency "to keep an eye on it"; he participated in a political environment that was avidly antiregulatory. And yet he testified in favor of a tougher Idaho certificate-of-need law because "there's not much sense in having the agency without one." He was willing to put aside political ideology and professional self-interest for the maintenance of the beleaguered organization. In a profound fashion, his experience is emblematic of the HSAs and their unexpected regulatory quest.

The lack of power that secured the legislation doomed the agencies. They did not have the political authority to achieve their policy goals. However, it is the process that mattered. The simple repetition of the HSAs' regulatory circus, year after year in every community, stripped the medical profession of its authority over medical politics.

By the early 1980s, the agencies had been swept from the political limelight to the bureaucratic periphery. A host of newer programs took their place, operating with an authority the HSA board members had unwittingly won. In many communities, lay interests that had entered health politics through health planning remained active. Business coalitions, chamber of commerce groups, corporate insurers, public officials, and consumer advocates who had sat on HSA subcommittees, debating the need for a new nursing home or hospital wing, maintained their interest in local health care politics. In addition, the state itself acquired a new legitimacy and new capacities: public officials had learned from the HSA process. The claims of professional judgment, which had once dominated medical politics, were no longer politically persuasive.[99]

By the early 1980s, a wide variety of new health policies had begun to emerge. For example, some states appropriated the authority to set all hospital rates for all payers—an extraordinary intrusion onto the most sensitive area of hospital management. In some cases, the government began not only to set the rates but to allocate the costs of uninsured patients among corporate payers—a complicated, hidden form of socialized medicine as sweeping as anything the AMA denounced when it was distributing the Reagan encomium to freedom in the early 1960s. Even the Reagan administration, caught between its free market rhetoric and its budget deficit, enacted powerful regulatory controls. Medicare payments—once set by the profession—are now computed on a new basis that profoundly penetrates the boundaries of professional authority. Rather than paying whatever hospitals charge, Medicare pays a fixed rate for each procedure, based crudely on the average charge for that treatment. Hospitals are reimbursed the fixed amount regardless of the care they actually provide. Ultimately, the change is designed to alter the practice of medicine. Rather than deferring to physicians over proper medical treatment, Medicare sets unambiguous incentives for them to do less. In the historical sweep of American health policy, it is a profound assertion of public authority. In 1983, less than twenty years after affirming the sanctity of medical judgment (in the first sections of Medicare), Congress empowered the bureaucrats in the Department of Health and Human Services to reshape it.[100]

The discourse of health care policy has been reconstructed. The medical profession has lost much of the public authority it once commanded. The health industry no longer even articulates a single perspective, but is fragmented into competing interests which have

319

little in common. The corporate payers—insurance companies, large employers, labor unions, state governments, Medicare—now exert more influence on health policy than do the physicians or the hospitals. The government itself operates with new legitimacy and capacity.[101]

None of this leads inevitably to new directions or policies. The American state remains fragmented and weak, new programs difficult to secure. Indeed, the democratic wish limited changes as much as it enabled them. The health-planning program introduced a wide variety of new political players; it subordinated an old élite. However, it did not pursue any powerful agenda at a time when many were calling for one. Canada enacted national health insurance and significantly reduced the problems of inflation and access. The United States invoked the democratic wish and injected a host of new interests into health care policy. If providers no longer dominate, the stalemate of the liberal state persists along with uncontrolled medical inflation; and the clutter of cost-cutting initiatives has helped create a new problem—some 38 million Americans without any health insurance.

At a high level of abstraction, American business might be said to have asserted control: a petit-bourgeois profession was subordinated to the rationalizing imperatives of large capital. In practice, business interests remain diffuse, their efforts at asserting control ineffectual. American corporations have found it difficult to articulate their health-sector interests, much less achieve their goals.[102] Most systemic changes—on both national and state levels—have been conceived and coordinated by government officials. Taken together they have amounted to an inchoate series of contradictory, incremental programs, alternately pursuing regulation and competition with little systematic purpose or consequence. The power that was taken from the profession has not been consolidated by any single political interest or institution.

Still, the political change should not be minimized. The next time national health insurance enters onto the political agenda (and in 1990, the liberal call is sounding), it will face the usual—daunting—political barriers to new programs. It will not, however, be damned as socialism. The state has extended its sphere of legitimate influence over the medical industry. It did so, in the 1970s, under the cover of the people.

The usual analysis is different. Powerful trends have been reshaping American medicine for decades: a huge growth in the number of physicians, what Paul Starr calls "a stunning loss of confidence" in the profession itself, the apparently inexorable inflation in medical costs, the rise of medical capitalism, the splintering of the profession into subspecialties.[103] All the trends put pressure on the medical profession and made the perpetuation of the old political patterns appear irrational. There is a diffuse belief that the trends within the profession and society are what led, inexorably, to the transformation of medical politics. As we have seen in every chapter of this book, however, great social pressures are not easily turned into new political patterns in a polity that fears its government. It was an apparently bizarre law, calling on communities to negotiate complex problems without any real authority (but with plenty of participation) that asserted public power over professional medicine. American policy makers used the democratic wish to reconfigure the power relations in the health care system. A decade later, in the 1990s, numerous political interests—corporations, governments, insurance companies—still struggle for control of health care policy; but the medical profession is scarcely among the contenders.

8

Elusive Community:
The People and the Limits of
American Government

The cure for the ailments of democracy is more democracy   —John Dewey, 1927

Where does the evolving quest for the people leave us as we face the twenty-first century? In this final chapter, I speculate about the American future and the role our democratic legacies might play in shaping it. I suggest that the old myths will have to be invoked in profoundly new ways if we are to address the challenges we face.

The democratic wish begins as a story of weak government: Americans declared their independence against "swarms of officers" and remain wary of state power two centuries later. Chaotic political institutions, marked by overlapping, uncoordinated authority, frustrate reform. I have focused on the populist urges that break the stalemate. Americans have negotiated their dread of government—and responded to a broad range of social and economic pressures—by chasing the elusive image of the people, by seeking participation in often imaginary communities. As we have seen, these democratic wishes led Americans to erect new insitutions, embrace new rules, and accept new groups.

322

The state and its bureaucracy grew; however, they never won a legitimate role at the center of our society. Instead, two centuries of state building produced a string of metaphorical legitimators for public administration: a mirror of the people (as the revolutionaries fancied their assemblies), a reflection of the people's choices (Jacksonians), the computation of disinterested science (Progressives), the outcome of the pluralistic political market (some New Dealers). Each formula was an effort to rest administrative authority on an external, automatically functioning source of legitimacy. Each was a different escape from the same threat—public officials who make independent judgments, ministers who think.

In the twentieth century, democratic wishes continue to offer Americans a potent yet partial mechanism of change. The lure of communal consensus overcomes the barriers to reform by prompting the design of new political arenas. The new institutions offer previously overlooked (or suppressed) interests an opportunity to enter American politics while focusing their struggle on representation at the political periphery. The pattern constrains the changes it enables. Despite the introduction of new interests and institutions, the process ends as it began: with the incoherent clash of private and public interests. Thus organized labor won its place in the political fray (in the 1930s) and professional medicine lost its (in the 1970s). Each reformation altered the political forces without articulating a definitive new policy; the new constellation of interests was left to thrash out incomes or social welfare or medical policy. John Dewey may have prescribed "more democracy for the ailments of democracy," but more democracy, as it has been attempted in the twentieth century, limits the oppressed at the same time as it legitimates them; it exacerbates the confusion of the American public sector at the same time as it permits the state to take on new tasks.

The often tumultuous, always unstable democratic urge does not introduce a workable notion of the people, or of the public interest, or of participatory community politics. Instead, it interrupts and reforms the regime. It leaves behind the underlying conditions it found: a political economy of self-seeking interests pushing ahead within a complex welter of political rules that advantage some citizens, disadvantage others, and seem almost invisible to all. Perhaps the essential images of the chaotic American individualism are those projected back onto the Jacksonian era by consensus historians: a dynamic, tumultuous, sweaty, ostensibly universal ambition to "get ahead, get ahead."

In the 1980s, President Ronald Reagan celebrated this ethos of American individualism with extraordinary political effect. The President won the sobriquet of the "great communicator." Perhaps he was. But what he was communicating was, as we have seen, among the most potent and persistent myths of American political life. If the democratic yearning for participation and community were not apparent in the Reagan rhetoric, the dread of government was its centerpiece. From the moment he assumed his office, the President conjured up and deprecated the oppressive swarms of officers: "We are a nation that has a government," he said at his inaugural, "not the other way around."[1]

Along with government bashing came the celebration of individualism—the "heroic dreams" of "entrepreneurs," "individuals," and "families." Citizens would, in this trusty Jacksonian construction, be free to "make their own way." And yet, amid the muscular Reagan rhetoric, there was a discordant, defensive note. A close look at his first inaugural address, for instance, yields the following: "I did not take the oath I've just taken with the intention of presiding over dissolution of the world's strongest economy." And, "We're not, as some would have us believe, doomed to an inevitable decline." And, "From time to time, we've been tempted to believe that society has become too complex to be managed by self-rule."[2] From the moment he took office, President Reagan offered Americans some of their sturdiest political conceits—usurpatious administrators, striving individuals—as counters to the frightening prospect of declining wealth and power.

Before the Reagan years, fears of decline were occasionally voiced. President Jimmy Carter, for example, diagnosed an American malaise (though, it is often said, he did not actually use the word) and was greeted with whoops of derision. Following the Reagan years, talk of decline seems ubiquitous. To cull just a handful of illustrations from the popular press: The *Wall Street Journal* routinely offers analyses of "the long decline" and "demise" of the American economy. *Time* magazine asks, "Is Government Dead?"—a question that gets a piquant turn by sharing the cover with the headline, "Wall Street Takes a Tumble." *Business Week* weighs in with "Congress: It Doesn't Work. Let's Fix It" (and again, unhappy economic news shares the cover: "Fallout from a Cheaper Yen"). The *Atlantic* offers "It's Time for an American Perestroika" (George C. Lodge) and the widely cited "The Morning After" (Peter Peterson). As their archenemies collapse, the ardent anticommunists (of the Committee for the Free World) meet and applaud speakers who lament the decline of American culture and urge that "we must be imaginative, innovative. We must do again what we did in 1945." Writing in the *New York Review of Books*, James Fallows summarizes the entire matter with "Wake Up, America!"[3]

The tales of distress fall, roughly, into three categories: the international economic order, domestic social trouble, and the deadlock of American politics. In the first category, commentary flows from the business class, focused primarily on the sudden transformation of the American economy—in a decade, the United States turned from the world's leading creditor into its largest debtor. (The business commentary should not be conflated with business interests, which often exacerbate the problem by moving their operations abroad.) The quick, macroeconomic fix was a fiddle with the currency rates; push the value of the dollar down, reasoned the policy makers, and American goods will be less expensive, foreign goods dearer, and the trade balance will right itself. However, a cheaper dollar (following the "Plaza Summit" in 1985) barely dented the trade deficit with Japan. Instead, it set off the "fire sale" of U.S. assets, snapped up by foreign investors who could now buy in the United States for less. Commented *Business Week* on relations with Japan: "You don't argue much with your banker, especially if he is also your landlord and employer." Robert Heilbronner articulated precisely what was getting on Wall Street's nerves: "The United States, for the first time in its history, is not in charge of its destiny."[4]

Underlying the trade deficit, say the declinists, is the hollowing out of the American manufacturing sector. Americans may be master salesmen, but they no longer manufacture hundreds of products—from bicycle tires to VCRs. "Within a few years," concludes one analysis, "the United States has lost positions of industrial and financial strength nurtured over the previous century."[5] Ultimately, the American economy looks, to these authors, frighteningly like a colonial one: importing high-technology items from Asia, exporting commodities (logs, soy-beans) and unfinished manufactured goods.

The international economic troubles are said to be sharpened by the massive federal budget deficit (though great jeremiads about that have been a staple of the American dread of government all along); by the piddling rate of personal savings—about 4 percent of disposable in-come (compared to 15 percent in West Germany, 20 percent in Japan, 35 percent in Taiwan); and by declining worker productivity.[6] Trans-portation networks decay, spending on research and development lags, the industrial infrastructure ages, the savings and loan industry self-destructs.

Domestic life has provoked a second literature documenting national decline. One in four children under the age of six lives in poverty (two in five for minorities). One out of four teens fails to finish high school. More than 30 million Americans are poor.[7] Roughly 37 million do not have health insurance; the uninsured have a difficult time getting health care, the hospitals that treat them are in financial trouble, and—at the same time—American health care costs are rising at eight times the Organization for Economic Cooperation and Development average (doubling the premiums for employer-sponsored health insurance in the last four years of the 1980s).[8]

We do not know how many people are homeless, nor do we agree on who fits into the category. (For example, should we count people who show up at a relative's door with no other place to live?) The most widely cited guesses suggest that 700,000 Americans are homeless on any given day, 2 million in the course of a year; perhaps 6 million are at "extremely high risk of homelessness." Judging by who shows up at the temporary shelters, roughly 1 in 3 homeless people are children under the age of twelve.[9] For all the tumult about drug abuse, treatment programs have long waiting lists (eight months for some); and there is little agreement, or even public argument, about the relative merits of different treatment strategies (drug-free versus drug-maintenance), about what to do about multiple addictions (so far, nothing), and about how such programs fit in with tough talk about punishment (so far, not at all).[10]

The litany continues, of course, and ranges from crumbling cities to rising crime. What bewilders many of the authors working this part of the "decline" field is the almost eerie quiet with which Americans seem to accept the spreading trouble. A National Academy of Science panel investigated homelessness and called it a "national disgrace"; academy officials edited the phrase out of the final report to "avoid politics" (though, in this case, the matter promptly landed in the *New York Times*). Why, wrote Michael Katz, is there so little "moral outrage at the persistence of . . . deprivation?"[11]

One answer may lie in the popular metaphor of an *underclass. U.S. News and World Report* introduced the concept (in 1977): "People who are more intractable, more socially alien, more hostile than anyone had imagined." The image of a self-destructive, probably undeserving, possibly irredeemable poor class helped isolate the reports of poverty from the American mainstream. It was more than a decade before William Julius Wilson popularized the idea that the trouble in the cities might be, simply, not enough jobs.[12]

Indeed, by the start of the 1990s, the reports of hardship had spread beyond the usual suspects (welfare recipients) and were fixing on the working class. Full-time work at a minimum wage got a family of three above the poverty line in 1980; it got them only 70 percent of the way there by 1989. Almost two million full-time workers (along with their dependents) were poor; many more, near poor.[13] These workers bear many of the burdens just described: they do not have health insurance, for example, and cannot afford to purchase it (even when they are not disqualified as poor risks in the first place).

The issue of jobs links American domestic troubles with the fears about international decline in two ways. On the one hand, the erosion of American manufacturing multiplies the problems of domestic poverty. On the other, shifting demographics mean that employers will increasingly have to rely on workers who grew up in poor families. As the population trend becomes clear, the business press frets about a work force "sufficiently skilled for jobs in the twenty-first century."[14] Platitudes about fostering better education are repeated like a mantra at each "What's Wrong with America?" gathering. Beneath the ills of education, however, lurk all the complex matters of youth and poverty in contemporary America—housing, health care, violence, drugs, racial antagonism, and on and on. A genuine revival of American education would require a sustained commitment of national energy directed at a multitude of problems.

Such reforming aspirations raise the third declinist motif: the apparent stalemate of American politics. Madison lamented the turmoil of constant turnover that plagued the Revolutionary legislatures: "half the faces" were new ones, year after year. Today's House of Representatives offers the opposite—the same faces, year after year. Better than 95 percent are now returned; short of scandal, incumbents are almost beyond reach, the Democratic party firmly entrenched. The Republicans appear to have an equally secure grasp on the executive branch, as quadrennial talk of their "lock" on the electoral college illustrates.

The public responds by disengaging: voters are vanishing. In 1960, 62.8 percent of the voting-age population turned out; in 1988, scarcely more than half. And in midterm elections, the proportion is down to one third (33.4 percent in 1986). Political scientists serve up all kinds of explanations: the decline of parties, the nature of the choices, the nature of the voters, rational calculations (it's not worth the time), and so forth.[15] Few argue that the apathy reflects a contented citizenry endorsing the status quo. In any case, political indifference contrasts sharply, both with our own past and with the ardor of the citizens of Europe and Asia in the late 1980s.

Waning electoral accountability pushes the bureaucracy still futher from public reach. The notion that elected officials control administrative chiefs who, in turn, hold subordinates to account ("overhead democracy") bears little relationship to the fragmented, far-flung American administration. A century-long parade of special commissions fruitlessly touting more efficient government offers ironic testimony against the theory. Today, as Morris Fiorina argues, members of Congress deflect problems into the bureaucracy, then assist constituents who get tangled in the administrative thickets—the essential strategy of individualized, interest-group politics.[16]

The political process, sum up the pessimists, offers Americans weak accountability, scant capacity to formulate good policy, and only feeble stabs at sustained public deliberation. American politics have always been organized to block precipitous action, but the inertia seems to have grown along with the problems we face. It is not clear whether any public official has the capacity (or the interest) to overcome the stalemate and address national needs. In a moment of frustration, Representative Charles Schumer of New York recently commented on the government's ability to address national problems: "The Founding Fathers didn't want to make it easy. They succeeded beyond their wildest dreams."[17]

Is the gloom warranted? After all, if the details are new, jeremiads about decline are older than the nation. Many colonists thought the tensions in their society were the result of lost virtue; contemporary society provokes its own version of rectitude. The old republican virtues have evolved into the bourgeois morality of hard work. Underlying our problems, in this view, are the corrosive effects of plenty on the sons and daughters of the entrepreneurs. The prophets of renewed economic probity warn that the old drive to "get ahead" by delaying gratification and working hard is being overwhelmed by the passion for instant gratification. "I told the Americans," writes Akio Morita (Sony Corporation's cofounder and chairman), "we [Japanese] are focusing on business ten years in advance while you seem to be concerned only with profits ten minutes from now. At that rate you may well never be able to compete with us."[18] National problems—from the savings and loan debacle to high school dropouts, from deficits to drugs—are said to follow from this lapse in the Protestant work ethic.

The deeper trouble, however, is just the other way round: not that Americans have lost their old habits but that a changing political universe will no longer accommodate them. The genius of American politics—government-bashing individualists pressing their own self-interest with only the loosest coordination from the center—offers few solutions to the kinds of problems I have catalogued. Frustration over that inadequacy—over the limits of American government—finds in this roster of public challenges the omens of fading national power.

Our political landscape has shifted radically from one that accommodated individualist, interest-group liberal arrangements to what I call a dense political environment. American institutions remain geared to the former. The American dilemma lies in a political process that is increasingly irrelevant to our policy problems.

The central feature of the traditional political establishment is, of course, weak and fragmented government—one not designed to focus national resources or mobilize the public for common projects. From that perspective, proposed industrial policies can be dismissed because, as skeptics enjoy repeating, it would get the government into picking business winners and losers—a spectacular flouting of the old dread of government. The suggestion that other nations have more effective medical care regimens is turned aside with the reflection that we do not have the civil service traditions necessary to import such reforms.

It is not, as we have seen, that the American government does nothing. Rather, the actions it takes are forged in a multitude of individualized agreements between public and private agents. Over time, they may sum to systematic policies (as in labor, race, and medical politics). In a fragmented, uncoordinated state, however, the pattern is difficult to discern and even more difficult to alter.

Thus, as frustrated trade negotiators keep pointing out, Americans already have an industrial policy: the state fosters entire industries with its defense and space agency contracts (through which, sure enough, government officials pick winners and losers). At the same time, a host of individual producers—the fishing or the lumber industries, for example—have negotiated their own benefits from their own public-sector clients. These arrangements reflect classic interest-group liberalism: the state disperses benefits to individual interests without regard to other claimants or systemic effects. It is precisely what a loosely organized government is adept at doing.

Once, an expanding economy—an expanding nation—accommodated an incoherent center. "Open spaces, empty jobs, and unmade fortunes," as Benjamin Barber puts it, were the right conditions for a government that offered occasional, uncoordinated, assistance and left the people to make their own way.[19] In the radically different dense environment of contemporary government, large interests and organizations—private and public, domestic and foreign—have grown interdependent. The actions of one affect numerous others, often those that seem only distantly related. Problems in such a setting are often not amenable to the simple striving of individual interests pressing ahead; there are too many consequences for too many others. Moreover, it is more difficult for government agents to assist one interest without re-

330

percussions for others. Decision making in such settings is far more complicated, marked by multiple and often unforeseen consequences. It requires policy makers to adopt a longer time horizon and to weigh an expanded range of factors.

For example, dams were once a pork barrel staple, a simple deal between public-sector suppliers and private development interests. Now, antidevelopment forces (with their feared battle cry "Not in my back yard") are likely to block these legislative boondoggles by taking them to the judiciary. More important, environmental concern—the essential illustration of "dense" politics—injects a wide number of new issues and actors into the calculus. What was once a simple transaction becomes complex and multifaceted. American political institutions are not well designed to cope with such conditions. What they produce is stalemate.

Consider a second illustration: The array of public and private institutions that are affected when hospitals dominate (or "capture," as political scientists used to say) the local rate-review board and win large rate hikes. Increased Medicaid costs raise the state's budget; Medicare increases worsen the federal deficit. Private insurance companies, their marketing decisions complicated by the uncertainties of inflation, pass the higher hospital costs on to their corporate clients. Corporations, in turn, either self-insure (as many large companies have done) or cut employee health benefits (the small-company response). When corporations self-insure, insurers lose business; when corporations cut benefits, hospitals face more patients with less insurance. In a dense political environment, even "capture" may rebound to the hospitals' disadvantage.[20] More generally, self-seeking behavior by each of these interrelated interests yields disadvantages for all of them: runaway inflation and great gaps in insurance coverage at the same time.

Precisely the same kind of complexity marks American trade policy. "There has to be someone in charge," laments Clyde Prestowitz, a former Commerce Department official. He then lists the agencies with a hand in trade policy decisions: Treasury, Commerce, Defense, Energy, Justice, the Office of the United States Trade Representative, the Export-Import Bank, the national laboratories, the National Aeronautics and Space Administration. And, of course, the corresponding muddle of congressional oversight committees.[21] Each agency (along with a host of private-sector clients) may appear somewhere in the trade-negotiating process—often in unexpected ways. Each agency, each exercise of American government power, is weak; few are coordinated with one another. Taken together, they comprise an enormously intrusive presence—assisting some, harming others, loading them all down with paperwork. The conclusion is not one Americans are used to drawing: a weak government is not just less competent; it is also more intrusive.

The new conditions lead me back to a theme I have traced through American history—the authority of public officials. The inventory of American problems, the gathering of intimations of decline, and the new political setting all press in the same unlikely direction: toward a stronger, more competent public sphere. The state lies at the heart of the issue.

Strengthening the government does not mean simply espousing particular programs and policies. Few solutions (in fact, few problems) can be placed uncontested on the political agenda. Some economists counsel, for example, against meddling with the federal deficit, or worrying about about foreign control of American assets, or venturing into national health insurance. The central issue is not that government should embark on (or eschew) any single program or strategy. It is rather that such judgments are best made by a competent, coherent, independent state. Even choosing not to intervene—saying no to well-organized claimants—requires public-sector strength. In short, a new political environment would require public officials with a far richer set of skills and a far greater discretion—bluntly, more power—than Americans have ever been willing to concede to their public officials.

Such reform implies a multitude of changes. For one thing, a more effective government would need to recruit bright, ambitious talent. To do so, we would have to change the rewards and standing of the public service. Most of our foreign competitors have long valued their civil servants. Japanese students, as James Fallows points out, compete for public posts in the same way that their American counterparts rush for openings in investment banking.[22]

Even this sea change in career aspiration is just the start. A government with the authority to make judgments would have to be less riddled with competing interests and agents, less fragmented. Harnessing national resources would require focused policies rather than the chaos of multiple, overlapping, often contradictory public- and private-sector projects that now bedevil the nation. Institutional coherence cannot be constructed with the old neo-Progressive tools—exhortations to coordination, efficiency, proper methodology, and the rest. Instead, it requires fundamental institutional reform: the Progressive–New Deal apparatus is ill constituted to meet contemporary challenges. A more competent government would require Americans to reconstruct their administrative state once again. Whatever the details, the general conception would have to put aside the checks and balances of multiple, competing authority. What we need is a state that could act—more directly, with less internal contradiction. It would, most unlikely of all, have to be a more authoritative state; as a result, perhaps most unexpectedly, it could be more accountable to the citizens for what their government does.

Finally, constructing a strong political center would require a profound change in American political thinking—a national reappraisal of ancient, powerful fears. The debate has not begun even on this conceptual level. American problems provoke long inventories of individual reformist items but rarely address the heart of the matter: the nature and power of American government.

On the contrary, politically successful reforms are likely to take the opposite tack: private-sector initiatives, metaphors of marketlike behavior, the search for consumer sovereignty. Reforms like deregulation (for all its fading popularity) stand in the ideological mainstream in that they limit the state. We can deregulate the skies; we have trouble overcoming the clash of interests required to construct a new airport.

After all, it is hard to imagine a more unlikely conclusion to the story of American state building. Stronger government means putting aside one of the most potent ideologies in America. Strong government is not necessarily more active and might well be less intrusive. It could offer Americans far more control over what their government does— and does not do. Yet, to Americans, such prospects generally have a whiff of tyranny about them. Patrick Henry smelled a rat when he got wind of the new Constitution. The notion of a strong public sphere is likely to provoke the same reaction again today. And yet the broad-ranging predicaments of our new political economy—trade, deficits, education, health care, homelessness, and so on—press for precisely this break with the American past. Once again, Americans are trapped between the imperatives for reform and the incapacity of their regime.

A vibrant society with a despised political center faces the task of transforming itself. How might it do so? If there is a single lesson in the preceding chapters, it is that great changes in American government come either with national emergencies or with great democratic movements.

The populist state building of the past, however, always led in the opposite direction—away from the state. Democracy lay "out of doors" or "in the streets" where it could be exercised directly by the people. Indeed, that has been the source of its power. "The people" appears—again and again, in all its variations—because it evokes the potent myths of yeomen citizens without provoking fears of state power. The democratic wish sidesteps the American dread, it pursues a communal unity which creates broad (always brief) coalitions that reform American politics. Democratic aspirations reinforced the weakness of the political center, as they reconstituted American government for each new era.

The present age requires stronger, more competent government. How might Americans even contemplate such an improbable prospect? One way to begin is by returning to the ideals that led Americans out of past perplexities: images of the people, community, and direct citizen participation. These are myths. But myths matter. Within each lies a crucial message for contemporary Americans.

The image of the people and their shared interest has been constructed in many fanciful ways. It has promised an objective shared interest—beyond the strife of race or class or interest group. But in the unattainable image of unity lies an important lesson. "The people" has afforded us a communal counter to self-interested individualism. For two hundred years we have tenuously balanced a republican faith with a liberal establishment (though it was not clearly articulated in that fashion for years). Americans have always managed to weigh the celebration of the individual with responsibility for community, market striving with civic sharing, the private sphere and the public good.

Communitarian values have always been more fragile; individualistic values always threaten to overwhelm them. Our current dilemma demonstrates what happens when they begin to do so. The American past offers us a rich tradition to draw on as we move to restore the balance. The first response to our present uncertainties ought to be not the quest for imaginary unity that can be discerned by some illusionary methodology, but an affirmation of our shared communal needs and aspirations.

Democratic hopes have always settled within notions of community. It is a mixed legacy. Americans have pursued genuine communal ideals—as the memory of Jefferson, Tocqueville, and Martin Luther King all testify. They have also sought community in imaginary rhetorical constructions—"the ideal hearth and fireplace of olden times" or beneficent industrial progress that would vitiate class tensions or economic need. And they have summoned the more malignant communal sentiments of race hatred or xenophobia to ugly purposes. Yet the communal image, too, suggests an alternative framework for the full range of contemporary policy troubles, a balance to the ubiquitous metaphors of the market. Every problem I have described is, at bottom, a common trouble—a challenge to our communal life. Thinking about education—or industrial decline or social insurance or the cities or the "underclass"—is impoverished, is fundamentally flawed, when it overlooks the shared nature of our troubles. The legacy of communal democracy offers us a way to think, not just about our problems, but about ourselves—about who we are and what we aspire to be.

Finally, democratic myths have always provoked popular ambitions for direct participation in politics. To be sure, the urge to reconstruct Jeffersonian wards in the grass roots have sent American reformers on great but chimerical crusades—like the War on Poverty. Or, to recall a different kind of example, bureaucratic reformers have aimed to reflect the people by mirroring the demographics of American society—as if a population sampler counted as a systematic representation of interests. The trouble with such participatory yearning is its innocence of organizational dynamics. It has been swept aside by the pressures of bureaucracy, by the dull imperatives of writing budgets and ordering paper clips. The search for a more workable form of popular participation returns us to the task of marrying democratic wishes to contemporary institutions. The present challenge is to infuse our institutions with broad, workable forms of popular participation; rather than pursing the ideal on the political fringes, linking it directly to the institutions that govern the political economy: the people indoors.

These reforming images can be, should be, tied into a political whole. Americans do not lack for policy advice. But proposals are offered individually, in an ad-hoc fashion, as if a single fix could restore the polity. Reformist notions range from technical fiddles to far-reaching improbables: currency adjustments, incentives to boost national savings, stronger parties, worker participation (a relic of early unionism, now in vogue as a Japanese management technique), or an infusion of parliamentary forms into our legislatures (briefly in vogue, perhaps as counter to celebrations of the Constitution's bicentenniel). The problem lies deeper than such solutions. The multiple glimmerings of decline all reflect the same imperative: Americans need a more powerful political center; we need to renew the public sphere.

Our past offers us an overarching ideal—the people. Contemporary challenges push us toward a more coherent government. These two— the people and the state, citizens and ministers—have balanced one another in a multitude of ways stretching back to the colonial era. Turning the American visions of community and participation into a stronger government requires a new variation of the old myths—one that leads more directly to the state Americans have long deprecated.

It is a daunting task. Change will not come, if the past is a guide, without broad populist agitation. Of course, public officials have often called the people out of doors; but contemporary leaders, on every level of government, demonstrate little appetite for reform. As we enter the 1990s, there is scant evidence of populism stirring or political leadership or sustained public debate about the strengths and weaknesses of the American system.

Still, the scope of the challenge should not obscure the force of the democratic urge. For two centuries, variations of an ancient, civic spirit have provoked the American imagination. The democratic wish has offered Americans a counter to both their individualism and their institutions, an ideological key for redefining and reconstructing the state. The communal impulse never found a permanent place within

336

our political institutions. Yet the call to community has recurred, again and again, repeatedly beckoning the American democrat. Can the search for the people be reconfigured? Can it lead Americans on still another populist crusade? One that embraces the minsters Americans have always revolted against? It is an unlikely aspiration—but the American future may depend on it.

Notes

Introduction: The Democratic Wish

1. On ironic state building, see Michael Nelson's wonderful "A Short Ironic History of American Bureaucracy," paper prepared for the annual meetings of the American Political Science Association, New York, 3–6 September 1981.

2. Although I am, of course, simplifying patterns that varied enormously across countries and centuries, the contrast to the American experience is instructive.

   The discussion follows Alexis de Tocqueville, *Democracy in America*, trans. George B. Lawrence (Garden City, N.Y.: Doubleday, 1966), 9ff.

   See also Charles Tilly, ed., *The Formation of National States in Western Europe* (Princeton, N.J.: Princeton University Press, 1975), 34–38; and, generally, the essays by Charles Tilly, Wolfram Fisher, and Peter Lundgren. Compare Tilly's more recent "War Making and State Making as Organized Crime," in Peter Evans, Dietrich Rueschemeyer, and Theda Skocpol, eds., *Bringing the State Back In* (New York: Cambridge University Press, 1985). See also Raymond Grew, ed., *Crises of Political Development in Europe and the United States* (Princeton, N.J.: Princeton University Press, 1978), especially the essays by Raymond Grew and Rogers Hollingsworth.

   For a sustained account of a more recent period, see R. R. Palmer, *The Age of Democratic Revolution* (Princeton, N.J.: Princeton University Press, 1964).

On administration more directly, see Ernest Barker, *The Development of Public Service in Western Europe* (Hamden, Conn.: Archon Books, 1966).

3. Tocqueville, *Democracy in America*, 18. Madison quoted by Gordon Wood, *The Creation of the American Republic: 1776–1787* (New York: W. W. Norton, 1969), 601.

The outstanding statement of the American liberal tradition and its escape from feudal and clerical traditions is Louis Hartz, *The Liberal Tradition in America* (New York: Harcourt, Brace & World, 1955).

This account of colonial America has come in for harsh treatment in the hands of colonial historians who demonstrate pervasive paternalistic hierarchies in both northern as well as southern colonies. See, for example, the essays in Jack Greene and J. R. Pole, *Colonial British America: Essays in the New History of the Early Modern Era* (Baltimore: Johns Hopkins University Press, 1984).

4. Declaration of Independence, 4 July 1776.

5. Tocqueville, *Democracy in America*, 60, 89. Hegel quoted by Stephen Skowroneck, *Building a New American State* (New York: Cambridge University Press, 1982), 6. James quoted by C. Vann Woodward, "The Comparability of American History," in C. Vann Woodward, ed., *Comparative Approaches to American History* (New York: Basic Books, 1968), 6.

For a now-classic effort to impart analytic bite to the concept of "stateness," see J. P. Nettl, "The State as a Conceptual Variable," *World Politics* 20 (1968): 563ff.

6. See, for example, Gaston Rimlinger, *Welfare Policy and Industrialization in Europe, America, and Russia* (New York: John Wiley, 1971). On the political uses of social welfare programs in Europe, see Paul Starr, *The Social Transformation of American Medicine* (New York: Basic Books, 1982), 237ff.

7. National Association of Manufacturers quoted by Thomas Anton, "Intergovernmental Change in the United States: An Assessment of the Literature," in Trudi Miller, ed., *Public Sector Performance* (Baltimore: Johns Hopkins University Press, 1984), 20.

Judge Tom Brady, "Communist Masses Howled with Glee on Black Monday," an editorial reprinted by Henry Steele Commager, ed., *The Struggle for Black Equality* (New York: Harper & Row, 1967).

"Our Children's Children," from a recording by Ronald Reagan distributed by the American Medical Association. Quoted by Max Skidmore, *Medicare and the American Rhetoric of Reconciliation* (University: University of Alabama Press, 1970), 127.

See Theodore J. Lowi's now classic discussion of "redistributive" politics in "American Business, Public Policy, Case Studies and Political Theory," *World Politics* 16 (July 1964): 677–715.

8. John Adams, "Thoughts on Government," in *The Political Writings of John Adams* (New York: The Liberal Arts Press, 1954), 86. See the discussion

in Hannah Pitkin, *The Concept of Representation* (Berkeley: University of California Press, 1972), 60 and, generally, chap. 4.

9. Quotations from Benjamin Barber, *Strong Democracy: Participatory Politics for a New Age* (Berkeley: University of California Press, 1984), 119–20.

10. Thomas Jefferson, Letter to Joseph Cabell (2 February 1816); Letter to John Tyler (26 May 1810); Notes on Virginia, Query XIX, all in *The Life and Selected Writings of Thomas Jefferson* (New York: Modern Library, 1944), 662, 605, 280.

11. Michael Zuckerman, *Peaceable Kingdoms: New England Towns in the Eighteenth Century* (New York: W. W. Norton, 1978). Tocqueville, *Democracy in America*, 189–90. The Progressive reformers, Wendell Phillips and G. S. Hall, quoted in William Nelson, *The Roots of American Bureaucracy, 1830–1900* (Cambridge, Mass.: Harvard University Press, 1982), 91–92.

12. The community participation literature is huge. See, for example, Carole Pateman, *Participation and Democratic Theory* (New York: Cambridge University Press, 1970); Barber, *Strong Democracy*. For a breathless and exuberant exhortation along these lines, see the Students for a Democratic Society, "The Port Huron Statement" (11–15 June 1962), reprinted in James Miller, *Democracy Is in the Streets* (New York: Simon & Schuster, 1987). The organizers' classic is Saul Alinsky, *Rules for Radicals* (New York: Vintage, 1972). For a range of recent efforts, try Robert Fisher, *Let the People Decide* (Boston: Twayne Publishers, 1984); Harry Boyte, *The Backyard Revolution* (Philadelphia: Temple University Press, 1980); Stuart Langton, *Citizen Participation in America* (Lexington, Mass.: D. C. Heath, 1978).

13. Wood, *Creation of the American Republic*, 56.

14. On adversarial democracy and its alternative, see Jane Mansbridge, *Beyond Adversary Democracy* (Chicago: University of Chicago Press, 1983); compare her "The Limits of Friendship," in Roland Pennock and John Chapman, *NOMOS XVI: Participation in Politics* (New York: Lieber-Atherton, 1975), 246.

15. For a lively articulation of the principle, see Michael J. Sandel's advice to Democratic candidates running in 1988, in "Democracy and Community: A Public Philosophy for American Liberalism," *New Republic,* 22 February 1988, pp. 20–23; Roosevelt quoted at 22.

16. James Madison, "Federalist No. 10" ("latent causes") and Alexander Hamilton, "Federalist No. 71" ("ardently wished"), in James Madison, Alexander Hamilton, and John Jay, *The Federalist Papers* (New York: Modern Library, no date).

17. Peter Marris and Martin Rein, *Dilemmas of Social Reform* (Chicago: Aldine Publishing, 1973), 7.

18. On sectional politics, see Richard Bensil, *Sectionalism and American Political Development* (Madison: University of Wisconsin Press, 1984); and Bar-

rington Moore, Jr., *Social Origins of Dictatorship and Democracy* (Boston: Beacon Press, 1966).

19. Computed from Ben Wattenberg, *Statistical History of the United States* (New York: Basic Books, 1976), 1083.

20. See Fred Block, "The Ruling Class Does Not Rule," in Thomas Ferguson and Joel Rogers, eds., *The Political Economy* (Armonk, N.Y.: M. E. Sharp, 1984).

21. "Despotic" from Thomas Jefferson, "Notes on Virginia," Query XIII, *Writings of Thomas Jefferson*, 237; "hot and heady" from James Bryce, *The American Commonwealth* (New York: Macmillan, 1888) I, 480; "Wild Irishmen" from Carl Russel Fish, *The Civil Service and Patronage* (Cambridge, Mass.: Harvard University Press, 1904), 502.

22. Daniel P. Moynihan, quoted by Marris and Rein, *Dilemmas of Social Reform*, 167.

23. *Federalist*, No. 51.

24. On idealism and liberalism, see Nancy Rosenblum, ed., *Liberalism and Moral Life* (Cambridge, Mass.: Harvard University Press, 1989), introduction. On pessimistic liberalism, see Hartz, *Liberal Tradition*; and John Diggins, *The Lost Soul of American Politics* (New York: Basic Books, 1984).

25. The most often cited works of the republican revisionism are Bernard Bailyn, *The Ideological Origins of the American Revolution* (Cambridge, Mass.: Harvard University Press, 1967); Wood, *Creation of the American Republic*; J. G. A. Pocock, *The Machiavellian Moment: Florentine Political Thought and the Atlantic Republican Tradition* (Princeton, N.J.: Princeton University Press, 1975).

Important additional work includes Drew McCoy, *The Elusive Republic: Political Economy in Jeffersonian America* (New York: W. W. Norton, 1980); Lance Banning, *The Jeffersonian Persuasion: Evolution of a Party Ideology* (Ithaca, N.Y.: Cornell University Press, 1978); Gerald Stourzh, *Alexander Hamilton and the Idea of Republican Government* (Palo Alto, Calif.: Stanford University Press, 1970).

Among the many works seeking to reconcile the traditions are Jean Yarborough, "Republicanism Reconsidered: Some Thoughts on the Foundation and Preservation of the American Republic," *Review of Politics* 41 (January 1979): 61–65; Joyce Appleby, *Capitalism and the New Social Order: The Republican Vision of the 1790s* (New York: New York University Press, 1984); Charles Taylor, "Cross Purposes: The Liberal-Communitarian Debate," in Rosenblum, *Liberalism and Moral Life*, 159–82.

26. On the critique of republicanism, see Issac Kramnick, "Republican Revisionism Revisited," *American Historical Review* 83 (June 1982): 629–64. The most agitated statement is surely Diggins, *The Lost Soul of American Politics*. Thomas Pangle, *The Spirit of Modern Republicanism* (Chicago:

University of Chicago Press, 1988), would seize republicanism away from Bailyn, Wood, and Pocock and fit it into the rubric established by Leo Strauss. See also Steven Dworetz, "The Rise of 'Cato' and the Decline of Locke," paper prepared for the annual meetings of the American Political Science Association, Washington, D.C., 1 September 1988.

The reviews in this area are great fun. See Gordon Wood on Diggins ("Hellfire Politics") and on the students of Leo Strauss ("Fundamentalists and the Constitution"), *New York Review of Books*, 28 February 1985, pp. 29–32, and 18 February 1988, pp. 33–40, respectively; Pocock on Wood and Stourzh, "Virtue and Commerce in the Eighteenth Century," *Journal of Interdisciplinary History* 3 (1972): 199–234.

27. Among the works in the nineteenth-century republican studies, see Sean Wilentz, *Chants Democratic* (New York: Oxford University Press, 1984); Christine Stansell, *City of Women* (Chicago: University of Illinois Press, 1987); Thomas James, "Rights of Conscience and State School Systems in Nineteenth-Century America," in Paul Tinkelman and Stephen Gottlieb, eds., *In Search of a Usable Past: The Origins and Implications of State Protections of Liberty* (Athens: University of Georgia Press, 1990); Jean Baker, *Affairs of Party: The Political Culture of Northern Democrats in Mid-Nineteenth Century* (Ithaca, N.Y.: Cornell University Press, 1983).

28. Samuel P. Huntington, *American Politics and the Promise of Disharmony* (Cambridge, Mass.: Harvard University Press, 1981), 24, 17, and passim.

29. Hartz, *Liberal Tradition*, is generally credited with articulating the most sweeping account of the consensus tradition and its roots. See generally the works of Daniel Bell, Seymor Martin Lipset, and David Potter for examples of the consensualist vision.

The pluralist argument was articulated in 1908 by Arthur Bentley, *The Process of Government* (Cambridge, Mass.: Harvard University Press, 1966). It was developed by David Truman, *The Governmental Process*—the title a conscious homage to Bentley—(New York: Alfred A. Knopf, 1951); Robert Dahl, *A Preface to Democratic Theory* (Chicago: University of Chicago Press, 1956); and Robert Dahl, *Who Governs?* (New Haven: Yale University Press, 1961).

For an outstanding analysis of the tradition, see J. David Greenstone, "Group Theory," in Fred Greenstein and Nelson Polsby, eds., *The Handbook of Political Science*, vol. II (Boston: Addison Wesley, 1975). See also Mark Kesselman, "The Conflictual Evolution of American Political Science: From Apologetic Pluralism to Trilateralism and Marxism," in J. David Greenstone, ed., *Public Values and Private Powers in American Politics* (Chicago: University of Chicago Press, 1982), 34–67.

The more critical neopluralists include Grant McConnell, *Private Power and American Democracy*; and Theodore Lowi, *The End of Liberalism* (New York: W. W. Norton, 1969).

30. Edmund and Helen Morgan, *The Stamp Act Crisis: Prologue to Revolution* (Chapel Hill: University of North Carolina Press, 1953). See also Edmund Morgan, "Conflict and Consensus in the American Revolution," in Stephen Kurtz and James Hutson, eds., *Essays on the American Revolution* (Chapel Hill: University of North Carolina Press, 1973). For a useful review of the early literature on conflict and consensus, see Jack Greene, "The Reappraisal of the American Revolution in Recent Historical Literature," in Jack Greene, ed., *The Reinterpretation of the American Revolution* (New York: Harper & Row, 1968). For a synthesis less hostile to the Progressives, see Gordon Wood, "Rhetoric and Reality in the American Revolution," *William and Mary Quarterly* 23 (January 1966): 3–32.

31. On the Jacksonians, see Marvin Myers, *The Jacksonian Persuasion* (New York: Vintage Books, 1960). On the Progressive era and the New Deal, see Richard Hofstadler, *The Age of Reform* (New York: Alfred A. Knopf, 1956).

32. The outstanding figure of Progressive historiography is Charles Beard. See, for example, *An Economic Interpretation of the Constitution* (New York: Macmillan, 1913). Compare the later Charles and Mary Beard, *The Rise of the American Civilization* (New York: Macmillan, 1927) and *American at Midpassage* (New York: Macmillan, 1939).

See also Vernon Parrington, *Main Currents in American Thought*, 3 vols. (New York: Harcourt, Brace & World, 1927, 1930); and John Simpson Penman, *The Irresistible Movement of Democracy* (New York: Macmillan, 1923).

See the contrast of consensualist and conflictualist historians laid out in David Noble, *The End of American History* (Minneapolis: University of Minnesota Press, 1985).

33. J. Franklin Jameson, *The American Revolution Considered as a Social Movement* (Princeton, N.J.: Princeton University Press, 1926); Beard, *Economic Interpretation of the Constitution*.

For an authoritative revision, see Wood, *Creation of the American Republic*.

34. Frances Fox Piven and Richard Cloward, *Regulating the Poor* (New York: Random House, 1971) and *Poor People's Movements* (New York: Random House, 1979).

For an earlier, neo-Progressive depiction, see Arthur M. Schlesinger, Jr.'s account of the labor and civil rights movements by comparing chap. 6 (especially "The Travail of Organized Labor") in *The Coming of the New Deal* (Boston: Houghton Mifflin, 1959) with chaps. 35 and 36 (especially "The Travail of Equal Rights") in *A Thousand Days* (Boston: Houghton Mifflin, 1965).

35. See Edward Pessen, *Riches, Class and Power Before the Civil War* (Lexington, Mass.: D. C. Heath, 1973), on the Jacksonians; Eric Foner, *Reconstruction*

(New York: Harper & Row, 1988); Walter Dean Burnham, *Critical Elections and the Mainsprings of American Democracy* (New York: W. W. Norton, 1970).

36. See Wood, "Rhetoric and Reality," 3–31.

37. Leonard White, *The Federalists, The Jeffersonians, The Jacksonians, The Republican Era* (New York: Macmillan, 1948, 1951, 1954, 1958). The best single-volume history is Paul Van Riper, *The History of the Civil Service* (Evanston, Ill.: Row, Peterson, 1958). For an article-length version, see Herbert Kaufman, "The Growth of the Federal Personnel System," in Wallace Sayre, ed., *The Federal Government Service* (Englewood Cliffs, N.J.: Prentice-Hall, 1965).

38. Matthew Crenson, *The Federal Machine: Beginnings of Bureaucracy in Jacksonian America* (Baltimore: Johns Hopkins University Press, 1975); Stephen Skowronek, *Building a New American State* (New York: Cambridge University Press, 1982); Theda Skocpol and Kenneth Finegold, "State Capacity and Economic Intervention in the Early New Deal," *Political Science Quarterly* 97 (2 [Summer 1982]): 255–77; Theda Skocpol and John Ikenberry, "The Political Formation of the American Welfare State in Political and Comparative Perspective," *Comparative Social Research* 8 (1983): 87–148; Sidney Milkis, "Programmatic Liberalism and the Rise of Administrative Politics in the United States," paper prepared for the annual meetings of the American Political Science Association, Washington, D.C., 1–4 September 1988.

39. Paul Van Riper, *History of The United States Civil Service*, 81.

Chapter 1. Representation, Revolution, and Republic

1. On the "conservative" label, see Edmund Morgan, "Conflict and Consensus in the American Revolution," in Stephen Kurtz and James Hutson, eds., *Essays on the American Revolution* (Chapel Hill: University of North Carolina Press, 1973), 290.

Many of the works cited earlier (see note 25, page 342) fit into the well-known rubrics noted in the text.

The best-known interpretation of the conflict school is Charles Beard, *An Economic Interpretation of the Constitution of the United States* (New York: Macmillan, 1913). See also J. Franklin Jameson, *The American Revolution Considered as a Social Movement* (Princeton, N.J.: Princeton University Press, 1926); and Arthur M. Schlesinger, Jr., *Prelude to Independence* (New York: Alfred A. Knopf, 1958). The contemporary critique of the Beardian view is often traced to Edmund and Helen Morgan, *The Stamp Act Crisis: Prologue to Revolution* (Chapel Hill: University of North Carolina Press, 1953).

The early literature on conflict and consensus is reviewed by Jack Greene, "The Reappraisal of the American Revolution in Recent Historical Literature," in Jack Greene, ed., *The Reinterpretation of the American Revolution* (New York: Harper & Row, 1968). For a more recent synthesis (less hostile to the Progressives), see Gordon Wood, "Rhetoric and Reality in the American Revolution," *William and Mary Quarterly* (3rd ser., 23, 1966).

2. Gordon Wood, *The Creation of the American Republic: 1776–1787* (New York: W. W. Norton, 1969), 11.

3. Bernard Bailyn, *Origins of American Politics* (New York: Random House, 1967), 59–64; and Bailyn, *The Ideological Origins of the American Revolution* (Cambridge, Mass.: Harvard University Press, 1967), 70–76.

4. See Samuel Beer, *British Politics in the Collectivist Age* (New York: Random House, 1965), 19–32; Pitt quoted at 23. See also Edmund Morgan, *Inventing the People* (New York: W. W. Norton, 1988), 146 and ff.

5. Beer, *British Politics*.

6. Both Penn and the settlers cited by Bailyn, *Origin of American Politics*, 64.

7. On the early American constitutions, see Willi Paul Adams, *The First American Constitutions: Republican Ideology and the Making of the State Constitutions in the Revolutionary Eras* (Chapel Hill: University of North Carolina Press, 1980). Quotation from the Declaration of Independence.

8. See Jack Greene and J. R. Pole, "Reconstructing British American Colonial History: An Introduction," in Jack Greene and J. R. Pole, eds., *Colonial British America: Essays in the New History of The Early Modern Era* (Baltimore: Johns Hopkins University Press, 1984), 5. Bernard Bailyn, *Origins of American Politics*, 87 (Hutchinson), 82 (Shirley). Hutchinson quote discussed in J. R. Pole, *Paths to the American Past* (New York: Oxford University Press, 1979), 232 and ff.

9. E. E. Schattschneider, *The Semisovereign People* (Hinsdale, Ill.: Dryden Press, 1960), 2.

10. Cited by Wood, *Creation of the American Republic*, 194–95.

11. Lawrence Henry Gipson, *The British Empire Before the American Revolution*, 15 vols. (New York: Alfred A. Knopf, 1958–76), vol. 9, *The Triumphant Empire: New Responsibilities Within the Enlarged Empire 1763–1766*, 18.

12. Edmund Morgan, *The Birth of the Republic: 1763–89* (Chicago: University of Chicago Press, 1977), 10–11.

13. See Michael Kammen, *People of Paradox* (New York: Random House, 1972), chap. 1; and Morgan, *Inventing the People*, 123.

14. Political scientists have often made this point. See James Q. Wilson, "The Rise of the Bureaucratic State," in Nathan Glazer and Irving Kristol, eds., *The American Commonwealth, 1976* (New York: Basic Books, 1976), 101. See also Michael Nelson, "A Short Ironic History of American Bureaucracy," paper prepared for the annual meetings of the American Political Science Association, New York, 3–6 September 1981, 4.

15. J. R. Pole, *Political Representation in England and the Origins of the American Republic* (New York: St. Martin's Press, 1966), xiv.

16. For discussion, see Pole, *Political Representation in England*, chap. 13; Whateley cited in Morgan and Morgan, *Stamp Act Crisis*, 77.

17. Edmund Burke, "The English Constitutional System," in Hannah Pitkin, ed., *Representation* (New York: Atherton Press, 1969), 175–76.

18. Cited by Hannah Pitkin, *The Concept of Representation* (Berkeley: University of California Press, 1972), 60–61 and chap. 4 generally.

19. Pitkin, *Concept of Representation*, chap. 4. See the discussion in Jean Yarborough, "Republicanism Reconsidered: Some Thoughts on the Foundation and Preservation of the American Republic," *Review of Politics* 41 (January 1979): 61–95; Thomas Jefferson, letter to John Taylor (28 May 1816), *The Life and Selected Writings of Thomas Jefferson* (New York: Modern Library, 1944), 670.

20. See Wood, *Creation of the American Republic*, chap. 5; on radicals and unicameralism in Pennsylvania, 83ff. See also Eric Foner, "Tom Paine's Republic: Radical Ideology and Social Change," in Alfred Young, ed., *The American in Revolution: Explorations in the History of American Radicalism* (DeKalb, Ill.: Northern Illinois University Press, 1976).

21. Wood, *Creation of the American Republic*, 192.

22. Ibid., 56. Chapter 2, sections 1–5 of Wood's book remain—for my money—the best introduction to civic republicanism. There are now a host of additional descriptions of the idea, most offering slightly different accounts and definitions. See, in addition to Wood, the works of Bailyn, Pocock, and Yarborough, cited earlier in this chapter. In addition, see Dorothy Ross, "The Liberal Tradition Revisited and the Republican Tradition Addressed," in John Hingham and Paul Conkin, eds., *New Directions in American Intellectual History* (Baltimore: Johns Hopkins University Press, 1979); Russell Hanson, *The Democratic Imagination in America* (Princeton, N.J.: Princeton University Press, 1985), chap. 2.

23. Wood, *Creation of the American Republic*, 62 ("multitude"), 57 ("emerge").

24. Morgan, *Inventing the People*, chap. 7; Edward Countryman, *The American Revolution* (New York: Hill & Wang, 1985), 141.

25. Thomas Jefferson, Notes on Virginia, Query XIX; Letter to Joseph Cabell (2 February 1816); Letter to John Tyler (26 May 1810), all in *The Life and Selected Writings of Thomas Jefferson* (New York: Modern Library, 1944), 280, 662, 605.

26. James Madison, "Federalist No. 10," in James Madison, Alexander Hamilton, and John Jay, *The Federalist Papers* (New York: Modern Library, no date). On the embodiment of Europe's utopian dream, see Henry Nash Smith, *Virgin Land* (Cambridge, Mass.: Harvard University Press, 1970), especially 126–32.

27. Wood, *Creation of the American Republic*, 16, 54.

28. Ibid., 57, 63.

29. On the critique of republicanism, see Issac Kramnick, "Republicanism Revisionism Revisited, *American Historical Review* 83 (June 1982): 629–64. The most agitated statement is surely John Diggins, *The Lost Soul of American Politics* (New York: Basic Books, 1984). See also Thomas Pangle, *The Spirit of Modern Republicanism* (Chicago: University of Chicago Press, 1988).

30. T. R. Malthus quoted by Jim Potter, "Demographic Development and Family Structure," in Greene and Pole, eds., *Colonial British America*, 129. For a discussion of the migrations, see Bernard Bailyn et al., *The Great Republic* (Boston: Little, Brown, 1977), 234–235.

31. Computed from Ben Wattenberg, *Statistical History of the United States* (New York: Basic Books, 1976), 1168.

32. Richard Maxwell Brown, "Violence and the American Revolution," in Kurtz and Hutson, eds., *Essays on the American Revolution*, 106ff.; Countryman, *American Revolution*, 79–87.

33. Lockridge quoted in James A. Henretta, "Wealth and Social Structure," in Greene and Pole, eds., *Colonial British America*, 280–81 and passim. Rowland Berthoff and John M. Murrin, "Feudalism, Communalism, and the Yeoman Freeholder: The American Revolution Considered as a Social Accident," in Kurtz and Hutson, eds., *Essays on the American Revolution*, 264ff.

34. Gary B. Nash, "Social Change and the Growth of Prerevolutionary Urban Radicalism," in Young, ed., *The American Revolution*, 278 and passim.

35. Richard Brown, "Violence and the American Revolution," in Kurtz and Hutson, eds., *Essays on the American Revolution*, 101ff. Dirk Hoerder, "Boston Leaders and Boston Crowds: 1765–1776," in Young, ed., *The American Revolution*, 244; Nash, "Social Change," 28, 29. Howard Zinn, *The People's History of the United States* (New York: Harper & Row, 1980), chap. 4.

36. Wood, *Creation of the American Republic*, 107–111.

37. Ibid., 112.

38. Dickinson quoted in Louis Hartz, *The Liberal Tradition in America* (New York: Harcourt, Brace & World, 1955), 48.

39. John Dickinson, "The Federal Convention: Madison's Notes of Debates," in Winton Solberg, ed., *The Federal Convention and the Formation of the American States* (New York: Bobbs-Merrill, 1958), 2 June (p. 95). Bailyn, *Origin of American Politics*, 131.

40. Morgan, *Birth of the Republic*, 36.

41. Ibid., 54, 4.

42. Bailyn, *Ideological Origins*, chap. 3; Bailyn, *Origins of American Politics*, 41–48.

43. Morgan and Morgan, *Stamp Act Crisis*, chap. 11.
44. Alfred Young quoted by Hoerder, "Boston Leaders and Boston Crowds," 242. See also Countryman, *American Revolution*, chaps. 3 and 5; Brown, "Violence and the American Revolution," 101ff.
45. Quoted by Wood, *Creation of the American Republic*, 102, 103.
46. Ibid., 102.
47. Quoted by Wood, *Creation of the American Republic*, 314. On the assemblies, see also Adams, *First American Constitutions*, 37 and, generally, chaps. 1 and 2. Ronald M. McCarthy, "Resistance Politics and the Growth of Parallel Government in America, 1765–1775," in Walter Conser, Jr., et al., eds., *Resistance in Politics, and the American Struggle for Independence, 1765–1775* (Boulder, Colo.: Lynn Reinner, 1986), 513.
48. Quoted by Wood, *Creation of the American Republic*, 317. Morgan, *Inventing the People*, 257.
49. Morris quoted by Countryman, *American Revolution*, 130. See also the discussion in Adams, *First American Constitutions*, 31; Foner, "Tom Paine's Republic," 196; Brown, "Violence and the American Revolution," 103.
50. See Countryman, *American Revolution*, 74–79 and passim; Pauline Maier, *From Resistance to Revolution* (New York: Alfred A. Knopf, 1974), especially chap. 1. See more generally George Rude, *The Crowd in History: A Study of Popular Disturbances in France and England, 1730–1848* (London: Lawrence and Wishart, 1981).
51. Foner, "Tom Paine's Republic," 195.
52. Bernard Bailyn et al., *The Great Republic* (Boston: Little, Brown, 1977), 259.
53. Wood, *Creation of the American Republic*, 102.
54. Frances Fox Piven and Richard Cloward, *Poor People's Movements; Why They Succeed, How They Fail* (New York: Random House, 1974); see also their *Regulating the Poor* (New York: Pantheon Books, 1971).
55. Patrick Henry, "Speech in the Virginia Ratifying Convention," 5 June 1788, in J. R. Pole, ed., *The American Constitution: For and Against* (New York: Hill & Wang, 1987), 119. Wood, *Creation of the American Republic*, 401. Annapolis Convention quoted in "Proceedings of Commissioners to Remedy Defects of the Federal Government," Annapolis, Maryland, 11 September 1786. Jefferson, Notes on Virginia, Query XIII, 237. Washington quoted in Wood, *Creation of the American Republic*, 482; and in Robert Wiebe, *The Opening of American Society* (New York: Vintage Books, 1984), 4.
56. Jefferson quoted in Wood, *Creation of the American Republic*, 136. On Pennsylvania, see Foner, "Tom Paine's Republic," quote from 208. See also Pole, *Political Representation in England*, 269ff. Page quoted in Leonard

White, *The Federalists* (New York: Macmillan, 1948), 22. Gerry quoted in "Madison's Notes on the Federal Convention," 31 May, 84.

57. James Madison, "Vices of the Political System of the United States," reprinted by Charles Beard, ed., *Readings in American Government and Politics* (New York: Macmillan, 1925), 43. The critique was later incorporated into *The Federalist Papers*; compare "Federalist No. 62": "It will be of little avail to the people that the laws are made by men of their own choice, if the laws be so voluminous that they cannot be read . . . if they be repealed or revised before they are promulgated. . . ."

58. Norman Jacobson, "Political Science and Political Education," *American Political Science Review* 57 (September 1963): 563. Congressional naval strategy discussed in Nelson, "A Short Ironic History," 4.

59. Madison, "The Federalist, No. 48," 332. Jefferson, "Notes on Virginia," Query XII, 237. "Bias of anger" from Wood, *Creation of the American Republic*, 404, 405.

60. Jackson Turner Main, "Government by the People: The American Revolution and the Democratization of the Legislatures," in J. R. Pole, ed., *The Advance of Democracy* (New York: Harper & Row, 1967), 78, 79, 80. "Every new election" in Madison, "The Federalist No. 62," 405.

61. Quoted by Bailyn et al., *The Great Republic*, 329. See the discussion in Countryman, *American Revolution*, 158–59.

62. Madison, "The Federalist, No. 10," 56. For a discussion of the Progressive interpretation and its critics, see Gordon Wood, "Rhetoric and Reality in the American Revolution," *William and Mary Quarterly* 23 (January 1966): 3–22. For a review of the standard literature, see Greene, "Reprisal of the American Revolution," which makes the attack on Progressive historiography its major (implicit) theme. For more recent work, see Countryman, *American Revolution*, bibliographic essay, 248–50; *New York Times* editorial on Beard noted by Zinn, *People's History*, 89.

63. Wood, *Creation of the American Republic*, chap 12; quotations at 481, 477. See also Main, "Government by the People," 62; Jackson Turner Main, *The Anti-Federalists* (New York: W. W. Norton, 1974), appendix E; James Madison, *Federalist*, No. 62.

64. Rush quoted by Wood, *Creation of the American Republic*, 426. See the discussion of Jefferson in Yarborough, "Republicanism Reconsidered."

65. Mason quoted in Madison, "The Federal Convention," 6 June, 2 May, and "Objections to this Constitution of Government," 107, 87, 338. Hamilton, *Federalist*, No. 35, 214, 216.

66. Roger Sherman ("want information," "misled," "little to do"), Elbridge Gerry ("dupes," "levelling spirit"), Edmund Randolph ("turbulence," "follies"), Madison, "Notes on the Federal Convention," 31 May, 84, 87.

For comments on this view, see Herbert J. Storing, *What the Anti-Federalists Were For: The Political Thought of the Opponents of the Constitution* (Chicago: University of Chicago Press, 1981), 39, 90, *n*19. Storing suggests that the contrasting diagnoses of danger to the republic constitute one of the major fissures between Federalists and Antifederalists.

67. Madison, "Notes on the Federal Convention," 31 May, 86, and *Federalist*, No. 10, 60, 58.

68. Wilson in Madison, "Notes on the Federal Convention," 31 May, 85; Washington described 14 September, 341 (the only time he entered into the debate). Antifederalist view from Brutus, "Essay IV: November 29, 1787," in J. R. Pole, ed., *The American Constitution: For and Against* (New York: Hill & Wang, 1987), 47.

69. Brutus, "Essay IV." Storing, *What Anti-Federalists Were For*, 44.

70. Madison, "Notes on the Federal Convention," 31 May, 86; *Federalist*, No. 10, 59, 60.

71. See Joyce Appleby, *Capitalism and a New Social Order: The Republican Vision of the 1790s* (New York: University Press, 1984); Drew R. McCoy, *The Elusive Republic: Political Economy in Jeffersonian America* (New York: W. W. Norton, 1980); Lance Banning, *The Jeffersonian Persuasion: Evolution of a Party Ideology* (Ithaca, N.Y.: Cornell University Press, 1978); Steven Watts, *The Republic Reborn: War and the Making of Liberal America, 1790–1820* (Baltimore: Johns Hopkins University Press, 1987).

72. Wood, *Creation of the American Republic*, passim; Storing, *What Anti-Federalists Were For*, 83, *n*7.

73. James Wilson, in Madison, "Notes on the Federal Convention," 31 May, 85.

74. Pole, *Political Representation in England*, 532. Diggins, *The Lost Soul of American Politics*, 19.

75. On Adams's fear that the Constitution left the chief executive too weak, see his letters to Roger Sherman, *The Works of John Adams*, Charles Francis Adams, ed. (Boston: Little, Brown, 1850–6), VI, 427–36.

76. Hamilton, *Federalist*, No. 68, 444.

77. Ibid., No. 27, 168–69.

78. Ibid., No. 17, 103; No. 27, 167; No. 46, 306; ratifying convention speech quoted by Storing, *What Anti-Federalists Were For*, 42. Both Storing and John Rohr describe the "rhetorical progress." John Rohr, *To Run a Constitution: The Legitimacy of the Administrative State* (Lawrence: University of Kansas Press, 1986), 2–3; see also Richard Sinnopoli, "Liberalism, Republicanism and the Constitution: American Citizenship Viewed from the Founder," Ph.D. dissertation, New York University, 1989.

79. Edward S. Corwin, *The President: Office and Powers* (New York: New York University Press, 1957), 12.

80. The couplet is from "An Essay on Man," Epistle IV, lines 303–304, in Aubrey Williams, ed., *Poetry and Prose of Alexander Pope* (Boston: Houghton Mifflin, 1969), 166. Hamilton, *Federalist*, No. 68, 444.

81. On Washington's appointments, see White, *Federalists*; Paul Van Riper, *History of the United States Civil Service* (Evanston, Ill.: Row, Peterson, 1958), 18–19.

82. White, *Federalists*, 514, 515.

83. Appleby, *Capitalism and a New Social Order*, 69.

84. Berthoff and Murrin, "Feudalism, Communalism, and the Yeoman Freeholder," 277–78. See also Appleby, *Capitalism and a New Social Order*, 70.

85. Hanson, *Democratic Imagination in America*, 84 ("control and influence"); Appleby, *Capitalism and the New Social Order*, 65 ("excellent when overturned").

86. Hanson, *Democratic Imagination in America*, 84 ("hateful," "hellish"); Appleby, *Capitalism and a New Social Order*, 65 ("phrenzy," "firebrands"). See also Richard Buel, Jr., *Securing the Revolution: Ideology and American Politics, 1789–1815* (Ithaca, N.Y.: Cornell University Press, 1972), 128–32.

87. For a decidedly different interpretation, see Appleby, *Capitalism and a New Social Order*. More generally, see the works cited in note 71, page 351.

88. Jefferson quoted by Leonard White, *The Jeffersonians* (New York: Macmillan, 1951), 550.

89. Wattenberg, *Statistical History of the United States*, 1104.

90. *New York Evening Post*, 13 March 1804. Quoted by Carl Russell Fish, *Civil Service and Patronage* (New York: Longmans, Green, 1905), 50.

91. White, *Jeffersonians*, 550. Sidney Aronson, *Status and Kinship in the Higher Civil Service: Standards of Selection in the Administration of John Adams, Thomas Jefferson and Andrew Jackson* (Cambridge, Mass.: Harvard University Press, 1964).

92. White, *Jeffersonians*, 546, 547. See also J. R. Pole, *The Pursuit of Equality in American History* (Los Angeles: University of California Press, 1978), 123; and Richard Hofstadter, *The Idea of a Party System* (Los Angeles: University of California Press, 1969), 159.

93. Declaration of Independence, 4 July 1776.

Notes

Chapter 2: The Resistible Rise of the Common Man: Jacksonian Democracy

1. Frederick Jackson Turner interpreted the period as sectional conflict, with Jackson as "the very personification . . . of the tenacious, vehement, personal West." *The Frontier in American History* (Tucson: University of Arizona Press, 1986), 252–53 and, generally, chap. 9. Vernon Parrington merged the revolt of "a city proletariat" to Turner's sectional argument, thus setting Jackson into the Progressive mold. See *Main Currents in American Thought*, vol. II: *The Romantic Revolution in America* (New York: Harcourt, Brace & World, 1927), 138–45, quoted on 139 ("broadcloth"). The dominant book of this literature is Arthur M. Schlesinger, Jr., *The Age of Jackson* (Boston: Little, Brown, 1945), quoted on 163 ("House of Want"). Schlesinger recasts the Progressive historiography into unabashedly New Deal terms (making Jackson a kind of neo-Progressive F.D.R.). See, for an unapologetic update, *The Cycles of American History* (Boston: Houghton Mifflin, 1986), 225–32.

   A large body of recent scholarship returns us to the themes laid out by the conflict school. See, in particular, Edward Pessen, *Riches, Class and Power Before the Civil War* (Lexington, Mass.: D. C. Heath, 1973); Edward Pessen, *Jacksonian America: Society, Personality and Politics* (Homewood, Ill.: Dorsey Press, 1978); Sean Wilentz, *Chants Democratic* (New York: Oxford University Press, 1984); and Alan Dawley, *Class and Community: The Industrial Revolution in Lynn* (Cambridge, Mass.: Harvard University Press, 1979).

2. The consensus school has, as its center work and sometime source of "data," Alexis de Tocqueville, *Democracy in America*, George B. Lawrence, trans. (Garden City, N.Y.: Doubleday, 1966); see also Louis Hartz, *The Liberal Tradition in America* (New York: Harcourt, Brace & World, 1955), part 3; Richard Hofstadter, *The American Political Tradition and the Men Who Made It* (New York: Vintage Books, 1973), chap. 3, quote on 71; Lee Benson, *The Concept of Jacksonian Democracy* (Princeton, N.J.: Princeton University Press, 1961).

3. Hartz, *Liberal Tradition*, 90; Schlesinger, quoting Abraham Lincoln, *Cycles of American History*, 232.

4. For a discussion of the "embodiment" theme, see John Ward, *Andrew Jackson: Symbol for an Age* (New York: Oxford University Press, 1953). Illustrations of the idea that Jackson physically embodied Western Democracy include Turner, *Frontier in American History*, 253; Parrington, *Romantic Revolution in America*, 139. For a popular Progressive rendition of Andrew Jackson, see Claude Bowers, *The Party Battles of the Jackson Period* (Boston and New York: Houghton Mifflin, 1922).

5. Marvin Meyers, *The Jacksonian Persuasion* (New York: Vintage, 1960), 10;

J. R. Pole, *The Pursuit of Equality in American History* (Berkeley: University of California Press, 1978), 141.

6. Wilentz, *Chants Democratic*, 63 ("over one another"). Jonathan Prude, *Coming of the Industrial Order* (New York: Cambridge University Press, 1983), 106 ("morning toddy"), and, generally, chap. 4.

7. Prude, *Coming of the Industrial Order*, 119, 120.

8. Ibid., 112.

9. Wilentz, *Chants Democratic*, 101 ("get forward"). Robert Rimini, *The Revolutionary Age of Andrew Jackson* (New York: Harper & Row, 1976), 5 ("go ahead").

10. Hofstadter, *American Political Tradition*, 78.

11. Fred Somkin, *Unquiet Eagle: Memory and Desire in the Idea of American Freedom, 1815–1860* (Ithaca, N.Y.: Cornell University Press, 1967); Robert H. Wiebe, *The Opening of American Society* (New York: Vintage Books, 1984), 136.

12. Computed from Ben Wattenberg, *Statistical History of the United States* (New York: Basic Books, 1976), 22.

13. Turner, *Frontier in American History*, 252–53.

14. Wattenberg, *Statistical History of the United States*, 106.

15. See Matthew Crenson, *The Federal Machine* (Baltimore: Johns Hopkins University Press, 1975), 162.

16. Marvin Meyers, "The Jacksonian Persuasion," in Douglas T. Miller, ed., *The Nature of Jacksonian America* (New York: John Wiley, 1972), 67, 68.

17. Meyers, *Jacksonian Persuasion*, 10 ("body of the people"); Hofstadter, *American Political Tradition*, 78 ("superior industry," "gratuities").

18. Jackson quoted by Meyers, *Jacksonian Persuasion*, 10–21.

19. Hofstadter, *American Political Tradition*, 82–85.

20. Wiebe, *Opening of American Society*, 239 ("purity"); Meyers, *Jacksonian Persuasion*, 26–27 ("morals"); James McPherson, *Battle Cry of Freedom* (New York: Oxford University Press, 1988), 27 ("enemies," etc.).

21. Paul Van Riper, *History of the United States Civil Service* (Evanston, Ill.: Row, Peterson, 1958), 55 ("bastion"); Williams Macdonald, *Jacksonian Democracy* (New York: Harper & Brothers, 1907), 45 ("unfaithful," etc.).

22. Schlesinger, *Age of Jackson*, 46 ("species of property"); Macdonald, *Jacksonian Democracy* ("quake in slippers"). See also Charles Beard, *The Rise of American Civilization* (New York: Macmillan, 1927), 555.

23. Crenson, *Federal Machine*, 164. On the Whigs and especially their articulation of the commonwealth theme, see Daniel Walker Howe, *The Political Culture of the American Whigs* (Chicago: University of Chicago Press, 1980).

24. Jackson's rhetoric taken from Meyers, *Jacksonian Persuasion*, 19–24.

25. Ibid.

26. Ibid., 24. Russell Hanson, *Democratic Imagination in America* (Princeton, N.J.: Princeton University Press, 1985), 132.
27. See Jean H. Baker, *Affairs of Party: The Political Culture of Northern Democrats in Mid-Nineteenth Century* (Ithaca, N.Y.: Cornell University Press, 1983), especially chap. 6 on the Democrats' racial attitudes.
28. On this view of the Jacksonian Democrats, see Harry Watson, *Jacksonian Politics and Community Conflict: The Emergence of a Second Party System in Cumberland County* (Baton Rouge: Louisiana State University Press, 1981); Wiebe, *Opening American Society*. Ronald Formisano, *The Transformation of Political Culture: Massachusetts Parties, 1790s–1840s* (New York: Oxford University Press, 1983), uses the concepts of core and periphery.
29. Wilentz, *Chants Democratic*, 211–14.
30. Voting percentages in Ronald Formisano, "Deferential Participant Politics: The Early Republic's Political Culture, 1789–1840," *American Political Science Review* 68 (1 [June 1974]): 482. See also Wiebe, *Opening American Society*, 348ff.
31. Formisano, "Deferential Participant Politics," 483.
32. Douglas Jaenicke, "The Jacksonian Integration of the Parties into the Constitutional System," *Political Science Quarterly* 101 (1 [1986]): 85–107, quoted at 94.
33. Van Buren quoted by Jaenicke, "Jacksonian Integration of Parties," 93. Marcy in Van Riper, *History of the Civil Service*, 30.
34. Biddle quoted in Wiebe, *Opening American Society*, 239. Webster in Richard Hofstadter, *Anti-Intellectualism in American Life* (New York: Alfred A. Knopf, 1962), 165. See Edward Pessen, *The Log Cabin Myth* (New Haven: Yale University Press, 1984), 19ff, for Harrison.
35. Computed from Wattenberg, *Statistical History of the United States*, 1072.
36. Alexis de Tocqueville, *Democracy in America*, Henry Reeve, trans., 2nd ed., 2 vols. (Cambridge, Mass.: Sever & Francis, 1863), I, 318, 319. The inauguration described in Margaret Bayard Smith, "President Jackson's Inauguration," in William Chute, ed., *The American Scene: 1600–1860* (New York: Bantam Books, 1964), 136–37. Amos Kendall quoted in Schlesinger, *Age of Jackson*, 6. James Fenimore Cooper, *The American Democrat* (New York: Alfred A. Knopf, 1956), 141.
37. Formisano, "Deferential Participant Politics," 474. See also Wiebe, *Opening American Society*, 348–52; Watson, *Jacksonian Politics and Community Conflict*; Wilentz, *Chants Democratic*.
38. An extended quote from Jackson's widely cited message can be found in Fish, *Civil Service and Patronage*, 111–12.
39. The reference to insolence in office is a quotation from Elbridge Gerry in Fish, *Civil Service and Patronage*, 81. James Bryce, *American Commonwealth* (New York: Macmillan, 1988), II, 482.
40. Pocock, *The Machiavellian Moment* (Princeton, N.J.: Princeton University

Press, 1975), 538. On New Orleans, see John William Ward, *Andrew Jackson—Symbol for an Age* (New York: Oxford University Press, 1953), chaps. 1–4.

41. Beard and Beard, *American Civilization*, 555. Sidney Aronson, *Status and Kinship in the Higher Civil Service: Standards of Selection in the Administration of John Adams, Thomas Jefferson, and Andrew Jackson* (Cambridge, Mass.: Harvard University Press, 1964), 195.

42. Lynn Marshall, "The Strange Still Birth of the Whig Party," *American Historical Review* 71 (January 1967): 445–68.

43. On Lincoln, see Van Riper, *History of the Civil Service*, 43, 47.

44. Bryce, *American Commonwealth*, vol. II, 484ff. Alexis de Tocqueville, *Democracy in America*, 89.

45. Tocqueville, *Democracy in America*, 208.

46. Leonard White, *The Jacksonians: A Study in Administrative History: 1829–1861* (New York: Macmillan, 1954), 304, 312, 314; see Ari Hoogenboom, *Outlawing the Spoils* (Urbana: University of Illinois Press, 1961), chap. 1, for a description of the offices that fell into the spoils.

47. See McPherson, *Battle Cry of Freedom*, 839, on the Thirteenth Amendment.

48. Crenson, *Federal Machine*, 170–71.

49. Ibid., 169–74.

50. Quoted in White, *The Jacksonians*, 426–27.

51. Computed from Wattenberg, *Statistical History of the United States*, 1103.

52. Ibid.

53. The argument that the Jacksonians put together an early American bureaucracy is laid out in Crenson, *Federal Machine*. For the citation to Jackson's address, see Fish, *Civil Service and Patronage*. The interpretation of Jackson's language is from Nelson, "Short Ironic History," 16; Marshall, "The Strange Still Birth of the Whig Party," 457–58 ("I want no discretion").

54. Crenson, *Federal Machine*, 164; Kendall quoted by Marshall, "The Strange Still Birth of the Whig Party," 452, "Placed and replaced" at 455–56. For the details of administrative development, see White, *The Jacksonians*, chap. 27 ("The State of Administrative Art"). Orestes Browning quoted by Schlesinger, *Age of Jackson*, 514. For a discussion, see Nelson, "Short Ironic History," 16.

55. Pessen, *Riches, Class and Power, 303*.

Chapter 3: Administrative Science and the People:
The Progressive Movement

1. Artemus Ward, cited by Paul Van Riper, *History of the United States Civil Service* (Evanston, Ill.: Row, Peterson, 1958), 60.

Notes

2. Stephen Skowronek, *Building a New American State* (New York: Cambridge University Press, 1982), 54. See also William E. Nelson, *The Roots of American Bureaucracy, 1830–1900* (Cambridge, Mass.: Harvard University Press, 1982), 88–89. See Gilbert Seldes, *The Stammering Century* (New York: John Day, 1928), for a taste of the enormous variety of reform movements.

3. Herbert Kaufman, "The Growth of the Federal Personnel System," in Wallace Sayre, ed., *The Federal Government Service* (Englewood Cliffs, N.J.: Prentice-Hall, 1965), 31.

4. A large literature seeks to sort out the multiplicity of goals and groups encompassed by Progressives. For an illustration, see the competing interpretations in Arthur Mann, *The Progressive Era*, 1st and 2nd eds. (New York: Holt, Rinehart & Winston, 1963, 1975). It is sometimes suggested that the Progressives ought to be dispensed with as a historical category; see Peter Filene, "An Obituary for 'the Progressive Movement,'" *American Quarterly* 22 (1970): 20–34.

5. On the rejection of Progressive democracy, see, for instance, John Thomas, "Nationalizing the Republic," in Bernard Bailyn et al., *The Great Republic* (Boston: Little, Brown, 1977), 900.

6. Frederick Jackson Turner, "The Significance of the Frontier in American History," *The Frontier in American History* (Tucson: University of Arizona Press, 1986), 1.

7. Quoted from *The Nation* 16 (30 January 1873): 65, in Leonard White, *The Republican Era* (New York: Macmillan, 1958), 368. For an account of the various frauds and scandals, see White, *Republican Era*, chap. 17.

8. See Robert Wiebe, *The Search for Order* (New York: Hill & Wang, 1967), 5; White, *Republican Era*, 367; Van Riper, *History of Civil Service*, 75.

9. The "offices" question quoted by James Bryce, *The American Commonwealth* (London: Macmillan, 1888), II, 455; and discussed in Van Riper, *History of Civil Service*, 60, *n.* 1

   The "Floaters" from Davis Rich Dewey, *National Problems, 1885–1897* (New York: Harper & Brothers, 1907), 144.

   Price of votes from White, *Republican Era*, 382.

10. Walter Dean Burnham, *Critical Elections and the Mainsprings of American Democracy* (New York: W. W. Norton, 1970), 75. The "orgies of office seekers" from Samuel P. Orth, *The Boss and the Machine* (New Haven: Yale University Press, 1921), 184. Garfield quoted by White, *Republican Era*, 94. Election turnouts from Ben Wattenberg, *Statistical History of the United States* (New York: Basic Books, 1976), 1072.

11. See Gerald W. McFarland, *Mugwumps, Morals, and Politics, 1884–1920* (Amherst: University of Massachusetts Press, 1975). See the description of the reformers in Ari Hoogenboom, *Outlawing the Spoils* (Urbana: University of Illinois Press, 1961), 112–13.

NOTES

12. The language of reform, including these quotations, is described in Van Riper, *History of Civil Service*, 81–82.

13. Quotations from Richard Hofstadter, *Anti-Intellectualism in American Life*, 188–89. See also George Washington Plunkett's view in William Riordan, *Plunkett of Tammany Hall* (New York: E. P. Dutton, 1863), especially chap. 4 ("Reformers Just Morning Glories").

14. See Robert Merton, "The Latest Function of the Machine," *Social Theory and Social Structure* (Glencoe, Ill.: Free Press, 1957), 71–82. For a discussion of the huge revisionist literature, see Jon Teaford, "Finis for Tweed and Steffens: Rewriting the History of Urban Rule," *Reviews in American History* (December 1982): 133–49.

15. Civil Service Reform Act, cited by Skowronek, *Building a New American State*, 57. See also Van Riper, *History of Civil Service*, 81–82.

16. See the account of this classic political battle in Skowronek, *Building a New American State*, 61–62.

17. Charles and Mary Beard, *The Rise of American Civilization* (New York: Macmillan, 1927), II, 551.

18. Michael Nelson, "A Short Ironic History of American Bureaucracy," paper prepared for the annual meetings of the American Political Science Association, New York, 3–6 September 1981, 22 ("ones to be remembered," "revealing description"); *Puck* quoted by Van Riper, *History of Civil Service*, 91. See also Edwin Erle Sparks, *National Development, 1877–1885* (New York: Harper & Brother, 1907), 192.

19. *Tribune* quoted in Hoogenboom, *Outlawing the Spoils*, 231–35; Sparks, *National Development*, 199 ("victory for people"); Van Riper, *History of Civil Service*, 94 ("devil was sick").

20. See Van Riper, *History of Civil Service*, chap. 5.

21. The argument of this and the next three paragraphs forms a major theme of Skowronek, *Building a New American State*; the numbers blanketed in are on 70–71.

22. Van Riper, *History of Civil Service*, 124.

23. Wattenberg, *Statistical History of the United States*, 1031.

24. See Burnham, *Critical Elections*, chap. 4.

25. Bryce, *American Commonwealth*, I, 158. Texas Representative John Reagan quoted in Wiebe, *Search for Order*, 8 ("there were no beggars").

26. James cited by Sparks, *National Development*, 157.

    For an analysis of the business role in municipal reform, see Samuel Hayes, "The Politics of Reform in Municipal Government in the Progressive Era," *Pacific Northwest Quarterly* 55 (1964): 157–69.

    For a more sweeping description, see Skowronek, *Building a New American State*, 50–52, and chap. 3, generally. Skowronek traces reform in this era to three sources: the patrician gentleman, merchants, the executive branch.

27. Carl Schurz, "Congress and the Spoils System," cited by Skowronek, *Building A New American State*, 55. See also *The Reminiscences of Carl Schurz* (New York: McClure, 1908), especially vol. III.

28. See Wattenberg, *Statistical History of the United States*, 1102–1103.

29. See Skowronek, *Building a New American State*, 192–93.

30. Robert La Follette, *Autobiography: A Personal Narrative of Political Experiences* (Madison, Wis.: Robert M. La-Follette, 1913), 22 ("thieving"); and Benjamin Parke De Witt, *The Progressive Movement* (New York: Macmillan, 1915; reissue, Seattle: University of Washington Press, 1968), 4–5 ("easier for the many"). De Witt remains one of the outstanding statements of the Progressive impulse.

31. Wattenberg, *Statistical History of the United States*, 1072. Classic accounts of the significance of this election include Burnham, *Critical Elections*, 73, and E. E. Schattschneider, *The Semisovereign People* (Hinsdale, Ill.: Dryden Press, 1960), 76–83.

32. Frances Parkman, "The Failure of Universal Suffrage," (1878), cited by Samuel Haber, *Efficiency and Uplift: Scientific Management in the Progressive Era* (Chicago: University of Chicago Press, 1964), 99.

33. Walter Lippmann, *The Good Society* (Boston: Little, Brown, 1937), 264 ("ideas from kings"). La Follette, *Autobiography*, 25 ("unconscious"). De Witt, *Progressive Movement*, 14 ("men realized"). The literature of the period is full of similar rhetoric. See especially the excerpts from Albert Beveridge's keynote address to the Progressive (or Bull Moose) party in Claude Bowers, *Beveridge and the Progressive Era* (New York: Literary Guild, 1932), 427 (on "invisible government"), chap. 7.

34. William Kent ("grub pile") quoted by George Mowry, *The Era of Theodore Roosevelt* (New York: Harper & Brothers, 1958), 53. La Follette quoted by Beard and Beard, *American Civilization*, 555.

35. De Witt, *Progressive Movement*, 143.

36. Jackson quoted by Beard and Beard, *American Civilization*, 554. A scandalized catalogue of the party faithfuls' professions is quoted in John Harrington, *Political Change in the Metropolis* (Boston: Little, Brown, 1981), 89. See also the description in Bryce, *American Commonwealth*, chap. 70, especially 560ff (including the appendix to the chapter). See, finally, De Witt, who complains of the "sharp practices" if not fraud of the party leaders, *Progressive Movement*, 149.

37. De Witt, *Progressive Movement*, 149–51.

38. Frederick Austin Ogg, *National Progress, 1907–1917* (New York: Harper & Brothers, 1918), 149 ("make no proper choice"). Wilson quoted by Richard Hofstadter, *The Age of Reform* (New York: Vintage Books, 1955), 266.

39. George Mowry, *The Era of Theodore Roosevelt, 1900–1912* (New York: Harper & Row, 1958), 80–81.

40. See, for instance, De Witt, *Progressive Movement*, 192.

NOTES

41. On "standing before the people," see Ogg, *National Progress*, 150, and Hofstadter, *Age of Reform*, 258.
42. Mowry, *Era of Roosevelt*, 118, 242.
43. La Follette, *Autobiography*, 64, 205, 302, 304.
44. De Witt, *Progressive Movement*, 143–49.
45. On judicial referenda, see De Witt, *Progressive Movement*, 156–61. On recall, see Mowry, *Age of Roosevelt*, 264–65.
46. Beveridge quoted by Thomas, *Great Republic*, 920. See also the discussion in Bowers, *Beveridge*, chap. 7.
47. See Herbert Croly, *The Promise of American Life* (New York: Macmillan, 1907), especially chaps. 1 and 7.
48. See the description in Mowry, *Era of Roosevelt*, chap. 3.
49. Edward Bellamy, *Looking Backward* (Boston: Houghton Mifflin, 1889), 48–49.
50. Wendell Phillips ("ideal civilization"), G. S. Hall ("educational environment"), Edward A. Ross ("solidarity"), all cited in Nelson, *Roots of American Bureaucracy*, 91. As Nelson demonstrates, there is a large Mugwump and Progressive literature of yearning for the "ideal hearth and fireplace of olden times."
51. Quoted in Mowry, *Age of Roosevelt*, 91–92.
52. Thomas Jefferson, "Notes on Virginia," Query XIX, Adrienne Koch and William Peden, eds., *The Life and Selected Writings of Thomas Jefferson* (New York: The Modern Library, 1944), 280–81.
53. Jones quoted by Thomas, *Great Republic*, 893; Haywood quoted at 970. Roosevelt quoted in Samuel P. Hays's penetrating *Conservation and the Gospel of Efficiency* (Cambridge, Mass.: Harvard University Press, 1959), 267.
54. Nelson, *Roots of American Bureaucracy*, 85–86.
55. Ibid.
56. Wiebe, *Search for Order*, 197–99.
57. See La Follette, *Autobiography*, 30–31. For comments on the Wisconsin idea, see Ralph H. Gabriel, *The Course of American Democratic Thought* (New York: Ronald Press, 1940), 332–37; and Haber, *Efficiency and Uplift*, 106.
58. The Pinchot Ballinger affair was one of the grand battles of the era, a showdown between the newly independent public administrators and a president "posing as a strong executive." Mowry, *Era of Roosevelt*, 250–59; and Skowronek, *Building a New American State*, 189–91 quoted at 191.
59. Haber, *Efficiency and Uplift*, 112.
60. James Q. Wilson, "The Rise of the Bureaucratic State," in Nathan Glazer and Irving Kristal, eds., *The American Commonwealth, 1976* (New York: Basic Books, 1976), 81–82.

61. Edward Purcell, "Ideas and Interests: Business and the Interstate Commerce Act," *Journal of American History*, 54 (December 1967): 561–78.
62. On the politics of regulation, see James Q. Wilson, *The Politics of Regulation* (New York: Basic Books, 1980), 357–94.
63. Among revisionists, see Gabriel Kolko, *Railroads and Regulation* (New York: W. W. Norton, 1965); and James Weinstein, *The Corporate Ideal in the Liberal State 1900–1908* (Boston: Beacon Press, 1968).
64. Walter E. Weyl, *The New Democracy* (New York: Macmillan, 1912), quoted in Skowronek, *Building a New American State*, 177.
65. Both proposals of Taft's Committee on Economy and Efficiency, cited by Ogg, *National Progress*, 145.
66. Quoted by Thomas, *Great Republic*, 930.
67. Hays, *Conservation*, 272–73 and passim.
68. Ibid., 274 and, generally, chap. 13.
69. Mowry, *Age of Roosevelt*, 201.
70. On the Progressives and antitrust, see Grant McConnell, *Private Power and American Democracy* (New York: Alfred A. Knopf, 1966), 38–60, good and bad trusts discussed on 40.
71. Haber, *Efficiency and Uplift*, 110.
72. Ibid., 107.
73. Robert Heilbroner, *The Economic Transformation of America* (New York: Harcourt Brace Jovanovich, 1977), 118.
74. Schattschneider, *Semisovereign People*; McConnell, *Private Power and American Democracy*; Theodore Lowi, *The End of Liberalism* (New York: W. W. Norton, 1967).

   On state-centered politics see Peter Evans, Dietrich Rueschemeyer, and Theda Skocpol, *Bringing the State Back In* (New York: Cambridge University Press, 1985); Eric Nordlinger, *On the Autonomy of the Democratic State* (Cambridge, Mass.: Harvard University Press, 1981); Samuel Beer, "Federalism, Nationalism and Democracy in America," *American Political Science Review* 72 (March 1978): 9–21.
75. Burnham, *Critical Elections*, 77.
76. Hofstadter, *Age of Reform*, 267–70.
77. Ogg, *National Progress*, 162–63.
78. Computed from Wattenburg, *Statistical History of the United States*, 1072.

Chapter 4: Progressive Administration without the People: The New Deal

1. Ben Wattenberg, *Statistical History of the United States* (New York: Basic Books, 1976). Discussed in A. J. Wann, *The President as Chief Administrator: A Study of Franklin D. Roosevelt* (Washington, D.C.: Public Affairs Press, 1968), 77–78. On the Overman Act, see Barry Karl, *Executive*

NOTES

Reorganization and Reform in the New Deal (Chicago: University of Chicago Press, 1963), 27.

2. James M. Landis, *The Administration Process* (New Haven, Conn.: Yale University Press, 1938), 24. David Lilienthal, quoted by Hofstadter, *Age of Reform*, 324 n. 8. See Lilienthal's *TVA: Democracy on the March* (New York: Harper & Row, 1944).

3. Landis, *Administrative Process*, 70.

4. Bruce Ackerman and William T. Hassler, *Clean Coal/Dirty Air* (New Haven, Conn.: Yale University Press, 1981), 6 and 4–7.

5. Landis, *Administrative Process*, 24.

6. Quoted in Hofstadter, *Age of Reform*, 307.

7. "More rapidly than causes" from Landis, *Administrative Process*, 14. "Addiction" and "nervous tic" from Arthur M. Schlesinger, Jr., *The Coming of the New Deal* (Boston: Houghton Mifflin, 1949), 535.

8. Barry Karl, *Executive Reorganization and Reform*, 197, 199.

9. On Johnson, see Schlesinger, *Coming of the New Deal*, 104–05. On Ickes and agriculture, see James McGregory Burns, *Roosevelt: The Lion and the Fox* (New York: Harcourt, Brace, 1956), 346. See also, Harold Ickes, *The Secret Diaries of Harold Ickes*, vol. II (New York: Simon & Schuster, 1954), 354–60.

10. Paraphrased from Hofstadter, *Age of Reform*, 307.

11. Quoted by William Leuchetenburg, *Franklin D. Roosevelt and the New Deal* (New York: Harper & Row, 1963), 178.

12. E. Pendleton Herring, *Public Administration and the Public Interest* (New York: McGraw-Hill, 1936), 3.

13. Bradley Behrman, "The Civil Aeronautics Board," in James Q. Wilson, *The Politics of Regulation* (New York: Basic Books, 1980), 81–88.

14. Dixon Wecter, *The Age of the Great Depression* (New York: Macmillan, 1948), 145–46. See also Grant McConnell, *Private Power and American Democracy* (New York: Alfred A. Knopf, 1966), chap. 7

15. Walter Lippmann, *Interpretations, 1933–35* (New York: Macmillan, 1936), 95 (originally published in the *Herald Tribune*, 27 July 1933). Darrow quoted by Eric Goldman, *Rendezvous with Destiny* (New York: Alfred A. Knopf, 1953), 348.

16. John Chamberlain, *Farewell to Reform: The Rise, Life and Decay of the Progressive Mind in America*, 2nd ed. (New York: John Day, 1933), 316 and, more generally, chap. 10. For a more narrow account of the Progressives in the New Deal, see Otis Graham, *An Encore for Reform: The Old Progressives and the New Deal* (New York: Oxford University Press, 1967). Graham develops a sample of major Progressive reformers and sorts out proponents and opponents of the New Deal, the latter forming a considerable majority (see especially appendix I).

17. Hofstadter, *Age of Reform*, 302–16.

Notes

18. H. L. Mencken, cited by Richard Hofstadter, *Anti-intellectualism and American Life* (New York: Alfred A. Knopf, 1953), 218, 214.

19. Rexford Tugwell, cited by Schlesinger, *Coming of the New Deal*, 534; and *Nation* 137 (4 October 1933): 371; discussed in Hofstadter, *Anti-intellectualism in American Life*, 218–19.

20. Quoted in Herring, *Public Administration*, 12.

21. Paul Van Riper, *History of the United States Civil Service*, 316–17.

22. Burns, *Roosevelt*, 363.

23. On pluralism, see note 29, p. 343.

It was not till the 1970s that the scholarly mainstream turned to examine the public sector as an autonomous power. See Samuel Beer, "The Adoption of Federal Revenue Sharing: A Case in Public Sector Politics," *Public Policy* 24 (2 [Spring 1976]): 127–95; Eric Nordlinger, *On the Autonomy of the Democratic State* (Cambridge, Mass.: Harvard University Press, 1981); and Peter Evans, Dietrich Rueschemeyer, and Theda Skocpol, *Bringing the State Back In* (New York: Cambridge University Press, 1985).

24. See the description in Burns, *Roosevelt*, chap. 15; or Leuchtenburg, *Franklin D. Roosevelt*, 231–38.

25. *The Public Papers and Addresses of Franklin D. Roosevelt*, Samuel Rosenman, ed. (New York: Random House, 1938), vol. 5, 670.

26. Karl, *Executive Reorganization and Reform*, 81.

27. Wann, *The President as Administrator*, 86.

28. Burns, *Roosevelt*, 344.

29. *Washington Star* quoted in Wann, *The President as Administrator*, 93. "Hitlerism" in Burns, *Roosevelt*, 344.

30. Ickes, *Secret Diaries*, vol. II, 360. See also the discussion in Wann, *The President as Administrator*, 96.

31. *The Public Papers and Addresses of Franklin D. Roosevelt*, Samuel Rosenman, ed. (London: Macmillan, 1941), 1938 volume, 179; see Burns, *Roosevelt*, quoted on 345, Congress described, 346. See also Wann, *The President as Administrator*, 94.

32. Margaret Weir and Theda Skocpol, "State Structures and the Possibilities for 'Keynesian' Responses to the Great Depression in Sweden, Great Britain, and the United States," in Evans, Rueschemeyer, and Skocpol, *Bringing the State Back In*, 108ff.

33. See Wattenberg, *Statistical History of the United States*, 1102.

Chapter 5. The Reconstruction of Working-Class Politics

1. Ben Wattenberg, *Statistical History of the United States* (New York: Basic Books, 1976), 178.

2. See Louis Adamic, "The Collapse of Organized Labor," *Harpers* 164

NOTES

(1932), quoted in Irving Bernstein, *The New Deal Collective Bargaining Policy* (Berkeley: University of California Press, 1950), 1. See the similar comments by George Barnett, "American Trade Unionism and Social Insurance," *American Economic Review* 23 (March 1933), quoted by David Brody, "The Expansion of the American Labor Movement," in Stephen Ambrose, ed., *Institutions in Modern America* (Baltimore: Johns Hopkins University Press, 1967), 11.

3. Lewis Lorwin, cited by J. David Greenstone, *Labor in American Politics* (New York: Alfred A. Knopf, 1969), 199. "Most violent" cited by Alan Altshuler, *Community Control: The Black Demand for Participation* (New York: Pegasus, 1970), 79.

4. Frances Perkins, *The Roosevelt I Knew* (New York: Viking Press, 1946), 221–22.

5. Quoted in Thomas P. Brooks, *Toil and Trouble: A History of American Labor* (New York: Dell Publishing, 1964), 98–99. The quotation is from a letter written to stockholders in 1902, though its spirit still guided industry at the start of the Depression.

6. See the discussion of paternalism in Amy Bridges, "Becoming American: The Working Classes in the United States before the Civil War," in Ira Katznelson and Aristide Zolberg, eds., *Working Class Formation* (Princeton, N.J.: Princeton University Press, 1986), 187–89.

7. Bernstein, *New Deal Collective Bargaining Policy*, 8–13.

8. The Interchurch Commission, cited by Frances Fox Piven and Richard Cloward, *Poor People's Movements* (New York: Random House, 1979), 104. Contrast the corporate response put out by Marshall Olds, *Analysis of the Interchurch World Movement Report on the Steel Strike* (New York: G. P. Putnam, 1923).

9. Figures reported by Piven and Cloward, *Poor People's Movements*, 103–4.

10. Josephus Daniels of North Carolina in a letter to President Franklin Roosevelt, reported in Schlesinger, *Coming of the New Deal*, 394.

11. Brooks, *Toil and Trouble*, 91.

12. *United Mine Workers* v. *Red Jacket Consolidated Coal and Coke Company*, 18 F. 2d 839, cert. den., 275 U.S. 536 (1927).

13. Brooks, *Toil and Trouble*, 92–97.

14. *Coppage* v. *Kansas*, 236 U.S. 1 (1915).

15. Samuel Gompers, *Seventy Years of Life and Labor: An Autobiography* (New York: E. P. Dutton, 1925), II, 209.

16. Brooks, *Toil and Trouble*, 97.

17. Cited in Philip S. Foner's exhaustive *History of the American Labor Movement in the United States*, vol. II (New York: International Publisher, 1955), 204.

18. Tobin and Collins both quoted in Schlesinger, *Coming of the New Deal*, 411.

19. Brody, "Expansion of the Labor Movement," 17.
20. Grant McConnell, *Private Power and American Democracy* (New York: Alfred A. Knopf, 1966), 303. *Fortune* editors quoted in Irving Bernstein, *The Lean Years: A History of the American Workers, 1920–1933* (Boston: Houghton Mifflin, 1960), 506.
21. Brody, "Expansion of the Labor Movement," 16.
22. Green quoted in Brody, "Expansion of the Labor Movement," 14. The jibe about labor statistics reported in McConnell, *Private Power and American Democracy*, 303. Role of Labor Secretary in Perkins, *The Roosevelt I Knew*, 215.
23. Wattenberg, *Statistical History of the United States*, 135.
24. Piven and Cloward, *Poor People's Movements*, 108.
25. Figures on U.S. Steel from Bernstein, *Lean Years*, 507. Stories of desperation from Leuchtenburg, *Franklin Roosevelt and the New Deal*, 2 (Philadelphia), 3 (Chicago); and Bernstein, *Lean Years*, 19 (Detroit).
26. Figures computed from Wattenberg, *Statistical History of the United States*, 164.
27. Bernstein, *Turbulent Years*, 23.
28. Jerome Frank, quoted in Schlesinger, *Coming of the New Deal*, 94. Note almost precisely the same language used by Progressives such as Walter Weyl.
29. The book by Raffaello Viglione described in Frances Perkins, *The Roosevelt I Knew*, 206.
30. Hugh Johnson, quoted by Schlesinger, *Coming of the New Deal*, 88.
31. Quoted by Robert Heilbroner, *The Economic Transformation of America* (New York: Harcourt Brace Jovanovich, 1977), 106.
32. On the business roots of New Deal industrial policy, see Robert F. Himmelberg, *Origins of the National Recovery Administration* (New York: Fordham University Press, 1976); Donald Brand, *Corporation and the Rule of Law* (Ithaca, N.Y.: Cornell University Press, 1988); and Schlesinger, *Coming of the New Deal*, 88–89.
33. United Mine Worker president, John Lewis, reported his conversion from voluntarism in Congressional hearings, quoted by Bernstein, *New Deal Collective Bargaining Policy*, 24.
34. Perkins, *The Roosevelt I Knew*, 192; and Bernstein, *Turbulent Era*, 24. Huey Long, the Louisiana Populist, describes his own influential version of the scheme in his autobiography, *Every Man a King* (New Orleans: National Book Co., 1933), chap. 31.
35. Perkins, *The Roosevelt I Knew*, 194.
36. Himmelberg, *Origins of the National Recovery Administration*, 203–4.
37. Harold Ickes, *The Secret Diaries of Harold Ickes* (New York: Simon & Schuster, 1954), vol. I, 95.

NOTES

38. See, for example, Schlesinger, *Coming of the New Deal*, 104; Perkins, *The Roosevelt I Knew*, 201.
39. Schlesinger, *Coming of the New Deal*, 99.
40. Bernstein, *Turbulent Years*, 32, 34.
41. The National Industrial Recovery Act of 16 June 1933, 48 stat., 195. For discussion of the passage, see Piven and Cloward, *Poor People's Movements*, 111–13; and Schlesinger, *Coming of the New Deal*, 98–100.
42. Quoted in Bernstein, *Turbulent Years*, 38.
43. Schlesinger, *Coming of the New Deal*, 146.
44. Ibid., 105.
45. Ibid., 110.
46. President Roosevelt quoted by Hugh Johnson, *The Blue Eagle: From Egg to Earth* (Garden City, N.Y.: Doubleday, Doran & Co., 1935), 260.
47. Ibid., 263.
48. Ibid., 264 ("one person"); Schlesinger, *Coming of the New Deal*, 115 (on Richberg).
49. Schlesinger, *Coming of the New Deal*, 116.
50. Persia Campbell, *Consumer Representation in the New Deal* (New York: Columbia University Press, 1940), 273; see, more generally, chap. 2 and conclusion.
51. Cited by Schlesinger, *Coming of the New Deal*, 130. See the more formal statement of the problem made by the Consumer Advisory Board itself, "Statement of June 10," appendix II, in Campbell, *Consumer Representation and the New Deal*, 289–90.
52. Schlesinger, *Coming of the New Deal*, 139.
53. Bernstein, *Turbulent Years*, 42. Piven and Cloward, *Poor People's Movements*, 114 (UMW membership).
54. Bernstein, *Turbulent Years*, 84–93.
55. Brooks, *Toil and Trouble*, 163.
56. Ibid., 164–65.
57. For accounts of the worker mobilization, see Bernstein, *Turbulent Years*, 93–94 (steel industry), 99–107 (rubber), 109–12 (oil).
58. Perkins, *The Roosevelt I Knew*, 210.
59. "Take it easy" quoted by Schlesinger, *Coming of the New Deal*, 140. "Mushmouth" quoted by Brooks, *Toil and Trouble*, 151.
60. Bernstein, *Turbulent Years*, 101–2.
61. Piven and Cloward, *Poor People's Movement*, 118.
62. Automobiles from Schlesinger, *Coming of the New Deal*, 395. See the same story told about miners in Bernstein, *Turbulent Years*, 106–9. See also Piven and Cloward, *Poor People's Movements*, 117–18.
63. Piven and Cloward, *Poor People's Movements*, 117. See also the descriptions in Bernstein, *Turbulent Years*, chap. 4.

64. Ford's reaction reported by Schlesinger, *Coming of the New Deal*, 117. The preference of the steel operators in Leuchtenburg, *Franklin Roosevelt and the New Deal*, 177. Employers "would be hanged," reported by Frances Perkins, *The Roosevelt I Knew*, 236.

65. Bernstein, *Turbulent Years*, 38–39.

66. Schlesinger, *Coming of the New Deal*, 147.

67. "Economic blackmail" in Schlesinger, *Coming of the New Deal*, 145. See Bernstein, *Turbulent Years*, 68. The Burns Company's enthusiasm unearthed by the La Follette Senate Subcommittee on Civil Liberties cited by Brooks, *Toil and Trouble*, 164.

68. Computed from Wattenberg, *Statistical History of the United States*, 179. The record of strikes during the summer months from Schlesinger, *Coming of the New Deal*, 145.

69. Bernstein, *Turbulent Years*, 273 *(San Francisco Chronicle)*; Hugh Johnson quoted in Schlesinger, *Coming of the New Deal*, 392.

70. Sevareid quoted in Bernstein, *Turbulent Years*, 217 and, generally, 229–52 on Teamsters' strike.

71. *Fibre and Fabric* quoted in Schlesinger, *Coming of the New Deal*, 394; figures from Piven and Cloward, *Poor People's Movements*, 126.

72. Figures from Bernstein, *Turbulent Years*, 172.

73. Schlesinger, *Coming of the New Deal*, 146.

74. Perkins, *The Roosevelt I Knew*, 238–39.

75. Bernstein, *Turbulent Years*, 183–84.

76. Quotations from Schlesinger, *Coming of the New Deal*, 149; see the description in Bernstein, *Turbulent Years*, 177–78.

77. Bernstein, *Turbulent Years*, 183–86.

78. Sloan in Bernstein, *Turbulent Years*, 185. *Times* cited by Piven and Cloward, *Poor People's Movements*, 127.

79. Bernstein, *Tubulent Years*, 197.

80. Smith quoted by Leuchtenburg, *Franklin Roosevelt and New Deal*, 178. Other quotes from Schlesinger, *Coming of the New Deal*, 404–5; Leon Keyserling, "Why the Wagner Act?" in L. G. Silverberg, ed., *The Wagner Act After Ten Years* (Washington, D.C.: The Bureau of National Affairs, 1945), 21.

81. Lewis quoted by Keyserling, "Why the Wagner Act?" 21; Garrison in Schlesinger, *Coming of the New Deal*, 404, American Communist party, 405.

82. Leuchtenburg, *Franklin Roosevelt and New Deal*, 151.

83. Charles Beard with Mary Beard, *America at Midpassage* (New York: Macmillan, 1939), 524.

84. *NLRB* v. *Jones and Laughlin Steel Corporation*, 301 U.S. 1 (1937).

85. Brooks, *Toil and Trouble*, 171.

86. Ibid., 180.

87. Wattenberg, *Statistical History of the United States*, 179.

88. For description of the strike, see Bernstein, *Turbulent Years*, 589–602; Brooks, *Toil and Trouble*, 181–82.

89. Figure from Piven and Cloward, *Poor People's Movements*, 140.

90. "Soda clerk" quoted in Brooks, *Toil and Trouble*, 180. For sitdown figures, see Bernstein, *Turbulent Years*, 500; Piven and Cloward, *Poor People's Movements*, 144.

91. Greenstone, *Labor in American Politics*, 45.

92. Green quoted by Schlesinger, *Coming of the New Deal*, 415.

93. Bernstein, *Turbulent Years*, 467.

94. Brody, "Expansion of the Labor Movement," 30; figures from Brooks, *Toil and Trouble*, 173.

95. Wattenberg, *Statistical History of the United States*, 177.

96. See, for example, the call for "broad executive power to wage war against the emergency," in his "Inaugural Address," *Congressional Record*, 73rd Congress, Special Session (4 March 1933), 77, pt. 5–6, reprinted in *Public Papers of Franklin Roosevelt*, vol. 2, 11–16.

97. Schlesinger, *Coming of the New Deal*, 110, 146.

98. For a brief but penetrating elaboration of these traditions, see Michael Goldfield, "Labor's Subordination to the New Deal," paper prepared for delivery at the 1985 annual meetings of the American Political Science Association, New Orleans, August 1985.

99. Schlesinger, *Coming of the New Deal*, 404–5.

100. McConnell, *Private Power and American Democracy*, chap. 9.

101. Quips taken, respectively, from Eric Goldman, *Rendezvous with Destiny*, 346; Schlesinger, *Coming of the New Deal*, 121; Leuchtenburg, *Franklin Roosevelt and the New Deal*, 185.

102. Michael Goldfield, *The Decline of Organized Labor in the United States* (Chicago: University of Chicago Press, 1987), xiv, 6.

Chapter 6. The Reconstruction of Racial Politics

1. Computed from Ben Wattenberg, *Statistical History of the United States* (New York: Basic Books, 1976), 422; see also the data from Tuskegee Institute, reprinted in Eric Lincoln, *The Negro Pilgrimage in America* (New York: Bantam Books, 1967), 81. See the discussion in John Hope Franklin, *From Slavery to Freedom: A History of the Negro Americans* (New York: Random House, 1969), 468–87.

2. Lucius J. Barker and Jesse J. McCorry, Jr., *Black Americans and the Political System* (Cambridge, Mass.: Winthrop Publishers, 1976), 17–19.

3. Median income from Barker and McCorry, *Black Americans*, 34. See also Wattenberg, *Statistical History of the United States*, 303–5. The figure

ranged from .51 (1947, 1949, 1958) to a high of .57 (1952). Life expectancy from Harvard Sitkoff, *The Struggle for Black Equality* (New York: Hill & Wang, 1981), 18. Poverty figures from Barker and McCorry, *Black Americans*, 8. Unemployment from Wattenberg, *Statistical History of the United States*, 135.

4. Gunnar Myrdal, *An American Dilemma* (New York: Harper & Row, 1944), 41.

5. "Nefarious design" from William A. Dunning, *Reconstruction and Political Economy, 1865–1887* (New York: Harper & Brothers, 1917), chap. 21, 117. Dunning is perhaps the author most often identified with the traditional view of Reconstruction which featured vindictive Northern Republicans, unscrupulous white Southerners, and gullible freemen. Perhaps what is most remarkable is how long this cartoon image survived. See Eric Foner, *Reconstruction* (New York: Harper & Row, 1988), chap. 1, for discussion.

   The astonishingly sympathetic defense of KKK violence in James Truslow Adams, *The March of Democracy* (New York: Charles Scribner, 1933), II, 129–32. See also Claude Bowers, *The Tragic Era: The Revolution after Lincoln* (Cambridge, Mass.: Houghton Mifflin, 1929). "This travesty" in Adams, *March of Democracy*, 130–32.

6. David H. Donald, "Uniting the Republic," in Bernard Bailyn et al., *The Great Republic* (Boston: Little, Brown, 1977), 811–12.

7. For a description of the Populist effort to construct an interracial coalition in the South, see C. Vann Woodward, *The Strange Career of Jim Crow* (New York: Oxford University Press, 1966), 60–65; "ditch" at 61.

   The precarious coalition was broken by a combination of distrust on the part of black and white Populists and massive fraud by the Bourbon Democrats.

8. V. O. Key, Jr., *Southern Politics* (New York: Alfred A. Knopf, 1949), 537. The income figure taken from Bailyn et al., *The Great Republic*, 811.

9. Key, *Southern Politics*, 567.

10. Louisiana figures from Woodward, *Strange Career of Jim Crow*, 85; 1940 figures compiled by the Southern Regional Council, cited at 141. The 1956 figures compiled by the Southern Regional Council, reprinted in John Hope Franklin and Isidore Starr, eds., *The Negro in Twentieth Century America* (New York: Random House, 1967), 329. The 6 votes out of 13,000 from Key, *Southern Politics*, 566. Figures from Selma in Woodward, *Strange Career of Jim Crow*, 186–87.

11. See Wattenberg, *Statistical History of the United States*, 95. See also Sitkoff, *Struggle for Black Equality*, 8. The 40-percent figure from Barker and McCorry, *Black Americans*, 3.

12. See Bette Woody, *Managing Crisis Cities: The New Black Leadership and the Politics of Resource Allocation* (Westport, Conn.: Greenwood Press, 1982),

chap. 3; and *The Report of the National Advisory Commission on Civil Disorders* (New York: Bantam Books, 1968), 57.

13. See the discussion in J. David Greenstone and Paul Peterson, "Racial Change and Citizen Participation: The Mobilization of Low Income Communities through Community Action," in Robert Havemen, ed., *A Decade of Federal Antipoverty Programs* (New York: Academic Press, 1977), 252; and Frances Fox Piven and Richard A. Cloward, *Regulating the Poor: The Functions of Public Welfare* (New York: Random House, 1971), 240.

14. See William Gould, *Black Workers in White Unions: Job Discrimination in the United States* (Ithaca, N.Y.: Cornell University Press, 1977), chap. 1.

15. Barker and McCorry, *Black Americans*, 8.

16. "Agitation" from Booker T. Washington's celebrated "Atlanta Exposition Address," reprinted in Franklin and Starr, *Negro in Twentieth Century America*, 87; "We shall prosper," at 86; "Cast down your buckets," at 86, emphasis added. "Merit . . . rewarded" from Booker T. Washington, *Up from Slavery*, in *Three Negro Classics* (New York: Avon Books, 1965), 50. "The best course" and "Be patient" quoted by Sitkoff, *Struggle for Black Equality*, 7.

17. C. Vann Woodward, *Origins of the New South 1877–1913* (Louisiana State University Press and The Littlefield Fund for Southern History, 1971), 357–60.

18. See Sitkoff, *Struggle for Black Equality*, 12–13, 18.

19. W. E. B. Du Bois, *The Souls of Black Folks* (New York: American Library, 1982) [written in 1903], quoted at 94; see generally 79–95. Kenneth Dolbeare, ed., *American Political Thought* (Chatham, N.J.: Chatham House, 1981), 420.

20. Ibid.

21. Benjamin Quarles, *The Negro in the Making of America* (New York: Collier Books, 1964), 216–17.

22. Harold Ickes, *The Secret Diary of Harold Ickes*, vol. III, *The Lowering Clouds* (New York: Simon & Schuster, 1954), 516.

23. Manning Marable, *Black American Politics: From the Washington Marches to Jesse Jackson* (London: Verso, 1985), 79–87; Garvey quoted at 63, 66, 65. Garvey's rejection of Du Bois from Sitkoff, *Struggle for Black Equality*, 9–10. Du Bois on Garvey, from *Souls of Black Folk*, 89.

24. Robert Hayden, "Fly Away Home," in the *Norton Anthology of English Poetry* (New York: W. W. Norton, 1970), 1096. For a delightful description of the myth, see Virginia Hamilton, *The People Could Fly: American Black Folktales* (New York: Alfred A. Knopf, 1985), 166–72.

25. The three strategic responses to black oppression are implicit in Du Bois, *Souls of Black Folks*, 88ff.

26. I am applying the classic categories laid out in Albert O. Hirschman,

Exit, Voice and Loyalty (Cambridge, Mass.: Harvard University Press, 1970).

27. Quoted in Howard Zinn, *A People's History of the United States* (New York: Harper & Row, 1980), 440.

28. Truman and the State Department both quoted by Robert Fisher, *Let the People Decide: Neighborhood Organizing in America* (Boston: Twayne Publishers, 1984), 97.

29. For concern with the new Africa, see, for example, John Hope Franklin, *From Slavery to Freedom*, 622; Stokely Carmichael and Charles Hamilton, *Black Power: The Politics of Liberation in America* (New York: Vintage, 1967), chap. 1. *Malcolm X Speaks*, George Breitman, ed. (New York: Grove Press, 1965), 72–87.

30. Arthur M. Schlesinger, Jr., *A Thousand Days* (New York: Houghton Mifflin, 1965), 866.

31. White primary first struck down in *Nixon* v. *Hernden* 273 U.S. 536, 47 S. Ct. 446 (1927). Private club struck down in *Smith* v. *Allwright* 321 U.S. 649, 64 S. Ct. 757 (1944).

   For a review of the cases leading up to *Brown*, see John H. McCord, ed., *With All Deliberate Speed: Civil Rights Theory and Reality* (Urbana: University of Illinois Press, 1969), 18. See also Richard Kluger, *Simple Justice: The History of Brown v. Board of Education and Black America's Struggle for Equality* (New York: Vintage Books, 1977).

32. Respectively, *Shelly* v. *Kramer*, 334 U.S. 1, 68 S. Ct. 836 (1948); *Morgan* v. *Virginia*, 328 U.S. 373, 66 S. Ct. 1050 (1946); *Henderson* v. *United States*, 339 U.S. 816, 70 S. Ct. 843 (1960).

33. The separate but equal doctrine was, of course, set out in *Plessy* v. *Ferguson*, 163 U.S. 537, 16 S. Ct. 1138 (1896).

34. *Missouri ex rel. Gaines* v. *Canada*, 305 U.S. 337, 59 S. Ct. 232 (1938); *Sweat* v. *Painter*, 339 U.S. 629, 70 S. Ct. 849 (1950); *McLaurin* v. *Oklahoma State Regents*, 339 U.S. 637, 70 S. Ct. 851 (1950).

35. *Brown* v. *Board of Education*, 347 U.S. 483, 74 S. Ct. 686 (1954).

36. See the discussion in Sitkoff, *Struggle for Black Equality*, 23–24.

37. Alexander Bickel, *The Least Dangerous Branch* (New York: Bobbs-Merrill, 1962), 256.

38. *Nashville Tennessean* and Vandiver both quoted in Woodward, *Strange Career of Jim Crow*, 150, 153.

39. Powell quoted in Louis E. Lomax, *The Negro Revolt* (New York: Signet Books, 1962), 85. Emancipation Proclamation reference in Sitkoff, *Struggle for Black Equality*, 23.

40. Judge Tom Brady, "Communist Masses Howled with Glee on Black Monday," in Henry Steele Commager, ed., *The Struggle for Racial Equality: A Documentary Record* (New York: Harper & Row, 1967), 71–72; East-

land cited in Judge Tom Brady, "The Press Charges the Court with Treason," 70.

41. The manifesto is reprinted in Franklin and Starr, *Negro in Twentieth Century America*. For discussion, see Bickel, *Least Dangerous Branch*, 256–57; and Anthony Lewis, *Portrait of a Decade: The Second American Revolution* (New York: Bantam Books, 1964), 38.

42. Quoted in Sitkoff, *Struggle for Black Equality*, 26; and Woodward, *Strange Career of Jim Crow*, 156 ("massive resistance").

43. The language of nullification drawn from an Alabama statute, cited in Woodward, *Strange Career of Jim Crow*, 156–57; Graves quoted at 159.

44. Lynching figure from Wattenberg, *Statistical History of the United States*, 422. For discussion, see Franklin, *From Slavery to Freedom*, 619.

45. Bickel, *Least Dangerous Branch*, 266.

46. See Lewis, *Portrait of a Decade*, chap. 4.

47. See Sitkoff, *Struggle for Black Equality*, 25.

48. *New York Times*, 24 September 1957, quoted in its entirety by Lewis, *Portrait of a Decade*, 43–47. The description of the black children from Bickel, *Least Dangerous Branch*, 267.

49. "Speech by President Eisenhower Explaining Why Federal Troops Were Being Sent to Little Rock," reprinted by Franklin and Starr, *Negro in Twentieth Century America*, 289–90.

50. For discussion of the political consequences of Little Rock, see Woodward, *Strange Career of Jim Crow*, 167; Lewis, *Portrait of a Decade*, 47; Sitkoff, *Struggle for Black Equality*, 33.

51. Quoted in Sitkoff, *Struggle for Black Equality,* 42.

52. Ibid., 50.

53. Ibid., 52.

54. *Browder* v. *Gayle*, 142 F. Supp. 707, aff'd per curiam, 352 U.S. 903, 77 S. Ct. 145 (1956).

55. For a general discussion of Montgomery, see Lewis, *Portrait of a Decade*, chap. 5; Lomax, *Negro Revolt*, chap. 8; and Sitkoff, *Struggle for Black Equality*, chap. 1.

56. Respectively, *Department of Conservation and Development* v. *Tate*, 231 F. 2d 615 (4th cir.), cert. den., 352 U.S. 838, 77 S. Ct. 58 (1956); *Muir* v. *Louisville Park Theatrical Assoc.*, 347 U.S. 971, 74 S. Ct. 783 (1955); *Dawson* v. *Mayor and City Council of Baltimore*, 220 F. 2d 396 (4th cir.), aff'd per curiam, 350 U.S. 877, 76 S. Ct. 133 (1955); *Holmes* v. *City of Atlanta*, 350 U.S. 879, 76 S. Ct. 141 (1955).

57. Franklin, *From Slavery to Freedom*, 622.

58. These widely cited figures are taken from the Southern Regional Council. See Quarles, *Negro in the Making of America*, 253.

59. Ibid.
60. Schlesinger, *A Thousand Days*, 855.
61. Woodward, *Strange Career of Jim Crow*, 170.
62. Schlesinger, *A Thousand Days*, 858–61.
63. Ibid., 861.
64. Woodward, *Strange Career of Jim Crow*, 174.
65. Wallace quoted in Woodward, *Strange Career of Jim Crow*, 175–76. See also the account in Schlesinger, *A Thousand Days*, 880. An enormous number of accounts document the extraordinary violence against black people: for instance, Farmer, "A Night of Terror in Plaquemine, Louisiana," in Commager, ed., *Struggle for Racial Equality*, 134.
66. Theodore White, *The Making of the President 1960* (New York: Atheneum, 1961), 354.
67. Students for a Democratic Society, "The Port Huron Statement," 353.
68. Schlesinger, *A Thousand Days*, 850.
69. See David Garrow, *Bearing the Cross* (New York: Vintage Books, 1986), chap. 4.
70. Sitkoff, *Struggle for Black Equality*, 130.
71. Martin Luther King, "Letter from Birmingham City Jail" (Philadelphia: American Friends Service Committee, May, 1963).
72. Schlesinger, *A Thousand Days*, 875.
73. Woodward, *Strange Career of Jim Crow*, 77.
74. Schlesinger, *A Thousand Days*, 875.
75. Figures from Woodward, *Strange Career of Jim Crow*, 179; and Piven and Cloward, *Regulating the Poor*, 245.
76. Schlesinger, *A Thousand Days*, 879.
77. Ibid., 881.
78. John F. Kennedy, "Radio and Television Report to the American People on Civil Rights," 11 June 1962, reprinted in Franklin and Starr, *Negro in Twentieth Century America*, 217–21.
79. Data from Schlesinger, *A Thousand Days*, 872; King quoted at 854.
80. Computed from United States Commission on Civil Rights, *Political Participation: A Study of Participation by Negroes in the Electoral and Political Processes in 10 Southern States since Passage of the Voting Rights Act* (Washington, D.C.: United States Government Printing Office, 1968), 12–13; and Lewis, *Portrait of a Decade*, 106–7.
81. Schlesinger, *A Thousand Days*, 885.
82. Lewis, *Portrait of a Decade*, 216ff.; *Times* article reprinted at 216; Baker quoted at 219.
83. See Marable, *Black American Politics*, 87–97; quotations cited at 92–93. Humphrey quoted by Lewis, *Portrait of a Decade*, 217.

84. Farmer, "A Night of Terror," 137.
85. Woodward, *Strange Career of Jim Crow*, 178.
86. The figures are widely cited: see Woodward, *Strange Career of Jim Crow*, 186.
87. Reprinted in Franklin and Starr, *Negro in Twentieth Century America*, 218.
88. Quoted in Sitkoff, *Struggle for Black Equality*, 211.
89. Schlesinger, *A Thousand Days*, 885.
90. Malcolm X, "Message to the Grass Roots," in *Malcolm X Speaks* (New York: Grove Press, 1965), 14–17.
91. Lomax, *The Negro Revolt*, 96.
92. Marable, *Black American Politics*, 97
93. See, for an example, Lomax, *Negro Revolt*, 100 and, generally on King, 96–111.
94. Malcolm X, in *Malcolm X Speaks*, 6. Carmichael quoted in Sitkoff, *Struggle for Black Equality*, 214. The philosophy of "black power" is perhaps most lucidly articulated in Carmichael and Hamilton, *Black Power*. The other books noted are James Baldwin, *The Fire Next Time* (New York: Dell, 1963); Robert F. Williams, *Negroes with Guns* (cited by Schlesinger, *A Thousand Days*, 874); Julius Lester, *Look Out, Whitey! Black Power's Gon' Get Your Mama!* (New York: Dial Press, 1968).
95. Woodward, *Strange Career of Jim Crow*, 183–84. Poll data from *New York Times*, 21 September 1964, reprinted in Franklin and Starr, *Negro in Twentieth Century America*, 212–13.
96. Daniel Bell writing in *Time* magazine, as quoted in Lewis, *Portrait of a Decade*, 228ff.
97. Michael Harrington, *The Other America* (Baltimore: Penguin Books, 1962), 11–12.
98. On Kennedy's reaction to poverty, see Richard Blumenthal, "The Bureaucracy: Anti-Poverty and the Community Action Program," in Alan Sindler, ed., *American Political Institutions and Public Policy*, 144–45. For discussion, see Peter Eisinger, in Havemen, *A Decade of Federal Antipoverty Programs*, 280–81.
99. Adam Yarmolinsky, in James Sundquist, ed., *On Fighting Poverty* (New York: Basic Books, 1969), 49.
100. John Strange, "Citizen Participation in Community Action and Model Cities Programs," *Public Administration Review* 22 (1972): 657. S. M. Miller and Martin Rein are more blunt: "poor meant black"' see "Participation, Poverty and Administration," *Public Administration Review* 29 (January–February 1969): 15–24.

   See also, John Wheeler, "Civil Rights Groups—Their Impact upon the War on Poverty," Robinson O. Everett, ed., *Anti-Poverty Programs* (Dobbs Ferry, N.Y.: Oceana Publications, 1966).

101. See Grace Olivarez, "Spanish Speaking Americans," *Public Administration Review* 22 (1972): 648–51.

102. Schlesinger, *A Thousand Days*, 922–23.

103. See James Sundquist, "Origins of the War On Poverty," in Sundquist, ed., *On Fighting Poverty*, 14 and, generally, 14–25.

104. Daniel Ylvisker, quoted in Peter Marris and Martin Rein, *Dilemmas of Social Reform* (Chicago: Aldine Publishing, 1967), 209.

105. The Ford Foundation's reform ideal is described in Marris and Rein, *Dilemmas of Social Reform*, 14–20 and 208–9.

106. "Obsessively" is Marris and Rein's term; see *Dilemmas of Social Reform*, 24.

107. Richard Cloward and Lloyd Ohlin, *Delinquency and Opportunity: A Theory of Delinquent Gangs* (New York: Free Press, 1960).

108. On the guerrillas, see Blumenthal, "Bureaucracy: Anti-poverty and the Community Action Program," 133ff. Sundquist provides a deft short description of the origins of the War on Poverty, in "Origins of the War on Poverty." For the best extended description, see Marris and Rein, *Dilemmas of Social Reform*.

   For a fascinating analysis of the War on Poverty from the perspective of its programmatic design, see Paul Schulman, *Large Scale Policy Making* (New York: Elsevier, 1980), chap. 5.

109. Mark Arnold, "The Good War That Might Have Been Won," *New York Times Sunday Magazine*, 29 September 1974, 56. See also Robert Plotnick and Felicity Skidmore, *Progress Against Poverty* (New York: Academic Press, 1975), 2–6.

110. Quoted by Paul Peterson and David Greenstone, "The Mobilization of Low Income Communities through Community Action," 253.

111. Mark Arnold, "Good War," 57.

112. For a full list of the programs and their budgets, see Felicity Skidmore, "The Establishment of the War on Poverty and OEO," in Robert Plotnick and Felicity Skidmore, eds., *Progress Against Poverty*, table 1.1, 7.

113. See the discussion in Schulman, *Large Scale Policy Making*, 93–94.

114. The community and consensus theme is ubiquitous. Lyndon Johnson quoted in Sundquist, "Origins of the War on Poverty," 23. The administrator quoted is John Wofford; see his "The Politics of Local Responsibility," in Sundquist, ed., *On Fighting Poverty*, 73–74 and passim. See also Sanford Kravitz, "The Community Action Program," in Sundquist, ed., *On Fighting Poverty*, 61; and Kravitz and Ferne Kolodner, "Community Action: Where Has It Been? Where Will It Go?" in *Annals of the American Academy of Political and Social Science* 385 (September 1969): 34.

115. Yarmolinsky, "Beginnings of OEO," 50.

NOTES

116. Daniel P. Moynihan, *Maximum Feasible Misunderstanding* (New York: Free Press, 1969), chap. 5.

117. See John C. Donovan, *The Politics of Poverty* (New York: Pegasus, 1967), 36–37 and chap. 2.

118. See Donovan, *Politics of Poverty*, 36; and Roger Davidson, "The War on Poverty: Experiment in Federalism," *Annals of the American Academy of Political and Social Science* 385 (September 1969): 2–3.

119. On the similar tone between the civil rights movement and the Community Action Program, see Kravitz, "Community Action Program," 63; and Richard Boone, "Reflections on Citizen Participation and the Economic Opportunity Act," *Public Administration Review* 22 (September 1972): 446.

120. The timing is described by Wofford in "Politics of Local Responsibility," 80. The study referred to is entitled "Community Representation in Community Action Agencies," conducted by the Florence Heller Graduate School; reported in David Austin, "Resident Participation: Political Mobilization or Organizational Cooptation?" *Public Administration Review* 11 (September–October 1972): 412.

121. Fisher, *Let the People Decide*, 114.

122. See the description in Wofford, "Politics of Local Responsibility," 80–81.

123. Ralph M. Kramer, *Participation of the Poor: Comparative Community Case Studies in the War on Poverty* (Englewood Cliffs, N.J.: Prentice-Hall, 1969), chap. 2.

124. Woody, *Managing Crisis Cities*, 69–70 and chap. 3 generally.

125. Ibid., 72.

126. Quoted in J. David Greenstone and Paul Peterson, *Race and Authority in Urban Politics: Community Participation and the War on Poverty* (Chicago: University of Chicago Press, 1973), 20.

127. "The Community Action Guide," described in Blumenthal, "Bureaucracy: Anti-poverty and the Community Action Program," 173.

128. Greenstone and Peterson, "Mobilization of Low Income Communities," 257. See also the description in Marris and Rein, *Dilemmas of Social Reform*, 216ff.; "Radical Democracy was in fashion," is their summary.

129. Greenstone and Peterson, "Mobilization of Low Income Communities," 258.

130. Lillian B. Rubin, "Maximum Feasible Participation: The Origins, Implications, and Present Status," *Annals of the American Academy of Political and Social Science* 385 (September 1969): 26, *n.* 2.

131. For an extremely penetrating analysis about the different electoral devices and their implications, see Greenstone and Peterson, *Race and Authority in Urban Politics*, chap. 6.

132. Marris and Rein, *Dilemmas of Social Reform*, 216.

133. Shriver quoted in Kramer, *Participation of the Poor*, 14.
134. The interpretation of the preceding three paragraphs draws heavily from Greenstone and Peterson, "Mobilization of Low Income Communities," 253ff. The comment regarding "the 1960s" comes from Strange, "Citizen Participation," 655.
135. Moynihan, *Maximum Feasible Misunderstanding*, 132–33.
136. *Report of the National Advisory Commission on Civil Disorders*, 56ff., especially 62. See also Woody, *Managing Crisis Cities*, chap. 3; and Moynihan, *Maximum Feasible Misunderstanding*, 156.
137. James Sundquist, with the collaboration of David Davis, *Making Federalism Work* (Washington, D.C.: Brookings Institution, 1969), 64.
138. Moynihan, *Maximum Feasible Misunderstanding*, 156–57.
139. Schlesinger, *A Thousand Days*, 878–79.
140. Moynihan, *Maximum Feasible Misunderstanding*, 149.
141. From a speech given by Moynihan, quoted by Marris and Rein, *Dilemmas of Social Reform*, 167.
142. Figures from *Report of the National Advisory Commission on Civil Disorders*, 57.
143. The description is quoted from a Senate hearing by Donovan, *Politics of Poverty*, 84; for a description of the case, generally, see chap. 6.
144. Sundquist and Davis, *Making Federalism Work*, 37. See also Donovan, *Politics of Poverty*, chap. 6.
145. See Blumenthal, "Bureaucracy: Anti-Poverty and the Community Action Program," 130; Sundquist and Davis, *Making Federalism Work*, 64.
146. Shelley quoted by Fisher, *Let the People Decide*, 119. For a similar list of agency activities, see Sundquist and Davis, *Making Federalism Work*, 63.
147. See the discussion of public-sector coordinators in T. R. Marmor and Elizabeth Kutza, *Analysis of Federal Regulations Related to Aging: Legislative Barriers to Coordination under Title III*, submitted to the United States Department of Health Education and Welfare, The Administration on Aging under grant No. DHEW (SRS) 90-A-364-01, October 1975.
148. For both a description and an analysis, see Piven and Cloward, *Regulating the Poor*, 306–312. Medicaid and housing cases treated in Marris and Rein, *Dilemmas of Social Reform*, 288. Durham noted in Austin, "Resident Participation: Political Mobilization or Organizational Cooptation?" 417.
149. Arnold, "Good War," 61. See also Piven and Cloward, *Regulating the Poor*, 312ff.
150. Greenstone and Peterson, "Mobilization of Low Income Communities," 271.
151. Sundquist and Davis, *Making Federalism Work*, 57.
152. Ibid., 49.

NOTES

153. See the participant observation account of Louis Zurcher, "Selection of Indigenous Leadership," reprinted in Hans B. C. Spiegel, *Citizen Participation in Urban Development* (Washington, D.C.: National Association for Applied Behavioral Science, 1968), 78–112. Zurcher observes a group of very suspicious native Americans; in this case, there was some success as the group began to get caught up in the process, almost despite themselves.
154. See the descriptions in Donovan, *Politics of Poverty*, 55; and Fisher, *Let the People Decide*, 117.
155. Davidson, "War on Poverty," 80.
156. Donovan, *Politics of Poverty*, 57.
157. The theme of contented black people being stirred up by outside trouble makers was ubiquitous, just as it had been after *Brown* v. *Board of Ed.* See, for just two examples, Blumenthal, "Bureaucracy: Anti-Poverty and the Community Action Program," 129; or Sundquist and Davis, *Making Federalism Work*, 65.
158. Marris and Rein, *Dilemmas of Social Reform*, 250.
159. Ibid.
160. Donovan, *Politics of Poverty*, 58.
161. Harry McPherson, quoted by Steven Lawson, *In Pursuit of Power: Southern Blacks and Electoral Politics, 1965–1982* (New York: Columbia University Press, 1985), 6.
162. Arnold, "Good War," 60.
163. Informal veto described by Roger Davidson, "War on Poverty," 9. Shriver comment printed in the *CAP Guide*, 7, quoted by Kramer, *Participation of the Poor*, 10, *n.* 13. Emphasis in the original.
164. Wattenberg, *Statistical History of the United States*, 1083.
165. See Davidson, "War on Poverty," 12.
166. The term "middle age" taken from Marris and Rein, *Dilemmas of Social Reform*, 253. The classic life cycle of government agencies in Marver Bernstein, *Regulating Business by Independent Commission* (Princeton, N.J.: Princeton University Press, 1955), chap. 2.
167. Fisher, *Let the People Decide*, 117.
168. Marris and Rein, *Dilemmas of Social Reform*, 254.
169. Sundquist and Davis, *Making Federalism Work*, 65–66.
170. Strange, "Citizen Participation in Community Action and Model Cities Programs," 658.
171. Quoted in Moynihan, *Maximum Feasible Misunderstanding*, 139.
172. Kravitz, "Community Action Program," 66.
173. See Howard Hallman, "Federally Financed Citizen Participation," *Public Administration Review* 22 (September–October 1972): 423.
174. Austin, "Resident Participation," 411–12.

175. "Unprecedented opportunity" from Strange, "Citizen Participation," 659. Moynihan, *Maximum Feasible Misunderstanding*, 129. Jobs estimate taken from Arnold, "Good War," 72. Piven and Cloward, *Regulating the Poor*, 261.

176. Greenstone and Peterson, "Mobilization of Low Income Communities," 262–63.

177. See Sundquist and Davis, *Making Federalism Work*, 62.

178. See Ronald Warren, "Model Cities First Round: Politics, Planning and Participation," *Journal of the American Institute of Planners* 35 (4 [July 1969]): 249. (The entire issue is on citizen representation.)

    For a discussion on model cities in the context of the War on Poverty, see Marris and Rein, *Dilemmas of Social Reform*, epilogue. See also Sundquist and Davis, *Making Federalism Work*, chap. 3.

    For a gripping account of the process described in the text, see "Maximum Feasible Manipulation," as told to Sherry Arnstein, the fight of a group of community leaders to influence the Philadelphia Model Cities program. See also the retort, "The View from City Hall," an unsigned, vaguely bureaucratic response that highlights the mayor's resolve not to lose control of the poverty program. Both articles in *Public Administration Review* 22 (September 1972): 377–401.

179. Moynihan, *Maximum Feasible Misunderstanding*, 129. The author cannot resist an extra shot—the full quote is "Tammany at its best (or worst) . . ."

180. *Examination of the War on Poverty*, prepared for the Subcommittee on Employment, Manpower and Poverty of the Committee on Labor and Public Welfare, United States Senate (Washington, D.C.: United States Government Printing Office, 1967), V, 1238, 1241–42.

181. Woody, *Managing Crisis Cities*, chap. 3.

182. Greenstone and Peterson, *Race and Authority in Urban Politics*, 37.

183. See Rufus Browning, Dale Rogers Marshall, and David Tabb, *Protest Is Not Enough: The Struggle of Blacks and Hispanics for Equality in Urban Politics* (Berkeley: University of California Press, 1984); Woody, *Managing Crisis Cities*, especially 24 and ff.; Greenstone and Peterson, "Mobilization of Low Income Communities," especially 271–73; Arnold, "Good War." And Peter Eisinger, "The Community Action Program and the Development of Black Political Leadership," in Dale Rogers Marshall, ed., *Urban Policy Making* (Beverly Hills, Calif.: Sage Publications, 1979), 127–44.

184. See *Statistical Abstract of the United States, 1984*, United States Commerce Department, Bureau of the Census (Washington, D.C.: United States Government Printing Office, 1983), 261 (for elected officials); Peter Eisinger, *Politics of Displacement* (New York: Academic Press, 1980), xvii (for mayors).

185. Piven and Cloward, *Regulating the Poor*, 267.
186. Figures on race and income are spotty before the 1950s, voluminous after the 1960s. Those presented in this paragraph are only illustrations. They are taken from Marable, *Black American Politics*, 104; and Jennifer L. Hochschild, *The New American Dilemma: Liberal Democracy and Social Desegregation* (New Haven: Yale University Press, 1984), 19–21. See also Hochschild, "Race, Class, and Power," in *Working Papers 10: Democratic Values* (Washington, D.C.: National Conference on Social Welfare, 1986). Michael Katz, *The Undeserving Poor: From the War on Poverty to the War on Welfare* (New York: Pantheon, 1989), 241.
187. Ira Katznelson, *Black Men, White Cities* (New York: Oxford University Press, 1973), 3.

Chapter 7: The Reconstruction of Medical Politics

1. Daniel Bell, *The Coming of Post Industrial Society* (New York: Basic Books, 1973), 31–33.
2. For discussions of medical professionalism, see Paul Starr, *The Transformation of American Medicine* (New York: Basic Books, 1982), chap. 1 and passim; and Eliot Freidson, *Profession of Medicine* (New York: Dodd, Mead, 1970).
3. The physician who tried the medical cooperative was Michael Shadid, discussed in Starr, *Transformation of American Medicine*, 303–4. See also Michael Shadid, *A Doctor for the People* (New York: Vanguard Press, 1939). On the more general issue of professional dominance over entry requirements, see George Stigler, "The Theory of Economic Regulation," *Bell Journal of Economics* 2 (1 [Spring 1971]): 3–21.
4. See the powerful critique of the American Medical Association by the editors of the *Yale Law Journal*, "The American Medical Association: Power, Purpose and Politics in Organized Medicine," *Yale Law Journal* 63 (May 1954): 933–1022, especially 950–53; quoted at 953. On the issue of racial discrimination, the authors note that four Southern medical societies reported no black members, n. 23.
5. Quoted in "The American Medical Association," *Yale Law Journal*, 955.
6. For the classic analysis of both Medicare and American interest-group politics, see T. R. Marmor, *The Politics of Medicare* (New York: Aldine Publishing, 1970); public opinion discussed at 111–12. Contrast the British case described by Harry Eckstein, *Interest Group Politics* (Palo Alto, Calif.: Stanford University Press, 1960).
7. "Compulsory" social insurance as "dangerous," quoted by Starr, *Transformation of American Medicine*, 253. "Forces representing," quoted by Odin Anderson, "The Legislative History of Medicare," in Eugene Feingold, ed., *Medicare: Policy and Politics* (San Francisco: Chandler Publishing, 1966), 90.

"Keystone" from Max Skidmore, *Medicare and the American Rhetoric of Reconciliation* (University: University of Alabama Press, 1970).

8. Starr, *Transformation of American Medicine*, 243–57.

9. The fear that the entire Social Security Act was endangered and the charge of "misrepresentation and vilification" both from Edmund Witte, *The Development of the Social Security Act* (Madison: University of Wisconsin Press, 1962), viii. The threat of boycotts discussed in Skidmore, *Medicare and the Rhetoric of Reconciliation*, 67.

10. See Starr, *Transformation of American Medicine*, 169. "Teeny weeny" from Arthur Altemeyer, *The Formative Years of Social Security* (Madison: University of Wisconsin Press, 1966), 38. Compare Frances Perkins, *The Roosevelt I Knew* (New York: Viking Press, 1946), 299.

11. For discussion, see Marmor, *Politics of Medicare*. The "final irrevocable step" from Skidmore, *Medicare and the Rhetoric of Reconciliation*, 71. The slavery notion and "Moscow" from Starr, *Transformation of American Medicine*, 282, 283–84.

12. "American way" discussed in Skidmore, *Medicare and the Rhetoric of Reconciliation*. For general discussions of the AMA as politically dominant, see Skidmore; and Richard Harris, *A Sacred Trust* (New York: New American Library, 1966).

13. For an outstanding description of Hill-Burton, see Rand Rosenblatt, "Health Care Reform and Administration Law: A Structural Approach," *Yale Law Journal* 88 (2 [December 1978]): 243–336, 264ff. "Argentina Model" is Frances Perkins's little-known appellation, *The Roosevelt I Knew*.

14. Rosenblatt, "Health Care Reform," 267.

15. Ibid.

16. On Hill-Burton financing of hospital construction, see Frank Thompson, *Health Care and the Bureaucracy* (Cambridge: M.I.T. Press, 1981), 36–42; Lester and Judith Lave, *The Hospital Construction Act: An Evaluation of the Hill-Burton Program* (Washington, D.C.: American Enterprise Institute, 1974), 2; and Starr, *Transformation of American Medicine*, 350.

17. See the instructive analysis in James Patterson, *The Cancer Crusade* (Cambridge, Mass.: Harvard University Press, 1987).

18. Starr, *Transformation of American Medicine*, 343–47.

19. For an an analysis of the liberal ideal and its political evolution, see Marmor, *Politics of Medicare*.

20. The tone of the debate is captured by Marmor, *Politics of Medicare*; Harris, *Sacred Trust*; Skimore, *Medicare and the Rhetoric of Reconciliation*; and Arthur M. Schlessinger, Jr., *A Thousand Days* (New York: Houghton Mifflin, 1965), 661–62.

21. Quoted in Skidmore, *Medicare and the Politics of Reconciliation*, 138.

22. Marmor, *Politics of Medicare*, 59.

23. Social Security Act, United States Senate Committee on Finance (Wash-

ington, D.C.: United States Government Printing Office, 1976), 399, Title XVIII, Sections 1801, 1802, 1803.

24. See Thompson, *Health Policy and the Bureaucracy*, chap. 5; Judith Feder, *Medicare: The Politics of Federal Hospital Insurance* (Lexington, Mass.: D.C. Heath, 1977).

25. Lyndon Johnson, *The Vantage Point: Perspectives on the Presidency*, 1963–1969 (New York: Holt, Rinehart & Winston, 1971), 220.

26. On Medicaid, see Robert Stevens and Rosemary Stevens, *Welfare Medicine in America* (New York: Free Press, 1974); Karen Davis and Cathy Schoen, *Health and the War on Poverty* (Washington, D.C.: Brookings, 1978), chap. 3; and Thompson, *Health Policy and the Bureaucracy*, chap. 4.

27. Starr, *Transformation of American Medicine*, quote at 371. See also Davis and Schoen, *Health and the War on Poverty*, chap. 6.

28. Ben Wattenberg, *Statistical History of the United States* (New York: Basic Books, 1976), 74; see the revised numbers in U.S. Bureau of the Census, *Statistical Abstract of the United States: 1986*, 106th edition (Washington, D.C., 1985).

29. Quotations from Starr, *Transformation of American Medicine*, 381.

30. Percentage of gross national product computed from Wattenberg, *Statistical History of the United States*, 74. Federal spending taken from Drew Altman, Richard Greene, and Harvey Sapolsky, *Health Planning and Regulation* (Washington, D.C.: AUPHA Press, 1981), 5.

31. See Paul Starr's penetrating "The Politics of Therapeutic Nihilism," *Hastings Center Reports*, October 1986, pp. 24–30. Perhaps the harshest critic of the profession was Ivan Illich, *Medical Nemesis: The Expropriation of Health* (New York: Pantheon, 1976). See also Rick Carlson, *The End of Medicine* (New York: John Wiley, 1975). For more mainstream worrying about the state of medicine, see John Knowles, *Doing Better and Feeling Worse* (New York: W. W. Norton, 1977).

32. Robert Evans and Greg Stoddart, *Medicare at Maturity* (Banff, Calgary: University of Calgary Press, 1987); Robert Evans et al., "Controlling Health Care Expenditures—The Canadian Reality," *New England Journal of Medicine* 320 (1989): 571–77.

33. On the CHPs, see Basil Mott, "The New Health Planning System," in Arthur Levin, ed., *Health Services: The Local Perspective* (New York: Academy of Political Science, 1977), 238–41; Parkum and Parkum, *Voluntary Participation in Health Planning* (Harrisburg: Bureau of Comprehensive Health Planning, Pennsylvania Department of Health, 1957). For a discussion of the amendments, see Altman, Greene, and Sapolsky, *Health Planning and Regulation*, 21–22.

34. Quoted by Starr, *Transformation of American Medicine*, 400–401.

35. The literature on competition is enormous. On HMOs in the 1970s see especially Lawrence Brown, *Politics and Health Care Organization: HMOs as*

Federal Policy (Washington, D.C.: Brookings, 1982); and Harold Luft, *Health Maintenance Organizations: Dimensions of Performance* (New York: John Wiley, 1981). On the 1970s version of the competitive ideal, see Alain Enthoven, "Consumer Choice Health Plan," *New England Journal of Medicine* 298 (23 March 1978): 650–58 (part I) and (30 March 1978): 709–20 (part II); or Walter McClure, "The Medical Care System Under National Health Insurance: Four Models," *Journal of Health Politics, Policy and Law* 1 (Spring 1976). McClure's article remains among the clearest expositions of the marketeer's hope.

36. Public Law 93-641, passed by Congress in December 1974; signed by President Ford, January 1975. Dominick quoted in *Congressional Record—Senate*, 19 December 1974. For a vague discussion of the vague congressional intent, see *The Report by the Committee on Interstate Commerce and Foreign Commerce on the National Health Policy, Planning and Resources Development Act of 1974*, report no. 93-1382 (Washington, D.C.: Government Printing Office, 26 November 1974).

37. The different mandates can be found in the following sections of the act: Preface (Purpose #1), 1513 (a) (2), 1513 (a) (5), 1502 (a) (9), 1502 (a) (2), and 1502 (a) (10).

38. *Report by the Committee on Interstate Commerce*.

39. Milton Roemer, "Bed Supply and Hospital Utilization: A Natural Experiment," *Hospitals* 35 (1 November 1961): 36–42.

40. PL 93-641, 1512 (b) (3) (c) (i). For an analysis of the implicit theories of representations, see James Morone and T. R. Marmor, "Representing Consumer Interests: The Case of National Health Planning," *Ethics* 91 (April 1981): 431–50.

41. Supporters quoted by G. Gregory Raab, "National/State/Local Relationships in Health Planning: Interest Group Reaction and Lobbying," *Health Planning in the United States*, vol. II (Washington, D.C.: National Academy Press, 1981), 120.

42. Daniel P. Moynihan, *Maximum Feasible Misunderstanding* (New York: Free Press, 1969), xx.

43. Raab, "National/State/Local Relationships," 117.

44. Quoted by Starr, *Transformation of American Medicine*, 402.

45. I include my own judgment in this litany as a gesture of conciliation to a group of scholars I admire enormously (despite their appearance here as something of straw men). The quotes are taken, respectively, from T. R. Marmor and James A. Morone, "Representing Consumer Interests: Imbalanced Markets, Health Planning and the HSAs," *Milbank Memorial Fund Quarterly: Health and Society* 58 (1 [Winter 1980]): 161 ("impossibly flawed"). Lawrence D. Brown, "Some Structural Issues in the Health Planning Program," *Health Planning in the United States*, vol. II (Washington, D.C.: National Academy Press, 1981), 1 ("fatuously," "back-

wards"). Harvey Sapolsky, "Bottoms Up Is Upside Down," *Health Planning in the United States*, 143. Frank Thompson, *Health Policy and the Bureaucracy*, 48, 50 ("awesome list").

46. Thompson, *Health Policy and the Bureaucracy*, 50.

47. See John Inglehart, "State, County Governments Win Key Role in New Program," *National Journal*, 8 November 1975, pp. 1533–39; and Raab, "National/State/Local Relationships," 114–42.

48. "Not capable" from Thompson, *Health Policy and the Bureaucracy*, 52–53. "Eleven people" from personal interview conducted in Washington.

49. Starr, *Transformation of American Machine*, 407. See the discussion in Thompson, *Health Policy and the Bureaucracy*, 57–58; and Inglehart, "State, County Governments," 1533.

50. On regulatory capture generally, see Barry Mitnick's literature review and taxonomy, *The Political Economy of Regulation* (New York: Columbia University Press, 1980). On the HSA case, see Lawrence Brown, who termed the effort "self-regulating localism," "Political Conditions of Regulatory Effectiveness: The Case of PSROs and HSAs," *Bulletin of the New York Academy of Medicine* 58 (1 [January 1982]): 78. The AMA view reported in "Repeal of Health Planning Act Urged," *American Medical News* 22 (15 [3–15 August 1979]): 1. The consumers' lament was voiced at public hearings held at the Institute of Medicine, National Academy of Sciences, Washington, D.C., 27 March 1980.

51. See Bruce Vladeck, "Interest Group Representation and the HSAs: Health Planning and Political Theory," *American Journal of Public Health* 67 (January 1977): 23–29. Still one of the best articles written on the agencies—despite predictions that were wrong.

52. Brown, "Some Structural Issues," 24.

53. The legislative mandate in PL 93-641, 1512 (b) (3) (c) (i). Green described in Moynihan, *Maximum Feasible Misunderstanding*, 92–93.

54. See James A. Morone, "The Real World of Representation," in *Health Planning in the United States*, vol. II (Washington, D.C.: National Academy Press, 1981), 273.

55. Infant mortality statistics from Guy Peters, *American Public Policy* (Chatham, N.J.: Chatham House, 1986), 185.

56. Barry Checkoway, *Citizens and Health Care: Participation and Planning for Social Change* (New York: Pergamon Press, 1981), ix. See, to take just two examples of his advocacy, "Citizens on Local Health Boards: What Are the Obstacles?" *Journal of the Community Development Society* 10 (Fall 1979): 101–6; and "Consumer Movements in Health Planning," *Health Planning in the United States*, 184–203.

57. "Business man's town" is Mayor Ivan Allen White's description. See Clarence Stone, *Economic Growth and Neighborhood Discontent* (Chapel Hill:

University of North Carolina Press, 1976), 25. The classic account of Atlanta's élite ("set the line") is by Floyd Hunter, *Community Power Structure: A Study of Decision Makers* (Chapel Hill: University of North Carolina Press, 1953), 102. For the view from the skeptics of the élite methodology, see Edward Banfield and James Q. Wilson, *City Politics* (Cambridge, Mass.: Harvard University Press, 1967), 273 *n.* 17.

58. Peter Eisinger, *The Politics of Displacement* (New York: Academic Press, 1980), 73.

59. Hunter, *Community Power Structure*, 109–12.

60. See Eisinger, *Politics of Displacement*, 65.

61. Stone, *Economic Growth and Neighborhood Discontent*, 31. See also Charlie Brown, *Charlie Brown Remembers Atlanta* (Columbia, S.C.: R. L. Bryan Co., 1982), 229.

62. Clarence Stone, *Regime Politics: Governing Atlanta, 1946–1988* (Lawrence: University Press of Kansas, 1989), 85–96.

63. Wayne Clark, *Placebo or Cure? State and Local Health Planning Agencies in the South* (Atlanta: Southern Regional Council, 1977), 29.

64. "Excess Beds Task Force Report," North Central Georgia Health Systems Agency, Atlanta, 1980.

65. "Taking Power in Georgia," *Health Advocate Newsletter of the National Health Law Program* 110 (July 1980): 3. The case was *Rakestraw et all.* v. *Califano et al.*, C.A. no. C77-635A (N.D. Ga., Atlanta div., filed 22 April 1977).

66. "Nursing Home Puts Squeeze on Taxpayers," *Idaho Statesman*, 9 July 1980, p. 1.

67. Idaho Health Systems Agency, Executive Committee, minutes, 10 April 1980 (mimeographed).

68. On Philadelphia's political style see J. David Greenstone and Paul Peterson, *Race and Authority in Urban Politics: Community Participation and the War on Poverty* (Chicago: University of Chicago Press, 1973), 25; Daniel Elazar, *Cities of the Prairies* (New York: Basic Books, 1970), chap. 4.

69. Banfield and Wilson, *City Politics*, 198, 271.

70. Conrad Weiler, *Philadelphia: Neighborhood Authority and the Urban Crises* (New York: Praeger, 1974), 41–44, 163–64. See also Banfield and Wilson, *City Politics*, 271.

71. On "blue ribbon" leadership factions, Banfield and Wilson, *City Politics*, 144. On Philadelphia, see James Reichley, *The Art of Government* (New York: Fund for the Republic, 1959).

72. Steven Neal, "Attila the Cop," *Nation*, 30 October 1976, p. 424.

73. On Ford and the Community Action Agencies, see Greenstone and Peterson, *Race and Authority in Urban Politics*. On Model Cities, see Sherry Arnstein, "Maximum Feasible Manipulation" and "The View from City Hall," *Public Administration Review* 22 (September 1972): 377–401.

74. Education Committee, Health Systems Agency of Southeastern Pennsylvania, minutes, 8 November 1978, p. 2 (mimeographed).

75. Richard Child Hill, "Crisis in the Motor City: The Politics of Economic Development in Detroit," in Susan Fainstein et al., *Restructuring the City* (New York: Longman, 1983), 83–84, 101.

76. See Bryan Jones and Lynn Bachelor, *The Sustaining Hand: Community Leadership and Corporate Power* (Lawrence: University of Kansas Press, 1986), 18–30; John C. Legget, *Class, Race, and Labor in Detroit* (New York: Oxford University Press, 1968); Greenstone and Peterson, *Race and Authority in Urban Politics*, 34–35.

77. See Eisinger, *Politics of Displacement*, 60ff.

78. Thomas Anton, *The Impact of Federal Grants on Detroit* (Washington, D.C.: Brookings Institution, 1981), chap. 5.

79. Quotes from Hill, "Crisis in the Motor City," 106–7.

80. See the analysis in Jones and Bachelor, *Sustaining Hand.*

81. "Hospital Council Losing Expansion Control," *Detroit News*, 27 May 1975, p. 16C.

82. "Large Scale Reduction Program Begins in Michigan," *Health Law Project: Library Bulletin* 4 (6 [June 1979]): 198.

83. "Bickering Perils Health Council," *Detroit Free Press*, 27 November 1978, p. 1. My analysis of the bluntly political agency (made possible by the underlying cohesion imposed by the auto industry) is the opposite view of one taken in Randolph Grossman's interesting analysis, "Voting Behavior of HSA Interest Groups," presented at the annual meeting of the American Public Health Association, Washington, D.C., 1 November 1977, pp. 9–11.

84. Mel Ravitz, "The Larger Issue," radio commentary on WJR Radio (Detroit). For an account of the battle, see "The U-M Proposal Is Back Inside the Proper Screening Process," *Detroit Free Press*, 26 July 1979. "Hospital to Get Second Review," *Michigan Daily*, 24 July 1979. "U of M Wins Approval for New Hospital," *Detroit Free Press*, 24 August 1979.

85. Alan Altshuler, *The City Planning Process* (Ithaca, N.Y.: Cornell University Press, 1965), 413.

86. Eric Black, "Quick Sweetheart, Get Me Rewrite, They Just Indicted the Donut Dunker," *Washington Monthly*, June 1982, pp. 24, 25, 26.

87. Ibid., 26.

88. For data and a discussion, see Odin Anderson et al., *HMO Development: Patterns and Prospects* (Chicago: Pluribus Press, 1985), tables 1.8 and 1.9 and chap. 2. On minorities, see also Theodore Kolderei, *More Care About the Costs in Hospitals* (Minneapolis: Citizens League, 16 September 1977). Unemployment figures from *Health Systems Plan for the Twin Cities Metro-*

politan Area, 1980–1981 (St. Paul, Minn.: Metropolitan Council and Metropolitan Health Board 1980), chap. 2.

89. Altshuler, *City Planning Process*, 194.

90. Kolderei, *More Care About Costs in Hospitals*, 121.

91. *Health Systems Plan*, chap. 8; "Elimination of 1,000 Hospitals Beds Urged," *Minneapolis Tribune*, 10 January 1978, p. B10; "Hospital Trustee Council Recommends Smaller Bed Cut," *Minneapolis Tribune*, 18 November 1978, p. A13.

92. Lewis Cope, "Study: 3 Area Hospitals Should Close or Merge," *Minneapolis Tribune*, 28 April 1981, p. 1; Virginia Rybin, "Public Hearing On Hospital Closing Set," *St. Paul Pioneer Press*, 25 June 1981, p. 25; Lewis Cope, "Hospitals Closing Proposal Advances," *Minneapolis Tribune*, 25 June 1981, p. A1. Quotations from "Coercing Hospitals to Consider Closing," *Minneapolis Tribune*, 7 June 1981, A14.

93. "Plan to Close Hospital Ignores Special Needs of Patients," *Minneapolis Star*, 4 June 1981, p. A8; "Coercing Hospitals to Consider Closing," *Minneapolis Tribune*, p. A14.

94. Virginia Rybin, "Health Board's Life-or-Death Power Causing Ill Will," *St. Paul Pioneer Press*, 20 December 1981, p. 1.

95. A. N. Johnson and David Aquilina, "The Competitive Impact of Health Maintenance Organizations and Competition in Minneapolis/St. Paul," *Journal of Health Politics, Policy and Law* 10 (4 [Winter 1985]): 659–75.

96. "Planners' new muscle" from Gay Sands Miller, "Agencies Act to Lower Health Bills by Saying No to Bigger Hospitals: Citizen Planners Turn Down Expansions, Push Clinics, Promote Shared Services," *Wall Street Journal*, 5 May 1977. On the New England agencies, see Altman, Greene, and Sapolsky, *Health Planning and Regulation*; and Codman Research Group, "The Impact of Health Planning and Regulation on the Patterns of Hospital Utilization in New England," executive summary, DHEW Contract 291-76-0003, September 1977. On national effects of certificates of need, see Andrew B. Dunham, "Health and Politics: The Impact of Certificate of Need Regulation," Ph.D. dissertation, University of Chicago, 1981.

97. On the railroads, see Gabriel Kolko, *Railroads and Regulation, 1877–1916* (Princeton, N.J.: Princeton University Press, 1965). The same view (from the other side of the political spectrum) informs George Stigler, "The Theory of Economic Regulation."

98. Uwe Reinhardt, "Paying the Doctor: Lessons from Home and Abroad," paper delivered at the annual conference of the New York Academy of Medicine, New York, 7 May 1987.

99. On the decline of professional power, see Starr, *Transformation of American Medicine*. For interesting lamentations over the trend, see Stanley

NOTES

Wohl, M.D., *The Medical Industrial Complex* (New York: Harmony Books, 1984); and Robert Cunningham, *The Healing Mission and the Business Ethic* (Chicago: Pluribus Press, 1982).

100. For the long-term political implications of recent developments, see James A. Morone and Andrew B. Dunham, "Slouching to National Health Insurance: The New Health Care Politics," *Yale Journal of Regulation* 2 (2 [Spring 1985]): 263–91. For a longer account of the development of the new payment mechanism, see Dunham and Morone, *The Politics of Innovation: Hospital Regulation in New Jersey* (Princeton, N.J.: Health Research and Education Trust, 1982).
101. The argument is elaborated in James A. Morone, "Beyond the N-Words: The Politics of Health Care Reform," *Bulletin of the New York Academy of Medicine* 55 (4 [July–August, 1990]): 344–65.
102. See Lawrence Brown, "The Painless Prescription: Influence without Power in Community Cost Settlement Programs," paper presented at the annual meetings of the American Political Science Association, Chicago, September 1987.
103. Starr, *Transformation of American Medicine*, 379.

Chapter 8. Elusive Community

1. The Inaugural Address of Ronald Reagan, January 20, 1981.
2. Ibid.
3. "Outlook: US Economy May Face Long Decline," *Wall Street Journal*, 17 August 1987, p. 1; *Time*, 23 October 1989; *Business Week*, 16 April 1990; George C. Lodge, *Atlantic Monthly*, April 1989; Peter G. Peterson, *Atlantic Monthly*, October 1987; David Frum, "The Anti-Communists Won't Concede Victory," *Wall Street Journal*, 1 May 1990, p. A18; James Fallows, *New York Review of Books*, 1 March, 1990. Perhaps the best-known statement of the theme is in the last chapter and epilogue of Paul Kennedy, *The Rise and Fall of Great Powers* (New York: Random House, 1987).
4. Bruce Nussbaum, "And Now the Bill Comes Due," *Business Week*, 16 November 1987, p. 161; Robert Heilbronner, quoted in Steven Schlossstein, *The End of the American Century* (New York: Congdon, 1989), 88.
5. Clyde V. Prestowitz, Jr., *Trading Places: How We Are Giving Our Future to Japan and How to Reclaim It* (New York: Basic Books, 1989), 491.
6. Savings figures reported in Schlossstein, *End of American Century*, 193; see the discussion in Frank Levy, *Dollars and Dreams: The Changing American Income Distribution* (New York: W. W. Norton, 1988), chap. 4.
7. Ford Foundation Project on Social Welfare and the American Future, *The Common Good: Social Welfare and the American Future: Policy Recommendations of the Executive Panel* (New York: Ford Foundation, 1989), 5, 6.
8. James A. Morone, "American Political Culture and the Search for Lessons

from Abroad," *Journal of Health Politics, Policy and Law* 15 (2 [Spring 1990]): 130.

9. Figures from Bruce Vladeck, "Health Care and the Homeless," *Journal of Health Politics, Policy and Law* 15 (2 [Summer 1990]): 306; see the range of estimates and general discussion in Michael Katz, *The Undeserving Poor: From the War on Poverty to the War on Welfare* (New York: Pantheon, 1989), 186–194. See also Institute of Medicine, National Academy of Sciences, *Homelessness, Health and Human Needs* (Washington, D.C.: National Academy Press, 1988).

10. James A Morone, "City Politics and AIDS," paper prepared for the annual meetings of the American Political Science Association, San Francisco, August 30–September 2, 1990.

11. Vladeck, "The Homeless," 314–16; Katz, *Undeserving Poor*, 238–39.

12. *US News And World Report*, quoted in Katz, *Undeserving Poor*, 197; William Julius Wilson, *The Truly Disadvantaged: The Inner City, the Underclass and Public Policy* (Chicago: The University of Chicago Press, 1987).

13. Ford Foundation, *Common Good*, 56, 64.

14. *Fortune*, quoted in Katz, *Undeserving Poor*, 197.

15. Richard M. Valelly, "Vanishing Voters," *The American Prospect* 1 (1 [Spring 1990]): 140–50.

16. Morris P. Fiorina, "The Case of the Vanishing Marginals: The Bureaucracy Did It," *American Political Science Review* 71 (1 [March 1977]): 180.

17. Linda Greenhouse, "Why the Public Housing Act of 1986 Isn't," *New York Times*, 25 August 1986, p. A22.

18. Akio Morita quoted by James Fallows, "Wake Up America," 14; the passage comes from Morita's *A Japan That Can Say No*, a book that, so far, has not been authorized for English translation or American distribution because, as Fallows quotes Morita, it was "intended for a Japanese audience."

Contemporary expressions of this view draw, often unwittingly, on the predictions made by Joseph Schumpeter, *Capitalism, Socialism and Democracy* (New York: Harper, 1947), and Daniel Bell, *The Cultural Contradictions of Capitalism* (New York: Basic Books, 1974).

19. Benjamin Barber, "The Compromised Republic: Public Purposelessness in America," in Robert H. Horowitz, ed., *The Moral Foundations of the American Republic*, 3rd ed. (Charlottesville: University Press of Virginia, 1986), 54.

20. This description is taken from James A. Morone and Andrew B. Dunham, "Slouching to National Health Insurance: The New Health Care Politics," *Yale Journal of Regulation* 2 (2 [Spring 1985]): 287ff.

21. Prestowitz, *Trading Places*, 511.

22. James Fallows, "Wake Up America!" 14. See the similar call by Arthur M. Schlesinger, Jr., "The Liberal Opportunity," *The American Prospect* 1 (1 [Spring 1990]): 18.

Index

Index

Index

Index

Index

Index

Monetary policy, 83
Monroe, James, 69
Morality, 54, 68, 82, 329
Morgan, Edmund, 20, 37–38, 50
Morgan, Helen, 20
Morita, Akio, 329
Morris, Gouverneur, 54
Moynihan, Daniel, 224–25, 234, 235, 250, 274
Mugwumps, 97, 101–2, 104, 105, 106, 297; and FDR's "brain trust," comparison of, 134; laments over the character of party politics, 110; and the Progressive coalition, 107–8, 109
Murphy, Frank, 176
Murray, James, 258
Murrin, John, 47
Mussolini, Benito, 154
Myrdal, Gunnar, 188

Nash, Gary, 20, 47
Nashville Tennessean, 200
National Academy of Science, 327
National Aeronautics and Space Administration, 331
National Association for the Advancement of Colored People (NAACP), 193–208 *passim*, 228, 233, 234
National Association of Governors, 270
National Association of Manufacturers, 4*n*, 154, 157, 158, 165, 171
National Association of Regional Councils, 277
National Defense Training Act, 194
National Guard, 166, 167
National Health Planning and Resources Development Act, 277–93 *passim*, 305, 308, 314, 316, 317
National Industrial Recovery Act (1933), 12, 29, 133, 156–84, 181, 221, 249; and the National Health Planning Act, comparison of, 317; section 7(a), 157–63, 164–65, 167, 170–71, 172, 173, 177, 180, 182, 227
National Institute for Mental Health, 261
National Institutes for Health, 261
National Labor Board (NLB), 168–73, 183, 184
National Labor Relations Board (NLRB), 171–73, 175, 183
National League of Cities, 277
National Livestock Association, 120
National Planning and Resources Development Act (1974), 271–75, 276, 277

National Recovery Administration (NRA), 131, 133, 153–63, 179–84, 202, 205, 274, 315; and civil rights, 197; coal code, 177, 178; and "consumer movements," 161, 162; and medical politics, 272, 280, 283, 285; and scientific planning, 221; and the Supreme Court, 174
National Rivers and Harbors Congresses, 120, 125
National Service Corps, 223
National Short Ballot Association, 97, 110
National Urban League, 192, 228
National Water Users Association, 120
Native Americans, 41, 46, 83, 282
Neighborhood Health Centers, 264
Neighborhood Legal Services, 237, 238
Nelson, Michael, 92
New Deal, 13, 220, 323; and the "dictator bill," 138–40; and labor relations, 13, 138, 145–85; and medical politics, 257–58; and Progressive reform, 26, 129–42, 257, 333; Skocpol on, 24, 141; and working-class politics, 145–85
Newsweek, 191, 213
New York Customs House, 97, 103
New York Federation of Labor, 151
New York Herald Tribune, 213
New York Review of Books, 325
New York Times, 60, 170, 203, 213, 223, 234, 241, 245, 256, 327
New York Tribune, 104
New York Working Men, 85
Nixon, Richard M., 266, 269, 270

Office of Economic Opportunity (OEO), 223–47 *passim*, 264–65, 317
Office of the United States Trade Representative, 331
Ohlin, Lloyd, 222, 225
Oil Field Workers Union, 163
Oliver, Andrew, 47
Olney, Richard, 149
Olson, Floyd, 166
Organization for Economic Cooperation and Development, 326
Other America, The (Harrington), 219

Page, John, 58
Palmer, Richard, 275

Index

Index

Index

Taiwan, 326
Taney, Roger, 81n
Tariffs, 50, 83, 84, 117
Tate, Jim, 297, 299
Taxation, 109; colonial, 39, 47, 50, 51–52; poll taxes, 189, 209; tax cuts, 210. *See also* Stamp tax; Tariffs
Taylor, Frederick, 116–17, 121
Taylor, Myron, 177–78
Taylor, Zachary, 90
Teamsters Union, 151, 164, 166, 178, 301
Tennessee Valley Authority, 130, 131
Tenure of Office Act, 102
Thurmond, Strom, 240
Tighe, Michael, 164, 177
Tijerna, 233
Tilden Commission, 109
Time, 218, 324
Tobin, Dan, 151, 164
Tocqueville, Alexis de, 6, 89, 335; egalitarian picture of early America, 2, 3; on Jacksonian democracy, 86, 87
Tory party, 45, 235
Townshend, Charles, 50n, 51
Townshend Act, 50
Trade, 50, 55, 333, 334, 335
Truman, Harry S., 196–97, 258–59, 261, 262
Tugwell, Rexford, 161
Turner, Frederick J., 97, 99n
Tyson, Cyril, 229

Unemployment, 152–53, 188
Union(s), 145–47, 167; black membership in, 151, 191, 304; doctrine of voluntary action, 155; and the majority principle, 169, 170, 171, 182; and yellow-dog contracts, 148, 149, 150. *See also* Labor; specific unions
United Auto Workers (UAW), 176–77, 303–4, 305–7
United Mine Workers (UMW), 149, 157, 162–63, 164, 168, 177, 182–83
United Mine Workers Journal, 162
United Rubber Workers, 176
United States Steel Corporation, 148, 153, 165, 177
U.S. News and World Report, 327

Van Buren, Martin, 85, 86
Vandiver, Ernest, 200
Van Riper, Paul, 135
Veterans Administration, 310–11
Vigilantes, 46
Vinson, Fred, 199
Volunteers in Service to America (VISTA), 223
Voting Rights Act, 218

Wagner, Robert, 162, 170–71, 258
Wagner Act, 168–74, 178, 182, 200; antidiscrimination clause in, 192; and the War on Poverty, comparison of, 231–32
Walker, Edwin, 208
Wallace, George, 202, 208–9, 211, 226n, 236
Wallace, Henry, 131
Wall Street Journal, 233, 324
Walsh, David, 138
Walsh, William, 240
War, Department of, 135
War on Poverty, 7, 12, 14–15, 21, 28, 187, 218–51, 298–99, 300, 335; and medical politics, 265, 268, 272, 274, 280, 282, 283, 289, 316, 317
Warren, Earl, 197, 199–200
Washington, Booker T., 192, 193, 195, 205, 251, 286
Washington, George, 42, 57, 68–69, 71, 101–2
Washington Star, 138, 213
Watergate scandal, 270
Webster, Daniel, 86
Weir, Ernest, 170
Weir, Margaret, 141
Weirton Steel, 169–70, 175
Welfare Administration, 223
Weyl, Walter E., 118, 221, 272
Whateley, Thomas, 39
Whig party, 30, 35n, 51, 57, 66–67, 72, 78n; Conscience Whigs, 79; emphasis on internal improvements, 82; and the expansion of government, 75; and Jacksonian Democrats, 82, 83–84, 86; and slavery, issue of, 95–96; victory of, in 1840, 89–90
Whiskey Rebellion (1794), 70
White, Ivan, 286
White, Leonard, 23, 68, 71, 89–90
White, Theodore, 209

401